AN ANOMALOUS JEW

An Anomalous Jew

Paul among Jews, Greeks,
and Romans

MICHAEL F. BIRD

WILLIAM B. EERDMANS PUBLISHING COMPANY
GRAND RAPIDS, MICHIGAN

Wm. B. Eerdmans Publishing Co.
2140 Oak Industrial Drive N.E., Grand Rapids, Michigan 49505
www.eerdmans.com

22 21 20 19 18 17 16   1 2 3 4 5 6 7

ISBN 978-0-8028-6769-8

Library of Congress Cataloging-in-Publication Data

Names: Bird, Michael F., author.
Title: An anomalous Jew : Paul among Jews, Greeks, and Romans / Michael F. Bird.
Description: Grand Rapids : Eerdmans Publishing Co., 2016. |
    Includes bibliographical references and index.
Identifiers: LCCN 2016022582 | ISBN 9780802867698 (pbk.)
Subjects: LCSH: Paul, the Apostle, Saint.
Classification: LCC BS2506.3 .B566 2016 | DDC 225.9/2—dc23
    LC record available at https://lccn.loc.gov/2016022582

Contents

Preface

This volume presents an attempt to understand Paul's Jewishness as it was expressed in relation to other Jews, to Paul's fellow Jewish Christians, and to Romans and the Roman Empire. Paul was clearly a Jewish person with a Jewish way of life and a very Jewish worldview. Even so, he still came into conflict with Jewish communities in both the Diaspora and Judea, aroused the angst of fellow Jewish Christians, and was eventually put to death by the Roman authorities as a Jewish agitator. My aim in this volume is to identify how Paul could be thoroughly Jewish and yet become a figure of notoriety and controversy among his Jewish compatriots. My answer, in short, is that Paul was an anomalous Jew, a strange figure with a blend of common and controversial Jewish beliefs that brought him into conflict with the socioreligious scene around him.

Chapters 1, 4, and 5 have been published before in an earlier form, and chapters 2 and 3 have been crafted especially for this volume. In many ways each chapter is itself an independent and stand-alone study. However, the collection has a common purpose in explaining how Paul postured himself in relation to common Judaism and how his approach resulted in both an affirmation and a transformation of his Jewish heritage. My hope is that these studies will contribute to further discussion of Paul as the Jewish Christian apostle to the Gentiles.

In developing this volume, I have incurred a debt to several people. First of all, I'm grateful to Bloomsbury, Mohr Siebeck, and InterVarsity publishers for permission to republish some of my previous studies in revised form. Second, Miss Elizabeth Culhane did a fine job of putting all of my chapters into a single and consistent format. Third, Michael Thomson and the editorial team at Eerdmans matched their usual high standard of work in bringing this volume to production and even indulged my tardiness in delivering the manuscript.

Fourth, Ridley librarian Miss Ruth Millard found several resources for me that aided in the completion of this work and did so with her usual diligence. Fifth, Ben Sutton compiled the abbreviations list and bibliography, and John Schoer prepared the indexes. Sixth, numerous learned friends, including Nijay Gupta, Joseph Fantin, Jason Maston, and Hefin Jones, read portions of this manuscript and offered wise corrections. Seventh, as always, my wife, Naomi, and our family have continued to offer me their love and support for my scholarship.

Finally, I dedicate this work to the board, faculty, and staff at Ridley College for their commitment to theological education and their partnership in the gospel of Jesus Christ. The encouragement of colleagues and supporters is vital when one is balancing teaching, administrative responsibilities, church ministry, and research. I'm glad to say that I feel like my colleagues are always cheering me on and always ready to help me in any way they can. In particular, it is very fortunate to be able to write a book about Paul with a bona fide Pauline scholar like Brian Rosner around the corner always ready to discuss all things Pauline.

Abbreviations

AB	Anchor Bible
ABD	*Anchor Bible Dictionary*
ABR	*Australian Biblical Review*
AGJU	Arbeiten zur Geschichte des antiken Judentums und des Urchristentums
AJEC	Ancient Judaism and early Christianity
ANRW	*Aufstieg und Niedergang der römischen Welt*
ANTC	Abingdon New Testament Commentary
AusBR	*Australian Biblical Review*
AYB	Anchor Yale Bible Commentaries
BBR	*Bulletin for Biblical Research*
BDAG	W. Bauer, F. W. Danker, W. F. Arndt, and F. W. Gingrich. *A Greek-English Lexicon of the New Testament and Other Early Christian Literature.* 3rd ed. Chicago: University of Chicago Press, 2000.
BECNT	Baker Exegetical Commentary on the New Testament
BI	*Biblical Interpretation*
Bib	*Biblica*
BJRL	*Bulletin of the John Rylands University Library of Manchester*
BNTC	Black's New Testament Commentary
BR	*Biblical Research*
BTB	*Biblical Theology Bulletin*
BZ	*Biblische Zeitschrift*
BZAW	Beihefte zur Zeitschrift für die alttestamentliche Wissenschaft
BZNW	Beihefte zur Zeitschrift für die neutestamentliche Wissenschaft
CBET	Contributions to Biblical Exegesis and Theology
CBNTS	Coniectanea biblica, New Testament Series
CBQ	*Catholic Biblical Quarterly*

CBR	*Currents in Biblical Research*
CD	Karl Barth. *Church Dogmatics*
CIL	*Corpus Inscriptionum Latinarum*
CITM	James D. G. Dunn. Christianity in the Making. 2 vols. Grand Rapids, MI: Eerdmans, 2003-9.
ConBNT	Coniectanea biblica. New Testament Series
COQG	N. T. Wright. Christian Origins and the Question of God. 4 vols. Minneapolis: Fortress, 1992-2013.
CUP	Cambridge University Press
DNTB	*Dictionary of New Testament Background*
DPL	*Dictionary of Paul and His Letters*
EvTh	*Evangelische Theologie*
FES	Finnish Exegetical Society
FGrH	*Fragments of the Greek Historians* (*Die Fragmente der griechischen Historiker*)
FilNT	Filología Neotestamentaria
GBS	Deutsche Bibelgesellschaft
GLAJJ	*Greek and Latin Authors on Jews and Judaism*
HBT	*Horizons in Biblical Theology*
HTR	*Harvard Theological Review*
IBS	*Irish Biblical Studies*
ICC	International Critical Commentary
IDBSup	*Interpreter's Dictionary of the Bible: Supplementary Volume*
IJST	*International Journal of Systematic Theology*
Int	*Interpretation*
JAJ	*Journal of Ancient Judaism*
JBL	*Journal of Biblical Literature*
JBTh	*Journal of Biblical Theology*
JES	*Journal of Ecumenical Studies*
JETS	*Journal of the Evangelical Theological Society*
JNES	*Journal of Near Eastern Studies*
JSHJ	*Journal for the Study of the Historical Jesus*
JSJ	*Journal for the Study of Judaism*
JSNT	*Journal for the Study of the New Testament*
JSNTSup	Journal for the Study of the New Testament Supplemental Series
JSOT	*Journal for the Study of the Old Testament*
JSOTSup	Journal for the Study of the Old Testament Supplement Series
JSP	*Journal for the Study of the Pseudepigrapha*
JSPL	*Journal for the Study of Paul's Letters*

JSPSup	Journal for the Study of the Pseudepigrapha Supplement Series
JSQ	*Jewish Studies Quarterly*
JTI	*Journal for Theological Interpretation*
KEK	Kritisch-exegetischer Kommentar über das Neue Testament
KNT	Kommentar zum Neuen Testament
LAE	*Light from the Ancient East*
L&N	J. P. Louw and E. A. Nida. *Greek and English Lexicon of the New Testament; Based on Semantic Domains.* New York: United Bible Societies, 1999.
LNTS	Library of New Testament Studies
LPS	Library of Pauline Studies
LSTS	Library of Second Temple Studies
NACSBT	New American Commentary Studies in Bible and Theology
NCCS	New Covenant Commentary Series
NDIEC	*New Documents Illustrating Early Christianity*
NIB	*New Interpreter's Bible*
NICNT	New International Commentary on the New Testament
NIGTC	New International Greek Testament Commentary
NovT	*Novum Testamentum*
NovTSup	Novum Testamentum Supplement Series
NSBT	New Studies in Biblical Theology
NTL	New Testament Library
NTM	New Testament Monographs
NTR	New Testament Readings
NTS	*New Testament Studies*
OGIS	*Orientis Graeci Inscriptiones Selectae*
OTL	Old Testament Library
OUP	Oxford University Press
PAST	Pauline Studies
PBM	Paternoster Biblical Monographs
PC	Pentecostal Commentary Series
PNTC	Pillar New Testament Commentary Series
P.Oxy	*Oxyrhynchus Papryi.* Edited by B. P. Grenfell, A. S. Hunt, et al.
PS	Pauline Studies
RB	*Revue biblique*
RBL	*Review of Biblical Literature*
RevExp	*Review and Expositor*
RTR	*Reformed Theological Review*
SBG	Studies in Biblical Greek

SBL	Society of Biblical Literature
SBLSS	Society of Biblical Literature Semeia Studies
SBT	Studies in Biblical Theology
SIG	Sylloge Inscriptionum Graecarum
SJT	*Scottish Journal of Theology*
SNTSMS	Society for New Testament Studies Monograph Series
SP	Sacra Pagina
ST	*Studia Theologica*
STDJ	Studies on the Texts of the Desert of Judah
TANZ	Texte und Arbeiten zum neutestamentlichen Zeitalter
TBei	*Theologische Beiträge*
ThLZ	*Theologische Literaturzeitung*
TNTC	Tyndale New Testament Commentary Series
TPI	Trinity Press International
TSAJ	Texts and Studies in Ancient Judaism
TynB	*Tyndale Bulletin*
VerbEccl	*Verbum et Ecclesia*
WBC	Word Biblical Commentary Series
WMANT	Wissenschaftliche Monographien zum Alten und Neuen Testament
WUNT	Wissenschaftliche Untersuchungen zum Neuen Testament
ZNW	*Zeitschrift für die neutestamentliche Wissenschaft*

Paul the Jew . . . of Sorts

Paul was Jewish. It is impossible to deny this basic fact, given Paul's own explicit testimony to his ethnic identity and religious heritage as a Jew,[1] Hebrew, and Israelite. Paul says:

> We ourselves are Jews by birth and not Gentile sinners. (Gal 2:15)

1. The meaning of Ἰουδαῖος ("Jew" or "Judean"), its lexical register, and its socioethnographic connotations are disputed. The crux of the debate is whether Ἰουδαῖος is principally an ethnic/territorial designation or a religious disposition. On lexical definitions, see BDAG, 478, with "one who is Judean (Jewish), with focus on adherence to Mosaic tradition, *a Judean . . .* Ἰουδαῖος frequently suggests conformity to Israel's ancestral belief and practice," and L&N 93.488, with "the ethnic name of a person belonging to the Jewish nation." See survey of secondary literature in David M. Miller, "Ethnicity, Religion, and the Meaning of *Ioudaios* in Ancient 'Judaism,'" *CBR* 12 (2014): 216-65; the multiauthor discussion in "Jew and Judean: A Forum on Politics and Historiography in the Translation of Ancient Texts," ed. T. Michael Law, *Marginalia Review of Books*, August 26, 2014, http://marginalia.lareviewofbooks.org/jew-judean-forum. Notable studies include Steve Mason, "Jews, Judaeans, Judaizing, Judaism: Problems of Categorization in Ancient History," *JSJ* 38 (2007): 457-512; Caroline Johnson Hodge, *If Sons, Then Heirs: A Study of Kinship and Ethnicity in the Letters of Paul* (Oxford: OUP, 2007), 11-15; John H. Elliott, "Jesus the Israelite Was Neither a 'Jew' nor a 'Christian': On Correcting Misleading Nomenclature," *JSHJ* 5 (2007): 119-54; Seth Schwartz, "How Many Judaisms Were There? A Critique of Neusner and Smith on Definition and Mason and Boyarin on Categorization," *JAJ* 2 (2011): 221-38; Cynthia Baker, "A 'Jew' by Any Other Name?," *JAJ* 2 (2011): 153-80; Michael Satlow, "Jew or Judaean?," in *"The One Who Sows Bountifully": Essays in Honor of Stanley K. Stowers*, ed. C. Johnson Hodge et al. (Providence, RI: Brown Judaic Studies, 2013), 165-75. John M. G. Barclay (*Jews in the Mediterranean Diaspora: From Alexander to Trajan [323 BCE–117 CE]* [Berkeley: University of California Press, 1996], 404) is probably right to identify "ancestry and custom" as the core of Jewish identity, or what it meant to be Ἰουδαῖος. A convenient summary and assessment of the options appear in Michael F. Bird, *Crossing Over Sea and Land: Jewish Missionary Activity in the Second Temple Period* (Peabody, MA: Hendrickson, 2010), 13-16.

[I was] circumcised on the eighth day, a member of the people of Israel, of the tribe of Benjamin, a Hebrew born of Hebrews; as to the law, a Pharisee. (Phil 3:5)

Are they Hebrews? So am I. Are they Israelites? So am I. Are they descendants of Abraham? So am I. (2 Cor 11:22)

For I could wish that I myself were accursed and cut off from Christ for the sake of my own people, my kindred according to the flesh. They are Israelites. (Rom 9:3-4)

I myself am an Israelite, a descendant of Abraham, a member of the tribe of Benjamin. (Rom 11:1)

And according to Luke:

Paul replied, "I am a Jew, from Tarsus in Cilicia, a citizen of an important city." (Acts 21:39)

Then he said: "I am a Jew, born in Tarsus in Cilicia, but brought up in this city at the feet of Gamaliel, educated strictly according to our ancestral law, being zealous for God, just as all of you are today." (Acts 22:3)

Paul believed that he belonged to the "race" (γένος) of the Jewish people (2 Cor 11:26; Gal 1:14), who are his "kin" (συγγενής) and brothers (ἀδελφοί) and even his very own flesh (σάρξ), so he passionately declares (Rom 9:3; 11:14). These sentiments should be unsurprising, since Paul was born into a Jewish family, he was educated in the Jewish religion, even becoming a Pharisee, and his zealous commitment to his ancestral traditions was demonstrated in his persecution of the church (Acts 9:4-5; 22:4-8; 26:14-15; 1 Cor 15:9; Gal 1:13, 23; Phil 3:6; 1 Tim 1:13). Even as a Christ-believer, Paul remained a devout monotheist (Rom 3:30; 1 Cor 8:4; Gal 3:20). He affirmed Israel's election, calling, and covenants (Rom 3:2; 9:4-5; 11:28-29), and he treated Israel's Scriptures as a divine revelation (e.g., 2 Cor 4:6; 6:16).

Even in his apostolic work as a Christ-believer, Paul remained thoroughly Jewish. He engaged in heartfelt lament for the Jews (Rom 9:1-3), prayed for their salvation (Rom 10:1), sought to win over and save some Jews (1 Cor 9:20-22), and even fashioned his apostolate in service to the Jews (Rom 11:14; 15:25-28; 1 Cor 16:1-4). Paul worked in partnership with the Judean churches (Gal

2:1-10) and included many Jews among his coworkers (Rom 16:7; 1 Cor 9:6; Col 4:11). He presented himself as a figure who functioned like a Jewish prophet (1 Cor 2:6-16; 2 Cor 4:1-6; 12:1-10), reminiscent of the Isaianic "servant" (Gal 1:15; 2 Cor 6:2; 2 Cor 7:6; Phil 2:16; see Acts 13:46-47), and even akin to a priest (Rom 15:16). Moreover, by preaching monotheism and messianism, and by insisting that his Gentile converts avoid idolatry and sexual immorality, Paul was, in a limited sense at least, judaizing the Gentiles (Rom 1:18-32; 1 Cor 5:10-11; 6:9; 8:4; 10:7, 14; 12:2; 2 Cor 6:16; Gal 5:19-21; 1 Thess 1:9).[2] Paul's call and apostolic mission to lead the Gentiles to praise Israel's God and to obtain a faithful obedience should be regarded as a very Jewish vocation.[3] Caroline Johnson Hodge even claims that "Paul's work as a teacher of gentiles is a part of the larger story of Israel, not a break from it."[4]

And yet Paul's self-description and praxis often make him look like he's moving away from the Jewish sphere. For example, Paul says things that no Torah-affirming Jew could seemingly say. Paul can lay out his inherited privileges as a Jewish-born Pharisee and claims that he now regards them as "crap" (Phil 3:4-8). He looks back on, and down on, his former "way of life in Judaism" (Gal 1:13-16). Paul declares that a Christ-believing Jew like himself (Gal 2:19) and even Christ-believing Gentiles (Rom 7:4) have died to the Torah by dying with Christ (Gal 2:20; Rom 6:1-14). He goes so far as to declare: "All who rely on the works of the law are under a curse" (Gal 3:10), which insinuates that all Jews who strive to please God by living a faithful life under Torah are merely rearranging the furniture in a house sent into exile. Furthermore, "The Torah brings wrath" (Rom 4:15); the Torah "was added because of transgression" (Gal 3:19), and "the Torah was brought in so that the trespass might increase" (Rom 5:20). The underlying premise is that Torah was part of a triumvirate of evil powers comprising Torah-Sin-Death, from which humanity needed deliverance (1 Cor 15:56; Rom 8:2). Such evidently radical statements are not limited to theology but shape social practices too. Paul can advocate Jews and Gentiles eating together (Gal 2:11-14) and eating food sacrificed to idols (1 Cor

---

2. See E. P. Sanders, "Paul's Jewishness," in *Paul's Jewish Matrix*, ed. T. G. Casey and J. Taylor (Rome: Gregorian & Biblical Press, 2011), 62-63; Paula Fredriksen, "Judaizing the Nations: The Ritual Demands of Paul's Gospel," in *Paul's Jewish Matrix*, ed. T. G. Casey and J. Taylor (Rome: Gregorian & Biblical Press, 2011), 327-54 (esp. 352).

3. See N. T. Wright, "Romans 2:17–3:9: A Hidden Clue to the Meaning of Romans?," *JSPL* 2 (2012): 1-28; Lionel J. Windsor, *Paul and the Vocation of Israel: How Paul's Jewish Identity Informs His Apostolic Ministry, with Special Reference to Romans* (BZNW 205; Berlin: Walter de Gruyter, 2014).

4. Hodge, *If Sons, Then Heirs*, 121.

8:1-10; 10:25-30), both of which other Christ-believing Jews regarded as clearly disloyal to the Jewish way of life (see Acts 11:1-3; Gal 2:12; Rev 2:14, 20). In an offhand remark he lays aside the entire scriptural regulation pertaining to *kashrut*, the Jewish dietary laws (Rom 14:14). A culinary flirtation with idolatry and disregard for food laws were sure ways to get oneself accused of apostasy in Diaspora communities (see 4 Macc 4:26!).[5] On rites and rituals, Paul did not merely fail to circumcise Gentiles but pronounced a curse on those who tried to force Gentiles to be circumcised (Gal 1:6-9; 5:6, 11; 6:12-15; Phil 3:2-3), which, not surprisingly, riled up many of his Christ-believing Jewish contemporaries (see Acts 15:1-5; Gal 2:1-5; 6:12-13). Now, because of Paul's qualifying remarks (see Rom 3:19-20, 21, 31; 7:12-14; 13:8-10; Gal 3:15-26), it would be wrong to conceive of this as a flat-out rejection of the Torah in toto. More properly, these statements look more like a repudiation of the Torah for certain ends, the relativization of the Torah for personal practice, and a retooling of the Torah as prophecy and wisdom in light of the revelation of the end of ages.[6] Yet no matter how animated one's defense of Paul as a Jewish thinker, none of such provocative comments can square with common Jewish beliefs about living a faithful life under the wings of Torah.

In addition, Paul received a violent and hostile response from his fellow Jews in both the Diaspora and in Judea. Just as Paul once persecuted the church, so too he came to be persecuted for his faith in Christ and service to the churches by his own Jewish compatriots (Acts 13:50; 1 Cor 4:12; 2 Cor 4:9; 12:10; Gal 5:11; 1 Thess 3:3-4, 7; 2 Tim 3:11). In the first letter to the Thessalonians, one of his earliest letters, he exhorts his audience to perseverance while they are under duress. Paul draws a correlation between the Thessalonians' persecution at the hands of local authorities and the persecution suffered by the Judean churches from the Jews:

> For you, brothers and sisters, became imitators of the churches of God in Christ Jesus that are in Judea, for you suffered the same things from your own compatriots as they did from the Jews, who killed both the Lord Jesus and the prophets, and drove us out; they displease God and oppose everyone by hindering us from speaking to the Gentiles so that they may be saved. Thus they have constantly been filling up the mea-

---

5. See John M. G. Barclay, "Who Was Considered an Apostate in the Jewish Diaspora?," in *Pauline Churches and Diaspora Jews: Beyond the New Perspective* (WUNT 275; Tübingen: Mohr Siebeck, 2011), 141-55 (esp. 151-54).

6. See Brian R. Rosner, *Paul and the Law* (NSBT; Downers Grove, IL: IVP Academic, 2013).

sure of their sins; but God's wrath has overtaken them at last. (1 Thess 2:14-16)[7]

Paul told the Corinthians that his apostolic credentials are validated by his list of travails, including the various persecutions he had received from the Jews.

Five times I have received from the Jews the forty lashes minus one. Three times I was beaten with rods. Once I received a stoning. Three times I was shipwrecked; for a night and a day I was adrift at sea; on frequent journeys, in danger from rivers, danger from bandits, danger from my own people, danger from Gentiles, danger in the city, danger in the wilderness, danger at sea, danger from false brothers and sisters. (2 Cor 11:24-26; see m. Mak. 3.14)

When Paul wrote to the Romans, he was preparing to embark on a return visit to Jerusalem to deliver the collection to the church before setting off for Spain via Rome. In this letter Paul asked the Romans to pray for his safety as he faced great peril by visiting Jerusalem, a peril confirmed by Luke's account in Acts 21:15–26:32. With the following words, he asked the Romans to pray for him:

I appeal to you, brothers and sisters, by our Lord Jesus Christ and by the love of the Spirit, to join me in earnest prayer to God on my behalf, that I may be rescued from the unbelievers in Judea, and that my ministry to Jerusalem may be acceptable to the saints, so that by God's will I may come to you with joy and be refreshed in your company. (Rom 15:30-32)

A complicating factor is that Paul did not regard being Jewish as the be all and end all of his identity. There was something about his Christ-faith that determined his identity and vocation, not only for himself, but for other Christ-believers too.

To the Jews I became as a Jew, in order to win Jews. To those under the law I became as one under the law (though I myself am not under the

---

7. On the background and authenticity of 1 Thess 2:14-16, see Markus Bockmuehl, "1 Thessalonians 2:14-16 and the Church in Jerusalem," *TynB* 52 (2001): 1-31, and J. A. Weatherly, "The Authenticity of 1 Thessalonians 2.13-16: Additional Evidence," *JSNT* 42 (1991): 79-98.

law) so that I might win those under the law. To those outside the law I became as one outside the law (though I am not free from God's law but am under Christ's law) so that I might win those outside the law. To the weak I became weak, so that I might win the weak. I have become all things to all people, that I might by all means save some. (1 Cor 9:20-22)

Paul's statement is sweeping in its rhetoric, even though it should not be reduced to a rhetorical remark of Paul's philosophical adaptability.[8] Paul can insert himself into the situation of a Jew, those under the law, or those outside the law or among the weak only because he believes that his own identity ultimately transcends them—he can flex in order to accommodate himself to them. That Paul is "not under the law" (μὴ . . . ὑπὸ νόμον) is rather striking, since being "under the law" is a signature way of describing a covenantally faithful Jew (see Gal 4:4, 21; cf. Rom 3:19; 7:6; Phil 3:6) and something Paul says that Gentile Christ-believers should not aspire to be (Gal 5:18; Rom 6:14-15). Believers are not, and should not be, "under law" because Paul locates his Jewish identity and that of other Christ-believers from other races in a position that is "in Messiah," where ethnic, social, and gender distinctions are *in some sense* nullified (Gal 3:28; Col 3:11).

Participation in this new creation means that the distinctions inherent in the old order, even those mandated "under the law," cease to have any intrinsic and ongoing validity. Hence his statements: "For in Christ Jesus neither circumcision nor uncircumcision counts for anything; the only thing that counts is faith working through love" (Gal 5:6) and "For neither circumcision nor uncircumcision is anything; but a new creation is everything!" (Gal 6:15). Similarly, he writes to the Corinthians, "Circumcision is nothing, and uncircumcision is nothing; but obeying the commandments of God is everything" (1 Cor 7:19). Circumcision was the sign of God's covenant with Abraham and Israel (Gen 17:10-14; Lev 12:3), and it was one the life-or-death issues that faithful Jews had to stand up for amid

---

8. Contra Mark A. Nanos, "Paul's Relationship to Torah in Light of His Strategy 'to Become Everything to Everyone' (1 Corinthians 9.19-23)," in *Paul and Judaism: Crosscurrents in Pauline Exegesis and the Study of Jewish-Christian Relations*, ed. R. Bieringer and D. Pollefeyt (LNTS 463; London: T&T Clark, 2012), 106-40, and idem, "Was Paul a 'Liar' for the Gospel? The Case for a New Interpretation of Paul's 'Becoming Everything to Everyone' in 1 Corinthians 9:19-23," *RevExp* 110 (2013): 591-608, who sees Paul not referring to his lifestyle without Torah and who espouses his rhetorical adaptability to argue from the viewpoints of others as a Torah-obedient Jew. A similar view is proffered by David J. Rudolph, *A Jew to the Jews: Jewish Contours of Pauline Flexibility in 1 Corinthians 9:19-23* (WUNT 2.304; Tübingen: Mohr Siebeck, 2011), who proposes that "scholars overstate their case when they assert that 1 Cor 9:19-23 is incompatible with a Torah-observant Paul . . . [since] 1 Cor 9:19-23 can be read as the discourse of a Jew who lived within the bounds of Mosaic law." Similar is Brian J. Tucker, *Remain in Your Calling: Paul and the Continuation of Social Identities in 1 Corinthians* (Eugene, OR: Pickwick, 2011), 100-109.

pressures to assimilate to Hellenistic culture (1 Macc 1:60-61). Even Philo could not conceive of reducing circumcision merely to the status of allegory (Philo, *Migr.* 89-93). And yet Paul can say that circumcision matters not. What counts for Paul is the new creation and the morally transformative realities that it engenders in subjects, including love and obeying commandments that amount to the "Torah of Christ" (Gal 6:2; 1 Cor 9:21). Such is the reason why Paul vouches for obedience as something that can be reckoned as circumcision (Rom 2:26-27), with the result that Jewishness is extended from circumcision of the heart by *pneuma* rather than extended from circumcision of the flesh by *Torah*. In other words, covenant membership is fictive rather than ethnic (Rom 2:28-29). For this reason, Paul can urge believers to resource righteous-living in union with the Messiah and life in the Spirit (Rom 6:1-23; 8:1-11; Gal 5:22-24), while accenting grace in antithesis to Torah (Rom 5:20-21; 6:14-15; Gal 2:21; 5:4).

Paul's matrix of Christology and eschatology leads to a decentering of the Torah. Even more shocking is the corollary of the fracturing of social structures that ordered relationships between Jews and Gentiles. Paul no longer sees himself "in Judaism" (Gal 1:13), nor does he consider his Gentile converts any longer in "paganism" (1 Cor 12:2; 1 Thess 1:10; 4:5). They have entered into a new social horizon (Gal 3:28; Col 3:11). They constitute a "third race," we could say, where Paul can divide humanity into the classes of "Jews . . . Greeks [and] the church of God" (1 Cor 10:32). Such language is even more scandalous as we remember that this is Paul speaking, the self-described Jew, Hebrew, and Israelite.

So, as Jewish as Paul was, he said and did things that provoked ire, umbrage, and violence from his fellow Jews. He conceived of his own identity and vocation as indelibly connected to Israel's sacred history, but determined more properly by his connection to Israel's Messiah. He paradoxically regarded the Torah as both repudiated and reappropriated in the new age that had dawned. He describes Christ-believers as sharing in Israel's blessings without the symbols of their covenantal belonging and incipiently experiencing the new creation ahead of the nation of Israel. Paul contributed to the gentilization of the church and, I suspect unconsciously, to the eventual "parting of the ways" between Christianity and Judaism.[9] By virtue of Paul's activities and

9. See Alan Segal, *Paul the Convert: The Apostolate and Apostasy of Saul the Pharisee* (New Haven: Yale University Press, 1990), 267: "Although it is possible to overemphasize the role of gentile Christianity in the early church, in Paul's writings we can see some of the reasons for its success"; and James D. G. Dunn, *The Parting of the Ways: Between Christianity and Judaism and Their Significance for the Character of Christianity* (London: SCM, 1990), 139: "Paul's stand at Antioch and thereafter *made a parting of the ways inevitable, and already probably a factor for the churches of his foundation*" (italics original). See similarly E. P. Sanders, *Paul, the Law, and the Jewish People* (Minneapolis: Fortress, 1983), 207-10.

legacy, he could be labeled as a Jewish apostate (just as he is accused of in Acts 21:20-21, 27-28; 24:5-6).[10]

As a result, we are faced with a number of questions about Paul and the Jews: Where in Judaism should we situate Paul? What kind of Jew was he? And how did he relate to contemporary Judaism as a Christ-believing Jew?

A whole industry of scholarship has attempted to map Paul in relation to Judaism and to show where he fit into the spectrum of Jewish beliefs and practices. A notion common in the nineteenth century and first half of the twentieth century was that Paul's "Christianity" was an intellectual construction that had burst through the confines of a Jewish particularism based on "works" to become a universal religion based upon "grace."[11] At the end of the nineteenth century, Adolf von Harnack declared that Paul "delivered the Christian religion from Judaism."[12] The next fifty years of scholarship offered little resistance to that position, as indicated by Rudolf Bultmann's use of the heading "Jewish legalism" to summarize the substance of Judaism as a backdrop to Christianity.[13] Paul was the first great Christian theologian!

A reassessment and even a recasting of the Jewish nature of Paul's thinking were precipitated by several things. First, there was scholarly recoil at the horrors of the European Holocaust, coupled with the observation that the grotesque evils of the Holocaust were at least partly perpetuated by a specifically Christian anti-Semitism. This point alone required a radical rethink of Paul and the Jewish people. Second, there was the discovery of the Dead Sea Scrolls and several scholarly comparisons of Paul with later rabbinic literature, with the result that Jewish sources eclipsed Hellenistic sources as the primary foil for Paul's thought. Third, the revolution in Pauline studies ushered in by E. P. Sanders in the 1970s spawned the subsequent "New Perspective on Paul" (NPP),[14] which

10. Udo Schnelle (*Apostle Paul: His Life and Theology*, trans. M. Eugene Boring [Grand Rapids, MI: Baker Academic, 2005], 362): "Not only for Jews but for strict Jewish Christians, there was no longer any difference between Paul and an out-and-out apostate who had betrayed the true spiritual home of both Jews and Christians, the synagogue." See discussion in John M. G. Barclay, "Paul among Diaspora Jews: Anomaly or Apostate?," *JSNT* 60 (1995): 89-120; James D. G. Dunn, "Paul: Apostate or Apostle of Israel?," *ZNW* 89 (1998): 256-71.

11. One thinks here of a trajectory of scholarship including F. C. Baur, Adolf von Harnack, and Rudolf Bultmann. See Anders Gerdmar, *Roots of Theological Anti-Semitism: German Biblical Interpretation and the Jews, from Herder and Semler to Kittel and Bultmann* (Leiden: Brill, 2009).

12. Adolf von Harnack, *What Is Christianity?* (New York: Harper & Row, 1957), 176.

13. Rudolf Bultmann, *Primitive Christianity in Its Contemporary Setting*, trans. R. H. Fuller (London: Thames & Hudson, 1956), 59-71.

14. See E. P. Sanders, *Paul and Palestinian Judaism: A Comparison of Patterns of Religion* (Philadelphia: Fortress, 1977); idem, *Paul, the Law, and the Jewish People*.

took as its starting point the view that Paul's problem with Judaism was not "legalism" but something else like "ethnocentrism." Scholars like James Dunn and N. T. Wright, each with their own particular vision, proffered a portrait of Paul that entailed a heavy revision of traditional Protestant interpretation in light of a fresh reading of Paul within his Jewish context. The NPP showed how deeply embedded Paul was in Jewish worldviews and practices, yet proponents of the NPP still stressed that Paul had a problem with Judaism, a critique of its covenant theology and social boundaries, which ensured that his relationship with the Jews remained permanently volatile.[15]

The NPP certainly set the agenda for Pauline studies in 1990s and 2000s. Some scholars felt that the NPP was a theological betrayal of the Reformation and justifiable only by a skewed reading of Paul's Christ vs. Torah antithesis.[16] Others tried to engage in a courageous task of holding together the theological depth of the old perspective and the historical insights of the new perspective.[17] Others still felt that the NPP was not radical enough, thinking that it is more accurate and more ethically responsible to emphasize that Paul did not think that Judaism had any problem and the Jews would be saved under the auspices of their own covenant. Paul was merely urging them to see the Messiah as the instrument for including Gentiles in God's saving purposes.[18] And then some have gone for a Barthian or apocalyptic position and constructed a theology of Paul that harnesses a mixture of post-Holocaust sensitivities, revamped apocalyptic categories, and deconstruction of Reformed theology.[19] The current state

---

15. See overview in Kent L. Yinger, *The New Perspective on Paul: An Introduction* (Eugene, OR: Cascade, 2011); Hans Hübner, "Zur gegenwärtigen Diskussion über die Theologie des Paulus," *JBTh* 7 (1992): 399-413; Don Garlington, *In Defense of the New Perspective on Paul: Essays and Reviews* (Eugene, OR: Wipf & Stock, 2004).

16. See, e.g., critical evaluation in D. A. Carson, Peter T. O'Brien, and Mark A. Seifrid, eds., *Justification and Variegated Nomism,* vol. 1, *The Complexities of Second Temple Judaism;* vol. 2, *The Paradoxes of Paul* (Grand Rapids, MI: Baker Academic, 2001-4); Simon J. Gathercole, *Where Is the Boasting? Early Jewish Soteriology and Paul's Response in Romans 1–5* (Grand Rapids, MI: Eerdmans, 2002); A. Andrew Das, *Paul, the Law, and the Covenant* (Peabody, MA: Hendrickson, 2004); Stephen Westerholm, *Perspectives Old and New on Paul: The "Lutheran" Paul and His Critics* (Grand Rapids, MI: Eerdmans, 2003); and Michael Bachmann and Johannes Woyke, eds., *Lutherische und neue Paulusperspektive: Beiträge zu einem Schlüsselproblem der gegenwärtigen exegetischen Diskussion* (WUNT 182; Tübingen: Mohr Siebeck, 2005).

17. Michael F. Bird, *The Saving Righteousness of God: Studies on Paul, Justification, and the New Perspective* (PBM; Milton Keynes, UK: Paternoster, 2006); idem, "What if Martin Luther Had Read the Dead Sea Scrolls? Historical Particularity and Theological Interpretation in Pauline Theology: Galatians as a Test Case," *JTI* 3 (2009): 107-25.

18. Lloyd Gaston, *Paul and the Torah* (Vancouver: University of British Columbia Press, 1987); John G. Gager, *Reinventing Paul* (Oxford: OUP, 2000).

19. Douglas A. Campbell, *The Deliverance of God: An Apocalyptic Rereading of Paul* (Grand

of Pauline scholarship is thoroughly pluralistic and includes proponents who are traditional Protestants, NPP, post-NPP, the apocalyptic school, the radically Jewish Paul, other blended perspectives, plus every perspective on Paul you can imagine, spawning a variety of readings on Paul vis-à-vis Judaism.[20]

The following survey of scholarship on Paul and Judaism is by no means exhaustive but is emblematic of attempts to situate Paul in relation to Jewish communities with their distinctive beliefs and practices. To that end I've adopted the following taxonomy: a former Jew, a transformed Jew, a faithful Jew, a radical Jew, and an anomalous Jew. This taxonomy is undoubtedly plastic and has fuzzy boundaries where authors could fit into more than one category, but it remains a heuristic paradigm for exploring Paul and Judaism.

A Former Jew

Several recent scholars have affirmed Paul's self-identification as a Jew, while simultaneously asserting the discontinuities between Paul and his Jewish contemporaries, not least in Paul's social location and the significance of his Christian identity as well. While Paul described himself as an ethnic Jew, even so, by virtue of his radical recasting of covenant boundaries and in light of his description of his participation in Christ, he is a *former Jew*. So for J. Louis Martyn, "The church, in short, is a family made up of former Jews and former Gentiles, not an enlarged version of a family that already exists."[21] Others have expanded upon this basic point.

Francis Watson, in a heavily revised version of his original publication, examines the social reality underlying Paul's statements about Judaism, the

---

Rapids, MI: Eerdmans, 2009); idem, "Christ and the Church in Paul: A 'Post–New Perspective' Account," in *The Apostle Paul: Four Views*, ed. M. F. Bird (Grand Rapids, MI: Zondervan, 2012), 113-43; and evaluation in Chris Tilling, ed., *Beyond Old and New Perspectives: Reflections on the Work of Douglas Campbell* (Eugene, OR: Cascade, 2014).

20. See Kathy Ehrensperger, *That We May Be Mutually Encouraged: Feminism and the New Perspective in Pauline Studies* (London: T&T Clark, 2004); Charles Cosgrove, Herold Weiss, and Khiok-Khng Yeo, *Cross-Cultural Paul: Journeys to Others, Journeys to Ourselves* (Grand Rapids, MI: Eerdmans, 2005); Mark D. Given, ed., *Paul Unbound: Other Perspectives on the Apostle Paul* (Peabody, MA: Hendrickson, 2010); Christopher D. Stanley, *The Colonized Apostle: Paul through Postcolonial Eyes* (Minneapolis: Fortress, 2011); Bird, *The Apostle Paul: Four Views*; Magnus Zetterholm, *Approaches to Paul: A Student's Guide to Recent Scholarship* (Minneapolis: Fortress, 2009), esp. 195-224.

21. J. Louis Martyn, *Galatians* (AB; New York: Doubleday, 1997), 382.

Torah, and Gentiles.[22] He sees Paul as a catalyst in transitioning certain Christ-believing communities from a reform movement within Judaism to becoming a sect that was deliberately independent and insulated from Jewish synagogues.[23] According to Watson, Paul regards "Judaism" as virtually synonymous with "Pharisaism," denoting the zeal for one's ancestral traditions, the very kind he experienced as a former persecutor of the church.[24] The debates that Paul had in Antioch and Galatia and that were reflected in his letter to the Romans show his concern to create a socioreligious space for Gentiles to exist as a community and to practice their faith without Torah observance, achieved largely by a reinterpretation of Jewish religious traditions.[25] Watson has the courage to set out Paul's radicalism and controversy without explaining it away or blunting its rhetorical edges.[26] Even so, I still wonder whether "sectarian separation" is really the best model for describing the social ethos of the Pauline communities. Paul's efforts to foster unity between Gentile Christ-believers and Jewish Christ-believers, where the latter were still attached in varying ways to Jewish communities and institutions, would make it impossible to absolutely sever a social connection between the two.[27] Indeed, the subsequent history of Jewish and Christian relations shows that the parting of the ways was never clean or absolute but always complex and malleable. Perhaps Paul understood his community as something like para-Jewish rather than post- or non-Jewish. While the identity and praxis of Christ-believers were defined by a mix of eschatology and Christology, there remained nonetheless an umbilical link between the Pauline churches and Jewish communities.

Love Sechrest engages in an ethnoracial study of Paul's thought, plotting the continuities (e.g., Rom 4:1-25; 11:25-32) and discontinuities (1 Cor 9:19-23; 10:32; Gal 6:16) that can be posited between Paul and Judaism on account of Paul's apocalyptic convictions about the new creation and his eschatological

22. Francis Watson, *Paul, Judaism, and the Gentiles: Beyond the New Perspective* (rev. ed.; Grand Rapids, MI: Eerdmans, 2007).

23. Watson, *Paul, Judaism, and the Gentiles*, 21-24, 51-53, 344-46; and see Barclay, *Jews in the Mediterranean Diaspora*, 386; Wayne Meeks, "Breaking Away: Three New Testament Pictures of Christianity's Separation from Jewish Communities," in *"To See Ourselves as Others See Us": Christians, Jews, and "Others" in Late Antiquity*, ed. J. Neusner and E. S. Frerich (Chico, CA: Scholars, 1985), 106; Segal, *Paul the Convert*, 271.

24. Watson, *Paul, Judaism, and the Gentiles*, 22-23.

25. Watson, *Paul, Judaism, and the Gentiles*, 52, 344-45.

26. Watson, *Paul, Judaism, and the Gentiles*, 24.

27. This is certainly the picture we get in Acts, with Paul beginning his preaching activities in synagogues, having Timothy circumcised, and even paying for two colleagues to take a Nazirite vow in the temple.

hope for Israel's salvation. She believes that, when the Pauline self-identity texts are interpreted against the framework of ancient Jewish constructions of race, it appears that Paul saw himself as someone who was born a Jew but no longer was one—not in the sense that his Jewishness was entirely negated, but it had been transcended by a deeper reality. Paul's perspective on the Christ-event apocalyptically changed his relationship with God, with his fellow Jews, and his disposition toward racial "others." According to Sechrest, "When Paul maintains that he can 'become *like* a Jew,' he clearly implies that he does not see himself as a Jew in the first place"; and "Paul and his Jewish-born and Gentile-born Christian family had become members of a new racial identity."[28] As will be seen later, I have a strong affinity with this position (see chapter 1), but some nuance might still be required, especially when it appears that the discontinuities between Paul and Judaism have been pressed too far.[29]

A Transformed Jew

Writers among the NPP, diverse as they are, have attempted to break the shackles of theological readings of Paul's letters that cast the Jews in the role of incipient medieval Catholic legalists by a fresh reading of Paul that has several characteristics:

1. engages in historically sensitive reading of Paul's letters that are insulated from anachronistic categories drawn from medieval and Reformed theologies;
2. reevaluates the soteriological patterns in Second Temple Judaism, with an accent placed on the nature of grace in Jewish religious belief;
3. undertakes a comparative study between Paul and other Jewish writers in relation to Jewish apocalypticism, first-century Jewish zeal and ethnocentrism, and sectarian debates about the interpretation of Torah.

To generalize, the result has been the portrayal of Paul as a more thoroughgoing Jewish figure whose Jewish worldview has been transformed rather than negated by his calling to be the apostle to the Gentiles.

28. Love L. Sechrest, *A Former Jew: Paul and the Dialectics of Race* (LNTS 410; London: T&T Clark, 2009), 156, 164.

29. See N. T. Wright, *Paul and the Faithfulness of God* (COQG 4; London: SPCK, 2014), 1448.

E. P. Sanders's landmark publication *Paul and Palestinian Judaism* changed the landscape of Pauline studies. While previous scholars had hinted at similar conclusions, Sanders effectively succeeded in ushering in a new view of Judaism and a new view of Paul within New Testament studies.[30] Sanders did two important things. First, instead of studying Paul as an object of theology to answer Christian questions concerned with "Am I saved by what I believe or by what I do?" he opted for a comparative-religious approach that attempted to trace the similarities between Paul's pattern of religion and the pattern of religion in Palestinian Judaism. Second, Sanders rejected the jaundiced and caricatured views of Second Temple Judaism inherited from the nineteenth century, which depicted Judaism as an externalized system of works righteousness and empty ritual. Accordingly, Sanders surveyed writings from rabbinic literature, the Dead Sea Scrolls, the Apocrypha, and pseudepigrapha, concluding that the sources show a heavy reliance on God's mercy and the efficacy of the covenant. Sanders sees that, "in all the literature surveyed, obedience maintains one's position in the covenant, but it does not earn God's grace as such. It simply keeps an individual in the group which is the recipient of God's grace."[31] Sanders summarized the Palestinian pattern of religion that was pervasive before AD 70 as teaching what he labels "covenantal nomism," that is, the view "that one's place in God's plan is established on the basis of the covenant and that the covenant requires as the proper response of man his obedience to its commandments, while providing means of atonement for transgression."[32] Or more fully, it can be enumerated as "(1) God has chosen Israel and (2) given the law. That implies both (3) God's promise to maintain the election and (4) the requirement to obey. (5) God rewards obedience and punishes transgression. (6) The law provides for means of atonement, and atonement results in (7) maintenance or re-establishment of the covenant relationship. (8) All those who are maintained in the covenant by obedience, atonement and God's mercy belong to the group which will be saved."[33] Accordingly, "election and ultimately salvation are considered to be by God's mercy rather than human achievement."[34]

---

30. On antecedents to E. P. Sanders, see Preston M. Sprinkle, "The Old Perspective on the New Perspective: A Review of Some 'Pre-Sanders' Thinkers," *Themelios* 30 (2005): 21-31, who includes G. F. Moore, Krister Stendahl, George Howard, and Joseph Tyson. To the list I would add N. A. Dahl, "The Doctrine of Justification: Its Social Function and Implications," in *Studies in Paul* (Minneapolis: Augsburg, 1977), 95-120, and Markus Barth, "Jews and Gentiles: The Social Character of Justification in Paul," *JES* 5 (1968): 241-67.

31. Sanders, *Paul and Palestinian Judaism*, 420.

32. Sanders, *Paul and Palestinian Judaism*, 75.

33. Sanders, *Paul and Palestinian Judaism*, 422.

34. Sanders, *Paul and Palestinian Judaism*, 422.

What this pattern has to do with Paul is that a new view of Judaism requires a new backdrop against which one must understand Paul's own pattern of religion centered on Jesus Christ. According to Sanders, the two most basic convictions that explain Paul's theology are (1) Jesus Christ is Lord, and in him God has provided salvation; and (2) Paul was called to be an apostle to the Gentiles.[35] Granted those basic convictions, Sanders thinks it follows that Paul's reasoning is not from plight to solution but from solution to plight. If God has sent Christ as Savior, then surely the world needed such a Savior in the first place. Paul's gospel is about the saving action of God in Christ and how his hearers can participate in it by faith.[36] Furthermore, Paul believes that salvation is attained in a mystical union with Christ, participating in his death and resurrection, where one submits to Christ's lordship. Paul's objection to the Torah is that it is not part of the way of salvation that God has staked out in Christ. The problem is not that the Torah is bad or that it is impossible to obey; it is simply not the locus of the divine saving action. Obedience to the Torah might produce a type of righteousness, but not the true goal of religion: a righteousness unto life, which comes by Christ and not by Torah. The Torah was indeed God-given, but it had the function of consigning everyone to sin so that everyone could be saved by God's grace in Christ.[37] Yet Paul can make that claim only if he has bypassed, if not denied, three crucial pillars of Judaism: Israel's election, the covenant, and Torah. Quite obviously for Sanders, then, Paul himself is not a covenantal nomist because he does not have a covenant theology per se, where God chooses Israel and makes a covenant with it that the people ratify by their subsequent obedience. Rather, the heart of Paul's thought is participation in Christ, with being "in the covenant" effectively replaced by being "in Christ."[38] Paul denies that election is efficacious, since one need not become Jewish to become a descendant of Abraham.[39] Paul denies that the Jewish notion of covenant can be effective for salvation, and he thus undermines the entire soteriological scheme of Judaism.[40] This consequence leads to Sanders's central claim: "In short, *this is what Paul finds*

35. Sanders, *Paul and Palestinian Judaism*, 441-42; idem, *Paul, the Law, and the Jewish People*, 152, 162.

36. Sanders, *Paul and Palestinian Judaism*, 442-47, 474-75, 497; idem, *Paul, the Law, and the Jewish People*, 138.

37. Sanders, *Paul and Palestinian Judaism*, 475-97, 505-6, 549-50; idem, *Paul, the Law, and the Jewish People*, 140-41.

38. Sanders, *Paul and Palestinian Judaism*, 513-15, 543.

39. Sanders, *Paul, the Law, and the Jewish People*, 160.

40. Sanders, *Paul and Palestinian Judaism*, 551.

wrong in Judaism: it is not Christianity."[41] Sanders teases out this conclusion later to mean that what Paul criticizes in his native religion is a lack of faith in Christ, a reliance on the efficacy of election "according to the flesh," and a lack of equality for Gentiles.[42]

Where Paul and his churches stand in relation to Judaism is ambiguous for Sanders. On the one hand, by drawing together Jews and Gentiles into a single body claiming Abrahamic sonship and experiencing the new creation, Paul created a "third entity," which became the functional equivalent of a "true Israel." On the other hand, Paul and the Jews who punished him with flogging must have regarded Paul as falling within Judaism, since punishment implies inclusion.[43] Paul had not intended to engineer a break between Christianity and Judaism, but he certainly contributed to it by denying that Abrahamic lineage was the basis of election and by insisting that faith in Christ and not proselytism was the means for joining the people of God. Sanders says, "We can see in the Pauline letters the nucleus of much of Christianity's understanding of itself. It would appropriate Israelite history and also claim to transcend it. It would rely on Jewish Scripture and find its truth therein, but it would not hesitate to dismiss unwanted parts and to supplement it with new words, some 'from the Lord' and some from human authority."[44]

James D. G. Dunn was the first to coin the phrase "New Perspective" for the post-Sanders wave of scholarship that tried to reevaluate Paul and Judaism.[45] In the aftermath Dunn claimed, "Nothing less became necessary than a complete reassessment of Paul's relationship with his ancestral religion, not to mention all the considerable consequences which were bound to follow for our contemporary understanding of his theology."[46] Of course, if, as Sanders claimed, Judaism was not a religion of inherent works-righteousness, it still remained puzzling as to precisely what Paul was reacting against in his affirmation of justification by faith apart from works of the Torah. Dunn's early work on Paul attempted to answer the question as to what Paul found wrong with Judaism that Jesus was supposedly the answer to. The conclusion that Dunn reached was that the Torah served to exclude Gentiles from the righteousness

41. Sanders, *Paul and Palestinian Judaism*, 552 (italics original).
42. Sanders, *Paul, the Law, and the Jewish People*, 155, 160.
43. Sanders, *Paul, the Law, and the Jewish People*, 171-79, 192.
44. Sanders, *Paul, the Law, and the Jewish People*, 209-10.
45. See the lifetime collection of essays in James D. G. Dunn, *The New Perspective on Paul* (rev. ed.; Grand Rapids, MI: Eerdmans, 2008).
46. James D. G. Dunn, *The Theology of Paul the Apostle* (Edinburgh: T&T Clark, 1998), 5.

of God now revealed in the Messiah.[47] Paul tried to dismantle the predominant Jewish view that Gentiles were sinners who had to be segregated from faithful Jews: "It was this characteristically Jewish 'attitude' to the law, or to Gentiles on the basis of the law, that Paul found it essential to challenge in order to maintain the gospel of justification by faith."[48] Paul's Jewish compatriots had been blinded by their zealous desire to reinforce the social boundaries that kept Israel separate from pagans. This in turn prevented them from seeing that, in Jesus, God had brought the Gentiles into the family of Abraham. Dunn's conclusion from Galatians and Romans is that, in Paul's eyes, "Israel had become, as it were, Judaism. It had shifted the focus of the covenant in which God chose Jacob by grace and made him Israel, and had focused the covenant in a law understood as limiting that grace and preventing the Jacobs of his day from participating in it."[49] The result for Dunn is that "Paul would by no means have regarded himself as outside Israel looking in. Outside Judaism, perhaps; but Judaism as defined by his Pharisaic contemporaries, Judaism as distinct from Israel; Paul [was] an Israelite still."[50]

Dunn's description of Paul vis-à-vis Judaism has four basic tenets:

1. Paul regarded his way of life in Judaism as something past, with "Judaism" defined as a mode of Pharisaic zeal for Israel's heritage.
2. Paul did not reject his own Jewishness but regarded it as functional rather than inalienable, as something to culturally distinguish himself from Gentiles, to denote a code of conduct or manner of living, and to describe an inner reality and relationship with God in which non-Jews could participate.
3. Paul designates himself as an Israelite, Hebrew, and descendant of Abraham; these labels, however, are primarily determined by one's relationship to God and thereby transcend ethnic and social distinctions and absorb ethnic and social diversity.
4. The primary rubric for Paul's self-identification is his self-description as one "in Christ," meaning that his identity was determined by his relationship to Christ, even though it did not entirely devalorize his other identities, such as that of a circumcised Jew.[51]

47. Dunn, *New Perspective*, 1-17.
48. Dunn, *New Perspective*, 31-32.
49. Dunn, *Parting of the Ways*, 147-48.
50. Dunn, *Parting of the Ways*, 149.
51. James D. G. Dunn, *Beginning from Jerusalem* (CITM 2; Grand Rapids, MI: Eerdmans,

Dunn's Paul is one who is thoroughly enmeshed in Jewish sectarian and halakic debates about Gentiles and the Torah, even while Paul adopts strategies that would move his converts away from Judaism.

N. T. Wright has emphasized across his career that Paul was a very Jewish thinker. In his more recent magnum opus he has devoted a mammoth 1,500 pages to describing how Paul redrew the Jewish worldview, symbols, and story around Jesus the Messiah.[52] The background story is that Israel was meant to be a light to the nations, but they recapitulated Adam's sin by their disobedience and found themselves in a protracted state of exile, resulting in the infliction of covenant curses. Many groups within Israel, including zealous Pharisees like Saul of Tarsus, had expected the pathway to Israel's deliverance to emerge through a regime of purity observance, separation from sinners and apostates, and militant resistance to pagan powers, which left them clinging to a "national righteousness." Yet the scriptural story was that God would remain faithful to his covenant promises to Abraham and bless the nations through his "seed," Israel and her Messiah, a promise that had come to pass in Jesus and his followers. Thus, Israel's problem is a mixture of an Adamic state, an exilic curse, and an ethnocentric disposition.[53] Given that narrative, Wright argues that Paul's intellectual current is not *against* Jewish religion as much as it is a *transformation* of Jewish beliefs around a particular messianic eschatology.[54] The sticking point was that Paul "believed that the Messiah had come, and had inaugurated the long-awaited new age, and they [i.e., his fellow Jews] did not."[55] While "Paul was born a Jew, and believed that the Jewish way of life and view of life were above all *true*," even so, Paul had a "complex and ambiguous relation to those of his Jewish contemporaries who did not believe that Jesus of Nazareth had been raised from the dead."[56] Paul had been transformed by his encounter with the risen Christ, which included both a call to his apostolic vocation but also a conversion to seeing the Messiah's death and resurrection as redefining the goal and meaning of the Jewish way of life.[57]

In terms of Paul's Jewish identity, there is no question of an "erasure," but a type of redundancy of the old order of life in light of the new event that had

---

2009), 522-30; idem, "Who Did Paul Think He Was? A Study of Jewish Christian Identity," *NTS* 45 (1999): 174-93.

52. Wright, *Paul and the Faithfulness of God*.

53. Wright, *Paul and the Faithfulness of God*, esp. 783-95 and 894-96, 1064-65, 1207-8, 1455.

54. Wright, *Paul and the Faithfulness of God*, 1407-72.

55. Wright, *Paul and the Faithfulness of God*, 1409.

56. Wright, *Paul and the Faithfulness of God*, 1410-11 (italics original).

57. Wright, *Paul and the Faithfulness of God*, 1423-26.

burst upon the world in Jesus. For Wright, "Eschatological messianism . . . is what counts, a vision rooted in the Jewish world, only comprehensive as a scripturally based variation on first-century visions of what it meant to be a loyal Israelite."[58] Consequently he can affirm that Paul saw the church as some kind of third entity, neither Jewish nor Gentile, but a new social reality (see 1 Cor 1:22-25; 10:32). To describe Paul's description of the church as a "third race" is neither a non-Jewish nor an anti-Jewish entity, since it presumes a Jewish way of dividing the world into Jews and Gentiles, and the new identity is one that is rooted in Israel's Messiah, even if redefined around a crucified and risen Messiah. To lean on Wright's metaphor, Christ-believing identity clearly has a Jewish DNA, so even if it has mutated somewhat, there is still a family resemblance. In the end, what ensures continuity of some sort—apart from Paul's olive tree metaphor in Rom 11—is that Wright sees Paul's account of the identity of the Messiah's people as grounded in the faithfulness of God to Israel.[59] Still, for Wright, discontinuity is more pronounced, since Paul sees his identity as christologically transformed. Hence Wright concludes: "Paul insisted that his primary self-definition was not, in fact, simply that of being Jewish. His primary self-understanding was that he was a Messiah-man. He was *en Christō*, and conversely the Messiah lived in him, so that Paul and all other Messiah people had 'the Messiah's mind.' These extraordinary claims, only comprehensible from within the Jewish worldview, nevertheless split that world open at the seams. They are those of man who has burnt his boats."[60]

Terence Donaldson, a much-neglected luminary in the NPP constellation, tackles the problem of how Paul came to launch the Gentile mission.[61] Donaldson took as his starting point Sanders's account of Judaism as covenantal nomism, in which election and salvation were considered to be by God's mercy rather than merited by human achievement. Paul himself was once a zealous Pharisee who believed that the only hope for Gentiles was to become a proselyte to Judaism, which is why he once preached circumcision to Gentile audiences (see Gal 5:11). Paul persecuted Christians for a range of reasons, yet paramount among them was the social reason that the Christ of the kerygma represented a rival to the Torah as demarcating the people who would be saved in the future.[62] The event

---

58. Wright, *Paul and the Faithfulness of God*, 1433.

59. Wright, *Paul and the Faithfulness of God*, 1443-49 (esp. 1447-48).

60. Wright, *Paul and the Faithfulness of God*, 1471.

61. Terence L. Donaldson, *Paul and the Gentiles: Remapping the Apostle's Convictional World* (Minneapolis: Fortress, 1997); idem, *Jews and Anti-Judaism in the New Testament: Decision Points and Divergent Interpretations* (London: SPCK, 2010), 109-38.

62. Donaldson, *Paul and the Gentiles*, 295-97.

on the Damascus road instilled in Paul a fundamental inversion in his convictions about Christ and Torah. Just as Paul viewed Christ and his followers as an alternative to the way to life under the Torah prior to his conversion, so too after his conversion he believed that Christ and Torah represented alternative and mutually exclusive paths to righteousness.[63] The inversion, however, was not total, since God had given Torah, and Paul could not reject it in the same way that he had formerly rejected Christ. Also, Paul's native convictional world was restructured around a new center, Christ, and key elements were reconfigured, including God, the election of Israel, Israel's role as a light to the Gentiles, and the consummation of God's reign on earth.[64] According to Donaldson: "While there can be no doubt that important things were left behind, and at substantial personal cost (see Phil 3:7-8), his shift from Torah to Christ has to be understood not as a total abandonment of one set of convictions in favor of another, different and distinct, but as the reconfiguration of one set of convictions around a new and powerful center. In the process, some individual native convictions were abandoned, others radically altered, still others carried over more or less intact, and additional Christian ones introduced."[65] A key transformation was Paul's idea of mission, which was that Gentiles could share in Israel's righteousness only by being "in Christ" and becoming full members of a redefined Israel. Paul's Gentile mission thus needs to be understood as a combination of two factors: models of apostleship already in operation within the nascent Christian movement, and the energy infused from his call to make Christ known to the Gentiles.[66] A final factor was Paul's belief in the nearness of the parousia. For Donaldson, this explains the "perplexing ambiguity" as to how Paul can, on the one hand, insist that old distinctions between Jew and Gentile are obsolete and, on the other hand, assume that ethnic Israel continues to be a significant entity. Paul could live with the tension of radically defining the boundaries of Israel while affirming Israel's place among the saved. In the end, Paul regarded Gentile Christians as eschatological proselytes in a newly defined family of Abraham. Subsequent generations would come to a fork in the road between an Israel defined by ethnicity and Torah and a Gentile church defining itself as a "new Israel."[67]

Critiques of the NPP with its view of Paul as a "transformed" Jew have been wide and varied. To generalize:

63. Donaldson, *Paul and the Gentiles*, 273-92, 297-98.

64. Donaldson, *Paul and the Gentiles*, 292, 297.

65. Donaldson, *Paul and the Gentiles*, 298.

66. Donaldson, *Paul and the Gentiles*, 298-99.

67. Donaldson, *Paul and the Gentiles*, 299, 305-7.

1. Some have challenged Sanders's summary of Palestinian Judaism as "covenantal nomism" on several grounds, such as that it is so broad as to be meaningless or that it fails to reckon with the fact that in some instances the emphasis could fall on Torah rather than on covenant, yielding a soteriological pattern based on obedience, or "works."

2. Many have been dissatisfied with Sanders's idiosyncratic statement that what Paul found wrong with Judaism was that it was not Christianity.

3. It has been complained that identifying works of the law as primarily signifying social boundary markers separating Jews and Gentiles and identifying justification by faith as a legitimation for the covenant membership of Gentiles simply collapses theology into sociology.

4. Others have objected that the NPP has still not escaped the tendency to depict Paul as an anti-Jewish figure who is characterized by an intractable supersessionism, and the old charge of Jewish legalism has merely been exchanged for new a charge of Jewish nationalism.

5. The NPP still operates with a Christianized Paul, whereas Paul was in reality a Torah-observant Jew writing to Gentiles and at no point expecting Jewish Christ-believers to cease obeying the Torah.

A Faithful Jew

Another cohort of scholars has attempted to reclaim Paul's Jewishness over and against anachronistic Christianizations of him and to utilize this more radically Jewish Paul as a catalyst for refreshing Jewish-Christian relations. Paul the apostle might be a misunderstood Jew, but he remained a *faithful Jew*.

Markus Barth was at the forefront of much of a rethink of New Testament studies in light of Christian-Jewish dialogue. Barth's study "St. Paul—a Good Jew,"[68] provocative in its day, was Barth-the-younger's take on the theological superiority complex that Christian theologians often lauded over the Jews and the caricature of Judaism that it engendered. For Barth, such a status quo in Pauline studies should be rejected for five reasons:

---

68. Markus Barth, "Der gute Jude Paulus," in *Richte unsere Füsse auf den Weg des Friedens*, ed. A. Baudis, D. Clausert, V. Schliski, and B. Wegener (FS Helmut Gollwitzer; Munich: Christian Kaiser, 1979), 107-37, repr. "St. Paul—a Good Jew," *HBT* 1 (1979): 7-45. See reflections on Markus Barth's article by Stanley E. Porter, "Was Paul a Good Jew? Fundamental Issues in a Current Debate," in *Christian-Jewish Relations through the Centuries*, ed. S. E. Porter and B. W. R. Pearson (JSNTSup 192; Sheffield: Sheffield Academic, 2000), 148-74.

1. The Old Testament background to the New Testament demonstrates that the coming of Jesus Christ and the Spirit can be understood only in light of the framework of the divine promises given to Israel.

2. Emerging Jewish scholarship identifies Paul as a "prodigal son" who is a challenge to the Jewish faith, but he remains nonetheless an authentic Jewish figure.

3. Recent scholarly works have shown just how enmeshed Paul was in the Jewish world, and the so-called anti-Judaism of Paul is blatant fiction.

4. Reluctance to acknowledge that Christian theology fostered an anti-Semitism that contributed to the Holocaust must be dismantled.

5. Criticism of Pauline interpretation need not mean a criticism of Paul himself. Barth's resulting point, which might seem prosaic now but was controversial back in 1960s, is that Paul needs to be rethought as a Jewish thinker and, accordingly, ecumenical relationships between Jews and Christians need to be refreshed.

The views of Markus Barth, who considered Paul a good Jew, form a natural segue into contemporary studies of Paul by an increasing number of Jewish scholars. Since the nineteenth century, a trickle of Jewish studies of Paul have appeared, which mainstream scholarship often ignores.[69] There is even now a Jewish study Bible of the Christian New Testament![70]

Mark Nanos, a Reform Jewish scholar, has ridden the tide of post-Holocaust scholarship, but with the aim of offering a revised portrait of Paul that sees him as thoroughly enmeshed in first-century Jewish life and is not condu-

---

69. See surveys in D. A. Hagner, "Paul in Modern Jewish Thought," in *Pauline Studies*, ed. D. A. Hagner and M. J. Harris (FS F. F. Bruce; Exeter: Paternoster, 1980), 143-65; idem, "Paul as a Jewish Believer—according to His Letters," in *Jewish Believers in Jesus: The Early Centuries*, ed. O. Skarsaune and R. Hvalvik (Peabody, MA: Hendrickson, 2007), 96-120; Stefan Meißner, *Die Heimholung des Ketzers: Studien zur jüdischen Auseinandersetzung mit Paulus* (WUNT 2.87; Tübingen: Mohr Siebeck, 1996); W. D. Davies, "Paul: From the Jewish Point of View," in *The Cambridge History of Judaism*, vol. 3, *The Early Roman Period*, ed. William Horbury, W. D. Davies, and John Sturdy (Cambridge: CUP, 1999), 3:678-730; Sung-Hee Lee-Linke, ed., *Paulus der Jude: Seine Stellung im christlich-jüdischen Dialog heute* (Frankfurt: Lembeck, 2005); Michael F. Bird and Preston Sprinkle, "Jewish Interpretation of Paul in the Last Thirty Years," *CBR* 6 (2008): 355-76; Daniel R. Langton, *The Apostle Paul in the Jewish Imagination: A Study in Modern Jewish-Christian Relations* (Cambridge: CUP, 2010); John Gager, "The Rehabilitation of Paul in Jewish Tradition," in *"The One Who Sows Bountifully": Essays in Honor of Stanley K. Stowers*, ed. C. Hodge, S. Olyan, D. Ullicci, and E. Wasserman (Providence, RI: Brown Judaic Studies, 2013), 29-41.

70. Amy-Jill Levine, ed., *The Jewish Annotated New Testament* (Oxford: OUP, 2011).

cive to (mis)appropriations of Paul that foster anti-Jewish ideologies.[71] Nanos does not regard Paul as a figure who misrepresented Judaism, but as a Torah-observant Pharisee who did not break with the essential tenets of Jewish belief.[72] According to Nanos, Paul believed that the death and resurrection of the Messiah had ushered in the new eschatological age, which set the time (now) and the mode (faith) for Gentiles to become members of God's people alongside the Jews. The result is that Gentiles need not become proselytes to Judaism through circumcision but should remain as Gentiles.[73] Nevertheless, Nanos sees Paul as urging Gentiles to adopt a minimal standard of Torah-adherence by observing the Noachide commandments in order to promote harmonious relationships with Jewish synagogal communities.[74] Whereas some interpreters regard Paul as trying to preserve the freedom of Gentile Christ-believers from the Torah, Nanos argues that Paul was trying to constrain the freedom of Gentile Christ-believers through halakah.[75] Paul's only negative remarks about the Torah are not about the Torah per se but about the proselytism of his fellow Jews who did not believe that the new age had dawned and who insisted on Gentile circumcision as the rite of entry into Israel.[76] Nanos perceives Paul as

71. Mark D. Nanos, *The Mystery of Romans: The Jewish Context of Paul's Letter* (Minneapolis: Fortress, 1996); idem, "The Jewish Context of the Gentile Audience Addressed in Paul's Letter to the Romans," *CBQ* 61 (1999): 283-304; idem, *The Irony of Galatians: Paul's Letter in First-Century Context* (Minneapolis: Fortress, 2002); idem, "How Inter-Christian Approaches to Paul's Rhetoric Can Perpetuate Negative Valuations of Jewishness—although Proposing to Avoid That Outcome," *BI* 13 (2005): 255-69; idem, "Paul between Jews and Christians," *BI* 13 (2005): 221-316; idem, "Paul and Judaism: Why Not Paul's Judaism?," in *Paul Unbound: Other Perspectives on the Apostle*, ed. M. D. Given (Peabody, MA: Hendrickson, 2010), 117-60; idem, "A Jewish View," in *Four Views on the Apostle Paul*, ed. M. F. Bird (Grand Rapids, MI: Zondervan, 2012), 159-93; idem, "To the Churches within the Synagogues of Rome," in *Reading Paul's Letter to the Romans*, ed. Jerry L. Sumney (Atlanta: SBL, 2012), 11-28; idem, "Paul's Polemic in Philippians 3 as Jewish-Subgroup Vilification of Local Non-Jewish Cultic and Philosophical Alternatives," *JSPL* 3 (2013): 47-92; idem, "Paul's Non-Jews Do Not Become 'Jews,' but Do They Become 'Jewish'? Reading Romans 2:25-29 within Judaism, alongside Josephus," *Journal of the Jesus Movement in Its Jewish Setting* 1 (2014): 26-53; Mark D. Nanos and Magnus Zetterholm, eds., *Paul within Judaism* (Minneapolis: Fortress, 2015). See evaluations of Nanos's work in Bird and Sprinkle, "Jewish Views," 365-69; Langton, *Apostle Paul in Jewish Imagination*, 89-91; Zetterholm, *Approaches to Paul*, 147-55.

72. Nanos, *Romans*, 3-10; idem, "Jewish View," 166-71.

73. Nanos, *Romans*, 9; idem, "Jewish View," 171-74.

74. Nanos, *Romans*, 34-36, 50-56, 177-79; idem, "Jewish View," 174-75; idem, "Paul and Judaism," 147-48.

75. Observed rightly by Langton, *Apostle Paul in Jewish Imagination*, 101n147.

76. Nanos, *Romans*, 9-10, 177-79.

defending Gentiles from proselytism, even while they joined Christ-believing Jewish groups that practiced Torah observance and adopted some token measures of Torah observance themselves. Thus, Nanos regards Paul as engaging in an intra-Jewish debate about the status of Christ-believing Gentiles within Jewish assemblies rather than engaging in an *adversus Israel* debate that pits the "Christian" Paul against the Jewish people.

Pamela Eisenbaum is a contemporary Jewish New Testament scholar who teaches at a Christian seminary and has published a number of studies on Paul.[77] She rejects the essentialist framework for understanding Paul, where Christianity is defined by devotion to Christ and Judaism by devotion to Torah. Such an approach squeezes Paul into Christianity from Judaism and makes him effectively "Christian."[78] The problem is that Paul was not a "Christian," according to Eisenbaum, for his primary anthropological categories are not "Christian" and "non-Christian" but Jew and Gentile. Paul was a "typical Jew,"[79] but one who believed that the eschatological ingathering of the Gentiles was being accomplished through the death of Christ. "To put it boldly," Eisenbaum comments, "Jesus saves, but he only saves Gentiles."[80] She finds the idea deeply offensive that Judaism is a flawed religion inherently linked to sin. In her thinking, this is not what Paul was about; rather, Paul provides a way to maintain the particularity of his ethnic and religious identity without denying the ethnic and religious identity of others. Paul is, then, a working model for religious pluralism.[81]

The lasting contribution of Nanos and Eisenbaum and their colleagues on the "Paul within Judaism" is their reclamation of Paul as a Jewish thinker, one who is a Torah-observant Jew, and his debates about Gentiles and circumcision can be understood as in-house Jewish debates about how to include Gentile outsiders in Jewish assemblies. That said, there is still something that just does not fit. A close reading of the Pauline letters suggests that Paul's problem with contemporary Jews is not merely the proper grounds for mutual relationships between Gentile

77. Pamela M. Eisenbaum, "A Remedy for Having Been Born of Woman: Jesus, Gentiles, and Genealogy in Romans," *JBL* 123 (2004): 671-702; idem, "Following in the Footnotes of the Apostle Paul," in *Identity and the Politics of Scholarship in the Study of Religion*, ed. S. Davaney and J. Cabezon (New York: Routledge, 2004), 77-97; idem, "Paul, Polemics, and the Problem of Essentialism," *BI* 13 (2005): 224-38; idem, *Paul Was Not a Christian: The Original Message of a Misunderstood Apostle* (New York: HarperCollins, 2009).

78. Eisenbaum, "Problem of Essentialism," 232.

79. Eisenbaum, *Paul Was Not a Christian*, 150.

80. Eisenbaum, *Paul Was Not a Christian*, 242.

81. Eisenbaum, *Paul Was Not a Christian*, 1-4.

Christ-believers and non–Christ-believing Jews to take place; rather, it is an anthropological problem. Precisely, what is the problem with humanity that Israel with its Torah and covenant cannot fix? Paul's narrative scheme concerns how (1) *both* Jews and Gentiles are locked into sin, whether with Torah or without it, and (2) the Messiah's death and resurrection provide reconciliation to God for sin for *both* Jews and Gentiles completely without Torah.[82] Paul's complex scriptural and rhetorical discourse would hardly be warranted if he were simply insisting on dissolving the category "God-fearer" in such a way that left the status of his fellow Jews intact. Nor would Paul have been flogged five times by synagogue leaders and voiced concerns for his own safety when arriving in Jerusalem (2 Cor 11:32; Rom 15:30-32) for promoting views that are hardly unprecedented in the Jewish world (Josephus, *Ant.* 20.17-48; Philo, *QE* 2.2).[83] However, if Paul was revisioning election within a new eschatological constellation, identifying Israel's story as summed up in a crucified and risen Messiah, asserting that Gentiles were experiencing the blessing of covenantal renewal perhaps not instead of Israel but certainly ahead of Israel, and insinuating the obsolescence of Torah when it comes to gaining praise from God, then Jewish anxiety about Paul and Jewish animosity toward Paul becomes entirely explicable.

A Radical Jew

Daniel Boyarin's provocative volume *A Radical Jew* argues that Paul sought to assimilate Jews and Gentiles into the Hellenistic ideal of "the One," a type of social monism, through an allegorization of the signs of Israel.[84] On Boyarin's account, Paul, as a Hellenistic Jew, was deeply concerned with the salvation of Gentiles on the same ground as Jews, yet he knew that Judaism could not provide the solution. Paul was troubled by and critical of the postbiblical religion of his contemporaries, which "implicitly and explicitly created hierarchies between nations, genders, social classes."[85] This was Paul's preconversion plight, to which his Damascus road experience became the solution. Paul conceived of faith in Christ as a way of bringing together a Platonic universalism and a Judean tribalism. In

---

82. Contra Hodge (*If Sons, Then Heirs,* 9), who believes that, for the most part, "Paul is speaking to *gentiles* and not to humanity" (italics original).

83. On Jewish debates about circumcision and proselytism, see discussion in Bird, *Crossing Over Sea and Land,* 24-40.

84. Daniel Boyarin, *A Radical Jew: Paul and the Politics of Identity* (Berkeley: University of California Press, 1994).

85. Boyarin, *Radical Jew,* 52.

Boyarin's mind, "Paul was motivated by a Hellenistic desire for the One, which among other things produced an ideal of a universal human essence, beyond difference and hierarchy."[86] A text like Gal 3:28 then becomes "the baptismal declaration of the new humanity of new difference" through Paul's messianic universalism.[87] Boyarin, a Talmudist and cultural critic, certainly offers an outside-of-the-box view of Paul as viewed through his lens of a postmodern Hegelian dialectic. He demonstrates why philosophers have seen Paul as something of a catalyst for species of universalism and equality. But therein lies the problem, as Bruce Hansen has noted: "Boyarin's post-structuralist, post-colonial culture criticism does not depend on his reading of Paul and can be appreciated or critiqued independently. It is, however, debatable whether Paul and his letters correspond to the universalizing pole to which Boyarin assigns them."[88] Boyarin's radical portrait of Paul is a wonderful entrée into the things that philosophers and cultural critics like Alain Badiou and Stanislas Breton can do with Paul, but it probably has very little to do with what Paul himself actually thought he was doing.[89] Several other criticisms can be leveled against Boyarin.[90] To begin with, Boyarin's reading of Paul itself is highly allegorical rather than authentic, Hegelian rather than historical. In addition, Boyarin's Paul is decidedly Christology-lite, and the cross also seems to figure very little in Boyarin's account, features which do not square with a thick account of Paul.[91]

An Anomalous Jew

John Barclay has argued that Paul was "an anomalous diaspora Jew."[92] For Barclay, Paul was a Diaspora Jew who was highly assimilated to Hellenistic

---

86. Boyarin, *Radical Jew*, 7.

87. Boyarin, *Radical Jew*, 5.

88. Bruce Hansen, *All of You Are One: The Social Vision of Galatians 3.28, 1 Corinthians 12.13, and Colossians 3.11* (LNTS 409; London: T&T Clark, 2010), 14.

89. Which is precisely where Boyarin is situated in scholarship by P. Travis Kroeker, "Recent Continental Philosophers," in *The Blackwell Companion to Paul*, ed. S. Westerholm (Malden, MA: Blackwell, 2011), 442.

90. Bird and Sprinkle, "Jewish Views," 363-65.

91. N. T. Wright, "Two Radical Jews: A Review Article of Daniel Boyarin, *A Radical Jew: Paul and the Politics of Identity*," *Reviews in Religion and Theology* 3 (1995): 15-23, repr. in N. T. Wright, *Pauline Perspectives: Essays on Paul, 1978-2013* (London: SPCK, 2013), 126-33.

92. Barclay, *Jews in the Mediterranean Diaspora*, 381-95 (esp. 384-86); idem, "Paul among Diaspora Jews," 103, 113. Ronald Charles (*Paul and the Politics of Diaspora* [Minneapolis: Fortress, 2014], 248) writes: "Paul was a diasporic male Judean of low social status negotiating

culture yet also a self-identifying Jew with a thoroughly Jewish worldview. This view itself is neither anomalous nor problematic. The incongruity is that Paul was highly antagonistic toward Hellenistic religion and culture, even while he engaged in a radical redefinition of traditional Jewish categories and adopted a lifestyle and a theology that questioned the normativity of his ancestral customs. According to Barclay, the truly anomalous character of Paul's theology and religion can be described as follows:

> In his conceptuality Paul is most at home among the particularistic and least accommodated segments of the Diaspora; yet in his utilization of these concepts, and in his social practice, he shatters the ethnic mould in which that ideology was formed. He shows little inclination to forge any form of synthesis with his cultural environment, yet he employs the language of a culturally antagonistic Judaism to establish a new social entity which transgresses the boundaries of the Diaspora Synagogues. By an extraordinary transference of ideology, Paul deracinates the most culturally conservative forms of Judaism in the Diaspora and uses them in the service of his largely Gentile communities.[93]

I take Barclay's point as proven and accept his description of Paul as an "anomalous Jew." My primary qualification is that Barclay's mapping of Paul in relation to Diaspora Judaism glosses over the close connection between Paul and Palestinian Judaism.[94] We must avoid the temptation to return to the old divide between a Hellenized Diasporan Judaism and a Hebraic Palestinian Judaism. It need not be denied that Jewish communities in the eastern Mediterranean, Africa, Arabia, Asia, and Palestine produced diverse expressions of Judaism—diverse from each other and even within themselves—shaped by local, linguistic, cultural, and sociopolitical forces. Nevertheless, all species of Judaism were to some degree homogenous insofar as they shared a commitment to a particular socioreligious framework that was characterized by ethnic kinship, common customs, and familiar beliefs.[95] Barclay's thick description of

different spaces; he was a devotee and interpreter of Christ among the nations; he was socially deviant, with little of an economic or political power base, and in the process of signifying a new empire under the authority of Christ in the first-century Mediterranean world."

93. Barclay, *Jews in the Mediterranean Diaspora*, 393.

94. To be fair, Barclay ("Paul among Diaspora Jews," 90-92) is aware of this problem.

95. For instance, J. Andrew Overman (*Church and Community in Crisis: The Gospel according to Matthew* [Valley Forge, PA.: TPI, 1996], 9) emphasizes diversity when he writes: "So varied was Jewish society in the land of Israel in this period, and so varied were the Jewish

the Jewish Diaspora provides a helpful backdrop to much of Paul's missionary activities, but we must add to the scenery the Palestinian context, which provides further texture and color to the portrait of Paul that interpreters draw. Otherwise we might fail to integrate elements of Palestinian Jewish life—halakic debates over Torah, Judean sectarianism, apocalypticism, and growing anti-Roman sentiment in Judea in the 40s and 50s—as the context in which Paul's beliefs and practices emerged. In other words, in addition to Barclay's "anomalous Jew" of the Diaspora, we must add the thoroughly Judean Paul of W. D. Davies and E. P. Sanders, among others.[96]

Mapping Paul and Judaism within the Greco-Roman World: The Way Ahead

Part of the problem is that elements of all the views surveyed above have something about them that is right. Paul did seem to partition Christ-believers away from synagogues and regard them as a new socioreligious entity that was not under Torah (a former Jew). Paul did transform elements of the Jewish worldview around faith in Jesus as the Messiah (a transformed Jew). Paul did remain faithful to much of the Jewish way of life in his own devotional practices, in the gospel he preached, and in the conduct he expected of Gentile believers (a faithful Jew). Paul's thought does include an inclusive social praxis that marks him out as peculiar in the very least (a radical or anomalous Jew).

I find the most helpful description of Paul to be that of an "anomalous Jew." Although, unlike Barclay, I do not see the essence of the Pauline anomaly to be

---

groups, that scholars no longer speak of Judaism in the singular when discussing this formative and fertile period in Jewish history. Instead, we speak about Judaisms. In this time and place, there existed a number of competing, even rival Judaisms." However, James C. VanderKam ("Judaism in the Land of Israel," in *Early Judaism: A Comprehensive Overview*, ed. J. J. Collins and D. C. Harlow [Grand Rapids, MI: Eerdmans, 2012], 91) responds to the nomenclature of "Judaisms" as follows: "The surviving evidence exhibits a richness and diversity in the Judaism of the Second Temple era, a diversity so great that some have resorted to the neologism 'Judaisms' to express it. Yet, despite the undoubted diversity present in the texts, there are fundamental beliefs and practices that would have been accepted by virtually all Jews during those centuries and that justify retaining the singular noun Judaism." See also E. P. Sanders, "Common Judaism Explored," in *Common Judaism: Explorations in Second-Temple Judaism*, ed. W. O. McCready and A. Reinhartz (Minneapolis: Fortress, 2008), 11-23, on balancing unity and diversity in ancient Judaism.

96. W. D. Davies, *Paul and Rabbinic Judaism: Some Rabbinic Elements in Paul's Theology* (London: SPCK, 1955); Sanders, *Paul and Palestinian Judaism*.

the paradoxes involved in Paul's attempt to negotiate his way within Diaspora Hellenism, but more properly related to the social epiphenomenon that follows on from his messianic eschatology, namely, his attempt to create a social space for a unified body of Jewish and Gentile Christ-believers worshiping God.[97] In brief, God had launched the new age through the cross and resurrection of Christ, which meant the launch of the new creation and the renewal of Israel, of which his assemblies were the vanguard.

If this summary is correct, then we can rule out what was *not* anomalous about Paul's beliefs and practices. First, belief that Jesus was the Messiah would not amount to a break with Judaism, any more than Rabbi Akiba's identification of Simon ben Kosiba as the Messiah would have entailed a break with Jewish beliefs.[98] Akiba may have backed the wrong horse of the apocalypse, but there is no question of his apostatizing from Judaism. Second, possessing a "realized" eschatology would not result in a parting from Judaism, since other groups, notably the Qumranites, especially in their commentaries and hymnody, could adopt "an eschatological understanding of the community's situation in history that places them at the end of the age and the telos of ancient prophecies."[99] Third, even proclaiming God to Gentiles without the condition of circumcision is hardly novel, as evidenced by the preaching activities of Jewish merchants to the royal family in Adiabene.[100] The anomaly belongs at a much deeper convictional level.

What we call Paul's "anomaly," he would probably call the "revelation of Jesus Christ" (Gal 1:12) that he received, which discloses how faith in Christ without Torah was the instrument that brings Jews and Gentiles into reconciliation with God and into the renewal of all things. In my estimation, the anomalous nature of Paul's thought consists of his apocalyptic interpretation of the Messiah's death and resurrection, which forced him into a rereading of Scripture and into a different praxis that yielded a transformation of "common Judaism" whereby the story and symbols of Judaism were now redrawn around Jesus the Messiah and his followers, who constituted the renewed Israel of an inaugurated eschaton.

Furthermore, the religious claims of Paul the anomalous Jew had the social

---

97. See Terence Donaldson ("Paul within Judaism: A Critical Evaluation from a 'New Perspective' Perspective," in *Paul within Judaism: Restoring the First-Century Context to the Apostle*, ed. M. Nanos and M. Zetterholm [Minneapolis: Fortress, 2015], 296): "In my view, the truly anomalous aspect is Paul['s] insistence that uncircumcised *ethnē*-in-Christ are at the same time full members of Abraham's 'seed' (*sperma*)."

98. y. Ta'an. 68d.

99. George W. E. Nickelsburg, *Ancient Judaism and Christian Origins: Diversity, Continuity, and Transformation* (Minneapolis: Fortress, 2003), 126-27.

100. Josephus, *Ant.* 20.17-96.

effect of making Paul a marginal Jew. This marginality is precisely what he embraced as part of his apostolate to the nations. As Calvin Roetzel suggests, "Paul actively embraced the margin and made it an instrument pregnant with possibility."[101] Whether it was inside the synagogue or on the outside, in an Ephesian prison or in the atrium of a Corinthian house church, Paul believed that God was calling a people of Gentiles and Jews to himself through Jesus Christ. This marginal place was fraught with peril, since it threatened the cultural norms and institutional structures overseen by leaders who were no doubt alarmed at Paul's dismantling of social boundaries and the consequences of his eschatological enthusiasm for Christ's lordship. It was a place full of ambiguities and tensions that required theological answers and pastoral responses, and yet Paul believed that this was exactly his calling. It was at the precipice of a new age and on the social margins that "Paul saw in this incandescent moment the prospect of reconciling an alien world to its Creator, and reconciling the 'outsider' to the 'insiders.'"[102]

I intend to test this hypothesis of Paul as an anomalous Jew on the margins in a number of areas that will highlight the jarring nature of Paul's thought and clarify the meaning and limits of Paul's Jewishness. First, in chapter 1, I examine the meaning of "salvation" for Paul and how Paul's conception of God's definitive act of rescue relates to the Judaism of his own day. Did Paul give an accurate representation of the soteriological architecture in common Judaism, and did Paul think that salvation was attainable within Judaism? Second, the meaning of Paul's apostolate to the nations is examined in chapter 2, where I suggest that Paul was far more active in Jewish evangelism than often recognized. The implication is that Paul's social partitioning of Christ-believing Gentiles from the synagogue could never be absolute, as Paul moved freely between both social horizons. Third, the contemporary debate about apocalypticism vs. salvation history in Paul's theology is taken up in chapter 3, and I offer a reading of Galatians that demonstrates the culmination of Israel's story in the apocalyptic revelation of Jesus Christ to include Gentiles in the family of Abraham. Fourth, Paul's abrasive relationship with other Jewish Christ-believers is examined in chapter 4, with an analysis of the incident at Antioch (Gal 2:11-14). My contention is that Paul was opposing an ethnocentric nomism of the procircumcision faction, and the episode gave expression to the raw and radical nature of Paul's *sola gratia* gospel. Finally, I tackle the subject of Paul and the Roman Empire in chapter 5 with an attempt to detect any anti-imperial resonances in Paul's letter to the Romans.

---

101. Calvin Roetzel, *Paul, a Jew on the Margins* (Louisville: Westminster John Knox, 2003), 3.
102. Roetzel, *Paul*, 2.

In sum, Paul was a religious anomaly. He appeared on the scene of the Greco-Roman world like a sudden yet small ripple moving upon the waters of a still river. He goes mostly unnoticed in his own time, and yet by the time the ripple reaches the shores of the modern age, it has become a tsunami. Paul's anomaly, offensive as it was to Jews and odd as it was to Greeks, became the Gentile Christianity that eventually swallowed up the Roman Empire and that, even to this day, two millennia later, casts its shadow upon the religious landscape of the world. Not bad for a Jewish tentmaker from Tarsus!

Excursus: Pauline Chronology

One should ideally attempt to map the contours of Paul's thought with a working knowledge of Pauline chronology. Here I lay out my basic understanding of the sequence of events in Paul's life and mission.

30	Death of Jesus
32-33	Persecution of Hellenistic Christ-believers
34	Conversion
34-36	Activity in Arabia and return to Damascus
37	Flight from Damascus and first visit to Jerusalem
37-48	Missionary of Church of Antioch
49/50	Jerusalem Council and incident at Antioch
50/51	Aegean mission
	1 & 2 Thessalonians, Galatians
52	Visit to Jerusalem and Antioch
52-54	Mission in Ephesus
	1 & 2 Corinthians, Philippians,
	Philemon, Colossians, Ephesians
55/56	Corinth
	Romans
57	Final trip to Jerusalem
57-59	Arrest and detention in Jerusalem and Caesarea
60	Arrival in Rome
60-62	House arrest in Rome
	Pastoral Epistles (?)
63/64	Execution

CHAPTER ONE

Salvation in Paul's Judaism

The title of this chapter is deliberately ambiguous.[1] Obviously there is the initial puzzle of what "salvation" meant to Jews, Christians, Greeks, and Romans. In addition, there is the more perplexing issue of the referent in the phrase "Paul's Judaism." Does that mean (1) the Judaism known to Paul or (2) the Judaism expressed in Paul's own *Christian* beliefs?[2] And therein the questions begin on either option: is Paul a reliable witness to the Judaism of his time, and are Paul's theological and religious beliefs to be situated within Judaism or external to it? I am interested in both of these questions. First, I am concerned in this study with how Paul described salvation in Judaism. Second, I am concerned with how that description is both continuous and discontinuous with Paul's articulation of salvation in his Christ-believing faith. As we will see, the rhetoric and reality of Paul's description of salvation in Judaism is much debated, as is the degree to which Paul and his communities are enmeshed in the matrix of "common Judaism."[3] In light of those questions, it is the task of this chapter to explore the relationship between Paul and Judaism in relation to salvation. That requires identifying how Paul's story of salvation in Jesus Christ relates to his narration of the story of Israel. I proceed by (1) briefly sur-

---

1. An earlier and much shorter version of this essay first appeared as Michael F. Bird, "Salvation in Paul's Judaism," in *Paul and Judaism: Crosscurrents in Pauline Exegesis and the Study of Jewish-Christian Relations*, ed. Reimund Bieringer and Didier Pollefeyt (LNTS 463; London: T&T Clark, 2012), 15-40.

2. I owe this distinction to Mark Nanos, "Paul and Judaism: Why Not Paul's Judaism?," in *Paul Unbound: Other Perspectives on Paul*, ed. M. D. Given (Peabody, MA: Hendrickson, 2009), 141-50.

3. On "common Judaism," see E. P. Sanders, *Judaism: Practice and Belief, 63 BCE–66 CE* (London: SCM, 1992), and discussion in Wayne O. McCready and Adele Reinhartz, eds., *Common Judaism: Explorations in Second-Temple Judaism* (Minneapolis: Fortress, 2008).

veying scholarly perspectives about Paul's presentation of Jewish soteriology and (2) discussing the socioreligious position of Paul and his Gentile Christ-believing communities in relation to Judaism. This chapter is thus an extension of the introductory chapter about Paul and Judaism, as we examine how the soteric architecture of Judaism provides a mixture of positive foundation and negative foil for the articulation of Paul's own view of salvation.

Paul, Judaism, and Salvation in Scholarship

There have been various proposals as to what kind of Judaism Paul knew and how faithfully he presented it. In what follows I summarize the main respective views.[4]

Paul and Jewish Legalism

A first perspective is that Paul, in his postconversion period, railed against a version of Judaism that, in the postexilic period, had degenerated into a form of legalism, merit-theology, and synergism, to which Christian grace was the divine solution. The long-standing Christian tradition of regarding Judaism as a religion of works-righteousness reached its zenith in the skewed Protestant history of early Judaism by Ferdinand Weber, Emil Schürer, and Wilhelm Bousset in the nineteenth century. Then, in the twentieth century, it was sustained by the caricature and cherry-picking of rabbinic writings by the Strack-Billerbeck *Kommentar*, canonized by Gerhard Kittel's *Wörterbuch*, fueled by the theological ingenuity of Rudolf Bultmann, and imbibed into the soul of twentieth-century Protestant theologians who took Judaism to be a cultural allegory for the phenomenon of human religion.[5] This line of scholarship led Günther Bornkamm to say that "Paul's opponent is not this or that section in a particular church, but the Jews and their understanding of salvation."[6] Similar was Ulrich Wilckens, who stated, "Paul was a Jew . . .

---

4. See other surveys in Douglas A. Campbell, *The Quest for Paul's Gospel: A Suggested Strategy* (London: T&T Clark, 2005), 139-40; Frank Thielman, *From Plight to Solution: A Jewish Framework for Understanding Paul's View of the Law in Galatians and Romans* (Leiden: Brill, 1989), 1-27; W. S. Campbell, "Perceptions of Compatibility between Christianity and Judaism in Pauline Interpretation," *BI* 13 (2005): 298-316.

5. Philip Sigal, *The Halakhah of Jesus of Nazareth according to the Gospel of Matthew* (Atlanta: SBL, 2007), 8.

6. Günther Bornkamm, *Paul*, trans. D. M. G. Stalker (New York: Harper & Row, 1971), 95.

but also an irreconcilable enemy of all 'Judaism' in Christianity."[7] For Ernst Käsemann, Paul's critique of religion strikes at "the hidden Jew in all of us, at the man who validates rights and demands over against God on the basis of past dealings with him and to this extent is serving not God but an illusion."[8] Here "Judaism" is simply a cipher for "religion," consisting of man-made rituals and legal codes that presume to merit divine favor by their dutiful performance. Judaism becomes the example par excellence of *Selbsterlösung* ("self-redemption"). It is a view of Judaism that remains common in churches and parts of the academy, yet it rests on a vexatious distortion of the actual evidence, which is far more messy and complex, something Jewish scholars have long protested against.

It is not hard to trace statements that strikingly emphasize God's mercy and election of Israel, expressed chiefly in the covenant, as the efficacious force in salvation (e.g., 1QS 11.11-15; 1QH 15.18-20; Tob 3:2-4; 4 Ezra 8:32; Jub. 16.26; Wis 12:16; m. Sanh. 10.1). Torah as story of salvation and Torah as rooted in the covenant relationship was the grid in which Torah as command was understood. According to George Nickelsburg, "A whole complement of Jewish texts . . . explicate Torah observance and the righteous life as functions of one's trust in the God who rewards the righteous. Although the observance of certain commands may be in focus, there is no evidence of legalism, slavish and fearful obedience, deprecating self-righteousness, or hypocrisy. To the contrary, the righteous are willing, exuberant, faithful servants of the covenantal God, whom they trust to reward the potentially dangerous actions that they carry out in obedience to God's commands."[9] As long as Jewish teachers remained in dialogue with their own sacred literature and traditions, they cannot have excised grace and covenant from their thinking. E. P. Sanders adds: "The charge of 'legalism' is empty if the Jews believed in the covenant—this belief having approximately the same role as the Christian idea of prevenient grace."[10]

I hasten to add that there is no term in antiquity that is translatable as "legalism," so its imposition upon ancient Jewish and Christian texts is somewhat

---

7. Ulrich Wilckens, *Rechtfertigung als Freiheit* (Neukirchen-Vluyn: Neukirchener, 1974), 7: "Paulus war ein Jude . . . war aber auch ein unversöhnlicher Feind jeglichen 'Judaismus' im Christentum."

8. Ernst Käsemann, "Paul and Israel," in *New Testament Questions of Today* (Philadelphia: Fortress, 1969), 186.

9. George W. E. Nickelsburg, *Ancient Judaism and Christian Origins: Diversity, Continuity, and Transformation* (Minneapolis: Fortress, 2003), 39.

10. E. P. Sanders, "Covenantal Nomism Revisited," *JSQ* 16 (2009): 27.

anachronistic.[11] Even if one prefers the more fashionable term "synergism,"[12] it still raises questions as to what it means and how it differs from Paul's own soteriological scheme, since Paul's scheme has its own tension between divine sovereignty and human responsibility and can be regarded as synergistic in some sense if the human response actually matters.[13] That is because Paul

11. The view that "works of the law" means something like "works done in a legalistic spirit" has a long and distinguished history (see, e.g., Daniel Fuller, *Gospel and Law: Contrast or Continuum?* [Grand Rapids, MI: Eerdmans, 1980], 95; Richard N. Longenecker, *Galatians* [WBC; Dallas: Word, 1990], 86; and survey in H. B. P. Mijoga, *The Pauline Notion of Deeds of the Law* [San Francisco: International Scholars Publications, 1999], 5-21). Yet it is far more likely that "works of Torah" means works that the Torah requires. That said, there are some grounds for claiming that the phrasing might reflect particular halakic perspectives on how to obey the totality of the Torah, since it appears in sectarian literature (see 4QMMT 31; 1QS 5.21, 6.18; 2 Bar. 57.2), as suggested by Michael Bachmann, *Anti-Judaism in Galatians? Exegetical Studies on a Polemical Letter and on Paul's Theology,* trans. R. L. Brawley (Grand Rapids, MI: Eerdmans, 2008), 1-31. Preston Sprinkle (*Paul and Judaism Revisited: A Study of Divine and Human Agency in Salvation* [Downers Grove, IL: IVP Academic, 2013], 79) gets it right: "For MMT, then, the works of law are the halachic deeds of the community by which they have escaped the covenant curse and obtained blessing." On the meaning of "legalism" in general, see Moisés Silva, "Historical Reconstruction in New Testament Criticism," in *Hermeneutics, Authority, and Canon,* ed. D. A. Carson (Grand Rapids, MI: Baker, 1986), 117-21; the wisely nuanced views of Richard N. Longenecker, *Paul, Apostle of Liberty* (New York: Harper & Row, 1964), 77-85, esp. on the difference between "nomism" and "legalism" (84); Stephen Westerholm, *Perspectives Old and New on Paul: The "Lutheran" Paul and His Critics* (Grand Rapids, MI: Eerdmans, 2004), 332-35, on "hard" and "soft" species of legalism; and for further references on the topic, see Michael F. Bird, *The Saving Righteousness of God: Studies on Paul, Justification, and the New Perspective* (PBM; Milton Keynes, UK: Paternoster, 2006), 89-90.

12. On Jewish "synergism," see Donald A. Hagner, "Paul and Judaism, the Jewish Matrix of Early Christianity: Issues in the Current Debate," *BBR* 3 (1993): 122; Timo Esko, "Paul, Predestination, and 'Covenantal Nomism'—Re-assessing Paul and Palestinian Judaism," *JSJ* 29 (1997): 390-412; Charles H. Talbert, "Paul, Judaism, and the Revisionists," *CBQ* 63 (2001): 20-22. Against the designation "synergism" is James D. G. Dunn, *The New Perspective on Paul* (Grand Rapids, MI: Eerdmans, 2008), 77-89; Kent L. Yinger, "Reformation *Redivivus*: Synergism and the New Perspective," *JTI* 3 (2009): 89-106; Campbell, *Quest,* 15; Sanders, "Covenantal Nomism Revisited," 49-50.

13. See Mikael Winninge, *Sinners and the Righteous: A Comparative Study of the Psalms of Solomon and Paul's Letters* (Stockholm: Almqvist & Wiksell, 1995), 334; Kari Kuula, *The Law, the Covenant, and God's Plan: Paul's Treatment of the Law and Israel in Romans* (FES 85; Göttingen: Vandenhoeck & Ruprecht, 2002), 5; Douglas Harink, *Paul among the Postliberals: Pauline Theology beyond Christendom and Modernity* (Grand Rapids, MI: Brazos, 2003), 32-38; Chris VanLandingham, *Judgment and Justification in Early Judaism and the Apostle Paul* (Peabody, MA: Hendrickson, 2005). But see objections of Peter T. O'Brien, "Was Paul a Covenantal Nomist?," in *Justification and Variegated Nomism,* vol. 2, *The Paradoxes of Paul,* ed. D. A. Carson, P. T. O'Brien, and M. A. Seifrid (Grand Rapids, MI: Baker Academic, 2004), 265.

prescribes a human response to the gospel in the form of "turning to God from idols" (1 Thess 1:9), "obey[ing] the gospel" (2 Thess 1:8), exhibiting the "obedience of faith" (Rom 1:5); persons need to "work out your salvation with fear and trembling" (Phil 2:12), and Paul knows of a judgment according to works (Rom 2:13-16; 14:12; 2 Cor 5:10). Paul's gospel is both a gracious gift and a demand for new-covenant loyalty.[14]

It can be granted that Paul's critique of Torah as a gateway to righteousness and life is certainly responding to perceived inadequacies within extant expressions of Judaism.[15] Yet he is still doing so using the framework, tradition, and grammar of the Jewish religion itself. Hence his appeal to key "faith" texts like Gen 15:6 and Hab 2:4, his allusions to the hope of covenant renewal in Deut 32, and his reliance on the restoration narrative within Isa 40–55. Paul's opponents in Galatia would have no doubt claimed that their soteriological pattern was rooted in the grace of the covenant. Paul himself believed that his gospel was not setting aside such grace, but he was amplifying it, since the coming of the Messiah had opened the way for Gentiles to share in salvation without the Torah (Gal 2:21). The chief difference that Paul had with his fellow Jews and with other Jewish Christ-believers was not the fact of divine grace but its object and instrument, that is to say, a different formula for divine and human agency in salvation. Paul evidently had his own *Jewish* configuration of *who* gets saved and *how* in light of the divine power of salvation operating through the Messiah's death and resurrection and through the gift of the Spirit.[16]

Paul and Diaspora Judaism

In another depiction, Paul did not experience true Judaism; rather, he knew only its Hellenistic counterpart, which was impoverished when compared to the talmudic Judaism of Palestine.[17] The obvious problem here is that it as-

---

14. I should add that πίστις belongs to the semantic domain that includes concepts like trustworthy, faithful, and loyal.

15. See Sir 17:11; 45:5; T. Dan. 6.11; 2 Bar. 67.6; Sib. Or. 3.580.

16. See esp. Francis Watson, *Paul, Judaism, and the Gentiles: Beyond the New Perspective* (rev. ed.; Grand Rapids, MI: Eerdmans, 2007), 15-19; John M. G. Barclay and Simon J. Gathercole, eds., *Divine and Human Agency in Paul and His Cultural Environment* (LNTS 335; London: T&T Clark, 2007); Jason Maston, *Divine and Human Agency in Second Temple Judaism and Paul: A Comparative Study* (WUNT 2.297; Tübingen: Mohr Siebeck, 2010); Sprinkle, *Paul and Judaism Revisited*.

17. Samuel Sandmel, *Judaism and Christian Beginnings* (Oxford: OUP, 1978); idem, *The Genius of Paul* (Philadelphia: Fortress, 1979); C. G. Montefiore, *Judaism and St. Paul: Two*

sumes that Diaspora Judaism was lax, whereas there is a great amount of evidence that Jews outside of Palestine were no less loyal to the pillars of Judaism than their Palestinian counterparts, even if they lived away from the land and far from the temple, even if they faced a different array of external pressures, and even if they expressed their piety in a different cultural idiom.[18] It also assumes an unhelpful dichotomy between Hellenism and Judaism, whereas it is now axiomatic that all Judaism of the first centuries BCE and CE was permeated by Hellenism in some form.[19] The notion of a liberal Judaism of the Diaspora in opposition to a conservative Judaism of Palestine is a scholarly myth no longer believed.

Paul's Misrepresentation of Judaism

On another account, Paul's view of Judaism was jaundiced and skewed, being unfair in his description of it.[20] In favor of this view we can say that (1) there is undoubtedly an element of rhetoric in Paul's polemics against his Jewish Christ-believing opponents and in his lament at the failure of Israel to embrace the Messiah; (2) he also reconfigures his biography to emphasize the inadequacies of his preconversion life in Pharisaic Judaism, and (3) his theological critique of Torah is somewhat atypical in Judaism. However, the content of Paul's language is hardly anti-Judaistic per se, as the form and content of his language reflect typical intra-Jewish disputes. His conversion was, in its immediate setting, a transference from one Jewish sect to another, even if the position of his Gentile converts vis-à-vis Judaism became subsequently ambiguous. Paul's remarks about the Torah oscillate between a peculiar hostility and loyal veneration, depending on the argumentative context, and Paul still remains far from a Marcionite perspective on the Torah as intrinsically unjust.

Essays (New York: Dutton, 1915); H. J. Schoeps, Paul: The Theology of the Apostle in the Light of Jewish Religious History (Philadelphia: Westminster, 1961).

18. The ubiquity of Jewish loyalty to their native customs throughout the inhabited world is stated frequently in Jewish and non-Jewish writings, e.g., Josephus, Ant. 17.26; 18.84; 19.290; Tacitus, Hist. 5.5.

19. Martin Hengel, Judaism and Hellenism, trans. J. Bowden (2 vols.; London: SCM, 1974), 1:104; I. Howard Marshall, "Palestinian and Hellenistic Christian: Some Critical Comments," NTS 19 (1973): 271-87; Troels Engberg-Pedersen, ed., Paul beyond the Judaism/Hellenism Divide (Louisville: Westminster John Knox, 2001); Anders Gerdmar, Rethinking the Judaism-Hellenism Dichotomy: A Historiographical Case Study of Second Peter and Jude (CBNTS 36; Stockholm: Almqvist & Wiksell, 2001).

20. Joseph Klausner, From Jesus to Paul (Boston: Beacon, 1939); Hyam Maccoby, Paul and Hellenism (London: SCM, 1991).

Furthermore, the New Testament generally and Paul specifically simply are among our best sources of knowledge for Judaism before 70 CE.[21]

Paul and Covenantal Nomism

Probably the most influential proposal in studies on Paul and Judaism in the last forty years has been E. P. Sanders's construal of Palestinian Judaism as "covenantal nomism."[22] This "pattern of religion" is now well known and is expressed by the dictum "grace to get in and works to stay in." In Sanders's own words, "Obedience maintains one's position in the covenant, but it does not earn God's grace as such. It simply keeps an individual in the group which is the recipient of God's grace. . . . Obedience is universally held to be the behaviour appropriate to being in the covenant, not the means of earning God's grace."[23] Paul's problem, then, with the Torah was that it had simply been superseded by Christ, and Paul himself reasoned from Christ's lordship to the human problem, that is, from solution (Christ) to plight (Torah).[24]

There has been an industry to critiques of Sanders's portrayal of Judaism and Paul; I include here only a few salient points.

First, there are undoubtedly documents from antiquity that exemplify the pattern of covenantal nomism that Sanders proposes, like the Testament of Moses, 1 Esdras, Pseudo-Philo, Rom 2:17-24, and 1QH. Yet the Jewish texts we encounter from the Second Temple and rabbinic periods are characterized by a wide-ranging diversity as to how they characterize divine agency and human

21. See Alan F. Segal (*Paul the Convert: The Apostasy of Saul the Pharisee* [New Haven: Yale University Press, 1990], 48): "Paul's texts provide information about first-century Judaism and Jewish mysticism, as important as the Jewish texts that have been found to establish the meaning of Christian texts. Indeed, Paul's letters may be more important to the history of Judaism than the rabbinic texts are to the interpretation of Christian Scriptures." Alan F. Segal, ("Conversion and Messianism: Outline for a New Approach," in *The Messiah: Developments in Earliest Judaism and Christianity*, ed. J. H. Charlesworth [Minneapolis: Fortress, 1992], 299): "The New Testament is . . . much better evidence for the history of Judaism [in the first century] than is rabbinic Judaism for the origins of Christianity." Geza Vermes (*Jesus and the World of Judaism* [London: SCM, 1983], 74-88): "Perhaps the N. T. itself is our best guide to Palestinian Judaism in the first century."

22. E. P. Sanders, *Paul and Palestinian Judaism: A Comparison of Patterns of Religion* (London: SCM, 1977), 422; idem, "Covenantal Nomism Revisited," 23-55.

23. Sanders, *Paul and Palestinian Judaism*, 420-21.

24. Sanders, *Paul and Palestinian Judaism*, 552; cf. Nickelsburg (*Ancient Judaism and Christian Origins*, 60), who thinks that the difference between Christianity and Judaism is not a pattern of soteriology but Christology.

response in salvation.[25] Apart from mammoth differences on what "salvation" might mean within this literature—individual vs. national, this-worldly blessing vs. otherworldly immortality, cosmic evil vs. personal evil, etc.—there are disparate views on the scope and instrument of salvation. There is, then, no single Jewish soteriology discernible apart from generalized hopes for God's granting something like peace, justice, and life to someone for some reason or another. Consequently, it is impossible to compress all narrations of the basis, agency, and scope of salvation in Judaism into a single soteric descriptor like covenantal nomism because the emphasis could fall upon either the "covenant" or the "nomism," depending on the peculiar dynamics of a given writing (and many writings themselves defy consistency in terms of their pattern of divine action and prescribed human response).[26] To justify this claim, one does not have to look far for contrary statements that declare that performance of righteous deeds are the basis of a person's standing before God or the condition of entering into the future age (e.g., Wis 5:15; 6:18; Pss. Sol. 9.3-5; 1QS 3-4; 4 Ezra 7.77; 8.33, 36; 2 Bar. 14.12; 51.7). To give a concrete example, the halakic letter 4QMMT, written from Qumran and probably sent to Jerusalem, describes the "works of the law" with the promise that, for those who observe them, "it will be reckoned to you as righteousness, in that you have done what is right and good before him, to your own benefit" (4QMMT C 31). Craig A. Evans comments on

---

25. Even Sanders (*Paul and Palestinian Judaism*, 427-28) conceded that 4 Ezra was an exception to the pattern he detected in extant literature. Gabriele Boccaccini ("Inner-Jewish Debate on the Tension between Divine and Human Agency in Second Temple Judaism," in *Divine and Human Agency in Paul and His Cultural Development*, ed. J. M. G. Barclay and S. J. Gathercole [London: T&T Clark, 2007], 23) says: "The author of 4 Ezra is a Paul without Christ."

26. Mark Adam Elliott, *The Survivors of Israel: A Reconsideration of the Theology of Pre-Christian Judaism* (Grand Rapids, MI: Eerdmans, 2000), 245-307; D. A. Carson, "Summaries and Conclusions," in *Justification and Variegated Nomism*, vol. 1, *The Complexities of Second Temple Judaism*, ed. D. A. Carson, P. T. O'Brien, and M. Seifrid (Grand Rapids, MI: Baker Academic, 2001), 543-48; Brendan Byrne, "Interpreting Romans: The New Perspective and Beyond," *Int* 58 (2004): 248; Bird, *Saving Righteousness*, 93-94; Watson, *Paul, Judaism, and the Gentiles*, xvii, 12-19; A. Andrew Das, "Paul and the Law: Pressure Points in the Debate," in *Paul Unbound: Other Perspectives on the Apostle*, ed. M. D. Given (Peabody, MA: Hendrickson, 2010), 101: "Jewish literature may be positioned somewhere between these two poles of mercy and demand with the exact formulation varying from author to author and genre to genre"; Daniel M. Gurtner, ed., *This World and the World to Come: Soteriology in Early Judaism* (LSTS 74; London: T&T Clark, 2011), esp. the conclusion by Nickelsburg (313): "There is no single Jewish soteriology," as salvation "shows its face in many different ways, sometimes in the same text"; Boccaccini, "Inner-Jewish Debate," 9-26; Sprinkle, *Paul and Judaism Revisited*, 208-38; Jacob Thiessen, *Gottes Gerechtigkeit und Evangelium im Römerbrief: Die Rechtfertigungslehre des Paulus im Vergleich zu antiken jüdischen Auffasungen und zur neuen Paulusperspektive* (Frankfurt: Peter Lang, 2014), 112-37.

this statement: "In sharp contrast to what Paul enjoins on the Galatians, the author of 4QMMT urges compliance with 'works of the Law': to guarantee a happy finish."[27] Preston Sprinkle agrees, seeing that the call of 4QMMT for "a return to the law in the eschatological age is a means of eliciting the covenant blessings, not merely a way to identify who the righteous really are."[28] Obviously following a specific sectarian halakah is said to be a way to eschatological deliverance. To these quotes I add the observation that Philo attests debates among Alexandrian Jews about whether God's blessings were earned or were freely bestowed (Philo, *Sacr.* 54-57). Similarly, when Josephus discusses the various sects of Judaism, he differentiates them by describing their diverse ways of conceiving of human destinies along a continuum of divine initiative and human self-determination (Josephus, *War* 2.119-66; *Ant.* 13.171-73; 18.11-25).[29] A diversity of soteric patterns was normative in common Judaism. Jason Maston concludes his comparison of Sirach and 1QH as follows: "Attempts to discover in these texts a single pattern, such as covenantal nomism, will inevitably flatten out the distinctions that are visible on the surface of the texts. Covenantal nomism runs counter to Sirach's insistence that life comes through Torah observance, and it misses out on the *Hodayot*'s stress on the continuing role of the Spirit. This study, therefore, has questioned the applicability of covenantal nomism as the basic soteriological structure of Second Temple Judaism."[30] The diversity of perspectives in these texts is evidently so expansive that by no stretch of the imagination can the majority of Jewish writings be lumped into any one soteriological pattern, regardless of whether some may label that pattern "legalism" or "covenantal nomism." This diversity means that we should not be surprised if we find instances where Torah obedience was treated as a pathway to eschatological life, even if it was not the perspective of all Jews, implying that Paul's representation of nomistic tendencies in Judaism cannot be dismissed as a distortion.[31]

In addition, although covenantal nomism is "a very flexible pattern,"[32]

27. Craig A. Evans, "Paul and 'Works of Law' Language in Late Antiquity," in *Paul and His Opponents*, ed. S. E. Porter (PS 2; Leiden: Brill, 2005), 223.

28. Sprinkle, *Paul and Judaism Revisited*, 78.

29. Watson, *Paul, Judaism, and the Gentiles*, 18; Maston, *Divine and Human Agency*, 10-18. According to Boccaccini ("Inner-Jewish Debate," 15): "The emphasis on theological and philosophical issues [in salvation] is not (only) a modern obsession of Christian scholars."

30. Maston, *Divine and Human Agency*, 176.

31. See Francis Watson, "Constructing an Antithesis: Paul and Other Jewish Perspectives on Divine and Human Agency," in *Divine and Human Agency in Paul and His Cultural Development*, ed. J. M. G. Barclay and S. J. Gathercole (London: T&T Clark, 2007), 99-116.

32. Richard Bauckham, "Apocalypses," in *Justification and Variegated Nomism*, vol. 1,

the attempt by some to affirm that covenantal nomism can accommodate highly nomistic schemes while simultaneously retaining the overall efficacy of the covenant makes the soteriological pattern so broad as to be practically meaningless.[33] Moreover, the grace-to-get-in-and-works-to-stay-in scheme still looks suspiciously centered on human action as determinative for one's position vis-à-vis God's blessings. As Peter Enns comments on soteric patterns in rewritten scriptural narratives, "It might be less confusing to say that *election* is by grace but salvation is by obedience." Such a statement exposes a conceptual weakness in Sanders's scheme, because if the covenant is the locus of salvation and if obedience maintains one's place in the covenant, then obviously obedience determines salvation.[34] Thus, covenantal nomism, depending on how it is worked out, can still be highly nomistic in the way that salvation is distributed to human recipients.

Second, I would also maintain that, under certain socioreligious circumstances, huge import can be assigned to human initiative and human effort in securing divine favor. This normally happens in discussions about the basis for persons entering the future eschatological age, amid sectarian disagreements over whose interpretation of the Torah avails before God, and around debates concerning the rites of entry for outsiders into Jewish groups. These settings arguably lead to soteric patterns that place an incredible amount of gravity on nomistic observances for determining one's salvation.[35] It is precisely issues like these that Paul confronts in places like the Jerusalem council (Gal 2:1-10// Acts 15:1-5), at the incident in Antioch (Gal 2:11-14), in Galatia (Gal 2:15–3:28), and in Rome (Rom 3:21–5:11). In other words, Paul engaged in the type of

---

The Complexities of Second Temple Judaism, ed. D. A. Carson, P. T. O'Brien, and M. Seifrid (Grand Rapids, MI: Baker Academic, 2001), 174.

33. C. F. D. Moule, "Jesus, Judaism, and Paul," in *Tradition and Interpretation in the New Testament*, ed. G. F. Hawthorne and O. Betz (Grand Rapids, MI: Eerdmans, 1987), 48; Douglas J. Moo, *The Epistle to the Romans* (NICNT; Grand Rapids, MI: Eerdmans, 1996), 215-16; Timo Eskola, *Theodicy and Predestination in Pauline Theology* (WUNT 2.100; Tübingen: Mohr Siebeck, 1998), 56; Bird, *Saving Righteousness*, 94-95; but see the objections of Bruce Longenecker ("On Critiquing the 'New Perspective' on Paul: A Case Study," ZNW 96 [2005]: 266-69), who understands "staying-in" as a multitemporal signifier that includes an eschatological component and believes that covenantal nomism includes an element of eschatological nomism.

34. Peter Enns, "Expansions of Scripture," in *Justification and Variegated Nomism*, vol. 1, *The Complexities of Second Temple Judaism*, ed. D. A. Carson, P. T. O'Brien, and M. Seifrid (Grand Rapids, MI: Baker Academic, 2001), 98 (italics original).

35. See Michael F. Bird, "What if Martin Luther Had Read the Dead Sea Scrolls? Historical Particularity and Theological Interpretation in Pauline Theology: Galatians as a Test Case," JTI 3 (2009): 107-25.

intra-Jewish disputes precisely where the accent was likely to be placed on Torah observance as determinative for salvation.

Third, it is likewise a matter of contention as to whether or not what Paul found wrong with Judaism was merely its redemptive-historical obsoleteness. Paul exhibits a strong anthropological pessimism and therefore has a more radical perspective on the efficacy of divine agency needed in salvation because of the inadequacies of the Torah in light of the frail and failed human condition.[36] The implication is, as Stephen Westerholm states, "Paul thought the salvific institutions of Judaism inadequate to cope with the problem of human sin," to the point that a solution had to be found in the revelation of the righteousness of God in Jesus Christ.[37] While Jewish authors had diverse perspectives on the origins of evil, human entrenchment in sin, and human capacity for good, Paul's claim that neither Jews nor Gentiles can be righteous before God is, according to Mikael Winninge, "something entirely new within Judaism."[38]

Fourth and finally, it is equally contestable that Paul's own pattern of religion was essentially in agreement with covenantal nomism.[39] That is, Paul may not so much have an idea of "staying-in" as he does of "going on" in what God had called people to be and do.[40]

---

36. See Timo Laato (*Paul and Judaism: An Anthropological Approach* [Atlanta: Scholars, 1995], 62), who believes that the chink in the argumentative armor of E. P. Sanders's *Paul and Palestinian Judaism* is its "inadequate coverage of the question of the capacity of humankind." According to Maston (*Divine and Human Agency*, 171-72): "Sanders is correct that Paul's rejection of the law as God's means of salvation arises from his conviction that God acted in Christ, and this point has not been adequately appreciated. Nevertheless, it does not follow that Paul did not develop a coherent anthropological explanation for why the law is not God's means to salvation. Paul's pessimistic anthropology may be a secondary deduction drawn from his belief that God acted in Christ to save, but it becomes an important point in his claim against Torah observance as the means to divine blessing."

37. Stephen Westerholm, "Paul's Anthropological 'Pessimism' in Its Jewish Context," in *Divine and Human Agency in Paul and His Cultural Development*, ed. J. M. G. Barclay and S. J. Gathercole (London: T&T Clark, 2007), 80; Sprinkle, *Paul and Judaism Revisited*, 125-44.

38. Winninge, *Sinners and the Righteous*, 264.

39. Sanders (*Paul and Palestinian Judaism*, 514, 543, 552) did not think that Paul's pattern of religion was a form of covenantal nomism, because of Paul's participationist transfer terminology. However, others like M. D. Hooker (*From Adam to Christ* [Cambridge: CUP, 1990], 155-64) do see a correlation between Paul and a covenantal nomistic scheme. In response, see Peter T. O'Brien, "Was Paul a Covenantal Nomist?," in *Justification and Variegated Nomism*, vol. 2, *The Paradoxes of Paul*, ed. D. A. Carson, P. T. O'Brien, and M. Seifrid (Grand Rapids, MI: Baker Academic, 2004), 249-96.

40. See Ben Witherington III, *Grace in Galatia: A Commentary on Paul's Letter to the Galatians* (Grand Rapids, MI: Eerdmans, 1998), 99.

Paul and Ethnocentric Judaism

A further cluster of perspectives holds that Paul's critique of his fellow Jews is for using the Torah to reinforce their own sense of ethnic superiority and to exclude Gentiles from God's saving purposes. The issue is not religious self-righteousness but a national righteousness.[41] A more radical perspective holds that Paul never challenged the mode of salvation for Jews within Judaism and that he never doubted the efficacy of the covenant and Israel's election. Such a position is typified by two aspects: postulating a Pauline *Sonderweg* ("special way") for Israel and regarding Israel's misstep as denying that God's salvation has come to the Gentiles.[42] Israel's failure, according to John Gager, "has nothing to do with accepting Christ as Israel's saviour. What Israel missed was understanding the goal of the Torah as it relates to the Gentiles."[43] In the specific case of Rom 11:25-27, it is said, "There is no mention of Israel's conversion, only Israel's salvation by God."[44]

One cannot properly regard Jewish exclusion of Gentiles from salvation as the sum total of Paul's critique of Judaism. Yes, Paul indeed rejected ethnocentric interpretations of the Torah as requiring Gentiles to become Jewish proselytes in order to become Christ-believers (e.g., Gal 2:11-15; Rom 3:21-31), and he mentioned Jewish resistance to his Gentile mission (1 Thess 2:15). Scholars habitually banter around the notion of Pauline universalism versus Jewish particularism, yet a better way of putting it would be to say that Paul believed that socioreligious kinship between Jews and Gentiles should be fictive rather than ethnic.[45] The gospel provided the narrative reinterpretation of the Jewish worldview necessary to provide the continuity and revision that made possible the inclusion of Gentiles

---

41. See, e.g., James D. G. Dunn, *The Theology of Paul the Apostle* (Edinburgh: T&T Clark, 1997), 119.

42. See, e.g., Klaus Haacker, "Das Evangelium Gottes und die Erwählung Israels: Zum Beitrag des Römerbriefs zur Erneuerung des Verhältnisses zwischen Christen und Juden," *TBei* 13 (1982): 70-71; Lloyd Gaston, *Paul and the Torah* (Vancouver: University of British Columbia Press, 1987); John Gager, *Reinventing Paul* (Oxford: OUP, 2000); Stanley K. Stowers, *A Rereading of Romans: Justice, Jews, Gentiles* (New Haven: Yale University Press, 1994); Eung Chun Park, *Either Jew or Gentile: Paul's Unfolding Theology of Inclusivity* (Louisville, KY: Westminster John Knox, 2003); Pamela Eisenbaum, *Paul Was Not a Christian: The Original Message of a Misunderstood Apostle* (New York: HarperCollins, 2009), 216-39.

43. Gager, *Reinventing Paul*, 135.

44. Bernhard Mayer, *Unter Gott Heilsratschluss: Prädestinationaussagen bei Paulus* (Würzburg: Echter, 1974), 290: "Es ist nicht die Rede von Israels Bekehrung, sonder vons Israels Rettung durch Gott."

45. See Eisenbaum, *Paul Was Not a Christian*, 108: "Not Family ties alone" determine membership in the Jewish *ethnos*, but "agreement in principles of conduct."

as Gentiles in Jewish assemblies. In any case, Paul's critique of Judaism goes far beyond social boundaries and rites of entry. Paul did not need the word of the cross to learn that God was the God of the Gentiles too. God's concern for the nations is attested from Genesis to Zechariah and is affirmed in Second Temple Jewish writings, with various patterns of universalism emerging.[46] Moreover, to what extent is it valid to call ancient Judaism ethnocentric or exclusivist? Jews did indeed accept Gentiles into their communities as proselytes; in fact, Philo, Josephus, and the rabbis speak glowingly of them![47] In addition, is not Christianity just as exclusivistic as Judaism in some respects in forbidding intermarriage with pagans, censuring sexual immorality, calling for the expulsion of apostates, avoiding pagan religious associations, and displaying a sectarian social perspective that rejects the values of its surrounding cultural environment?[48]

Paul ultimately deals with a more fundamental issue, namely, what the problem with humanity is that Judaism, with its Torah and covenants, cannot solve.[49] The answer for Paul is the cosmological problem of evil, which is focused in the precise anthropological problem of human corruption and death, i.e., the Adamic condition shared by all humanity.[50] Jews need the gos-

46. See Ronald Feldmeier, Ulrich Heckel, and Martin Hengel, eds., *Die Heiden: Juden, Christen und das Problem des Fremden* (WUNT 70; Tübingen: Mohr Siebeck, 1994); Terence Donaldson, *Judaism and the Gentiles: Jewish Patterns of Universalism (to 135 CE)* (Waco, TX: Baylor University Press, 2007); David C. Sim and James S. McLaren, eds., *Attitudes to Gentiles in Ancient Judaism and Early Christianity* (LNTS 499; London: Bloomsbury, 2014).

47. See Michael F. Bird, *Crossing Over Sea and Land: Jewish Proselytizing Activity in the Second Temple Period* (Peabody, MA: Hendrickson, 2009).

48. Watson, *Paul, Judaism, and the Gentiles*, 53, 232; N. A. Dahl, "The One God of Jews and Gentiles (Rom. 3:29-30)," in *Studies in Paul* (Minneapolis: Augsburg, 1977), 191; E. P. Sanders, *Paul, the Law, and the Jewish People* (Minneapolis: Fortress, 1983), 160; idem, "Jewish Associations with Gentiles and Galatians 2:11-14," in *The Conversation Continues: Studies in Paul and John in Honor of J. Louis Martyn*, ed. Robert T. Fortna and Beverly R. Gaventa (Nashville: Abingdon, 1990), 181; Anders Runesson, "Particularistic Judaism and Universalistic Christianity? Some Critical Remarks on Terminology and Theology," *ST* 54 (2000): 55-75.

49. Bruce Longenecker, *The Triumph of Abraham's God: The Transformation of Identity in Galatians* (Nashville: Abingdon, 1998), 120-21; Mark A. Seifrid, *Christ, Our Righteousness: Paul's Theology of Justification* (NSBT 9; Downers Grove, IL: InterVarsity, 2000), 19-21; Graham Stanton, "The Law of Moses and the Law of Christ," in *Paul and the Mosaic Law*, ed. James D. G. Dunn (Grand Rapids, MI: Eerdmans, 2001), 103-4; Seyoon Kim, *Paul and the New Perspective: Second Thoughts on the Origin of Paul's Gospel* (Grand Rapids, MI: Eerdmans, 2002), 55-56; Westerholm, *Perspectives Old and New on Paul*, 367-68; idem, "Paul's Anthropological 'Pessimism' in Its Jewish Context," 77-78.

50. N. T. Wright, *Paul and the Faithfulness of God* (COQG 4; London, SPCK, 2014), 547-50, 747-72.

pel because they are part of a world enthralled to evil powers; Israel too is in Adam! For this reason Paul can say things like the gospel being for the Jew first and then the Gentile (Rom 1:16); it explains his assumption of a continuing mission to the Jewish people (Rom 10:14-21; 11:14; 1 Cor 9:20; Gal 2:9), and it accounts for his celebration at the existence of a current remnant of Jewish believers in Jesus, with whom Gentile believers are united (Rom 9:27-29; 11:1-10). For Paul there no διαστολή ("difference") between Jew and Gentile in either condemnation (Rom 3:22-23) or justification (Rom 10:12); both need faith in Jesus Christ.[51]

In relation to the *Sonderweg* view, although it is appealing to postmodernists, pluralists, and post-Holocaust interpreters, it is unlikely to be what Paul was actually thinking.[52] While Paul did not envisage a *Sonderweg* for Israel apart from the Messiah, he did foresee in Rom 11 a *Sonderplatz* ("special place") for the Jewish nation in God's eschatological plans as he looked forward to the deliverance of ethnic Israel at the Messiah's return.[53]

Summary

From the foregoing survey we have seen that some authors think Paul regarded salvation as consisting of freedom from a legalistic Judaism because the prescriptions of the Torah were the antithesis of grace and mercy. Alternatively, other scholars think that Paul did not really understand Judaism and its mode of salvation, since either he knew only a distorted Diasporan Judaism or else he com-

---

51. Against Caroline Johnson Hodge (*If Sons, Then Heirs: A Study of Kinship and Ethnicity in the Letters of Paul* [Oxford: OUP, 2007], 141), who supposes that in Rom 10:12 "there is no difference between a *Ioudaios* and a Greek *with respect to God's impartiality*" (italics original). In contrast, I'd say that divine impartiality is not the qualification to the lack of difference, but the premise for it. Therefore, because God is impartial, there is ultimately no privileged position outside of faith in Christ for either Jews or Gentiles.

52. Segal (*Paul the Convert*, 281) is one who wishes Paul had advocated cultural pluralism but remains certain that Paul himself most probably did not. Wright (*Paul and the Faithfulness of God*, 1175) is biting in his criticism that, on the *Sonderweg* view, "Jews are saved by being good Jews and gentiles are saved by becoming Christians."

53. See further critiques in Reidar Hvalvik, "A 'Sonderweg' for Israel: A Critical Examination of a Current Interpretation of Romans 11:25-27," *JSNT* 38 (1990): 87-107; Terence L. Donaldson, "Jewish Christianity, Israel's Stumbling, and the *Sonderweg* Reading of Paul," *JSNT* 29 (2006): 27-54. In addition, while interpreters of the "radical Paul" are trying to avoid supersessionism, in many ways they imply a supersession with Paul's congregations superseding Israel's role to be a light to the Gentiles. See Bruce Longenecker, "On Israel's God and God's Israel: Assessing Supersessionism in Paul," *JTS* 58 (2007): 26-44.

pletely misrepresented Jewish beliefs and practices. Others have suggested that Paul's critique of Judaism consists of its ethnocentrism, with Gentiles wrongfully excluded from the people of God. Others go a bit further and postulate the church as remaining part of Israel's Gentile clientele and Israel as being saved under the auspices of its own covenantal economy. Still others see Paul as remaining within the orbit of Judaism but engaging in some creative configurations of Jewish beliefs around his Christocentric faith. Paul was part of a wing of the church that initiated a shift from a renewal movement within Judaism to a sectarian community beside Judaism and postulated a theological legitimation for the freedom of Gentile converts from Jewish proselytism. In any case, everyone admits that Paul still has some degree of tension with his Jewish compatriots in general and with his Jewish Christ-believing contemporaries in particular. In modern interpretation these tensions seem to revolve around various conceptions of nomism, supersessionism, and ethnocentrism, and they can be configured with a Paul external to Judaism or with a Paul still within Judaism.

Israel's Problem	Nomism	Supersessionism	Ethnocentrism
Paul *contra* Judaism	Paul possessed a Torah-gospel antithesis developed in contrast to the religion of Judaism.	Paul conceived of Christians as a replacement of Israel as God's people.	Paul established Christian communities separate from Judaism and resisted attempts at bringing them into closer socioreligious proximity to Judaism.
Paul *intra* Judaism	Many Jews and Jewish Christians would concur with Paul's critique of nomistic stances; nomism arises only in the context of admitting Gentiles into mixed Jew/Gentile fellowships.	Paul conceived of Jewish and Gentile Christ-believers as a remnant within Israel who occupy a special place within an irrevocably elected Israel.	Paul believed that the eschaton had dawned in Jesus' resurrection and that Jesus had become the way for Gentiles to enter into Israel without having to actually become Jews themselves; Israel must accordingly accept this fact.

Most of these perspectives imply some kind of disjunction between Paul's articulation of salvation in Jesus Christ and his perception of the scope and means of salvation according to his fellow Jews. It is the degree of discontinuity that is debated, and whether that discontinuity removes Paul from common Judaism altogether.

My own view is that Paul very much straddles the "contra" and "intra" Judaism fence, depending on what part of his career one looks at, and contingent upon what specific issue we analyze. Paul is intra-Judaism insofar as most of his debates can normally be paralleled in halakic discussions, and they are often analogous to similar debates that took place among Jews in the Diaspora. (Paul was not the first Jew to argue about food and circumcision in relation to the Gentiles!) Furthermore, Paul's rhetoric fits the sectarian context of Second Temple Judaism with rancorous polemics between sects, and Paul never intended to set up a new religious entity. Yet Paul can also be seen to be contra-Judaism in a very radical sense, as he seems to be willing to go where very few Jews would wish to follow—namely, to lower the currency of Israel's election through the inclusion of Gentiles as part of the "Israel of God." Furthermore, Paul's exegesis of Lev 18:5, his anthropological pessimism, his placement of Jesus *within* the Shema, and the triadic link of Torah-Sin-Death that he makes are too blunt for most of his contemporaries to accept as "in-house" debates. Charles Freeman states that Paul did not convert from one religion to another religion, but he was venturing beyond the margins of conventional Judaism. He writes, "He was in theological no-man's-land and the boundaries between traditional Judaism, Jewish Christianity as it was emerging in Jerusalem and his own teachings remained without clear definition."[54]

In any case, Paul's contrariety will depend entirely on which salvation scheme in Judaism we are comparing him with, for it seems that Paul knew several such schemes. In Rom 1:18-32 his critique of idolatry and pagan immorality mirrors the "ethical monotheism" of Philo, Wisdom of Solomon, and Sirach.[55] Yet, in contrast to Ben Sira and the author of Wisdom, Paul does not think that Torah is God's final answer to the floundering folly of Gentile idolatry. And unlike Philo, Paul doubts the existence of enlightened philosophers who, by their pursuit of virtue and assent to monotheism, have set themselves

---

54. Charles Freeman, *A New History of Early Christianity* (New Haven: Yale University Press, 2009), 50.

55. See Jacob Neusner, *The Emergence of Judaism* (Louisville: Westminster John Knox, 2004), 74-75, who lists four tenets of ethical monotheism: (1) creation, Torah as the plan; (2) the perfection of creation and justice; (3) God's will and humanity's will in conflict; and (4) restoration of perfection. See also Donaldson, *Judaism and the Gentiles*, 493-98.

on course towards a heavenly Jerusalem. There is no noble savage and no saintly pagan for Paul; rather, all people, the Greek as well as the Barbarian, are entrenched in contamination, corruption, and condemnation and desperately need God's deliverance through the Messiah. In addition, Paul evidently knows of a "covenantal nomism" whereby grace is embedded in the covenant and obedience is merely the appreciative response to maintain one's election. His objection, however, consists in the assertion that covenantal grace is efficacious only in the context of covenantal obedience, which is precisely what the Jews lack (Rom 2–3; 9–10). Paul responds most virulently to an "ethnocentric nomism" (Gal 2:1–3:29; Rom 3:27-31; Phil 3:1-9), whereby Christ is merely an add-on to the Sinaitic covenant, so that Christ tops up rather than displaces the salvific function of portions of the Torah. This view effectively keeps the butterfly in the cocoon and locates salvation exclusively within the Jewish constituency. Paul strenuously objects to the view that the gospel is the good news that Greeks can be saved by becoming Jews. Paul also responds to a "sapiential nomism" (1 Cor 1:10–3:23; 2 Cor 3) arising in Corinth that perceives in Christ and the Torah a means to wisdom, power, and glory. Finally, Paul opposes an "apocalyptic mysticism" that locates salvation as something acquired through Torah observance, coupled with visionary ascents to heaven couched in the language of Hellenistic philosophy (Col 2).[56]

If we are to understand Paul's critical stance toward the various schemes of salvation in the Judaism that he knew, then I think that we need to identify the particular socioreligious location of Paul and his converts, as well as the theological texture of his argumentation. Only then can we place Paul's soteriology in relation to that of Judaism.

The Identity of Paul and the Socioreligious Location of Paul's Communities

In his conversion/call, Paul shifted from a Pharisaic sect to a messianic sect within Judaism (albeit soon to be on the fringes of Judaism). Even so, I sense that Paul, at least by the 50s, did not regard the socioreligious ethos of the Judean *ethnos* as the most determining elements of his identity and beliefs. In Gal 1:13-14 Paul writes, "You have heard, no doubt, of my former way of life in Judaism [ἐμὴν ἀναστροφήν ποτε ἐν τῷ Ἰουδαϊσμῷ]. I was intensely perse-

---

56. See Michael F. Bird, *Colossians and Philemon* (NCCS; Eugene, OR: Cascade, 1999), 15-26.

cuting the church of God and was incessantly trying to destroy it. I advanced in Judaism beyond many among my kinsmen of the same age, for I was far more zealous for the traditions of my ancestors." "Judaism" was something that Paul excelled in, to the point of advancement over others, and this Judaism is defined in terms of violent zeal and adherence to a particular tradition. Most likely, then, "Judaism" means a cross of general ancestral customs and a sectarian quest for religious purity of a Pharisaic form. (Perhaps a colloquial gloss like "Judean fanaticisim" captures this sectarian sense.)[57]

However, the crux of the issue is how Paul's current life ἐν Χριστῷ differs from his former way of life ἐν Ἰουδαϊσμῷ. He clearly posits a biographical disjunction and theological distance between his former life in Judaism and his present life in Christ.[58] Despite the immense implications of his apparent rupture with Judaism, Paul did not cease speaking of himself as an Israelite or a Hebrew on other occasions (Rom 11:1; 2 Cor 11:22; Phil 3:5). Given these statements, we can appreciate that the subject of Paul's identity,[59] and Christian and Jewish identity in antiquity for that matter,[60] is incredibly complex.

57. On the sectarian nature of "Judaism" as "the judaizing movement," see Matthew V. Novenson, "Paul's Former Occupation in *Ioudaismos*," in *Galatians and Christian Theology: Justification, the Gospel, and Ethics in Paul's Letter*, ed. M. W. Elliott, S. J. Hafemann, and N. T. Wright (Grand Rapids, MI: Baker Academic, 2014), 24-39.

58. See Georg Strecker, *Theology of the New Testament*, trans. M. E. Boring (Louisville: Westminster John Knox, 2000), 21-22; Thomas R. Schreiner, *Paul, Apostle of God's Glory in Christ: A Pauline Theology* (Downers Grove, IL: InterVarsity, 2001), 45; Giorgio Jossa, *Jews or Christians?* (WUNT 202; Tübingen: Mohr Siebeck, 2006), 12, 95-102; Watson, *Paul, Judaism, and the Gentiles*, 96-99; E. P. Sanders, "Paul's Jewishness," in *Paul's Jewish Matrix*, ed. T. G. Casey and J. Taylor (Rome: Gregorian & Biblical Press, 2011), 64—all to be contrasted with Nanos, "Paul and Judaism," 141-44.

59. See K.-W. Niebuhr, *Heidenapostel aus Israel: Die jüdische Identität des Paulus nach ihrer Darstellung in seinen Briefen* (WUNT 62; Tübingen: Mohr Siebeck, 1992); Daniel Boyarin, *A Radical Jew: Paul and the Politics of Identity* (Berkeley: University of California Press, 1994); James D. G. Dunn, "Who Did Paul Think He Was? A Study of Jewish Christian Identity," *NTS* 45 (1999): 174-93; Jörg Frey, "Paul's Jewish Identity," in *Jewish Identity in the Greco-Roman World*, ed. J. Frey, D. R. Schwartz, and S. Gripentrog (AGJU 71; Leiden: Brill, 2007), 285-321; Caroline Johnson Hodge, "Apostle to the Gentiles: Constructions of Paul's Identity," *BI* 13 (2005): 270-88; William S. Campbell, "Religion, Identity, and Ethnicity: The Contribution of Paul the Apostle," *Journal of Beliefs and Values* 29 (2008): 139-50; idem, *Paul and the Creation of Christian Identity* (London: T&T Clark, 2006).

60. See, e.g., E. P. Sanders et al., eds., *Jewish and Christian Self-Definition*, vol. 2, *Aspects of Judaism in the Graeco-Roman Period* (London: SCM, 1981); W. C. van Unnik, *Das Selbstverständnis der jüdischen Diaspora in der hellenistisch-römischen Zeit* (Leiden: Brill, 1993); Shaye J. D. Cohen, *The Beginnings of Jewishness: Boundaries, Varieties, Uncertainties* (Berkeley: University of California Press, 1999); Jörg Frey, Daniel R. Schwartz, and Stephanie Gripentrog,

In what follows, I analyze Paul's own conception of his identity and the socioreligious location of the Pauline communities in relation to Judaism. I look at several aspects of Paul's letters that point to continuities and discontinuities with his Jewish milieu under the headings of Pauline identity, Christology and covenant, and church and synagogue.

The Pauline Identity

Paul's biography was a matter of seismic changes in personal identity: beginning life as a diaspora Jew, then a Palestinian Pharisee, and finally a Jewish Christ-believing apostle of Jesus Christ to the Gentiles. So who was he? Paul's representation of himself in his letters is that he is just as Jewish as his Jewish contemporaries and that he holds ethnic descent from Israel. Paul's rebuke to Cephas in the Antioch episode included the comment that "we who are Jews by nature and not Gentile sinners," which clearly marks Paul and Cephas as Jewish Christians rather than Gentile adherents to faith in Christ (Gal 2:15). In Philippians Paul famously states that he was "circumcised on the eighth day, a member of the people of Israel, of the tribe of Benjamin, a Hebrew born of Hebrews; as to the law, a Pharisee" (Phil 3:5). Paul can even affirm that his own ethnography as Hebrew, Israelite, and Abrahamic is equal to that of the "superapostles" who visited Corinth (2 Cor 11:22). In Romans he says that Israel is "my own people, my kindred according to the flesh" (Rom. 9:3) and comments about himself, "I myself am an Israelite, a descendant of Abraham, a member of the tribe of Benjamin" (Rom 11:1). Paul's conceptual framework including particularized notions of God as one, as well as his perspective on intermediary figures, his view of the afterlife, his sacred texts and their interpretation, his theopolitics and mission strategy, his denunciation of idolatry and pagan sexual practices, and his piety and gospel, are all rooted in the Judaism of the Greco-Roman world. It seems that he even submitted himself to synagogue discipline on multiple occasions (2 Cor 11:24). He strove to remain in amicable relations with the Jerusalem church, which was still within the orbit of Palestinian Judaism (Gal 2:1-10; Rom 15:25-31; 1 Cor 16:1-3), and he chided a predominantly Gentile congregation for anti-Judaism in favor of the interlocking destiny of Jews and Gentiles in salvation history (Rom 1:16; 11:1-32; 15:8-9). Paul thus identified his own genealogical and religious origins

---

eds., *Jewish Identity in the Greco-Roman World* (AGJU 71; Leiden: Brill, 2007); Judith Lieu, *Christian Identity in the Jewish and Graeco-Roman World* (Oxford: OUP, 2004); Bengst Holmberg, *Exploring Early Christian Identity* (Tübingen: Mohr Siebeck, 2008).

in Israel and in Judaism, he endeavored to maintain affable links with the Jerusalem church and Jewish Diaspora communities, and his own thought world was firmly rooted in Jewish texts and traditions. Furthermore, even in his post-Damascus state he continued to have a particular bond of solidarity with the Jewish nation, as witnessed in his eschatological expectations (Rom 11:25-32), his prayer for Israel's salvation (Rom 10:1), and his heartfelt anguish to the point of wishing for vicarious self-anathematization on their account (Rom 9:3). Nevertheless, much of the cerebral furniture in Paul's mind had been significantly rearranged since his conversion to his new point of view, so that several of Paul's ideological fixtures were now clearly at odds with those of his Jewish contemporaries.

A good example of Paul's theological calibration from Pharisee to Christ-believer is seen in his view on circumcision, for Paul no longer required circumcision of Gentile converts to Christ-faith. Circumcision was the distinguishing mark of the Jewish male, ordinarily the rite of entry into the commonwealth of Israel for male proselytes and commanded in the Mosaic legislation (Lev 12:3).[61] Paul, however, dissolved the category of Jewish adherent (i.e., "God-fearers") and accepted uncircumcised persons as full and equal members of Christ-believing assemblies and demanded their acceptance, even in mixed Jewish/Gentile Christ-believing settings (Gal 2:1-14). In which case, Paul has replaced the Mosaic covenant (e.g., Gal 2:11-21) with a messianic pneumatology for his Gentile converts (e.g., Gal 4:6-7; Rom. 8:14-17). Paul strikes hard and fast against the soteric invalidity of circumcision (Gal 5:2, 6; Rom 4:11; 1 Cor 7:19; see Acts 15:1, 5).[62] He even contends that membership in the people of God is no longer defined by circumcision, rather, through faith in the Messiah and by a concomitant inward transformation by the Holy Spirit (Rom 2:25-29; 8:9-17; Gal 3:26-29; 6:15; Phil 3:3). The obedience of the uncircumcised can be "imputed" (λογίζομαι) as "circumcision" (Rom 2:26; see Phil 3:3; 1 Cor 7:19). In Rom 2:28-29 the apostle explicitly redefines being a Ἰουδαῖος ("Jew") as something that is not φανερός ("outward") but κρυπτός ("hidden"), thus implying a redefinition of the designation so as to include those who are not circumcised (i.e., those who have neither ethnic descent from Israel nor possess the chief emblem of Israel's covenant identity). The privilege of circumcision and ethnic Jewish descent are not denied, but they

---

61. See Bird, *Crossing Over Sea and Land*, 17-43.

62. In a strange feat of irony, the teachers in Galatia aver that Paul usually preached circumcision but that, being fickle or expedient, he misinformed them by omitting their obligation to be circumcised (Gal 1:10; 5:11). In turn, Paul alleges that the teachers are themselves fickle and false when they omit the obligation to obey the whole Torah (Gal 5:3; 6:13).

are of little benefit in the face of disobedience to God and rejection of his Son (Rom 2:25; 3:1-20; 9:1-29). What separated Paul from other more revisionist approaches to circumcision and Gentiles (e.g., Ananias in Josephus, *Ant.* 20.34-42, or the allegorizers in Philo, *Migr.* 89-94) was three things: (1) the soteriological singularity of God's apocalyptic deliverance wrought in Jesus' death, resurrection, and exaltation (e.g., Gal 2:21; Rom 8:3), (2) the experience of the Spirit being poured upon the uncircumcised (e.g., Gal 3:2-5, 14; 4:6; Rom 8:4-17), and (3) the salvation-historical priority of the Abrahamic promise over the Mosaic covenant (e.g., Gal 3:6-14, 29; Rom 4:10-11).[63]

This reconfiguration of Jewish beliefs was not an absolute disjunction, as Paul believed that Christ-believing communities remained in continuity with Israel's sacred history. The designations "Israel" and "Israelite" were evidently positive for Paul, as they denoted continuity with God's purposes first announced to the patriarchs and fulfilled in the economy of God's action in Jesus Christ.[64] These terms relate to God's electing purposes, and yet they are used in such a way as to transcend ethnic categories. For instance, Paul's "Israel of God" (Gal 6:16) is analogous to Philo's "Israel who sees God," which is a philosophical rather than an ethnic category for the Alexandrian philosopher (Philo, *Migr.* 113-14; *Conf.* 56; *Her.* 78).[65] Paul considers the patriarchs and Israelite history to be the ancestry and story belonging to Jewish and Gentile Christ-believers (Rom 4:1; 1 Cor 10:1). Paul envisages salvation for the renewed Israel, which comprises believing Jews and Gentiles, centered on Christ (Rom 9:4-8; see Rom 3:30; 4:10-12; Eph 2:11-22), and the whole or part of national Israel in the eschatological future (Rom 11:26, 32).[66]

Further to this theological transformation, Paul's explication of his own identity moves in a direction away from the key nodes of Jewish identity. Let me first say that I think that Paul is self-consciously of Jewish origin, and he

63. Terence Donaldson, *Paul and the Gentiles: Remapping the Apostle's Conviction World* (Minneapolis: Fortress, 1997), 215-48.

64. See James D. G. Dunn (*The Parting of the Ways: Between Christianity and Judaism and Their Significance for the Character of Christianity* [London: SCM, 1990], 148-49): "Paul may have been disowning the *Judaism* in which he had been brought up (Gal. 1.13-14), but he did so self-consciously as an *Israelite*—that is, as one who sought to maintain and promote the true character of Israel's election against the majority of fellow Israelites who were currently interpreting it in a more narrowly particularistic or ethnic sense" (italics original).

65. See Ellen Birnbaum, *The Place of Judaism in Philo's Thought: Israel, Jews, and Proselytes* (Providence, RI: Brown University Press, 1996), 11-12.

66. I think this idea of equality in fellowship rules out the idea prevalent among some scholars (e.g., Mark Nanos, Caroline Johnson Hodge) that Gentile Christ-believers constitute companions to Israel without actually being part of Israel.

gives the impression of being committed to Israel's way of life, Scriptures, and hope. I would suggest that his own default setting for personal conduct would be Torah observance; he did nothing to discourage Jewish Christians from Torah observance, and he even obligated Gentiles to heed specific scruples of concern to Jews about avoiding idolatry and sexual immorality and about adhering to monotheism. The question of who was a Jew in antiquity is complex. But if we define Judaism in terms of ethnicity and shared custom, then it is evident that Paul relativized the former and denied the efficacy of the latter in view of the saving event of God executed in Jesus Christ. In addition, if ethnicity is also defined with reference to a religious culture, as it was in Judaism, then Paul's critique of Judaism as a religion implies a rupture within his own biological origins and current religious disposition.[67] Several features of Paul's construal of his identity suggest that being ἐν Χριστῷ does not negate his Jewish origins, but it does transcend it and even relativizes it in relation to a new Christ-given and Spirit-endowed identity. That new identity is continuous with his Israelite ancestry, but also consciously distinct from it in some regards.

For instance, in Phil 3:7-8, Paul can consider his nationally inherited Jewish privileges as ζημία ("loss") and σκύβαλον ("filth") when *compared to* Christ. It is evident from 1 Cor 9:20-23 that he considered "becoming" (γίνομαι) a Jew (i.e., living like a Jew) just as much a compromise as becoming one "without law" (ἄνομος) or becoming "weak" (ἀσθενής) for the sake of his missionary call to herald the gospel.[68] The exhortation in Gal 3:28, with its οὐκ . . . οὐδέ

67. Love L. Sechrest, *A Former Jew: Paul and the Dialectics of Race* (LNTS 410; London: Continuum, 2009), 105-9.

68. See Richard Hays (*First Corinthians* [Interpretation; Louisville: Westminster John Knox, 1997], 153): "Since Paul was in fact a Jew, this formulation shows how radically he conceives the claim that in Christ he is . . . in a position transcending all cultural allegiances"; Wolfgang Schrage (*Der erste Brief an die Korinther* [Neukirchen-Vluyn: Neukirchener Verlag, 1991-99], 2:340): "Paulus wird nicht einfach Jude oder Heide, sondern *wie* ein Jude und *wie* ein Heide, ihnen vergleichbar. Er läßt sich auf sie ein, wird in bestimmter Weise mit ihnen solidarisch. Das erweist gerade das Ἰουδαίοις ὡς Ἰουδαῖος. Denn wie kann Paulus, der geborene Jude (vgl. Gal 2,15 ἡμεῖς φύσει Ἰουδαῖοι), erst ein Jude *werden*? Nicht zufällig fehlt ein μὴ ὢν Ἰουδαῖος in Analogie zu den beiden folgenden Beispielen. Aber kann er nicht nur etwas werden, was er in bestimmter Weise nicht mehr ist? In der Tat. Weil es in Christus weder Juden noch Griechen gibt (Gal 3,28; vgl. zu 12,13), *ist* Paulus auch als geborener Jude nicht mehr einfach Jude, sonder wird es, 'um Juden zu gewinnen.'" Dunn ("Who Did Paul Think He Was?," 182): "Paul speaks as one who does not acknowledge 'Jew' as his own given identity, or as an identity inalienable from his person. . . . Instead, the term 'Jew' is being treated almost as a role which one might assume or discard." Wright (*Paul and the Faithfulness of God*, 1435-36): "Paul understood himself to possess what in our jargon we might call a new 'identity'—the word is slippery, but it is hard to think of a better one—in which his previous 'identity' as a 'Jew,' as one 'under the

construction framing the binary pairing of Jew/Greek, slave/free, and male/female, is not a negation of the ontological and cultural existence of the respective tags (e.g., believers do not suddenly cease to be Greek-speaking male freedmen), as much as it stipulates their transformation into a shared meta-identity defined by being ἐν Χριστῷ Ἰησοῦ. The various identities are spliced together, creating a socioreligious hybrid identity.[69] What is negated is the effectiveness of these tags to become vehicles of separation and superiority. The emphasis in Gal 3:28-29 (and Gal 2:19-21; 5:6; 6:15; 1 Cor 7:18-19; 12:13; Col 3:11) is not the obliteration of different human identities but the *inclusion* and *transformation* of multiple identities under a single meta-identity marked by Christ and the new creation. But this new entity can be true only if the existing identities, which are a means of distinction and status, are themselves negated in value and lessened in their ability to cause differentiation.[70] Paul's

---

law,' had been, to say the least, drastically modified. It no longer defined who he was, and what he could and could not do." In contrast, Nanos ("Paul and Judaism," 139) states, "I understand Paul to be expressing *a rhetorical strategy*, not a change of halakic behaviour.... I propose that 'becoming like' signifies 'arguing from the premises' of each." But I wonder whether Nanos has simply exchanged a legal duplicity for a philosophical one (see Schrage [*Der erste Brief*, 342]: "Aber V20b ist auch nicht einfach eine Tautologie oder eine bloß rhetorische Wiederholung von V20a. Eher wird es sich um eine Explikation und Steigerung handeln. Explikation insofern, als das Gesetz den Juden zum Juden macht und das Sein ὑπὸ νόμον für Paulus das ist, was den Juden von Christen unterscheidet. Steigerung aber insofern, als Paulus erklärt, selbst unter den Nomos getreten zu sein, um die Gesetzesleute zu gewinnen. Wie ungewöhnlich und alles andere als selbstverständliche das ist, zeigt die konzessive Partizipialbestimmung μὴ ὢν αὐτὸς ὑπὸ νόμον. Christliches Leben wird nicht mehr durch die Tora konstituiert und determiniert"). Furthermore, 1 Cor 9:20-23 is not merely about accommodation to the standard of those without law, because Paul is well aware of the potential charge of antinomianism that his activity can foster, hence his plea that he remains constricted and constrained by the law of Christ, even in his temporary identification with the lawless.

69. See similarly Sze-kar Wan ("Does Diaspora Identity Imply Some Sort of Universality? An Asian American Reading of Galatians," in *Interpreting beyond Borders*, ed. F. F. Segovia [Sheffield: Sheffield Academic, 2000], 126): "This new 'people' is reconfigured not by erasing ethnic and cultural differences but by *combining these differences into a hybrid existence*" (italics original). Joshua Garroway (*Paul's Gentile-Jews: Neither Jew nor Gentile, but Both* [New York: Palgrave MacMillan, 2012]) argues that Paul creates his own hybrid identity "Gentile-Jews" because he did not have a third category like "Christian" to use.

70. Bird, *Colossians and Philemon*, 102-6. See discussion in Mark D. Nanos, *The Irony of Galatians: Paul's Letter in First-Century Context* (Minneapolis: Fortress, 2002), 99; Mark Seifrid, "For the Jew First: Paul's Nota Bene for His Gentile Readers," in *To the Jew First: The Case for Jewish Evangelism in Scripture and History* (Grand Rapids, MI: Kregel, 2008), 26-27, 37; Pauline Nigh Hogan, *"No Longer Male and Female": Interpreting Galatians 3:28 in Early Christianity* (LNTS 380; London: T&T Clark, 2008). I'm singularly curious about, but unsure

Jewishness is retained but is subsumed beneath and subordinated to being in Christ. When this formulation is combined with Paul's remarks in 1 Cor 10:32 that divide persons into Jews, Greeks, and the church of God, and the "us" who are differentiated from Jews and Gentiles in Rom 9:24 and 1 Cor 1:18-24, it seems hard to avoid the conclusion that Paul conceived of Christ-believers as a τρίτον γένος, or *tertium genus*: a third race.[71] Based on her study of ethnicity and race in Paul's letters, Love Sechrest writes:

> Contrary to scholars who use an anachronistic definition of race or ethnicity and take it for granted that Paul continued to think of himself as [a] Jew, Pauline self-identity texts interpreted against the framework of ancient Jewish constructions of race suggest that Paul identified himself as

---

of, Hodge's claim (*If Sons, Then Heirs*, 126-31) that Paul is simply reordering identities within an existing hierarchy of multiple identities, since this view fails to grapple with the negation that Paul makes.

71. See Clement of Alexandria, *Strom.* 6.5.41.6; Aristides, *Apol.* 2.2. According to E. P. Sanders (*Paul, the Law, and the Jewish People*, 178): "Paul's view of the church, supported by his practice against his own conscious intention, was substantially that it was a third entity, not just because it was composed of both Jew and Greek, but also because it was in important ways neither Jewish nor Greek." Sanders elsewhere adds ("Paul's Jewishness," 66): "The terminology reflects the *social fact* that Paul inhabited a tri-partite world: there were Jews, pagans and those who belonged to Christ, some of whom had belonged to Judaism, and some to paganism." Wright (*Paul and the Faithfulness of God*, 1443-49 [esp. 1448]) thinks the notion of a third race is a quintessentially Pauline and characteristically Jewish way of conceiving of the church. Segal (*Paul the Convert*, 263): "What Paul did not wish and what he fought against is what eventually happened: The church became a new, third entity." David J. Rudolph (*A Jew to the Jews*, 33-35) tries to rebut an analogy with a third race but can do so only by denying what Paul clearly says in places like 1 Cor 12:2, where he calls believers former Gentiles. Magnus Zetterholm ("Paul within Judaism: The State of the Questions," in *Paul within Judaism*, ed. M. D. Nanos and M. Zetterholm [Minneapolis: Fortress, 2015], 47-51) wrongfully thinks that identifying the Pauline churches as a "third race" necessitates complete abandonment of Torah observance by Jews and Gentiles, a point I would contest. Interestingly, Garroway (*Paul's Gentile Jews*, 8) believes that Paul had no consistent way to describe his congregations who were Jews yet not Jews and Gentiles yet not Gentiles, an observation that comports with E. P. Sanders's *Encyclopedia Britannica* article "Paul," which claims, "Moreover, since Paul's converts did not become Jewish, they were, in general opinion, *nothing*: neither Jew nor pagan" (italics original). Garroway surmises: "When interpreters retrospectively provide Paul that *tertium quid* by introducing 'Christians,' they resolve what is left unresolved in Paul's own discourse. That catachrestical term 'Gentile-Jew,' on the other hand, *reflects* rather than *resolves* Paul's incapacity to describe the identity of his charges with a consistent, coherent term" (italics original). Of course, if "Gentile-Jew" is a new entity, differentiated from "Gentiles" and "Jews," a "third race" for all intents and purposes, and if it is indeed a hybrid ethnic category that underlay the invention of "Christian" as a name for this new identity, then, "a rose by any other name. . . ."

an Israelite who was born a Jew but no longer was one. Paul's perspective on and response to the Christ event apocalyptically altered his relationship with God, his relationship to his kinsmen, and his interactions with the radically Other. That is to say, Paul and his Jewish-born and Gentile-born Christian family had become members of a new racial entity.[72]

So can we ask with Markus Barth whether Paul's life "was a good Jewish life: a struggle for the right of the other?"[73] Paul himself could have conceivably said so, but I doubt whether that would have been agreed by all Jews or by all Christ-believing Jews who may have regarded him as an apostate or schismatic.[74] Paul's construal of his identity is paradoxically affirming of his Israelite ancestry but also relativizes his Jewishness to the point that many of his coreligionists would wonder whether, so to speak, he had given away the family store.

Is Paul, then, in Judaism any longer? The answer to this question is again notoriously difficult to state absolutely one way or the other. On the one hand, I have to warn against Harnackian portraits of a Paul who is all but done with Judaism. Paul was not using messianism as an excuse to turn Judaism into some kind of monotheistic pagan philosophy with a universal scope and good ethics. If that were the case, we would be at a loss to understand why he would circumcise Timothy (Acts 16:3), pay for a colleague's Nazirite vow (Acts 21:23-26), make an apology for the Torah (Rom 7:1-25), defend

72. Sechrest, *A Former Jew*, 164.

73. Markus Barth, "Der gute Jude Paulus," in *Richte unsere Füsse auf den Weg des Friedens*, ed. A. Baudis, D. Clausert, V. Schliski, and B. Wegener (FS Helmut Gollwitzer; Munich: Christian Kaiser, 1979), 132 ("Sein Leben war eines guten Juden Leben: ein Kampf für das Recht des Nächsten"). Nanos ("Paul and Judaism," 124) characterizes the consensus of Pauline scholarship as supposing that Paul "may have thought of himself as a 'good Jew,' but no other practicing Jews would have."

74. Paul's experience of synagogue punishments (2 Cor 11:24), having his mission hindered by Jewish groups (1 Thess 2:16), praying for deliverance from Jews in Jerusalem (Rom 15:31), accusations of antinomianism (Rom 3:8; Acts 21:21), and antagonism from Jewish Christians (Gal 6:17; Phil 1:17) do not bode well for Paul being considered a "good Jew" by others. That said, Paul did have a cohort of Jewish Christian supporters, and we can safely assume that not all Jews would have been automatically hostile to him (e.g., Acts 28:17-24). See John M. G. Barclay, "Paul among Diaspora Jews: Anomaly or Apostate?," *JSNT* 60 (1995): 89-120; Stanley E. Porter, "Was Paul a Good Jew? Fundamental Issues in a Current Debate," in *Christian-Jewish Relations through the Centuries*, ed. S. E. Porter and B. W. R. Pearson (JSNTSup 192; Sheffield: Sheffield Academic, 2000), 148-74; J. Ross Wagner, *Heralds of the Good News: Isaiah and Paul "in Concert" in the Letter to the Romans* (Leiden: Brill, 2003), 4; Michael F. Bird and Preston M. Sprinkle, "Jewish Interpretation of Paul in the Last Thirty Years," *CBR* 6 (2008): 355-56.

those weak in conscience (Rom 14:1-15:1; 1 Cor 8:7-13), and uphold the Torah (Gal 3:21; Rom 3:31). Paul is firmly at home within the symbolic universe of ancient Judaism; he affirms certain practices and basic theological premises, even if he reprioritizes and reinterprets certain beliefs in light of a Jewish messianism.[75] On the other hand, I likewise have to warn against presentations of Paul where he is so devoutly Jewish that one can scarcely imagine rabbis raising their voice against him. The Pauline epistles and Acts confirm that Paul managed to excite debate, division, and even violence by his missionary work among Jewish communities. The question is why? Most likely, it was because Paul's unique concoction of Christology, eschatology, and the transformation of identity was deemed to be pushing the boundaries of a common Judaism to the breaking point. In addition, we must add that Paul consistently characterizes Judaism as "Pharisaic Judaism" and regards this as fundamentally incompatible with the gospel (Gal 1:13-14; Phil 3:6-8).[76] Paul found in the Judaism of his compatriots both a treasure of riches and a tragic story of repeated failure.

Let us remember that ethnic identity is something that is privately enacted and publicly validated. Paul was enacting his own model of Israelite identity centered on Jesus as Messiah and the inclusion of Gentiles as part of the mandate of the Abrahamic covenant. Paul can vehemently criticize contemporary Jewish interpretations of what it means to be and belong to Israel when his enactment of his Israelite identity comes under opposition from Jewish and Jewish Christ-believing detractors. Collective identities are not static and are constantly in flux as they negotiate their sociocultural environment. The problem for Paul was that he was trying to negotiate the seemingly nonnegotiable symbols and subjects of the Jewish way of life in order to accommodate them to his messianic faith. Paul's self-understanding, mission, theology, and praxis were expressions of a Jewish worldview that we can legitimately call "early

---

75. Gabriele Boccaccini (*Roots of Rabbinic Judaism: An Intellectual History, from Ezekiel to Daniel* [Grand Rapids, MI: Eerdmans, 2002], 35) alleges that, if Judaism is defined as the "monotheistic religion of YHWH," then Christianity "has never ceased to be a Judaism."

76. In this instance Paul seems at one with Josephus, who also regards Pharisaism as the default position of the Jewish masses (*Ant.* 13.288, 297-98; 18.15). Roland Deines ("The Pharisees between 'Judaisms' and Common Judaism," in *Justification and Variegated Nomism*, vol. 1, *The Complexities of Second Temple Judaism*, ed. D. A. Carson, P. T. O'Brien, and M. A. Seifrid [Grand Rapids, MI: Baker Academic, 2001], 503) calls Pharisaism "the fundamental and most influential religious movement within Palestinian Judaism." Dunn ("Who Did Paul Think He Was?," 185) thinks that Paul regarded Judaism as too much identified with Maccabean views of circumcision and food laws.

Christianity," but it resulted in a way of life that many regarded as a departure from a perceived norm on how to live as a faithful Jew. Paul knew that Christ-faith created a divide from his fellow Jews, and he placed the blame squarely at the feet of *their* Judaism rather than to *his* messianic faith.[77]

To use a dramatic metaphor, it was as if he and his Jewish colleagues were a troop of actors who shared one and the same script. The problem was that they had completely botched the performance of the last act of the play by missing the cameo appearance of the playwright's son. The cast then decided to co-opt a zealous dramaturge to be the director, and he decided to lock out half of the cast from the show and added lines to the script. The actors trusted in their possession of the script rather than in its performance; they were seemingly unaware that their membership in the actors union did not automatically guarantee them immunity from critical reviews by the author, nor did they believe what several cast members said, that the author himself is going to step onto the stage at any moment.

From the theatrical back to the historical, the point of contention was a fundamental divergence between what it meant to be the people of God in the aftermath of the advent of the Messiah. Non–Christ-believing Jews could dispute that the Messiah had come, since the world looked to them entirely unredeemed, and so no cause to reconfigure any beliefs could be justified. Jewish Christ-believers could agree that the Messiah had come, but they disagreed as to how to configure their beliefs about Torah, Israel, and the Gentiles in light of his advent. And so herein lay the crux. It is precisely the question of Messiah and Judaism—the crucified and risen Lord in relation to the emblems, ethos, and ethnicity of the Jewish people—that perplexed the early Christian interpreters, and it became a matter of contention in their own communities. The focal point of debate revolved around how the God-given instruments of Torah and Christ related to each other. Should one interpret God's Messiah in light of God's Torah, or interpret God's Torah in light of God's Messiah?[78] This is very much the question that Paul wrestles with on several fronts. The resulting issue, then, is what takes priority: Christology or covenant? This, I submit, is the primary point of contention between Paul and his Jewish Christ-believing competitors.

---

77. This paragraph was stimulated by reading James C. Miller, "Paul and His Ethnicity: Reframing the Categories," in *Paul as Missionary: Identity, Activity, Theology, and Practice*, ed. T. J. Burke and B. S. Rosner (LNTS 420; London: T&T Clark, 2011), 37-50 (esp. 49-50).

78. J. Louis Martyn, *Galatians: A New Translation, with Introduction and Commentary* (AB; New York: Doubleday, 1997), 124.

Christology and Covenant

For Paul, it seems that what had been a Torah-centered way of life in the context of Israel's Sinaitic covenant has become a Christ-centered way of life in the context of the (re)new(ed) covenant that is the fulfillment of the Abrahamic promises. Paul, paradoxically, strove to demonstrate tangible links between the Jesus movement and Israel's religious antiquity, principally through his use of Scripture, yet he also intended to provide an ideological legitimation for the separation of his Gentile converts from the synagogue and their freedom from certain Torah observances that some Jewish Christ-believers wanted to foist upon them. While precise elements of continuity and discontinuity between the Sinaitic covenant and the new covenant are many and debatable, I intend here to focus on two key texts from Paul that engage this subject: 2 Cor 3:6-13 and Rom 9:30–10:6 as indicative of the macrostructure of Paul's covenantal thinking.[79]

In 2 Cor 3 Paul provides an "allusive homily"[80] in defense of his apostolate by reference to the superiority of the ministry of the new covenant over that of the old covenant. There is no problem of proselytizing Jewish Christ-believers in Corinth à la Galatians, but the intrusion of Jewish Christ-believers still occasions Paul's efforts to distance his own ministry from the pattern of ministry represented by the intruding visitors to Corinth. In 2 Cor 3:6 Paul asserts that God has made him and others sufficiently capable to serve in the dispensation of the new covenant, which is defined not by the "letter" (γράμμα)[81] but by the "Spirit" (πνεῦμα). He immediately adds an explanatory remark: "for the letter kills, but the Spirit gives life" (τὸ γὰρ γράμμα ἀποκτέννει, τὸ δὲ πνεῦμα ζῳοποιεῖ). Paul's subsequent argument in 3:7-11 uses a series of qal wāhômer (a minori ad maius) comparisons, built around the imagery of Exod 32–34, to the effect that if the ministry that

---

79. Barth ("Der gute Jude Paulus," 113) cites these same two texts and argues that anyone who takes them to imply that Paul regarded the law/covenant as obsolete, canceled, annulled, or replaced "despises and condemns the Jews along with the law" ("verachtet und verurteilt mit dem Gesetz die Juden"), and consequently, if such an interpretation is true, then "together the old covenant and its testament as well as God's promises fall by the wayside" ("mit dem Alten Bund und Testament fallen dann auch die Gottesverheissungen dahin betreffend Nachkommenschaft").

80. Richard B. Hays, Echoes of Scripture in the Letters of Paul (New Haven: Yale University Press, 1989), 132.

81. Here γράμμα refers to the Ten Commandments, given the reference to "tablets of stone" in v. 3.

brought death and condemnation was glorious (i.e., the Sinai covenant), *then* how much more glorious is the ministry that bequeaths the Spirit and grants righteousness (i.e., the new covenant). The doxological inferiority of the old ministry compared to the new ministry is particularly stressed in 3:10-11. Paul asserts that what once appeared as glorious, when compared to the new glory, now appears to be utterly lacking in glory. The diminishing nature of the Mosaic glory in v. 7 leads in v. 11 to the supersession of the Mosaic service. Paul reasons that the fading glory that reflected from Moses' face indicates the transitory nature of the Mosaic legislation, which is replaced with something yet more glorious and more permanent. Consequently, the fading nature of the Mosaic glory becomes allusive for the limitation or ineffectiveness of the Mosaic covenant itself.[82]

The same pattern emerges in 3:13-14, with the stress on the transitory and therefore redundant nature of the old covenant. Paul says that Moses wore a veil to prevent the Israelites from gazing "at the end that was being set aside" (εἰς τὸ τέλος τοῦ καταργουμένου), indicating the Israelites' fascination with something that was both hidden and already diminishing. In effect, Israel's error was its mesmerizing fixation on a face that symbolized a ministry that was already on the way out. In v. 14 Paul applies the analogy to his own time, contending that the hardening of the Israelites' minds means that the same veil that covered Moses' face now covers Israel when they read the old covenant, and thus they fail to understand its transitory nature. That veil is lifted when one turns to the Lord through Christ (3:14-16). The net point underling 2 Cor 3:6-18 is that the fading/diminishing nature of Moses' "glory" is allusive of the end of the ministry of the old covenant and the rule of the letter of the Torah. Several key implications for Paul and Judaism emerge from this analysis of 2 Cor 3:6-18.

First, the sociorhetorical function of this passage must be mapped into Paul's own social context. The intruding superapostles (2 Cor 11:5; 12:11), who have come to Corinth with letters of recommendation, are ministers of this letter that kills. That is not to say that the intruders are proselytizers like Paul's opponents in Galatia—indeed, they probably have a more sapiential and so-phistic form of discourse.[83] Nevertheless, Paul postures himself as an antitype to their ministry by making a stark contrast between the old covenant and

---

82. Scott J. Hafemann, *Paul, Moses, and the History of Israel: The Letter/Spirit Contrast and the Argument from Scripture in 2 Corinthians 3* (WUNT 81; Tübingen: Mohr Siebeck, 1995), 329-30.

83. See discussion in N. H. Taylor, "Apostolic Identity and the Conflicts in Corinth and Galatia," in *Paul and His Opponents*, ed. S. E. Porter (PAST 2; Leiden: Brill, 2005), 115-22.

the new covenant, covenants that mirror Jewish and Christ-believing communities respectively, and Paul thereby insulates his Christ-believing Gentiles from anyone who would seek to draw them into the orbit of the Sinai covenant. Rejection of these superapostles necessitates Paul's constructing a paradigm of how the new covenant supersedes the old and thus providing an ideological justification for the separation of Christ-believing communities from the synagogues.[84]

Second, Paul asserts the negative soteriological effect of the "old covenant" and the positive soteriological effects of the "new covenant." The "letter" (i.e., Torah) kills, and the old covenant is associated with death and condemnation. In contrast, the new service brought about by the Spirit brings righteousness and life. The glory of the new covenant also eclipses the glory of the old covenant in several ways. First, the hope that the righteous would share in God's glory at the eschaton was widespread in postbiblical Judaism, and Paul attributes its realization to the advent of the new covenant.[85] Second, the hope for transformation and glorification is brought by the Lord and Spirit, thus showing that the new covenant brings in the new creation (2 Cor 3:18). Sprinkle aptly sums up the contrast Paul makes, referring to "the law in its old covenant function of offering life conditioned on obedience, whereas the spirit is the divine agent who grants the covenant blessing of life unilaterally."[86] For this reason Paul does not minister "like Moses, who put a veil over his face" (2 Cor 3:13), but in a different order of service associated with hope, life, freedom, righteousness, transformation, and glory (2 Cor 3:17-18).[87]

Third, Paul implies the renewal of the old covenant with the advent of the new covenant. The precise meaning and application of the words τέλος (3:13) and καταργέω (3:7, 11, 13, 14) are of course disputed. What is clear, however, is that Paul regards the old covenant as comparatively inglorious, transitory, and ineffective next to the new covenant. The focus in 3:6-14 is ultimately on the discontinuity between the two covenants. Otfried Hofius correctly suggests that, already in v. 6, it is assumed that the new covenant relates antithetically to the old covenant, even if "old covenant" does not appear until v. 14.[88] The new

---

84. Watson, *Paul, Judaism, and the Gentiles*, 156-59.

85. Peter Stuhlmacher, "Erwägungen zum ontologischen Charakter der καινὴ κτίσις bei Paulus," *EvTh* 27 (1967): 1-35.

86. Sprinkle, *Paul and Judaism Revisited*, 101.

87. Hafemann, *Paul*, 352-53.

88. Otfried Hofius, "Gesetz und Evangelium nach 2. Korinther 3," in *Paulusstudien* (WUNT 51; Tübingen: Mohr Siebeck, 1994), 75.

covenant is the eschatological deed of God executed in Jesus Christ, mediated through the Spirit, and enacted by the apostolic ministers.

Fourth, the logic of Paul's covenant theology is that the position of Jews under the Torah is implied to be dire. In 3:14-15 the synagogues in which Torah is read continue to exacerbate the problem of Moses' original audience. As Francis Watson states: "There, each Sabbath, Moses is read and heard without any awareness that, beneath the surface of the veil, the glory has departed."[89] Furthermore, a metaphoric veil covers their hearts and impairs their understanding of the very words before them. Those of the synagogue, then, need to turn to the Lord and have Christ remove the veil for them. That way, they will participate in the freedom bequeathed by the Spirit and so enter into the transforming glory of the new creation, which has no reason to be veiled (3:17-18). It is probable that Χριστός as the remover of the veil in v. 14 is to be identified with the κύριος of v. 16, meaning that turning (ἐπιστρέφω) to the Lord is essentially conversion to Christ (see 2 Cor 4:3-4).[90] In other words, the noetic liberation of Israel and their doxological transformation occurs through their conversion to Jesus the Messiah.

An additional key document for exploring Paul's covenant theology is Romans. Paul writes this epistle to a predominantly Gentile church in order to garner support for his future mission to Spain, to return to Jerusalem with the Gentile churches of Rome behind him, to defend himself against allegations of being antinomian or even anti-Israel, and to engage in some preventive pastoral care of a cluster of congregations that he suspects could fracture over ethnic lines or over halakic issues.

The vital passage is Rom 9:30–10:6, where Paul explains why Israel has not obtained righteousness and yet the Gentiles have. His focus is largely apologetic: if God is faithful, then why has Israel failed to believe in its own Messiah? Paul must deal with the problem of Israel's unbelief in order to settle the question of whether God's faithfulness is really faithful and whether God's righteousness will at last triumph even over Israel's obduracy.

One thing we should note is that the ideas expressed in 9:30-33 are essentially restated anew in 10:1-6.[91] The parallel includes:

---

89. Watson, *Paul, Judaism, and the Gentiles*, 159.

90. Cf. Richard H. Bell, *The Irrevocable Call of God* (WUNT 184; Tübingen: Mohr Siebeck, 2005), 238-43.

91. Tobin, *Paul's Rhetoric in Its Contexts*, 309-11, 341-42.

A	9:30 What then are we to say? Gentiles,	10:1-2 Brothers and sisters, my heart's desire and prayer to God for them is that they may be saved. I can testify that they have a zeal for God, but it is not enlightened.
B	who did not strive for righteousness, have attained it, that is, righteousness through faith;	3 For, being ignorant of the righteousness that comes from God, and seeking to establish their own,
C	31 but Israel, who did strive for the righteousness that is based on the law, did not succeed in fulfilling that law.	they have not submitted to God's righteousness.
D	32 Why not? Because they did not strive for it on the basis of faith, but as if it were based on works.	4 For Christ is the end of the law so that there may be righteousness for everyone who believes.
E	They have stumbled over the stumbling stone, 33 as it is written, "See, I am laying in Zion a stone that will make people stumble, a rock that will make them fall, and whoever believes in him will not be put to shame."	5-6 Moses writes concerning the righteousness that comes from the law, that "the person who does these things will live by them." But the righteousness that comes from faith says, "Do not say in your heart, 'Who will ascend into heaven?' (that is, to bring Christ down)."

A. Paul juxtaposes the response of the Gentiles (9:30) and Israel (10:1-2) to God's righteousness.

B. The contrast is twofold: first, between Gentiles who did not seek righteousness with an Israel that did seek righteousness; second, between the Gentiles who received a righteousness from faith, whereas Israel sought to establish its own righteousness (9:30; 10:3).

C. Despite Israel's efforts, it did not attain a righteousness from Torah (9:31); as such, it did not submit to the righteousness of God (10:3).

D. The operating assumption of Paul is that righteousness is from faith and not from works (9:32), and the reason is that Christ is the "end" (τέλος) of the Torah so that righteousness would come to everyone who believes (10:4). In parallel, "by faith" (ἐκ πίστεως) seems to be a metonym for "Messiah" (Χριστός), and righteousness by means of "by works" (ἐξ ἔρ-γων) has ended with the culmination of the νόμος ("law" or "covenant").

E. This argument is validated with scriptural citations, including a conflation of Isa 8:14 and 28:16 (9:32-33) about Israel's stumbling, and then again by Lev 18:5, Deut 9:4 and 30:12-14 concerning the inability of persons to satisfy the Torah, in contrast to the efficacious advent of God's saving word (10:5-6).

Matters about the discontinuity between the dispensations of Christ and Torah permeate Romans (see 3:21; 5:21; 6:14-15; 7:1-6), and the disjunction between the two reaches a climax in the much-discussed text Rom 10:4, that "Christ is the end/goal/terminus of the Torah/covenant so that there might be righteousness for everyone who believes" (τέλος γὰρ νόμου Χριστὸς εἰς δικαιοσύνην παντὶ τῷ πιστεύοντι). Israel's stumbling in the wake of Christ consists of its failure to know that Christ is the *goal* of the Torah itself[92] and that Scripture points in the direction of a righteousness for Jews and Gentiles. Righteousness is not the exclusive property of Israel because the Torah itself cannot properly be a source of righteousness. Rather, it is the righteousness of God, revealed in Christ and apprehended by faith, that provides righteousness for all. Continuity is not fully obviated, however, as Paul endeavors to show the conformity of his message to Israel's Scripture (esp. from Deuteronomy and Leviticus), and the parallels between 10:3-4 and 3:20-23 qualify the antithesis as forecast in Israel's sacred traditions. We can conclude that the Torah is no more because its *goal* has been attained, and therefore its operation has *terminated*. This means, as Paul goes on to argue, that salvation is located in the word of faith about Christ and not in the covenantal structures of the Mosaic economy (Rom 10:6-14).

In effect, what Paul was trying to achieve in 2 Cor 3:6-18 and Rom 9:30–10:6 was to provide the ideological legitimacy of a partition between the Sinaitic covenant and his Gentile converts by demonstrating that the bridge between God's ancient promises and the nations is through Christ rather than the Mosaic economy. The Mosaic dispensation was necessary and good, but it was ultimately preparatory for the event that would lead to the salvation of both Israel and the nations. But what does one do if Israel at large will not accept Paul's view of the people of God as comprising Jesus-believing Jews and Gentiles? Where does one go if this message finds only mixed or minimal success in the synagogues of the Diaspora?

---

92. In Pauline usage τέλος ordinarily denotes cessation (1 Cor 15:24), a gradual closure (1 Cor. 10:11), or a goal or result (Rom 6:21, 22; 2 Cor 11:15; Phil 3:19), or it can be used adverbially (1 Thess 2:16; 1 Cor 1:8; 2 Cor 3:13). It is striking, however, that Rom 10:4 occurs in a context filled with athletic imagery (in 9:30-33), so a translation of "goal" may be the meaning most contextually appropriate.

Church and Synagogue

Paul's articulation of the Christ/Torah antithesis and his concomitant defense of Gentile believers as Gentiles emerge out of a particular social location. Paul's missionary career appears to have included periods of missionary activity oriented to Jews in Damascus/Arabia (Gal 1:17; 5:11), then to Jews and Gentiles in Diasporan synagogues while connected with the Antioch church (Gal 1:21), and focused intensively on Gentiles in his later Aegean mission (e.g., 1 Thess 1:10). Furthermore, all of Paul's disputes over circumcision and Jewish observances in relation to Gentiles can be situated within intra-Diasporan Jewish debates over halakah for Gentiles. Still, it appears that Paul soon began establishing Christ-believing assemblies that were separate from Judaism and included some persons who had never been part of the Jewish synagogues. As Wayne Meeks states: "Socially the Pauline groups were never a sect of Judaism. They organized their lives independently from the Jewish associations of the cities where they were founded, and apparently, so far as the evidence reveals, they had little or no interaction with Jews."[93] I hesitate in following Meeks on the degree of interaction between Jews and Christians, as I think it was far more dynamic and varied, depending on the individual contexts in Galatia, Corinth, Philippi, Thessalonica, and Ephesus, yet his central point of independence from Jewish social centers probably holds true. Though Paul usually began his work within the orbit of Jewish synagogues, by either painful ejection or voluntary departure, he eventually took his followers out of the synagogue in order to avoid their simply becoming a chapter within the local synagogues.[94] This action led to small house-church communities composed of Jews, Gentiles with previous degrees of Jewish association, and some Gentiles with no previous Jewish association.

This admittedly elastic socioreligious location is best described as a post- or

---

93. Wayne Meeks, "Breaking Away: Three New Testament Pictures of Christianity's Separation from Jewish Communities," in *"To See Ourselves as Others See Us": Christians, Jews, and "Others" in Late Antiquity*, ed. J. Neusner and E. S. Frerich (Chico, CA: Scholars, 1985), 106; see John M. G. Barclay, *Jews in the Mediterranean Diaspora: From Alexander to Trajan (323 BCE–117 CE)* (Berkeley: University of California Press, 1996), 386: "In social reality Paul's churches were distinct from the synagogues, and their predominantly Gentile members unattached to the Jewish community."

94. That is not to say that some Jews and/or Gentiles completely ceased interactions with Jewish communities and abandoned attendance at synagogues/prayer houses. Participation in a house church with meeting for meals, instruction, and worship did not rule out attending Jewish meetings on other occasions.

parasynagogue position. Consequently, Paul's ecclesiology is really a form of sectarianism that is built on a mixture of *socioreligious partitioning* and *theological reconfiguration* in relation to Jews and Judaism. Paul seeks to maintain amiable relations between Gentile Christ-believers, Jewish Christ-believers, and nonbelieving Jews because he knows full well that they occupy a shared socioreligious space in the polis, and they share a common religious heritage. Even so, if one of Paul's central convictions was that the "dividing wall" between Jew and Gentile had been broken down in Christ, then, as a matter of course, he was committed to providing a social space for that unity to flourish, and he was also committed to providing an ideological defense of his thesis in order to preserve the ethnic diversity of the churches under his apostolate. That position meant protecting the idea of Gentiles as equals and not simply as guests, not burdening Gentiles with the Torah but insisting on an appropriate moral law suitable to their Gentile identity. This protection was not possible in most synagogues, as far as Paul believed. Thus, the ideological texture of Galatians and parts of Romans is that of a religious leader justifying separation from the social structures of Judaism.[95] Likewise, Paul's manner of *deviant labeling* relates to those who endeavored to bring his converts under the aegis of Torah as determinative for their identity and salvation (e.g., Phil 3:2; Gal 5:12). Similarly, his *reinterpretation* of Israel's sacred traditions locates divine election through a route other than Jewish ethnicity and postulates divine reconciliation as manifested in Christ and not a return to Torah (e.g., 2 Cor 3:6-18; Gal 3:10-29; 4:22-31; Rom 4:1-25; 9:1-29).

Paul, then, marks a transition from a renewal movement within Judaism to the establishment of a sect on the fringes of Judaism.[96] These communities are not versus Judaism but are para-Judaism in the social and theological sense. Paul does not deliberately take his communities out of Judaism per se but deliberately shifts them to the margins, away from the influence and authority of Jewish teachers—yet they are still socially involved to varying degrees with Jewish communities. The "parting of the ways" between Chris-

---

95. Watson, *Paul, Judaism, and the Gentiles*, 51-56.

96. Martin Hengel (*Paul between Damascus and Antioch*, 200) argues that this social separation took place even before Paul's conversion at the church in Antioch, where "this new enthusiastic message in the long run formally compelled the separation from synagogue communities, since such eschatological communities were difficult to accept for a fixed religious association which also exercised social and religious functions, not the least in a tense situation which was getting increasingly worse and therefore politically uncertain." I think the house churches probably did eventually separate from the synagogues at Antioch, but I doubt that it was an absolute and total break; some members probably moved between both communities.

tianity and Judaism was a complex matter and differed through the centuries in various geographic locales and in different sociohistorical contexts. Nonetheless, it is hard to avoid the conclusion that Paul inadvertently contributed to that partings.[97]

Conclusion: Salvation from Judaism to Jesus

This chapter has provided a summary of the different ways in scholarship that Paul's perception of the soteriology of Judaism has been articulated and to what extent Paul's own soteriological convictions are continuous with Judaism. All commentators recognize that Paul had some point of contention with the way that salvation for Gentiles was expressed by his Jewish and Jewish Christ-believing contemporaries. That conflict led us to explore the socioreligious location of Paul and his communities in relation to Judaism. We saw, first, that Paul's own identity is umbilically related to Judaism as Paul explicitly retains its Israelite component, but his Jewishness is transcended and subsumed by being "in Christ" and is set in antithesis to Pharisaic Judaism. Second, it is evident from 2 Cor 3:6-18 and Rom 9:30–10:6 that Paul emphasized the discontinuity between the epochs of Christ and Torah/Moses in order to provide an ideological justification for maintaining the Gentileness of his Gentile converts in their own assemblies. Yet the discontinuity is qualified and not absolute, as Paul sees his Christ-faith as an extension of Judaism's scriptural heritage, not an alternative to it. Third, the Pauline communities eventually became separate from the institution of the synagogues. Though Paul himself seems to have engaged in some spasmodic evangelistic activity toward Jews and pursued unity with Jewish Christ-believers, he established predominantly Gentile Christ-believing communities that became deliberately independent of the synagogue.

What can we conclude about salvation in "Paul's Judaism"? For a start, Paul teaches that salvation comes *from* Judaism in a positive sense in terms of its point of origin because Christ himself came from Israel and to Israel (esp. Rom 9:4-5; 15:7-8). In Pauline language, Gentiles have been grafted into a Jewish olive tree, and they receive the patriarchal promises only because the Messiah

---

97. See Barclay (*Jews in the Mediterranean Diaspora*, 395): "Thus, mostly unwittingly, Paul fostered the fateful division between Christianity and Judaism"; Frey ("Paul's Jewish Identity," 321): "Even though Paul relentlessly worked for the unity of Jewish and Gentile Christians, it may well be the case that he actually contributed more to the later split between the increasingly Gentile church and Jewish Christianity."

served the circumcision (Rom 11:17-24; 15:8-9). Salvation will always be "for" Israel as well, since the messianic age gains currency from the efficacy of Israel's covenant promises. Still, there is no denying the tensions between Paul and his Jewish and Jewish Christ-believing contemporaries when it comes to the means of salvation. Paul knows of several soteric schemes in Judaism, such as "ethical monotheism" (Rom 1:18-32), "covenantal nomism" (Rom 2–3; 9–11), "ethnocentric nomism" (Galatians), "sapiential nomism" (1 Cor 1:10–3:23), and "apocalyptic mysticism" (Colossians). Against all of these, salvation comes *from* Judaism in an antithetical sense because (1) the Torah has served to antagonize rather than solve the Adamic condition of humanity in its state of alienation from God, and one should not impose a deadly and defunct force upon Gentile converts; (2) the majority of Israel, including its leaders, have vigorously opposed the message of the gospel; and (3) the Torah's temporal and ethnographic character did not lend itself to being the mechanism by which God achieved his purpose of extending salvation to the nations.

I want to stress that such an antithesis should not be pressed so as to evacuate Judaism, Israel, and the genuinely salvific role of the Torah in Paul's narrative about the culmination of salvation in Christ. Paul is announcing the good news of salvation by announcing the fulfillment of Israel's eschatological hopes. Still, Paul's point of contention was not simply that Judaism needs to let the Gentiles into a Christ-religion while the Jews themselves continue on under the Mosaic religion, nor is it that the eschatological sands had simply shifted and Israel was yet to catch up. It is far more problematic than that: for both Jews and Gentiles, the end had come in Christ, not in Torah. Furthermore, when Torah's role in salvation history is viewed retrospectively through the lens of messianic faith, it is seen as oppressive, ineffectual, and temporary. "Paul's soteriology," says Sprinkle, "remains within the Jewish spectrum of beliefs," rooted as it is in prophetic restoration eschatology. However, "Paul's Damascus road encounter would entail a rereading of salvation history—a transposition of the divine and human dynamics in bringing eschatological salvation into the present through the death and resurrection of the Messiah," with the result that "the most unique element in Paul's soteriology, one that used to offend his Pharisaic sensibilities and no doubt continued to sound outlandish, is the sacrificial death, bodily resurrection, subsequent enthronement, and personal indwelling, intercession and love that the risen Messiah accomplishes in and for wicked people, Jesus' enemies, whom God stubbornly sought to justify."[98]

---

98. Sprinkle, *Paul and Judaism Revisited*, 243-47, 249.

Finally, as was formerly and famously said by E. P. Sanders: "In short, this is what Paul finds wrong in Judaism: it is not Christianity."[99] Similarly, Lloyd Gaston said: "This is what Paul finds wrong with other Jews: that they do not share his revelation in Damascus."[100] More recently, Mark Nanos has wryly written: "This is what Paul would find wrong in Paulinism: it is not Judaism."[101] But I say unto you: This is what Paul finds wrong with Judaism: it looks to the Torah rather than to the Messiah for the revelation of God's righteousness, for the reconciliation of the world, and for the renewal of creation. Yet the Torah was at best a holding pattern for sin, and at worst it exacerbated the reign of sin over the flesh in the present evil age. And what the Torah could not do because of its temporary nature and its restriction to the Jewish *ethnos,* also on account of fleshly weakness, God did by sending his Son in the likeness of a human being, to carry sin's curse on the cross, to be raised for the vindication of a new people, a people comprising Jews and Gentiles, just as God had promised the patriarchs, so that this renewed people of God will dwell in a gloriously refashioned creation. Consequently, for Paul, salvation is of Judaism, but not the zealous Judaism of the Pharisees; rather, salvation is manifested in the Israelite religion, which climaxes in the story of Jesus Christ.[102]

99. Sanders, *Paul and Palestinian Judaism,* 552.

100. Gaston, *Paul and Torah,* 140.

101. Nanos, "Paul and Judaism," 159.

102. This paragraph has been heavily revised since the original version, influenced by the task of writing a Romans commentary and twice reading through Wright's *Paul and the Faithfulness of God.*

CHAPTER TWO

Paul: Apostle to the Gentiles and Jews?

The apostle Paul has been a common subject of Christian art featured in count-less icons, mosaics, sculptures, and paintings. Artistic representations of Paul have focused on his Damascus road Christophany, such as Caravaggio's two paintings of the event *The Conversion of Saint Paul* (1600/1601) and *The Conversion of Saint Paul on the Road to Damascus* (1601). Or else he is depicted as the graying old man at the writing desk, as in Rembrandt's *The Apostle St. Paul* (1657). One of the most popular artistic depictions of Paul, if the dust covers of modern books on Paul are anything to go by, is Raffaello Santi's *Paul Preaching in Athens* (1515-16). It is popular precisely because it depicts Paul doing exactly what he is most remembered for: preaching to the Gentiles as the apostle to the Gentiles. The description of Paul in the Areopagus in Acts 17:22-34 con-jures up images of Paul as the learned Christian orator preaching the gospel to Greeks in Athens. In Luke's actual narrative, however, Paul begins his ministry in Athens, not among the Epicurean and Stoic philosophers (17:18), but with the Jews and God-worshipers in the local synagogue (17:16). While Luke skirts over this event in the lead-up to Paul's speech in the Areopagus, Paul's ministry to the Jews in Athens is not insignificant because it conforms to Luke's overall literary pattern of Paul as the apostle to Gentiles *and* Jews.

Even though Paul the apostle to the Gentiles has dominated the Christian artistic imagination, recognition of Paul as the apostle among the Jews has not entirely evaded readers of the Pauline letters and Acts either. The Byzantine mosaic *St. Paul Preaching to the Jews in the Synagogue at Damascus* (ca. 1180), located in Duomo, Monreale, Sicily, is a helpful reminder of a forgotten facet of Paul's ministry, namely, that Paul was remembered as also preaching to his fellow Jews. The painting obviously takes its inspiration from Acts 9:20-25, Luke's account of Paul's ministry in Damascus. Yet within Acts this is no iso-lated instance; preaching to Jews becomes something typical of the Lukan Paul, who, "as was his custom" (Acts 17:2), commenced his evangelistic endeavors in a new territory by addressing Jews and Greeks in the synagogue. One might object that Paul's own representation of himself in his letters is that he is the apostle to the Gentiles and not to the Jews (see Rom 11:13; 15:16; Gal 1:16; 2:2), supported by the observation that his audiences consisted primarily of former pagans (Gal 4:8; 1 Cor 12:2; 1 Thess 1:9), and reinforced by the demarcation of the jurisdiction set between himself and Cephas at the Jerusalem council (Gal 2:7-9).[1] However, Tertullian's summary of the Jerusalem council reads differently: "Then, at last, having conferred with the primitive authors, and having agreed with them touching the rule of faith, they joined hands in fellowship, and divided their labours thenceforth in the office of preaching the gospel, so that they were to go to the Jews, and St. Paul to the Jews and the Gentiles."[2] Obviously, Tertullian is anachronistic in his reference to the "rule of faith," and he smoothes over the clear frictions of the Jerusalem meeting. However, I would not dismiss Tertullian's remark as merely a harmonization of Gal 2:1-10 with the Paul of Acts. The Lukan portrayal of Paul as a sometime Jewish evangelist can actually be mapped onto the undisputed Pauline letters. I hope to show that there remain credible grounds for seeing the Jews as having an evolving and yet constant place for Paul over the course of his ministry.

Such a thesis is likely to meet resistance because the notion of Jewish evangelism, ancient and modern, is something of an embarrassment to recent interpreters of Luke and Paul.[3] Regardless, the thesis of this chapter is that, although Paul was indeed the apostle to Gentiles, an earlier phase of his career included evangelistic work among Jewish communities; and even after his turn

---

1. See E. P. Sanders, *Paul, the Law, and the Jewish People* (Minneapolis: Fortress, 1983), 179-90.

2. Tertullian, *Adv. Marc.* 4.2.

3. For example, Robert Tannehill, who understands Luke's view that a mission to the Jews "is assumed to continue even beyond the end of Acts," adds the caveat, "I caution my readers now that this emphasis does not mean that Acts reflects my own opinion about Christian mission toward Jews. It seems to me that the centuries of history since the writing of Acts should teach Christians something, namely, that God's covenant loyalty and promise for the Jewish people cannot be dependent on acceptance of Jesus as Messiah. I would not myself advocate a Christian evangelistic mission to Jews" (*The Narrative Unity of Luke-Acts: A Literary Interpretation* [2 vols.; Minneapolis: Fortress, 1990], 3; see idem, *The Shape of Luke's Story: Essays on Luke-Acts* [Eugene, OR: Cascade, 2005], 143-44, 253). Similarly, E. P. Sanders (*Paul, the Law, and the Jewish People*, 197) writes that Paul "thought that the only way to be saved was through Christ Jesus. If it were to be proposed that Christians today should think the same thing, and accordingly that the Jews who have not converted should be considered cut off from God, and if such a proposal came before a body in which I had a vote, I would vote against it. I still would. I am now inclined to think that Paul would too."

to the Gentiles, he never stopped sharing the gospel with Jews when he had the chance. I will argue this point by (1) demonstrating the malleable nature of the terms "Gentile" (ἔθνος, plural ἔθνη), "Greek" (Ἕλλην), "uncircumcised/circumcised" (ἀκροβυστία/περιτομή), and "lawless" (ἄνομος) in the context of studies on ethnicity and cultural identity, and (2) describing literary evidence from Paul's letters and the Acts of the Apostles for the evolution of Paul's audience in his evangelistic activities. These efforts will, I hope, illuminate the place of the *Jews* in Paul's apostolate to the *Gentiles*.

Ethnic and Social Descriptions of Jews and Gentiles

A study of the designators for non–Christ-believing non-Jews is a tedious but necessary preliminary task as we begin to unpack the meaning of Paul's apostolate to the ἔθνη. For if Paul is the apostle to Gentiles, Greeks, pagans, and the uncircumcised, exactly who are these people, and how are they to be distinguished from Jews? I suggest that some of these designations for Gentiles are somewhat more flexible than is often recognized and that such labels can be embedded with socioreligious connotations beyond purely ethnic and tribal affiliations. I shall do so by examining the standard terms for non–Christ-believing non-Jews in Paul's letters.

ἔθνη

The term ἔθνη is Paul's preferred term for referring to non–Christ-believing non-Jews. In English translations ἔθνη is varyingly rendered as "Gentiles" (an ethnic term), "nations" (a territorial term), or "pagans" (a religious term). As a point of background, our English words "Gentile" and "pagan" reflect a specifically Jewish and Christianized form of ethnography. The non-Jews of antiquity did not call themselves "Gentiles" or "pagans" but were more properly self-identified as Romans, Greeks, Phoenicians, Syrians, Phrygians, Galatians, and so forth, usually using tribal or city-state designators, as opposed to religious or ethnic descriptors. Even the term "nations" is hardly neutral, since what we think about nations owes much to the formation of nation-states in the eighteenth to twentieth centuries. In one standard lexicon ἔθνος refers to "a body of persons united by kinship, culture, and common traditions."[4] In Jewish tradition this term (the

---

4. BDAG, 276. On the Jews as a particular ἔθνος, see Luke 7:5; 23:2; John 11:48, 50-52; 18:35; Acts 10:22; 24:2, 10, 17: 26:4.

Old Testament word גּוֹיִם; see, e.g., Exod 34:24; Lev 18:24; cf. 2 Macc 8:9; Wis 10:15) refers principally to a foreign people who do not worship Israel's God. This is clearly the linguistic background that Paul shares, as he knows of the ἔθνη as distinct from Jews (Rom 3:29; 9:24; 11:13-15; 15:8-10; 1 Cor 1:23; Gal 2:15; 1 Thess 2:16). Paul evidently regards "Greeks" and "Barbarians" as two distinct subclasses of the ἔθνη as well (Rom 1:13-14). In a complex web of intertextual argumentation, Paul asserts that it had always been God's aim to bring the ἔθνη into the family of Abraham (Rom 4:17-18; 15:8-12; Gal 3:6-14). In some cases, the ἔθνη have received salvation ahead of (not instead of!) Israel (Rom 9:30; 10:19; 11:11-13, 25-26). The relationship of non-Jewish Christ-believers to the ἔθνη is ambivalent, as they are clearly distinct from the ἔθνη (Rom 16:4; Gal 2:12), and yet they are now called to live apart from the ethos of the ἔθνη (1 Cor 5:1; 12:2; 1 Thess 4:5; Eph 4:17).

However, it remains interesting that, when Paul describes the breadth of his apostolate to τὰ ἔθνη in Rom 15:15-20, he defines it geographically rather than in ethnographic terms. Paul's priestly service of presenting the Gentiles as an offering to God (Rom 15:16) had its beginnings in Jerusalem, according to Rom 15:19: "by the power of signs and wonders, by the power of the Spirit of God, so that from Jerusalem and as far around as Illyricum I have fully proclaimed the good news of Christ." Most probably Paul's time in Jerusalem reflects a prior period of his ministry that included preaching briefly to Greek-speaking Jews (see Gal 1:18-19; Acts 9:26-29), and yet it stands in organic unity with his current array of missionary activities, which include testifying in Jerusalem, going to Rome, and traveling onward to Spain (Rom 15:18-24). In fact, Paul's desire to go to Spain might imply that he was influenced by Isa 66:19-20, assuming that Tarshish can be identified with Spain, spelling out his ambition to declare God's glory to *Jews and Gentiles* among the ἔθνη as part of the Isaianic script for the end of Israel's exile and the beginning of the new creation (see Rom 15:22-25, 28).[5] Paul is sent to the provinces of the ἔθνη to herald the gospel of Christ, and the ethnic and tribal constitution of his audience does not seem to matter all that much. Perhaps the central feature of the ἔθνη is the "where," not the "who."

The geographic horizon of Paul's apostolate can be reinforced by reference to Rom 1:5, 13. In v. 5 Paul mentions Jesus Christ as the one "through whom we have received grace and apostleship to bring about the obedience of faith ἐν πᾶσιν τοῖς ἔθνεσιν for the sake of his name" (see similarly Gal 2:2, with ἐν τοῖς ἔθνεσιν). The questions are whether (1) ἔθνη here should be translated "Gentiles" (excluding Jews) or "nations" (including Diaspora Jews) and (2) whether

5. See Rainer Riesner, *Paul's Early Period: Chronology, Mission Strategy, Theology,* trans. Doug Stott (Grand Rapids, MI: Eerdmans, 1998), 245-53, 305-6.

the dative prepositional phrase ἐν πᾶσιν τοῖς ἔθνεσιν is telic ("to all the Gen-tiles/nations") or locative ("among all the Gentiles/nations"). While virtually all translations accept the locative sense (e.g., NRSV, NIV, NJB, ESV), most com-mentators resist the notion that Paul's apostolate is oriented toward a geographic signifier of the "nations" rather than simply to ethnic "Gentiles."[6]

Yet why is "among the nations" an illegitimate framework for Paul's mis-sion? In Rom 15:15-20 Paul is clearly thinking of ἔθνη as territories rather than as non-Jewish individuals because his mission in the East can be "finished" only if he has preached in all of the provinces of that region, and not in the sense that he has converted all individual Gentiles.[7] In addition, Paul laments in Rom 1:13 that he has not yet been to Rome, but he hopes to get there in order that "I might have some fruit among you just as I have had ἐν τοῖς λοι-ποῖς ἔθνεσιν." Obviously Paul is not suggesting that the Roman churches are made up exclusively of Gentile Christ-believers or that he has preached only to Gentiles in the past. Paul is interested in gathering fruit from among both Jews and Gentiles in Rome, and he intends to work cooperatively with the entire breadth of the churches in Rome.[8] I would add that including the Diasporan Jews within this apostolic remit is hardly incredulous when

- the gospel is for the "Jew first" in Rom 1:16,
- Paul knows of a remnant of Jewish believers in Rom 9:24-29 and 11:1-10,

6. See, e.g., James D. G. Dunn (*Romans 1–8* [WBC; Dallas: Word, 1988], 18): "(τὰ) ἔθνη certainly means 'the Gentiles' (and not 'the nations' including the Jews)"; Robert Jewett (*Romans* [Hermeneia; Minneapolis: Fortress, 2007], 111): "This [meaning of 'nations'] seems highly unlikely in view of Paul's description of his calling to be an apostle to the 'Gentiles' (Gal. 1:16; 2:8) and also in view of Paul's purpose in writing his letter, namely, the mission to Spain, where there were yet no Jewish settlements." See in contrast Don B. Garlington (*"The Obedience of Faith": A Pauline Phrase in Historical Context* [WUNT 2.38; Tübingen: Mohr Siebeck, 1991], 234), who thinks that ἔθνεσιν includes "Jews," and James M. Scott (*Paul and the Nations: The Old Testament and Jewish Background on Paul's Mission to the Nations, with Special Reference to the Destination of Galatians* [WUNT 84; Tübingen: Mohr Siebeck, 1995], esp. 27-61) focuses on "nations" rather than "Gentiles" and proposes that Paul was influenced by the "table of nations" in Gen 10 and 1 Chr 1:1–2:2. Ksenija Magda ("Unity as a Prerequisite for a Christian Mission: A Missional Reading of Rom 15:1-12," *Kairos* 2 [2008]: 47) writes: "It is much more plausible to believe that he uses the term neutrally and universally, i.e., in most cases it should include the Jews" (see further his *Paul's Territoriality and Mission Strategy: Searching for the Geographical Awareness Paradigm behind Romans* [WUNT 2.266; Tübingen: Mohr Siebeck, 2009]).

7. See Donaldson, *Paul*, 361n15; Johannes Munck, *Paul and the Salvation of Mankind* (Lon-don: SCM, 1959), 52-55.

8. Rick Strelan, *Paul, Artemis, and the Jews in Ephesus* (Berlin: Walter de Gruyter, 1996), 304-5.

- a continuing Jewish mission is implied in Rom 10:12-21,
- hope for Israel's salvation emerges climactically in Rom 10:1 and 11:26-32,
- a list of Jewish Christ-believing friends and colleagues is supplied in Rom 16:1-16, and
- Romans is filled with Paul's concerted effort to assuage explicitly Jewish objections to his gospel (e.g., 3:7-8; 6:1-3; 7:1-25; 9:1-5; and 10:1-3).

Furthermore, Luke presents James informing Paul that the Jewish anger at him is caused by the perception that "you teach all the Jews living among the Gentiles/nations [ἐν τοῖς ἔθνεσιν] to forsake Moses" (Acts 21:21). The similarities in the phrasing between Rom 1:5, 13, and Acts 21:19 are remarkable. However apologetically contrived the Lukan account may be, Luke asserts that the Pauline mission in the geographic territory of non-Jews encompassed Jewish audiences as well (see Acts 13:43; 14:1; 17:4, 11-12; 18:4; 19:10, 17).[9]

In sum, if the preceding analysis about the geopolitical frame of Paul's apostolate is correct, and if the implied reference to ἔθνη as regions beyond Judea in Rom 1:5, 13, and Acts 21:19 hold firm, then Paul the apostle to the ἔθνη understood his missionary work to consist of the announcement and persuasion of all people that Israel's God has disclosed his salvation through Jesus Christ for Greeks, Barbarians, and Jews *among the nations*. While it is an overstatement to think that Paul saw himself as an Israelite prophet sent to the Jewish Diaspora of the ἔθνη, as Bruce Malina and John Pilch do, it is equally wrong to think that Paul and the other apostles had no special provision in mind for Diaspora Jews, as E. P. Sanders supposes.[10]

Ἕλλην

Ἕλλην ("Greek," plural Ἕλληνες) ordinarily denotes a person influenced by Greek culture, learning, and religion (e.g., 3 Macc 3:8; 4 Macc 18:20; Acts

---

9. James's words likely convey a false accusation against Paul from Jewish critics, specifically, that "you teach all the Jews living among the Gentiles to forsake Moses, and that you tell them not to circumcise their children or observe the customs," an allegation that is false of both the Paul of the Epistles and the Paul of Acts. Undoubtedly, though, regardless of the historicity of Luke's reporting of James's words, that Paul was "teaching" Jews and that he held controversial views on "law" and "circumcision" can be taken as historical, and therefore so can Jewish reservations about his ministry.

10. Bruce J. Malina and John J. Pilch, *Social-Science Commentary on the Letters of Paul* (Minneapolis: Fortress, 2006), 1-25; Sanders, *Paul, the Law, and the Jewish People*, 189.

21:28)[11] and can be specifically distinguished from Jews in some instances (e.g., 2 Macc 4:36; 11:2; Acts 14:1; 16:1, 3; 18:4; 19:10, 17; 20:21). The Jew/Greek contrast derives from the cultural divisions in the East emerging between the Judean and the Hellenized groups of the Seleucid and Maccabean periods. But it also constitutes a Jewish appropriation of the well-known division of the world into the categories of Greek and Barbarian. Philo knows of the Greek/ Barbarian sociopolitical construction, and yet the place of the Jews in this construction is ambiguous, as they stand outside a complete bifurcation (*Cher.* 91; *Ios.* 56; *Legat.* 8, 83, 292). For Philo, the Jews are geographically Barbarians but philosophically Greeks.[12] No wonder some authors preferred to make the categories tripartite, consisting of Ἑλληνικός/βαρβαρικός/Ἰουδαῖος ("Greek/ Barbarian/Jew").[13] In Paul's letters, we observe that Paul uses Ἕλληνες most commonly as a contrast with Jews (1 Cor 1:22; Rom 1:16; 2:9-10; 3:9; 10:12; 1 Cor 1:22, 24; 10:32; 12:13; Gal 3:28), but he also knows the Greek, Barbarian, and Jew classification (Rom 1:14, 16; Col 3:11).[14]

In some cases, however, there cannot be an absolute divide between "Jew" and "Greek."[15] Throughout the New Testament, Ἕλληνες can signify non-Jewish Greeks who have some affiliation with Judaism (e.g., John 12:20; Acts 14:1) and designate Jews of the Diaspora (John 7:35; Acts 9:29). Timothy was a Ἕλλην who had not been circumcised, even though he was technically Jewish, since his mother was Jewish (Jewish identity was transmitted through the mother, Acts 16:1-3). There were various degrees of acculturation and assimilation in the Greek polis. Hellenism was not necessarily inimical

11. Herodotus (*Hist.* 8.144.2) defined "Greekness" as consisting of common purpose, kinship, shared language, shared sanctuaries of the gods, and similar customs.

12. Eric Gruen, *Diaspora: Jews amidst Greeks and Romans* (Cambridge, MA: Harvard University Press, 2002), 227.

13. See Martin Hengel, *Jews, Greeks, and Barbarians,* trans. J. Bowden (Philadelphia: Fortress, 1980).

14. On Christian appropriations of these distinctions, see Paul, who writes that the Corinthians should "give no offense to Jews or to Greeks or to the church of God" (1 Cor 10:32). Aristides identified Christians as a "third race" among "idolaters, Jews and Christians" (*Apol.* 2.2 [some MSS add "fourth race" and include "Barbarians"]). In the *Kerygma Petrou* frag. 2 (= Clement of Alexandria, *Strom.* 6.39.4; 41.2.6), it says, "For the ways of the Greeks and the Jews are old, but we Christians . . . worship him in a new way as a third race." The *Epistle of Diognetus* (1.1) implies a similar tripartite classification of Jews, Greeks, and Christians. Interestingly enough, Christians could also be accused of being "Barbarians" by Greek critics (Tatian, *Or. Graec.* 35; Origen, *Contra Celsus* 8.73-92).

15. See esp. Lucio Troiani, *Il perdono cristiano e altri studi sul cristianesimo delle origini* (Brescia: Paideia, 1999).

to Jewish customs but often brought Jewish culture to new expressions. No doubt, some Jews went so far as to be more recognizably Hellenist than Hebrew in the eyes of their Jewish contemporaries (e.g., 2 Macc 4:12-13; 3 Macc 1:3; Josephus, *Ant.* 12.240; Philo, *Migr.* 89-93). After all, many Jews attended the gymnasium, theater, and games; also they intermarried, made oaths under the names of Greek gods, and used magical papyri, and some even offered sacrifices to pagan gods.[16] The Ἑλληνισταί ("Hellenists") of Acts were probably Greek-speaking Jews of the Jerusalem church (Acts 6:1),[17] and it was they who initiated the mission to Greek-speaking Gentiles (Acts 11:20).[18] Thus, the Gentile mission formally began with Jewish *Greeks* sharing the gospel with Gentile *Greeks* in Antioch. In fact, the Acts of the

16. See Stephen G. Wilson, *Leaving the Fold: Apostates and Defectors in Antiquity* (Minneapolis: Fortress, 2004), 23-65; John M. G. Barclay, *Jews of the Mediterranean: From Alexander to Trajan* (Edinburgh: T&T Clark, 1996), 88-93.

17. There is much debate as to who the "Hellenists" of the early church were; proposals include Gentile Christians, Jewish proselytes, liberal Jews, and Diasporan Jews. Yet the Hellenists are probably to be defined linguistically as Greek speakers who were sociologically oriented toward other Greek-speaking Jewish communities. Between Hebrew and Hellenistic Jewish Christ-believers, we may speak tentatively of a theological diversity based on various appropriations of the Jesus tradition because of a complexity of sociolinguistic frameworks among the first Christians, but not yet of an internecine theological division fermented by different *religionsgeschichte* locations. See T. W. Martin, "Hellenists," *ABD* 3:136; Martin Hengel, *Between Jesus and Paul* (London: SCM, 1983), 1-27; Craig Hill, *Hellenists and Hebrews: Reappraising Division within the Earliest Church* (Minneapolis: Fortress, 1994); Alexander J. M. Wedderburn, *A History of the First Christians* (London: T&T Clark, 2005), 41-58; Peter J. Russell, *Heterodoxy within Second-Temple Judaism and Sectarian Diversity within the Early Church: A Correlative Study* (Lewiston, NY: Edwin Mellen, 2008), 240-57.

18. Anna Maria Schwemer ("Paulus in Antiochien," *BZ* 42 [1998]: 167 [similarly Hengel, *Between Jesus and Paul*, 8]) follows 𝔓⁷⁴, ℵ², A, and D* in preferring Ἕλληνας; she writes: "'Griechen' (Ἕλληνας, nicht Ἑλληνιστάς) ist hier sicher gegen NA²⁷ die ursprüngliche Lesart." The appearance of Ἑλληνιστάς is confusing, since earlier in Acts it refers to Greek-speaking Jews in 6:1 and 9:29. Yet here the context evidently supports a reference to Gentile Greeks, given the contrast with Ἰουδαῖοι ("Jews") in 11:19. It seems more likely that scribes would change Ἑλληνιστάς for the better-known Ἕλληνας than the other way around. Objections that Ἑλληνιστάς means "Greek-speaking Jew" and is therefore inappropriate overlooks the fact that ἑλληνίζειν simply means to speak Greek and can apply to Jews and Gentiles alike. See further F. F. Bruce, *The Acts of the Apostles: The Greek Text, with Introduction and Commentary* (Grand Rapids, MI: Eerdmans, 1951), 235-36; Bruce M. Metzger, *A Textual Commentary on the Greek New Testament* (2nd ed.; Stuttgart: Deutsche Bibelgesellschaft, 1994), 340-42; C. K. Barrett, *Acts of the Apostles* (2 vols.; ICC; Edinburgh: T&T Clark, 1994), 1:550-51. Thus, these "Greek-speakers" are not Greek-speaking Jewish Christians (Acts 6:1) or Greek-speaking Jews (Acts 6:9; 9:29); rather, they are Greek-speaking Gentiles, probably "Griechen um heidnische Sympathisanten" (Schwemer, "Paulus," 168).

Apostles shows just how plastic and malleable the designation "Greek" is, for Greek-speaking Jewish Christ-believers (6:1), Greek-speaking Jews (9:29), Greek-speaking Gentile adherents to Judaism (Acts 11:20; 14:1; 17:4, 12; 18:4; 21:38), and Greek-speaking non-Jews (16:1, 3; 19:10) can all be described as a Ἕλλην or Ἑλληνιστής. These various uses indicate that Ἕλλην possesses a degree of socioreligious flexibility and is not insulated from that which is "Jewish." In which case, Paul's gospel orientation toward the Ἕλλην (Rom 1:16) can *potentially* include a diverse audience of (1) uncircumcised Greek-speaking Gentiles (i.e., "pagans"), (2) Greek-speaking Gentile adherents to Jewish practices (i.e., "God-fearers"), and even (3) Greek-speaking Jews of the Diaspora (i.e., "Hellenistic Jews"). Undoubtedly, the "pagans" and "God-fearers" seem to have occupied most of his missionary activity, but the actual practice of this missionary campaign meant that linguistically, culturally, socially, and geographically, these three groups were not insulated; Paul would be dealing with Greeks in all three categories in his missionary endeavors.

ἀκροβυστία, περιτομή

The terms ἀκροβυστία ("uncircumcised) and περιτομή ("circumcised") refer to the state of the male genitalia, and the latter to the excision or slitting of the foreskin.[19] Circumcision obviously has symbolic significance for Jews as a sign of the covenant with Abraham (Gen 17:9-14) and a signifier of loyalty to the Mosaic covenant (Lev 12:3; Josh 5:1-9).[20] Greco-Roman authors could revile the practice as barbaric, unnecessary, and even un-Roman.[21] During the Maccabean period circumcision became a symbol of national resistance to Hellenism and the chief identifier of a Judean male.[22]

The extent to which circumcision was the determinative signifier for Jewish identity was open to some debate within Jewish communities. For a start, circumcision was practiced by others groups, including Egyptians and Syrians, so while it was characteristic of male Jews, it was not unique to them.[23] For women, their Jewishness was established either maternally or by marriage. Yet

---

19. See Andreas Blaschke, *Beschneidung: Zeugnisse der Bible und verwandter Text* (TANZ 28; Tübingen: Francke, 1998).

20. See Exod 4:24-26; Sir 44:20; Jub. 15.28; Philo, *QG* 3.51-52; m. Ned. 3.11; Acts 7:8.

21. Philo, *Spec.* 1.1-3; Tacitus, *Hist.* 5.5.2; Juvenal, *Sat.* 14.99 (Stern, *GLAJJ* 2, §301); Martial, *Epigr.* 7.30, 82; 11.94 (Stern, *GLAJJ* 1, §§240, 243, 245); Petronius, *Sat.* 68.4-8; 102.14; *Frag.* 37 (Stern, *GLAJJ* 1, §193, 194, 195); Suetonius, *Domitian* 12.2 (Stern, *GLAJJ* 2, §320).

22. 1 Macc 1:48, 60; 2 Macc 6:10; Josephus, *Ag. Ap.* 1.171; *Ant.* 1.192-93, 214; Tacitus, *Hist.* 5.5.

23. Josephus, *Ant.* 8.262; *Ag. Ap.* 1.169-70; 2.140-43; Ep. Barn. 9.6.

without the rite of circumcision and in the absence of marriage to a Jewish male, female adherents to Judaism had a slightly ambivalent position as to exactly when they formally became constituent members of a Jewish community.[24] The lines between adherent and convert were probably more flexibly drawn for women who frequented the synagogues and embraced elements of the Jewish way of life.[25] In other cases, even those who were maternally Jewish (i.e., born from a Jewish mother, but with a non-Jewish father) could still exhibit an anomalous status if they were not circumcised, as in the case of Timothy (Acts 16:1-3).[26] Timothy was circumcised by Paul, not to become a Jew, but to put his Jewishness beyond question. Additionally, we should also observe that the necessity of proselytes being circumcised was debated in some quarters. Philo asserts that what constitutes a proselyte is not circumcision but submission to God, "because the proselyte is one who circumcises not his uncircumcision but his desires and sensual pleasures and the other passions of the soul" (*QE* 2.2). Philo also knows of Jewish teachers in Alexandria who interpreted the ceremonial laws in a strictly allegorical fashion (*Migr.* 89-94). Josephus's account of the conversion of King Izates of Adiabene to Judaism includes Izates's encounters with two Jewish teachers, Ananias and Eleazar, who differed over the matter as to whether Izates was required to be circumcised (*Ant.* 20.34-48).[27] Generally speaking, circumcision was regarded as the threshold to be traversed in male conversion to Judaism in Diaspora communities (e.g., Esth 8:17; Jdt 14:10; Josephus, *War* 2.454; Tacitus, *Hist.* 5.5.2;

24. See Shaye J. D. Cohen, *Why Aren't Jewish Women Circumcised? Gender and Covenant in Judaism* (Berkeley: University of California Press, 2005).

25. Michael F. Bird, *Crossing Over Sea and Land: Jewish Missionary Activity in the Second Temple Period* (Peabody, MA: Hendrickson, 2009), 42-43.

26. Shaye J. D. Cohen (*The Beginnings of Jewishness: Boundaries, Varieties, Uncertainties* [Berkeley: University of California Press, 1999], 268-340) notes that the principle of matrilineal descent was not formally operative in the first century. However, Gerd Lüdemann (*Early Christianity according to the Traditions in Acts: A Commentary,* trans. J. Bowden [London: SCM, 1989], 175) suggests that it was already part of Jewish halakah at the time. Cohen does not think that Timothy was Jewish (*Beginnings of Jewishness,* 363-77), but the ambiguity of the scholarship that he surveys reflects the ambiguity of Timothy's status. Whether Timothy was Jewish would depend finally on a community consensus, and there obviously was no consensus about the status of the offspring of mixed marriage between Jews and Greek, which is precisely why Paul had Timothy circumcised.

27. On the relevance of Josephus's account of the "conversion" of King Izates, see Mark Nanos, "The Question of Conceptualization: Qualifying Paul's Position on Circumcision in Dialogue with Josephus's Advisors to King Izates," in *Paul within Judaism: Restoring the First-Century Context to the Apostle,* ed. M. D. Nanos and M. Zetterholm (Minneapolis: Fortress, 2015), 105-52.

Petronius, *Sat.*, Frag. 37). Nevertheless, there were some who, for various reasons, wished to treat Gentile guests/adherents more or less as equals on some plane or another.[28]

Physical circumcision was integrally bound up with the national rituals and ethnic identity of the Jews, yet it could also evoke particular religious values and motifs. As a *sign,* circumcision *signified* covenant identity, loyalty to YHWH, election, and separateness. Even so, there was a tendency in some circles to detach the sign from what it signified. This process is already underway in the Hebrew Bible, with the command to interiorize the commandments beyond external performance (Deut 10:16; 30:6; Jer 4:4; 9.25-26; Ezek 44:7), and many looked ahead to the inward renewal of the Torah in Israel (1QS 5.5; cf. 1QpHab 11.13). Philo could regard "ethical monotheism" as relatively more important than, though not necessarily a substitute for, physical circumcision (*Spec.* 1.304-6; *QE* 2.2; *QG* 3.46, 48). There is a lengthy exposition of the theme of the "circumcised heart" in Ep. Barn. 9.1-9, where Christians are depicted as the partakers of a true circumcision, and physical circumcision is disparaged as now defunct and not even unique to Israel.

Paul's references to circumcision and uncircumcision must be placed in this context about the extent to which circumcision determined Christian identity and the detachment of circumcision from its ritual and ethnic context. Paul is evidently aware of the ethnic and covenantal dimensions of circumcision (Rom 3:1-2; 4:11-12; 15:8; Gal 2:7-9; Phil 3:5); his interlocutors were labeled as οἱ ἐκ περιτομῆς ("those from the circumcision") and constituted a Jewish Christ-believing faction in the early church who opposed his teachings about Gentiles in some way (Gal 2:12; Col 4:11; Tit 1:10), and Paul also knows of the contrast between persons who are ἀκροβυστία and those who are περιτομή (Rom 2:26-27, 30; 4:9-11; 1 Cor 7:18-19; Gal 2:7; 5:6; 6:15; Eph 2:11). Paul responds to the attempted imposition of circumcision on his Gentile converts by way of several complex arguments.

First, Paul diminishes the value and validity of circumcision for Gentiles through his narration of Israel's sacred history. In Gal 3–4 Paul regarded circumcision as indelibly connected to the Torah, and the Torah bound up with the Deuteronomic curses that penalize all transgressors. Abraham's exemplary faith is what God demands of Gentiles in the messianic age, and the later coming of Torah with the Sinai covenant did not erase the Abrahamic promises (esp. Gal 3:23-39). Similarly, in Rom 4 Paul argued that the Abrahamic promises of righteousness by faith are for the circumcised and the uncircumcised

---

28. See further discussion in Bird, *Crossing Over Sea and Land*, 24-43.

(Rom 4:9). Circumcision was the seal of the righteousness that Abraham had by faith, not the means toward it (Rom 4:10-11). In this way, Abraham is not the prototype of the ideal proselyte; rather, he is the paradigmatic pagan who believes in the divine promises fulfilled in Jesus Christ.

Second, Paul denies the efficacy of circumcision for covenant identity and salvific inclusion. An important qualification we need to make is that Paul does not make an in-toto erasure of the binary identities of Jew and Greek.[29] The "neither/nor" text of Gal 3:28-29 is not espousing a Platonic androgyny or an egalitarian manifesto to feed modernist sensitivities to equality, since the emphasis falls squarely on unity with distinction, not sameness (see also Rom 10:12; 1 Cor 12:13; Col 3:11).[30] Paul's stress falls on the *inclusion* and *transformation* of multiple subidentities (Jew, male, circumcision, etc.) under a single meta-identity marked by Christ and the new creation. Of course, that status can be true only if the existing identities, which are a means of distinction and status, are themselves negated in value and lessened in their ability to cause differentiation.[31] In which case, circumcision may have value on a cultural plane, but it does not translate into any form of eschatological security or signify election.

Third, what matters most is not circumcision but a Spirit-wrought obedience and the experience of the new creation through Jesus Christ, which substitutes for circumcision (1 Cor 7:19; Rom 2:25-29; Gal 5:6; 6:11-16).

Fourth, Paul redefines "circumcision" as a transferable marker denoting a life pleasing to God; for this reason, circumcision is "a matter of the heart, by Spirit, not the letter" (Rom 2:29). Circumcision becomes ethical rather than ethnic in Paul (see Col 2:11-13). Physical uncircumcision can thus be "reckoned" (λογίζομαι) as circumcision where obedience appears in its stead

29. Contra, e.g., Douglas A. Campbell, *The Quest for Paul's Gospel: A Suggested Strategy* (London: T&T Clark, 2005), 97, 101-2; Daniel Boyarin, *A Radical Jew: Paul and the Politics of Identity* (Berkeley: University of California Press, 1994), 19-23.

30. David J. Rudolph, *A Jew to the Jews: Jewish Contours of Pauline Flexibility in 1 Corinthians 9* (WUNT 2.304; Tübingen: Mohr Siebeck, 2011), 30-33.

31. Michael F. Bird, *Colossians and Philemon* (NCCS; Eugene, OR: Cascade, 2009), 103-4. See also Mark D. Nanos, *The Irony of Galatians: Paul's Letter in First-Century Context* (Minneapolis: Fortress, 2002), 99; Mark Seifrid, "For the Jew First: Paul's Nota Bene for His Gentile Readers," in *To the Jew First: The Case for Jewish Evangelism in Scripture and History* (Grand Rapids, MI: Kregel, 2008), 26-27, 37; Pauline Nigh Hogan, *"No Longer Male and Female": Interpreting Galatians 3:28 in Early Christianity* (LNTS 380; London: T&T Clark, 2008); Caroline Johnson Hodge, *If Sons, Then Heirs: A Study of Kinship and Ethnicity in the Letters of Paul* (Oxford: OUP, 2007), esp. 129; Pamela Eisenbaum, "Is Paul the Father of Misogyny and Antisemitism?," *Crosscurrents* 50, no. 4 (2000-2001): 515.

(Rom 2:26). In the extreme sense, obedient Gentiles who embrace God's saving action in Christ and live lives worthy of the gospel have more claim to be the "circumcision" (i.e., the covenant people of God) than their Jewish counterparts (Rom 2:25-29; Phil 3:3). Paul is fully aware of the covenantal privileges of circumcision (Rom 3:1-4), yet he argues that covenantal signs of God's favor are effective only in the context of covenantal obedience, which Israel has distinctly lacked (Rom 2:25; 3:19-20).

Paul creates a framework in which one can postulate uncircumcised Gentiles as inwardly circumcised, and circumcised Jews as uncircumcised in the flesh of their heart. Paul invests circumcision with ethical meaning, something already known in Diaspora Judaism, but he also proceeds to sever any positive connotation of its ethnic and ritual meaning for non-Jews.[32] The effect that this has is that the meaning of circumcision is not merely broadened or spiritualized but is radically inverted by Paul in order substantiate his view of Christ-believing identity as something that transcends and transforms ethnic identity.

ἄνομος

The final term to explore is ἄνομος ("without law"). Paul employs the word in 2 Thess 2:8 to refer to the "Lawless One" and also in 1 Cor 9:21, where he himself becomes "outside of the law" to win those "outside of the law." In 1 Cor 9:20-21 when ἄνομος is juxtaposed with the reference to Paul's ministry to the Jews, it certainly means non-Jews (see Wis 15:17; Sir 39:24). At the same time, we should observe that ἄνομος is a general ethical quality in exhortations and warnings in the LXX (e.g., Ps 24:3; Mal 3:18, 21; Isa 1:31; 53:12) and used explicitly of compromised Jews in later periods (1 Macc 2:44; 3:5-6; 7:5; 9:58; 11:25; 14:14; Dan 11:32; 12:10 [Theod.]). In extreme cases, one who is ἄνομος ("without law") can also be called a παράνομος ("lawbreaker"). The latter term was applied both to the Hellenizer Menelaus (2 Macc 13:7) and to James the Just (Josephus, *Ant.* 20.200). Both ἄνομος and παράνομος were thus also vituperative accusations in intra-Jewish debates.[33]

The discussion so far has focused on the elasticity of certain terms that are

---

32. I take Rom 3:1 to be Paul's affirmation of circumcision as a sign that Jews belong to the people who received the oracles and promises of God, which demonstrate God's faithfulness and witness to the revelation of God's righteousness in the Messiah's death and resurrection.

33. See Michael F. Bird, "Jesus as Law-Breaker," in *Who Do My Opponents Say That I Am? An Investigation of the Accusations against the Historical Jesus*, ed. S. McKnight and J. B. Modica (LNTS 358; London: T&T Clark, 2008), 4-7.

thought to designate non-Jews (ἔθνος, Ἕλλην, ἀκροβυστία, and ἄνομος). They do indeed denote non-Jews most of the time, but as we have seen, there are exceptions. My argument, however, does not run:

1. Paul is apostle among the ἔθνη.
2. The ἔθνη can include Jews.
3. Ergo, Paul is apostle to the Jews as well.

Rather, I am suggesting that the fluidity of the language is indebted to the complex social and sectarian context of early Judaism in the Greco-Roman world. Jews could occupy, interact, and flourish in the social space of the ἔθνη; many Jews could to varying degree become Ἑλληνισταί; and in polemical contexts prestige terms like περιτομή and pejorative terms like ἀκροβυστία and ἄνομος could be applied to both Jews and Gentiles. Given this environment, the identity of Paul's audience is not always cut-and-dried.

A further complicating factor is that "ethnicity" is a complex matter. To say that Paul is the apostle to the ἔθνη means that he is the apostle to the non-Jews. However, "Jew" and "non-Jew" cannot be reduced to any particular essence that is obvious or measurable. While we are perhaps accustomed to thinking of ethnicity as a mix of race, tribe, and territory, ethnicity in many cases is a social construction. According to Thomas Eriksen, "Ethnicity is an aspect of social relationships between agents who consider themselves as culturally distinctive from members of other groups with whom they have a minimum of regular interaction. It can thus also be defined as a social identity (based on a contrast vis-à-vis others) characterised by metaphoric or fictive kinship."[34] Fictive kinship is precisely what many Jewish communities extended to Gentile guests and converts. The objection that many Jewish Christ-believers and perhaps even some Jews had against Paul was that, by refusing to circumcise Gentiles as a condition of full membership in Jesus-believing assemblies, he was divesting this fictive kinship of all fiction. In other words, the kinship of Gentile Christ-believers vis-à-vis Jewish Christ-believers was intended to be the same as Jews vis-à-vis other Jews. Paul did not have two classes of "insiders"—adherents/proselytes and Jews; he knows of only those who are "in Christ." For that reason, Paul was perceived to be lowering the currency of Israel's election by extending the privileges of Jewish identity to non-Jews, entirely apart from the covenantal and ethnic markers of Jewish

---

34. Thomas Hylland Eriksen, *Ethnicity and Nationalism: Anthropological Perspectives* (2nd ed.; London: Pluto, 2002), 12.

identity. Paul could do so because he began investing ethnic identities with religious meanings.

The religionizing of ethnic identity was nothing new. One can make the case that Ἰουδαῖος transformed from "Judean" to "Jewish religionist" during the post-Hasmonean period.[35] Isabella Sandwell contrasts John Chrysostom and Libanius on religious identity in antiquity. She notes that clear-cut religious identities and labels were central for Chrysostom and his preaching, while Libanius disengaged loyalty to particular gods from civil, political, and cultural duties.[36] Denise Kimber Buell further indicates the common link of religion and ethnicity in the ancient world: "Early Christians frequently portray religiosity and ethnicity/race as mutually constituting and, like their contemporaries, treat ethnicity/race as both fixed and fluid."[37] In terms of conversionist practices, this reality meant: "By construing Christianness as having an 'essence' (a fixed content) that can be acquired, early Christians could define conversion as both the transformation of one's ethnicity and the restoration of one's true identity. And by portraying this transformation as available to all, Christians universalized this ethnoracial transformation."[38] The significance of this development is that, just as Paul invests ἔθνη with the socioreligious capital of the Ἰουδαῖοι through the gospel, so too does he then place the Ἰουδαῖοι into the religious category of the ἔθνη by their disobedience (esp. in Rom 2:1–3:20, though far more nuanced in Rom 9–11). Among those who are "other" than believers in the Lord (i.e., unbelieving Jews and Gentiles), Paul focuses his primary attention on Gentiles (see Gal 2:7-9; 1 Thess 1:9; 2:15), yet the ultimate goal of his apostolic vocation remained the transformation of Gentiles and Jews into the "Israel of God" (Gal 6:16) and provoking Israel to jealousy through the Gentile engrafting, "so that all Israel may be saved" (Rom 11:26).

In sum, in the later phase of his missionary endeavors, Paul described himself as the apostle to the non-Jew, i.e., to Gentiles, Greeks, Barbarians,

---

35. Love L. Sechrest (*A Former Jew: Paul and the Dialectics of Race* [LNTS 410; London: T&T Clark, 2009], 61-109) accentuates the role of religion in ancient accounts of ethnographic and racial identity, especially for Jewish identity. She comments that "the central criterion of Jewish identity for the Jews studied here was *the Torah-ordered worship of the God of Abraham, Isaac and Jacob*" (105 [italics original]).

36. Isabella Sandwell, *Religious Identity in Late Antiquity: Greeks, Jews, and Christians in Antioch* (New York: CUP, 2007).

37. Denise Kimber Buell, *Why This New Race: Ethnic Reasoning in Early Christianity* (New York: Columbia University Press, 2005), 36.

38. Buell, *Why This New Race*, 138.

those without Torah, and the uncircumcised. I wish to point out, however, that sometimes Jews can be identified with the classifications ἔθνος, Ἕλλην, ἀκροβυστία, and ἄνομος as well (see diagram below). Jews who belonged to the web of socioreligious commitments known as Judaism still lived among the ἔθνη, and geopolitically speaking, they were often regarded as part of them. For those Jews influenced by Hellenistic culture, they sat on a continuum ranging from resistance to acculturation to assimilation to apostasy and were in some sense Ἕλληνες. Hence, "the cultural boundaries between Israelites and non-Israelites were often quite blurred, indicating far more diversity than generally imagined."[39] Furthermore, while circumcision was the distinguishing mark of the Jewish male, there were some anomalous Jews and proselytes who, because of the circumstances of their birth or because of competing views on rites of entry for converts, were not circumcised. It should also be apparent that ethnic identity is something that is partly inherited, but it also is socially constructed. It was consequently possible to invest ethnic identities with religious significance. Hence, Paul creates a religious framework in which Jews can be regarded *as if Gentiles* and Gentiles can be regarded *as if Jews*.

Let it be known that I am not contesting the existence of lines of demarcation between Jews and Gentiles in antiquity. Distinctions were made between Jews and non-Jews then whether by essentialist definitions of identity based on religious activity (e.g., Gentiles practice idolatry, while Jews follow Torah; or from another perspective Romans honor the gods, while those Jewish atheists ignore them) or distinguished by social belonging and boundaries (e.g., Jews live here and do this, while Gentiles live over there and do that).[40] My point is that the designating words were elastic and were often placed on insiders as a pejorative label for practical exclusion (You call yourself a Jew, but you're a lawless Greek!) or given to outsiders as a prestige label for fictive inclusion (Despite being a Gentile, you're an inward Jew or part of the Israel who sees God!). We must be cognizant of this linguistic fuzziness and social blurring when we examine Paul's descriptions of his ministry to non–Christ-believing non-Jews.

39. Malina and Pilch, *Social-Science Commentary on the Letters of Paul*, 15.

40. To attempt to define "Judaism" as a sharable body of beliefs and practices does not necessarily warrant the charge of "essentializing"; rather, it is simply part of the attempt to arrive at a set of observable characteristics that distinguish Jews as a social entity. See E. P. Sanders, "Common Judaism Explored," in *Common Judaism: Explorations in Second-Temple Judaism*, ed. W. O. McCready and A. Reinhartz (Minneapolis: Fortress, 2008), 21-23.

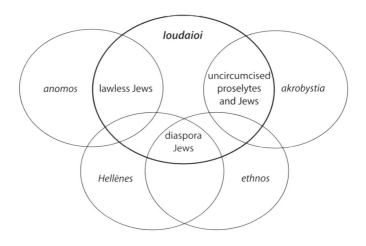

Jewish Evangelism in the Apostolate of Paul

The contention of this study is that Paul, even as apostle to the ἔθνη, remained engaged in spasmodic evangelistic activities within the orbit of Jewish communities of the Diaspora. In addition, I argue that the target audience for his ministry evolved over the course of his career. While his early missionary work was probably carried out primarily if not exclusively to Greek-speaking Judeans in Palestine and Arabia, eventually it became oriented primarily toward Gentiles. If that hypothesis is valid, then it raises the question as to precisely when Paul received his commission to go to the Gentiles. The evidence from his epistles and Acts is ambiguous. (See appendix 2 at the end of this chapter.) In Gal 1:15-16 Paul identifies himself as "set apart" by God, and he received a revelation of the Son from God "in order that [ἵνα] I might gospelize him among the Gentiles." Traditionally, this statement has been taken to mean that, at his conversion, Paul received a commission to be an apostle to the Gentiles.[41] Yet Paul does not explicitly say that, at his Christophany, the resurrected

41. See Jerome Murphy-O'Connor (*Paul: A Critical Life* [Oxford: OUP, 1997], 80): "He was called precisely in order to bring the good news to those who did not belong to the Jewish people. Both Galatians 1:11-12 and 1:15-16 unambiguously indicate that Paul's mission to the Gentiles was not a late development, nor a mere extension of a presumed outreach of Hellenists in Jerusalem. It should be unnecessary to stress this obvious point, but it has in fact been challenged"; Martin Hengel and Anna Maria Schwemer (*Paul between Damascus and Antioch,*

Jesus directed him to preach to the Gentiles, only that the Gentile mission was the goal of this revelation. The ἵνα may be logical and imply that this aspect of his calling became apparent to him only later.[42] In Acts it becomes even more opaque. In the first presentation of Paul's conversion narrative, the information about Paul's future ministry is given not to Paul but to Ananias, and it is said to include "Gentiles and kings and the sons of Israel" (Acts 9:15). Paul and Barnabas are "set apart" by the church of Antioch (Acts 13:2) for a missionary journey that focuses predominantly on the synagogues of Cyprus and southern Galatia (Acts 13:1–14:28), but it closes with the results among the Gentiles being celebrated (Acts 14:27). In Luke's second rendition of Paul's conversion narrative, the divine directive to go to the Gentiles occurs during a revelation in the temple in Jerusalem (Acts 22:21). Then, in the third account, the Lukan Paul describes his Christophany as including his appointment to be sent and to testify before the people of Israel and to the Gentiles (Acts 26:16-17). Acts is notoriously opaque when it comes to *when* Paul received his missionary

---

trans. J. Bowden [London: SCM, 1997], 97): "His mission to the 'Gentiles' appears as a direct consequence of the 'revelation of Jesus Christ' before Damascus and the commission to preach the gospel which he was given them"; Terence L. Donaldson (*Paul and the Gentiles: Remapping the Apostle's Convictional World* [Minneapolis: Fortress, 1997], 271): "Paul's convictions about the Gentile mission were the direct result of the Damascus experience; there is no solid reason to believe that they were preceded by a preliminary phase in which he either preached only to Jews or preached a 'Torah plus Christ' gospel to Gentiles"; James D. G. Dunn (*Beginning from Jerusalem,* [CITM 2; Grand Rapids, MI: Eerdmans, 2009], 354): "He saw himself as first and foremost 'apostle to the Gentiles'; and so far as Paul himself was concerned, that had been the case from his commissioning itself"; Seyoon Kim (*Paul and the New Perspective* [Grand Rapids, MI: Eerdmans, 2002], 104): "This immediacy militates against the view that he began to interpret his Damascus experience years later or that Gal. 1:15-17 represents only a later interpretation of it for an apologetic, rhetorical, or paradigmatic purpose"; Riesner (*Paul's Early Period*, 235): "It is perfectly clear that when composing the letter to the Galatians the apostle was convinced that the self-revelation of the resurrected Jesus near Damascus already contained his commission to the Gentiles." Riesner (*Paul's Early Period*, 236-41) goes on to suggest that (1) Paul's echo of prophetic texts to describe his calling (e.g., Isa 49:1 = Gal 1:15; Isa 52:15 = Rom 15:20-21; Isa 49:8 = 2 Cor 6:2) stem from parts of Isaiah that refer to the salvation of the Gentiles (see Acts 13:47; 26:16-18) and, (2) in light of Jewish and Jewish Christian traditions about Damascus, the shining of the messianic light at his calling may have led him to believe that the time for the eschatological ingathering of the Gentiles had begun. While this line of thought is certainly interesting, it is circumstantial and hardly decisive.

42. See Theodor Zahn, *Der Brief des Paulus an die Galater* (KNT; Leipzig: Deichert, 1907), 63-68; Martin Hengel, *Acts and the History of Earliest Christianity,* trans. J. Bowden (Philadelphia: Fortress, 1979), 88; Alexander J. M. Wedderburn, *A History of the First Christians* (London: T&T Clark, 2005), 85; Francis Watson, *Paul, Judaism, and the Gentiles: Beyond the New Perspective* (2nd ed.; Grand Rapids, MI: Eerdmans, 2007), 59-60, 70-71, 73, 79.

calling and to *whom* he was to direct his message. In light of Paul's ambiguity and Luke's opacity about the origins of the Pauline Gentile mission, it will be profitable to look at the contours of Paul's ministry in two stages: before and after the Jerusalem council. If we examine *who* Paul ministered to during these respective periods, it might tell us something of *when* he received his call, or when he became conscious of his calling to go the Gentiles. That in turn will inform us further of the place of Jews in Paul's apostolate.

Jewish Evangelism in Paul's Early Ministry

The period between Paul's conversion and the Jerusalem council is when our sources are the scarcest, but we do have some material to work with. In Gal 1:17 Paul recounts that, after his conversion/call, "I did not go up to Jerusalem to see those who were apostles before I was, but I went into Arabia. Later I returned to Damascus." What Paul was doing in Arabia is one of the most perplexing matters of Pauline chronology. Arabia (Ἀραβία) denotes the region west of Mesopotamia, south and east of Syria, and extends as far as the Sinai Peninsula.[43] Paul could have stayed in any number of the Hellenistic cities that existed between Damascus and Babylon, among the northern cites of the Decapolis, or as far south as Petra. But Paul's mention of Arabia in relation to Damascus means that he probably visited the Nabatean kingdom to the immediate south of Damascus, which is why he was brought to the attention of King Aretas (2 Cor 11:32). We do not know how long Paul was in Arabia, how much of the "three years" mentioned in Gal 1:18, or what he was doing there: respite, learning,[44] or mission? If mission, then to whom? To Gentile Arabs,[45] the Nabateans who were ethnic cousins of the Jews (i.e., Ishmaelites),

---

43. See BDAG, 127-28; Murphy-O'Connor, *Paul*, 81-84; Hengel and Schwemer, *Paul between Damascus and Antioch*, 120-26.

44. See J. B. Lightfoot, *Saint Paul's Epistle to the Galatians* (London: Macmillan, 1982), 87-90; Harald Riesenfeld, *The Gospel Tradition* (Oxford: Blackwell, 1970), 17-18; Richard N. Longenecker, *Galatians* (WBC; Dallas, TX: Word, 1990), 34; Nicholas H. Taylor, *Paul, Antioch, and Jerusalem: A Study in Relationships and Authority in Earliest Christianity* (JSNTSup 66; Sheffield: JSOT Press, 1992), 73; Riesner, *Paul's Early Period*, 259-60; Wedderburn, *First Christians*, 87.

45. See F. F. Bruce (*Paul: Apostle of the Free Spirit* [Carlisle, UK: Paternoster, 1980], 81): "The implication of his own narrative relates his Arabian visit rather closely to his call to preach Christ among the Gentiles"; Murphy-O'Connor (*Paul*, 81-82): "Paul must have been doing something to draw attention to himself and arouse the ire of the Nabataeans because he had to return to Damascus. . . . The only explanation is that Paul was trying to make converts. This first act subsequent to his conversion confirms his understanding of his conversion as a commission to preach the gospel among pagans"; Wayne A. Meeks (*The First Urban Christians:*

or to Jews in the region.[46] It is impossible to say for certain. We know that Paul returned to Damascus and had to leave there quickly to avoid capture by the local ruler, King Aretas, sometime around 37 CE. Such disturbances may well imply that his activities in Damascus and Arabia were incendiary or controversial; if so, I think that they were probably evangelistic (Gal 1:17; 2 Cor 11:32-33).[47] This idea may partially authenticate the narration of Paul in Acts, where, during his time in Damascus, he lodged with the disciples and was preaching Jesus as the Messiah and Son of God in the synagogues (Acts 9:19b-25).[48] Such activity is perfectly plausible, given the concentration of Jews in the city of Damascus at the time.[49]

The Social World of the Apostle Paul [New Haven: Yale University Press, 1983]): "It is evident that Paul had stirred up this official hostility not by meditating in the desert nor by wandering from village to village, but by preaching in flourishing Hellenistic cities such as Petra, Gerasa, Philadelphia, and Bostra"; Martin Hengel ("The Stance of the Apostle Paul toward the Law in the Unknown Years between Damascus and Antioch," in *Justification and Variegated Nomism*, vol. 2, *The Paradoxes of Paul* [Grand Rapids, MI: Baker Academic, 2004], 89): "'Why Arabia?' is simple. *As the offspring of Israel the 'Arabians' were the genealogically and geographically closest physical relatives of Israel among the 'Gentiles,' since they, too, were descendents of Abraham.* The offspring of Esau, the Edomites, had already become Jews under Hyrcanus and were no longer 'Gentiles'" (italics original). Paul Barnett (*Jesus and the Rise of Early Christianity: A History of New Testament Times* [Downers Grove, IL: InterVarsity, 1999], 255): "While we may reasonably assume that, as in Damascus, Saul preached to Jews in the Nabataean synagogues . . . Aretas' hostility toward him implies that he had also evangelized indigenous Nabataeans." Eckhard J. Schnabel (*Early Christian Mission*, vol. 1, *Jesus and the Twelve*; vol. 2, *Paul and the Early Church* [Downers Grove, IL: IVP Academic, 2004], 2:1037): "The intervention of Nabatean officials suggests that Paul did not limit his preaching to Jewish audiences, but that he reached pagan Nabateans as well." More cautious is Riesner (*Paul's Early Period*, 260), who wonders whether Paul lived in Arabia "reclusively," engaged in a possible "sojourn with a group of Jewish Christians" and perhaps "did mission work under the Jews living in the Nabataean territory."

46. On Jews in Nabataea, see David Graf, "Nabateans," *ABD* 4:972-73; Hengel and Schwemer, *Paul between Damascus and Antioch*, 112-13.

47. We should also recognize that tensions between the two Roman client-kingdoms of Judea and Nabataea may also have given Paul reason to cut his mission short (see Josephus, *Ant.* 18.109-26).

48. It is likely that Luke has telescoped Paul's initial and later periods in Damascus and omitted any reference to his time in Arabia. Paul's evangelical work in and escape from Damascus occurred *after* his time in Arabia and led to his journey to Jerusalem (2 Cor 11:32-33; Gal 1:17-18; Acts 9:24-26).

49. Murphy-O'Connor (*Paul*, 85) tendentiously rejects Luke's account in Acts 9:20-23 about Paul preaching to Jews in Damascus, since it is "incompatible with Paul's conviction that his mission was to the Gentiles." Yet Damascus was part of Eretz Israel according to several Jewish authors (e.g., Josephus, *Ant.* 5.86). The "land of Damascus" was eschatologically significant for the Qumranites (CD 6.5, 19; 8.21; 19.34; 20.12), and the messianic star of Num 24:17 was thought

After some time in Arabia/Damascus, Paul also made a brief visit to Jerusalem and soon afterward left Jerusalem and entered into the regions of Syria and Cilicia (Gal 1:18, 21; see Acts 9:26, 30). Besides making a visit to Cephas and James, what else was Paul doing in Jerusalem? An answer is hinted at in Rom 15:19, containing "a remark to which too little attention has been paid."[50] There Paul states that he has fully proclaimed the gospel "from Jerusalem all the way around to Illyricum." Significantly, Paul does not identify Damascus or Antioch as the starting point for his apostolic mission, but Jerusalem. Commentators have been puzzled as to how Paul, the apostle to the Gentiles, can place the origin of his proclamation in Jerusalem. Scholars have thus tried to explain away this reference to preaching *from* Jerusalem in a number of creative ways. Some argue that, although Paul refers to Jerusalem, he actually means the area of Damascus and Arabia.[51] Or Jerusalem is mentioned because it is the epicenter of Israel's worship and the ultimate location for the eschatological pilgrimage of the Gentiles (e.g., Isa 2:2-4; Mic 4:1-4; Zech 8:20-23).[52] Or it is plain hyperbole.[53] Or because it was in Jerusalem that the Christ-movement

---

to arise near Damascus (CD 7.14-18). According to Josephus (*War* 2.561; 7.368), though the numbers are obviously inflated, eighteen thousand Jews were massacred in the gymnasium in Damascus ca. 66 CE. Thus, Damascus was fitting and fertile territory for a Jewish Christian mission. Note Hengel and Schwemer (*Paul between Damascus and Antioch*, 50), who regard Paul's "messianic preaching in the synagogues of Damascus" as "historical." See the reconstruction of events listed in Schnabel, *Early Christian Mission*, 2:1032. While Luke may have a narrative impetus to portray Paul as a new Stephen, a Hellenistic preacher to fellow Jews, and while Luke consistently emphasizes Paul's ministry to Jews *then* Gentiles, it is most unlikely that this proclivity and pattern have led him to invent the story of Paul's messianic preaching in Damascus. The story is full of social realism, it accords with what Paul hints at in his letters about his ministry among Jews, and it conflicts with Luke's own extolling of Paul as the apostle of the Gentiles par excellence.

50. Hengel, *Acts*, 87.

51. Barnett (*Jesus and the Rise of Early Christianity*, 248) thinks that, by "Jerusalem," Paul probably included Damascus and Arabia in his thinking. However, the "land of Israel" (אֶרֶץ יִשְׂרָאֵל) would be far more likely to evoke the wider area of Judea and Syria than "Jerusalem."

52. Bruce, *Paul*, 322. The obvious problem here is that Paul's missionary work is centrifugal not centripetal and is done ahead of any eschatological pilgrimage of the nations to Zion (see Bird, *Jesus and the Origins of the Gentile Mission*, 162-68). In addition, if Jerusalem's geotheologic significance were the point, then Paul would perhaps bracket the terminus point of his apostolic travels with somewhere more theologically significant than Illyricum, an outer province of the Roman Empire. Somewhere like Ephesus, Corinth, or even Athens were far more appropriate as representative cities of the Gentile world in the East.

53. Sanders, *Paul, the Law, and the Jewish People*, 186-87.

began.[54] Or that it was in Jerusalem that Paul received his vision in the temple to go to the Gentiles (Acts 22:17-21).[55] More likely, in Rom 15:19 Paul is speaking literally and geographically about his former preaching ministry in Jerusalem, however brief it may have been.[56] Paul's ministry in Jerusalem was not among Jewish Christ-believers, since he confesses that he was unknown to the churches of Judea at this time (Gal 1:22-23), and Jerusalem does not ordinarily hold a sizable contingent of Gentiles, except perhaps during festivals. It is far more likely that, just as Acts 9:26-29 says, Paul proclaimed Jesus as Messiah to Greek-speaking Jews in Jerusalem.[57] After that, as Gal 1:21 and Acts 9:30 largely agree, Paul journeyed to Syria and Cilicia to do more of the same.[58] Overall, the evidence from Gal 1:17-23 and Acts 9:19-30 demonstrates that Paul's early ministry in Arabia, Damascus, and Jerusalem was oriented toward Jews. That is exactly what Luke appears to describe in Acts 26:20, where he writes, "First to those in Damascus, then to those in Jerusalem and in all Judea, *and then to the Gentiles* [καὶ τοῖς ἔθνεσιν], I preached that they should repent and turn to God and demonstrate their repentance by their deeds." Even in the context of Luke's description of Paul's immediate commission at his Christophany to preach to the Gentiles (Acts 26:16-16), Luke still regards the Gentile component of Paul's apostolate as something subsequent to his period of ministry in Damascus and Jerusalem. Luke, even while extolling Paul's exploits among the Gentiles, knows full well that Paul's early ministry was geared toward the Jews of Damascus and Jerusalem.[59]

The Pauline and Lukan accounts both agree that Paul left Jerusalem and went to Syria and Cilicia (Gal 1:21; via Caesarea to Tarsus, according Acts 9:30). Paul's return to his city of origins (Acts 9:11; 21:39; 22:3) may have constituted an attempt to indigenize this new Jesus movement among his family and compatriots. Importantly, there is no indication that Paul's activity was limited to Syria/Cilicia; he merely indicates the point from which he began

---

54. F. F. Bruce, *Romans* (TNTC; rev. ed.; Leicester: InterVarsity, 1985), 247; C. E. B. Cranfield, *Epistle to the Romans* (2 vols.; ICC; Edinburgh: T&T Clark, 1975-79), 2:760-61. But it is the origins of Paul's ministry and not that of the Christian movement as a whole that is under discussion here.

55. Riesner, *Paul's Early Period*, 263.

56. See Hengel, *Acts*, 87; Moo, *Romans*, 894.

57. See Schnabel, *Early Christian Mission*, 2:1045-46.

58. Gerd Lüdemann, *Paul, Apostle to the Gentiles: Studies in Chronology* (Philadelphia: Fortress, 1984), 59-60.

59. Luke's use of πρῶτος in Acts 26:20 might reflect an early Christian redemptive-historical scheme that assumed that the gospel was for the Jews "first" (see Mark 7:27; Rom 1:16; 2:9-10; 3:2).

his missionary work.[60] It is not necessarily the case that, as Ernst Haenchen imputed to Luke, Paul remained quiet for a while in his hometown of Tarsus.[61] Though we have to wait until 1 Thessalonians (ca. 51 CE) before we have any concrete evidence of Paul's activities, there is no reason why Paul's work in the initial period of his time in Syria/Cilicia was different from his former work in Damascus, Arabia, and Jerusalem. Tarsus and Syrian Antioch both possessed a substantial Jewish population.

During this period Luke reports that Barnabas sought out Paul and brought him to Antioch (Acts 11:25-26). The occasion for this was the Gentile "break-through" in Antioch. The expulsion of the Hellenists from Jerusalem, facilitated by the death of Stephen, led to the establishment of a Christ-believing assembly within or beside the synagogues of Antioch. It is apparent that Luke has projected the story of the Hellenists at Antioch to a later point in Acts in order to prioritize Paul's conversion (Acts 9:1-30) and Peter's "Gentile Pentecost" with Cornelius (Acts 10:1–11:18). That rearrangement is plausible, for Acts 9:1–11:18 seems to interrupt what was probably a continuous account of the beginnings of the Hellenistic mission started in Acts 6:1. Luke does this in order to provide apostolic precedent to the Gentile mission, whereas the inclusion of non-Jews into the Jesus movement was probably more piecemeal, sporadic, and less controlled than what Luke depicts.[62]

The transition from a purely Jewish mission to a mission toward a Jewish and Gentile audience was not a single event but a process with antecedents in Jerusalem (Nicolaus the proselyte, Acts 6:5), replicated by other Christ-believing Hellenists (Philip, Acts 8:4-40) and paralleled by other analogous happenings (Peter and Cornelius, Acts 10).[63] In Antioch it was genuinely unique; there, the Greek-speaking Jewish Christ-believers seem to have integrated Gentiles into their ranks as full and equal members without requiring proselytism (Acts 11:26). Dropping circumcision for Gentiles was not entirely unknown in the Diaspora (see Josephus, *Ant.* 20.40-42), and neither did the Antiochene church suddenly become hyper-Lutheran with a law/gospel antith-

60. See John Knox, *Chapters in a Life of Paul* (rev. ed.; Macon, GA: Mercer University Press, 1987), 59; Lüdemann, *Paul,* 61; Jewett, *Dating,* 82-83; Hengel and Schwemer, *Paul between Damascus and Antioch,* 151-61; Riesner, *Paul's Early Period,* 264-68; Murphy-O'Connor, *Paul,* 95; Schnabel, *Early Christian Mission,* 2:1046-48.

61. Ernst Haenchen, *Acts of the Apostles: A Commentary* (Oxford: Blackwell, 1971), 333.

62. Bird, *Jesus and the Origins of the Gentile Mission,* 5-6; Schnabel, *Early Christian Mission,* 1:672; Riesner, *Paul's Early Period,* 108; Wedderburn, *First Christians,* 60, 68-69, 71-72.

63. Hengel, *Acts,* 79-80; Riesner, *Paul's Early Period,* 109-10; Schnabel, *Early Christian Mission,* 1:1071.

esis that meant ceasing observance of the distinctive Jewish way of life. What was different was a concerted outreach to Greek-speaking Gentiles already associated with Jewish communities, ceasing the obligation of circumcision for membership, and engaging in mixed table fellowship. The motivation for this relaxing of the rules was probably (1) the Jesus tradition, which furnished believers with stories of Jesus' encounters with non-Jews, his table fellowship with sinners, and his teaching about covenantal righteousness in relation to halakic purity regulations; (2) the visible manifestation of the Spirit being poured upon non-Jews; and (3) scriptural exposition of key texts that refer to the eschatological ingathering of the Gentiles in the final days. In addition, the designation χριστιανοί ("Christians") in Acts 11:26 is not a Lukan anachronism but emerged probably as a term created by local officials to designate a Jewish messianic group with their Gentile clientele in and around the synagogues of Antioch.[64] In any event, the Hellenists were the "needle's eye" through which the Christian message found a mouthpiece into the Greco-Roman world.[65] Barnabas brought Paul to Antioch probably because Paul was uniquely suited for working in a mixed ethnic context with non-Jews and had a suitably enthusiastic faith that lent itself to outreach.

The Jewish Christ-believing Hellenists were among the first to launch a deliberate mission into the wider Mediterranean, by sending Barnabas and Paul as delegates (Acts 13:1-3) for missionary work in Cyprus and southern Asia Minor (Acts 13–14).[66] Galatians 1:21 seems to cover the period between Paul's first and second visits to Jerusalem and allows time for the "first missionary journey," since Pamphylia, Pisidia, and Lyconia bordered Cilicia.[67] We are entirely reliant on Luke for this period, and the picture that emerges is that of Paul as operating initially among Jews and only gradually making concerted steps toward Gentiles. In Cyprus at Salamis "they" proclaimed the word of God in the Jewish synagogues, then in Paphos they encountered the Jewish magician Elymas/Bar-Jesus, and they were summoned by (not seeking after) the proconsul Sergius Paulus, who became a believer (Acts 13:4-12).

In Pisidian Antioch, Paul and Barnabas entered a synagogue and were

---

64. See Acts 26:28; 1 Pet 4:16; Tacitus, *Ann.* 15.44; Suetonius, *Nero* 16; Pliny, *Ep.* 10.96.1-5; Josephus, *Ant.* 18.64; Ignatius, *Rom.* 3.2. On the authenticity of this designation, see Lüdemann, *Early Christianity*, 138-39; Riesner, *Paul's Early Period*, 111-14.

65. Hengel, *Between Jesus and Paul*, 26-27, 53-54.

66. See Schnabel, *Early Christian Mission*, 2:1073-1124; Dunn, *Beginning from Jerusalem*, 417-38.

67. Hengel and Schwemer, *Paul between Damascus and Antioch*, 261; Dunn, *Beginning from Jerusalem*, 371.

asked for a "word of exhortation." Paul preached a sermon to the Israelites and God-fearers (Acts 13:16, 26) predicated on the premises of Jewish covenant history, with a narration of Jesus' life and the apostolic interpretation of his death and resurrection (Acts 13:16-41). Luke notably reports that many Jews and devout proselytes "followed" Paul and Barnabas (Acts 13:43). The subsequent Sabbath meeting does not go anywhere near as well with the Jews, who were "filled with jealousy." Paul and Barnabas responded by citing Isa 49:6 to the effect that, because of such recalcitrance, they will take their message to the Gentiles. The Gentiles rejoice at this news, and then the Jews petition God-fearing women and leading men to expel Paul and Barnabas (Acts 13:44-52). As such, the Pisidian Antioch episode is paradigmatic of Lukan theology. Paul's speech is somewhat akin to Stephen's in Acts 7, with its covenant history narration (though it retains clear points of contact with authentic Pauline tradition).[68] The pattern of an initially positive reception among a small cohort of Jews, God-fearers, and proselytes, followed by Jewish antagonism and Roman complicity to persecution, occurs repeatedly throughout Paul's missionary journeys. The Isa 49:6 theme also permeates Luke/Acts, to the effect that the role of Jesus as "light" to the Gentiles is continued in the ministry of Paul.[69]

Ironically, though Paul and Barnabas turn to the Gentiles (Acts 13:46),[70] they still continue the pattern of starting with Jewish synagogues in the very next location—Iconium, where they speak to "Jews and Greeks" (Acts 14:1), with a similar cycle of opposition and persecution ensuing (Acts 14:2-7). The account of Paul and Barnabas in Lystra is anomalous, as they do not make it

68. See Dunn, *Beginning from Jerusalem*, 438.

69. Michael F. Bird, "'Light to the Nations' (Isaiah 42:6 and 49:6): Intertextuality and Mission Theology in the Early Church," *RTR* 65 (2006): 127-28.

70. On these passages about "turning" to the Gentiles, Paul, later on in Corinth, utters a similar polemical remark indicting the Jews for their failure to believe and announces that he will instead focus on the Gentiles (Acts 18:6). Afterward, however, he again returns to the synagogues in Ephesus (Acts 18:19-20; 19:8-10). After his arrival in Rome, Paul takes the initiative in summoning the Jewish leaders to hear his message (Acts 28:17-28). In Rome there is another "turning" to the Gentiles after disagreements among the Jews in Rome between those who believed his message and those who did not. That experience leads Paul to a citation from Isa 6:6-10 about Jewish hardness of heart, and he announces that God's salvation will be sent to the more attentive Gentiles (Acts 28:26-29). Still, during a period of house arrest in Rome Paul welcomed "all who came to see him" and proclaimed the kingdom of God without hindrance. Overall, then, the Lukan Paul's "turning" to the Gentiles (13:46; 18:6; 28:28-29) appears to be temporary and localized and never final. There is no definitive and absolute abandonment of a mission to the Jewish people, which is emphasized further by the summarizing statements of Paul's ministry to Jews and Gentiles at key points (Acts 9:15; 20:21; 26:17, 20).

into a synagogue. Instead, the healing of a man and their gospel announcement ferment another Jewish-instigated riot before they head off to Derbe and then retrace their steps (Acts 14:8-21). The objects of their ministry in Derbe and Perga are not stated, and Luke quickly places Paul and Barnabas back in Antioch, where their report focuses not on the Jews but on "all that God had done with them, and how he had opened a door of faith for the Gentiles" (Acts 14:27).

The Antioch-based mission of Paul highlights Luke's theological creativity, seen through his ordering of events to highlight Jewish opposition to the gospel, the Spirit-driven nature of the mission, and the emerging role of Paul as apostle to the Gentiles. That said, the Lukan sequence is hardly his own creation, and though we cannot reconstruct Luke's sources and clearly identify his redaction of them, he appears to be providing accounts of traditional material related to Paul's Antioch-based missionary exploits (which on some points can be partially cross-referenced to Paul's epistles). What is fairly secure is that Paul and Barnabas's activities began with the synagogues in a given city, and gradually it became apparent that the Gentiles in association with the synagogues represented fertile soil for the gospel message.

Jerusalem Council and the Antioch Incident

There never seems to have been any resistance to the view that Gentiles could participate in the Jesus movement. The only dispute was the terms of their entrance into the church and subsequently the parameters for their social fellowship with Jewish Christ-believers. Galatians 2:4-5 and Acts 15:1-2 agree that Paul's second visit to Jerusalem was necessitated by dissensions related to "liberty" (Gal 2:4) and "circumcision" (Acts 15:1, 5) caused by the prevalence of Gentiles in the church at Antioch. The Jerusalem council described in Gal 2:1-10/Acts 15 resolved this issue by determining that Gentile believers were free from proselytism (i.e., conversion by circumcision), and the validity of Paul's mission to the uncircumcised was recognized. What was not settled or foreseen was the mode of fellowship between Gentile Christ-believers and Jewish Christ-believers when they occupied the same social space. This lack of foresight led to the incident at Antioch described in Gal 2:11-14 (cf. Acts 15:35-41/18:22-23?).[71]

The Antioch incident was a watershed in the early church. It forced Paul

---

71. For what follows, see Michael F. Bird, *The Saving Righteousness of God: Studies on Paul, Justification, and the New Perspective* (PBM; Milton Keynes, UK: Paternoster, 2006), 119-36.

to split from the Antiochene church, to pursue mostly Gentile converts in his ensuing ministry, and to socially separate his Gentile-believing majority assemblies from Jewish communities. On coming to Antioch, Peter (Cephas) initially engaged in table fellowship with Christ-believing Gentiles, but then, at the arrival of "certain men from James" and in fear of "those of the circumcision," he withdrew and separated himself. The Antioch incident has been varyingly understood. My take on the episode is that nationalistic fervor fermenting in Judea in the 40s forced James to send a delegation to Antioch to urge Jews there to avoid excessively fraternizing with Gentiles unless the Gentiles were circumcised. Taking this position would enable Jewish Christ-believers in Jerusalem to escape persecution from Judean groups.[72] The other thing we must consider is whether the Christ-believing fellowship in Antioch was already separate from the local synagogues of Antioch. These mixed Christ-believing groups may well have been an intra-Jewish entity that still functioned as a small chapter within a wider Jewish association. That would explain the presence of "those of the circumcision" who comprised Christ-believing Jews *and* non–Christ-believing Jews who were still committed to the soteric and social function of circumcision and the Jewish way of life. This "circumcision" group within Antioch was alarmed at Jews eating with non-Jews so brazenly.

Paul's response to Cephas was that the Jewish Christ-believers had chosen purity over unity and were proposing a view of "equal but separate, unless circumcised."[73] Paul saw this position as a compromise of what the Antiochene church and its daughter churches stood for, and he parted ways with Peter, Barnabas, and Antioch. (If he had won the debate, I suspect that he would have said so in Gal 2). Paul belonged to the old Antioch school and was determined to continue his ministry in such a way that did not require Gentiles to become Jews either for salvation or as a condition of full eucharistic fellowship. In the rest of his apostolic career he remained committed to ensuring the equality of

---

72. On anti-Gentile sentiment, see 1 Thess 2:15-16; the persecution of Christians described in Gal 6:12 may be due to reports of Christians outside of Judea consorting with non-Jews. This pool of Judean nationalism was created by the fiasco over Caligula's attempt to place a statue of himself in the Jerusalem temple. Herod Agrippa's reign over a united kingdom (41-44 CE) may have aroused certain hopes of a powerful Eastern monarchy. The following procurators were often incompetent or harsh. Cuspius Fadus (44-46 CE) demanded that the priestly vestments be returned to Roman custody and confronted a sedition under Theudas (Josephus, *Ant.* 20.6, 97-99; Acts 5:36). The Jewish apostate Tiberius Alexander (46-48 CE) crucified the sons of Judas the Galilean (*Ant.* 20.102). The subsequent period saw several incidents such as riots in the temple, increasing banditry, and the rise of the Sicarii (Josephus, *War* 2.223-38; *Ant.* 20.105-24, 208).

73. Ben Witherington III, *Grace in Galatia: A Commentary on Paul's Letter to the Galatians* (Grand Rapids, MI: Eerdmans, 1998), 158.

his Gentile converts, even while attempting to build bridges with the Jerusalem church through his collection.

Jewish Evangelism during Paul's Aegean Mission

During his Aegean mission, Paul established churches in Philippi, Thessalonica, and Corinth between ca. 50 and 52 CE.[74] During this period the two Thessalonians letters were written, and Paul corresponded several times with the Corinthians. Paul and his coworkers wrote letters to the Galatians, Philippians, Philemon, Colossians and Ephesians, and Romans between 51 and 57 CE after the Jerusalem council and the Antioch incident. In these later letters we find indications of Paul partitioning his Gentile-majority churches away from the synagogues in order to avoid both Jewish opposition and interference from Jewish Christ-believers varyingly associated with the Jerusalem church. Although Paul always possessed a call to proclaim Jesus Christ and had a certain sense of independence in his calling, only in this later period did Gentiles become the primary object of his missionary work. In any case, from these letters we still find echoes of Paul's interaction with Jewish groups and several remarks pertinent to Jewish evangelism.

The Corinthian correspondence contains several allusions to Paul's evangelistic interactions with Jews. The exposition of the foolishness of the cross in 1 Cor 1:18–2:5 recognizes that the cross is a stumbling block to Jews, and yet the same message calls Jews to find in Christ the power and wisdom of God (1 Cor 1:22-24). In 1 Cor 9 Paul discourses about his apostolic ministry; it includes his claim that he does all things to promote the gospel among Jews and Gentiles:

> To the Jews I became as a Jew, in order to win Jews. To those under the law I became as one under the law (though I myself am not under the law) so that I might win those under the law. To those outside the law I became as one outside the law (though I am not free from God's law but am under Christ's law) so that I might win those outside the law. To the weak I became weak, so that I might win the weak. I have become all things to all people, that I might by all means save some. (1 Cor 9:20-22)

The Pauline mission is comprehensive in scope, as seen in Paul's urgency

---

74. This is because Paul was in Corinth when the expulsion of Jews from Rome (49 CE) was relatively recent (Acts 18:2), and he encounters Gallio (Acts 18:14-17), who is placed in Corinth in 51 CE by an inscription.

to save persons who are Jews ("under law"), Gentiles, ("without law"), and Gentile adherents to Judaism ("weak"). This results in rhetorical strategies and social behaviors undertaken by Paul tantamount to "becoming" a Jew or a Gentile for the sake of promoting the gospel, though Paul himself appears to regard both transformations as compromises of his own identity, which is defined by being in Christ. Regardless of one's ethnic makeup and independent of one's degree of adherence to the Torah, Paul regards "all people" as objects of salvation. Sanders's dismissal of Paul's language here as "hyperbolic" is premature, given the surrounding evidence from the Corinthian correspondence as a whole.[75] Francis Watson is much better: "Paul's commission extends not just to the non-Jewish world of the ἄνομοι but also to Jews and those drawn to Jewish practices. This is most plausibly understood as referring to the type of missionary practice represented in Acts. Even if the Acts portrayal is unhistorical, however, Paul could hardly have written as he does in 1 Cor 9 if he had *always* preached exclusively to Gentiles and had *never* seen Jews as the direct objects of his missionary endeavors."[76] There is no reason to deny that Paul believed that Jews, much like himself, needed to be converted to Christ and transformed by the Spirit. Gentiles would have to give up their idolatry and impurity, and Jews give up the practices that separated them from Gentiles. They would be drawn together into a single community, not two separate sects, worshiping and living together, with Paul as leader. Alan Segal hits the nail on the head as to what this means for Paul's ambitions: "If Paul's call for unity is taken seriously, he did not merely want to be the apostle to the gentiles. He wanted to be an apostle of all the church, for his vision was for a new community formed of all gentiles and Jews."[77]

Several similar snippets are found in 2 Corinthians. The arrival of the su-

---

75. Sanders, *Paul, the Law, and the Jewish People*, 186-89.

76. Watson, *Paul, Judaism, and the Gentiles*, 73 (italics original). Note also the comment of Karl Olav Sandnes ("A Missionary Strategy in 1 Corinthians 9.19-23?," in *Paul as Missionary: Identity, Activity, Theology, and Practice*, ed. T. J. Burke and B. S. Rosner [LNTS 420; London: T&T Clark, 2011], 141): "The more Acts is taken into account, the more 'real' 1 Corinthians 9 becomes. In three fundamental ways Acts corroborates the implications of 1 Corinthians 9. First, Paul speaks regularly in the synagogues. He travels to Jerusalem to celebrate Jewish Pentecost (Acts 20.16), and he circumcises Timothy. Second, he converses in the *agora*. He gives a speech where pagan poets are cited thus aligning himself with persuasive Greek style. Third, Acts witnesses to the difficulties inherent in living according to the dictum. Paul instantly ran into difficulties with the synagogues; he is ridiculed in Athens. His performance there even earned him accusations of being an idolater."

77. Alan Segal, *Paul the Convert: The Apostolate and Apostasy of Saul the Pharisee* (New Haven: Yale University Press, 1990), 265.

perapostles in Corinth, even if their teaching was sophistic rather than no-mistic, led Paul to buttress his own apostolic authority by juxtaposing the old covenant with the new covenant in 2 Cor 3. Paul laments that the Jews who read the old covenant are unaware that the glory of Moses has departed. The veil that covers their minds is "removed" (καταργέω) in Christ when one "converts" (ἐπιστρέφω) to the Lord (2 Cor 3:15-16). This remark about those who are veiled should be coordinated with what Paul states in 2 Cor 4:3-4, "And even if our gospel is veiled, it is veiled to those who are perishing. In their case the god of this world has blinded the minds of the unbelievers, to keep them from seeing the light of the gospel of the glory of Christ, who is the image of God." Paul places the Jews in the category of those who are perishing (ἀπόλ-λυμι) and are unbelievers (ἄπιστοι) and therefore are in need of salvation. Finally, in 2 Cor 11:24 Paul claims that he has five times received the thirty-nine lashes from the Jews. That implies his willingness to submit to the discipline of a synagogue, also that he was evidently doing something that prompted a call for severe discipline for his activities. We do not know whether evangelistic, social, or legal reasons led to Paul's receiving this penalty, but it does prove that he remained within the orbit of Jewish synagogues at one time or other.

Romans contains further material that relates the Jews to Paul's gospel.[78] The *propositio* of Rom 1:16 that "the gospel is the power of salvation for every-one who believes, the Jew first, and then the Greek" is not reflecting purely a salvation-historical scheme of how the gospel came to the Gentiles via the Jews, but it mirrors Paul's actual missionary practice of beginning with the Jews in a local synagogue. The diatribes in Romans may reflect actual instances of debates with real Jewish persons (e.g., Rom 2:1–3:9; 6:1-3; 7:1-25; 9:1-5; 10:1-3). The climax of Paul's midrashic argument about Abraham is that the saving event in Jesus Christ includes both Jews and Gentiles: "The promise comes by faith, so that it may be by grace and may be guaranteed to all Abraham's offspring—not only to those who are of the law but also to those who have the faith of Abraham. He is the father of us all" (Rom 4:16). Paul certainly looks ahead to the eschatological salvation of Israel in the future (Rom 10:1; 11:12, 26), yet he does not leave their salvation to a matter of time. Paul believes that, despite Israel's rejection of the message, God has still called Jews and Gentiles into salvation (Rom. 9:24) and that they are the remnant of God's faithful peo-

---

78. See Leander E. Keck, "The Jewish Paul among the Gentiles: Two Portraits," in *Early Christianity and Classical Culture: Comparative Studies in Honor of Abraham J. Malherbe*, ed. J. T. Fitzgerald, T. H. Olbricht, and L. M. White (NovTSup 110; Leiden: Brill, 2003), 461-81; James C. Miller, "The Jewish Context of Paul's Gentile Mission," *TynB* 58 (2007): 101-15.

ple (Rom 9:25-29; 11:1-6). There is no distinction between Jew and Gentile, and all who call upon the name of the Lord will be saved (Rom 10:12-13). Indeed, Rom 10:14-21 appears to assume a continued mission to Israel despite their obstinacy. Israel's "failure" has a positive consequence in that it has allowed the Gentiles the opportunity to respond to the message, and Paul hopes that the salvation of the Gentiles will make Israel jealous and prompt their change of mind (Rom 11:13-15). On this jealousy motif, note the words of Richard Bell: "Paul's theology *demands* a mission to the Jewish people. Provoking Israel to jealousy is no replacement for mission. It is just one possible precursor for mission. The gospel must be preached for it is only the gospel, God's reconciling word, which can make someone a Christian (Rom 10.17)."[79] In addition, the list of names in Rom 16:1-16 may include reference to persons who are also missionaries or apostles who work primarily among the Jewish people. Paul not only knows of such persons, but he also extols their efforts and sees himself as working independently, but cooperatively with them. Although Paul writes directly to the Gentiles in Rome, he remains keen to maintain affectionate relations with the Jewish Christ-believers in Rome as part of his comprehensive vision for a unified network of churches among the ἔθνη.

Acts provides its own picture, which essentially corresponds with the Pauline materials about Paul working among both Jews and Gentiles during his later Aegean mission. In Philippi, Paul began his work in a "place of prayer" where he met the "God-worshiper" Lydia (Acts 16:11-15). The work in Thessalonica, Berea, and Athens all commenced in the synagogues (Acts 17:1-5, 10-12, 16-17). The Athens account is quite interesting, with Paul in the synagogue with the Jews and God-worshipers and then in the Agora and Areopagus with pagans, which represents the exact type of thing we might expect (Acts 17:17-19). Paul's actions in Corinth were equally as realistic and pragmatic. There he preached to Jews and Greeks in the synagogue; after opposition, however, he was forced to take his converts elsewhere (Acts 18:4-8). During his time in Ephesus, Paul attended the synagogues to reason with the Jews (Acts 18:19-21), and when he returned there, he continued on in the synagogue until he encountered resistance and then took his followers to a lecture hall to continue a ministry to Jews and Greeks (Acts 19:8-20). The Lukan Paul's summary statement of his ministry to the Ephesian elders is that he "testified to both Jews

79. Richard H. Bell, *Provoked to Jealousy: The Origin and Purpose of the Jealousy Motif in Romans 9–11* (WUNT 2.63; Tübingen: Mohr Siebeck, 1994), 354-55 (italics original). See similarly N. T. Wright ("Romans," in *NIB*, ed. L. E. Keck [12 vols.; Nashville: Abingdon, 2002], 10:697): "To imagine that Jews can no longer be welcomed into the family of the Messiah . . . [that] for Paul, would be the very height of anti-Judaism."

and Greeks about repentance toward God and faith toward our Lord Jesus" (Acts 20:21). All of this indicates that "Luke *at no point* envisages a distinctive Pauline mission to Gentiles—unless perhaps at the very end of his work."[80]

Commentators have asked, How plausible and historical is the Lukan picture of Paul working, at least initially, in the synagogues?[81] If many of Paul's converts had "turned to God from idols" (1 Thess 1:9) and were former pagans (Gal 4:8; 1 Cor 12:2), then perhaps a great many of them had never been associated with the synagogues of Jewish communities. Several scholars argue that Paul did not use synagogues as a base for his evangelistic teaching and instead used his tentmaking activities as a means of contact with non-Jews and meeting in the homes of patrons, in rented spaces, or even in tenements for instruction, meals, and prayer.[82] There is some truth to Jerome Murphy-O'Connor's claim: "As Paul's ministry expanded, particularly among God-fearers, the enmity of the Jews increased, and it became progressively impossible to preach in the synagogue; he had only to open his mouth to be shouted down," meaning that Paul's workshop might have become a main avenue of his evangelistic operations at certain times.[83] E. P. Sanders goes even further: "There is no hint that Paul's converts attended synagogues."[84]

But I am not convinced. On the whole, we have no reason to doubt that Paul began his work in the synagogues, as this accounts for the large number of God-worshipers in the early church and explains why issues such as food, fellowship, and circumcision were the continuing points of contention that Paul had to address, even when writing to Gentile-majority churches. Likewise, his exposition of Scripture suggests that his audiences were varyingly aware of synagogal ways of expositing the Jewish Scriptures. Furthermore, from a sociological vantage point, conversions are usually made through social networks, and the conversion of Gentiles or God-fearers would emerge out of communities like synagogues, where they interacted with Jews.[85] Paul

---

80. Watson, *Paul, Judaism, and the Gentiles*, 70 (italics original).

81. According to Sanders (*Paul, the Law, and the Jewish People*, 181), the Lukan narration of Paul beginning his preaching activities in a synagogue is "either uncertain or dubious."

82. See, e.g., Ronald Hock, *The Social Context of Paul's Ministry: Tentmaking and Apostleship* (Philadelphia: Fortress, 1980); S. K. Stowers, "Social Status, Public Speaking, and Private Teaching: The Circumstances of Paul's Preaching Activity," *NovT* 26 (1984): 68-73; Lüdemann, *Early Christianity*, 159, 185; Segal, *Paul the Convert*, 271; J. Louis Martyn, *Galatians* (AYB; New Haven: Yale University Press, 1997), 213-16.

83. Murphy-O'Connor, *Paul*, 263.

84. E. P. Sanders, "Paul's Jewishness," in *Paul's Jewish Matrix*, ed. T. G. Casey and J. Taylor (Rome: Gregorian & Biblical Press, 2011), 66.

85. See James G. Crossley, *Why Christianity Happened: A Sociohistorical Account of*

conducted his evangelistic activities with his coworkers in major urban centers of the eastern Mediterranean, where these Jewish networks were the most vibrant. It is little wonder, then, that most of Paul's coworkers were Jewish, that he invests so much effort on Jewish halakic matters and scriptural exegesis, and that he can still retain some opposition to the politics and paganism of the Greco-Roman pantheon: Paul was working among Jews, Romans, and Greeks. Paul's message might have particularly appealed to Diasporan Jews because it enabled them to retain the essential religious capital of Judaism like monotheism, Torah observances, election, covenant, eschatology, and avoidance of idolatry, yet they were able to have a free degree of cultural assimilation with their environs, which would have been very attractive.[86]

It is highly probable, then, that Paul commenced his evangelistic work in the synagogues and would sometimes be compelled to leave with a small cohort of Jews and God-worshipers to alternative premises, just as Acts describes happening. In Robert Jewett's words: "There is widespread consensus that despite the apologetic interests of the book of Acts, it is realistic to expect that wherever possible he would begin his missionary activities in local synagogues and move to an independent base of operations after troubles erupted or patrons and patronesses emerged."[87] So it seems that "the way to the 'Gentiles' led through the synagogue."[88]

Summary

There do not appear to have been any "missions" in the early church that were completely independent from either Jews or Gentiles. Peter as the apostle to the circumcision came into close social contact with Gentiles in Antioch

Christian Origins (26-50 CE) (Louisville: Westminster John Knox, 2006), 157-61, although Crossley seems unduly skeptical of the accuracy of Luke's accounts of Gentiles attracted to the synagogues.

86. Rodney Stark, *Cites of God* (San Francisco: HarperSanFrancisco, 2006), 119-39. Against Malina and Pilch (*Letters of Paul*, 1-25), it is impossible to go along with their contention that Paul was an Israelite prophet sent to Israelites living among non-Israelites.

87. Jewett, *Romans*, 75; also Segal, *Paul the Convert*, 269-71.

88. Hengel and Schwemer, *Paul between Damascus and Antioch*, 107; similarly James D. G. Dunn, *The Parting of the Ways: Between Christianity and Judaism and Their Significance for the Character of Christianity* (London: SCM, 1991), 125-26; Segal, *Paul the Convert*, 269-70; Christopher Rowland, *Christian Origins* (London: SPCK, 1985), 216-17; Schnabel, *Early Christian Mission*, 2:1300-1301; Miller, "Jewish Context," 101-15; Reidar Hvalvik, "Paul as a Jewish Believer—according to the Book of Acts," in *Jewish Believers in Jesus: The Early Centuries*, ed. O. Skarsaune and R. Hvalvik (Peabody, MA: Hendrickson, 2007), 123-35.

and perhaps also in Corinth (if he visited there). The proselytizers in Galatia were Jewish Christ-believers concerned with bringing Paul's Gentile converts under the aegis of Torah. Paul paradoxically strove to provide an ideological justification for the separation of his Gentile-majority assemblies from the local synagogues, while simultaneously making exhortations to unity between Jewish and Gentile Christ-believers. We do not have a "Gentile mission" and a "Jewish mission" in the early churches; rather, we are confronted with a number of interlocking missions that included persons who worked evangelistically among Judean and Diasporan Jews, God-worshipers, and Greeks with competing views of the degree of adherence of Torah for Gentiles and the mode of social relations between believing Jews and believing non-Jews. The division of labor between Paul and Cephas in Gal 2:9 about the "circumcised" and "uncircumcised" was not absolute and implied emphases rather than strict boundaries, since it would have been impossible to definitively separate these two groups.[89] Thus, the Pauline mission, even in its mature form in the 50s, cannot be isolated from missionary activity among Jewish communities. Furthermore, we detected a development in Paul's missionary activities from (1) an early Jewish mission in Damascus, Arabia, and Jerusalem that might have featured some Gentiles in the mid-late 30s; (2) an ethnically mixed mission to Jews and Gentiles undertaken with Jewish Greek-speaking Christ-believers in Antioch, beginning with synagogues in Syria, Cyprus, and southern Asia Minor during 37-50 CE; and (3) a predominant Gentile mission independent of the Antiochene church in the 50s. A focus on the Gentiles in Paul's later missionary work was not a reaction to a failed Jewish mission; instead, it was attributable to the parting with the Antiochene church, where Paul attempted to move into a sphere where Jewish and Gentile divisions would be minimized, and to also move into new territories like Spain, where a negligible Jewish presence existed.

Conclusion

Martin Hengel wrote: "It was never possible to draw a neat division between mission to the Gentiles and mission to the Jews in the church."[90] I think this

---

89. See, e.g., Rowland, *Christian Origins*, 217; Ferdinand Hahn, *Mission in the New Testament* (SBT 37; London: SCM, 1965), 81; Günther Bornkamm, *Paul*, trans. D. M. G. Stalker (London: Hodder & Stoughton, 1971), 39-40.

90. Martin Hengel, *The Four Gospels and the One Gospel of Jesus Christ*, 154.

assertion is justified in light of the evidence set out above. Paul's conversion included a call to preach Jesus as the Son of God, Messiah, Image of God, and Lord of Glory. As far as we can tell, a missionary commission was attached to his conversion experience from the very beginning. However, only through the fallouts and the fruitfulness of his missionary work in Asia and the Aegean did it become apparent to Paul that his apostolic calling was to focus on non-Jews. We could summarize the evidence as follows.

First, the key terms that Paul uses to identify non-Jews like ἔθνος, Ἕλλην, ἀκροβυστία, and ἄνομος are plastic and flexible designations that can, under some circumstances, include Jews. That conclusion is supported by the fluid nature of these labels in sectarian contexts and the propensity of some ancient writers to embed religious meanings in ethnic labels.

Second, the Jews had a significant place in Paul's missionary work in both its early and its later stages.

1. The sources are ambiguous as to when Paul actually received his missionary call to go to the Gentiles. Solid evidence coordinated between the Pauline letters and Acts, however, indicates that Paul's time in Damascus, Arabia, and Jerusalem included preaching primarily, though maybe not exclusively, to Jews.

2. In association with the Antioch church, Paul started to engage in more concerted missionary activity orientated toward Gentiles in Syria, Cyprus, and Asia, but always beginning with Jewish synagogue communities.

3. The capitulation of the church of Antioch to pressure from the Jerusalem church to adopt a model of proselytism as a basis for table fellowship resulted in a split between Paul and others, with Paul retaining the "old Antioch" position. The subsequent result was that Paul focused thereafter more fully on Gentile converts and also attempted to socially insulate them from spheres of Jewish influence where they would not be pressured to judaize to the point of circumcision.

4. In the later stages of Paul's missionary work, where the call to the Gentiles finally worked itself out in mature form, Paul still saw the Jews as objects of his missionary preaching (1 Cor 9:20-23; 2 Cor 3:14-15; 4:3-6). He retained a belief in the necessity of a continued preaching mission to the Jews (Rom 10:14-21), and he knows of the church as made up of Jews and Gentiles who have been "called" and who "believe" (1 Cor 1:24; Rom 1:16; 9:24; 10:12-13).

Third, the portrait of Paul in Acts as ordinarily beginning his missionary ventures in the synagogues is historically authentic and socially plausible.

Finally, let me be clear about what I am saying and not saying. I am not advocating that Paul was apostle to the Jews in the same way that Peter was the apostle to the circumcision. I maintain that, during his Asian and Aegean missions, the Jews were a subset of Paul's apostolate because of their place *among* the ἔθνη and because of Paul's modus operandi of beginning with synagogue communities in the Diaspora. All of this is perhaps attributable to his intention to follow the missional script set out in Isa 66:19-20, which required heralding the good news to Jews and Gentiles among the nations. In which case, Paul's vocation to proclaim Christ Jesus to the ἔθνη was inexplicable and even impossible without some kind of missionary work among the Jews as well. While doors opened up among the Gentiles, they were never closed to the Jews. An anomalous aspect of Paul's career is that, even while he attempted to protect his Gentile converts from Jewish proselytism, he never ceased to proclaim Christ to his fellow Jews and persisted in seeking amicable relations with Jewish Christ-believing communities. Thus, I conclude that Luke and the early church's portrayal of Paul as the apostle to Gentiles *and to Jews* is essentially correct.

Appendix 1

Paul as Apostle to Nations/Gentiles, Greeks, and Uncircumcised/Lawless

Nations/Gentiles

Now I am speaking to you Gentiles. Inasmuch, then, as I am an apostle to the Gentiles. . . . (Rom 11:13)

Nevertheless on some points I have written to you rather boldly by way of reminder, because of the grace given me by God to be a minister of Christ Jesus to the Gentiles in the priestly service of the gospel of God, so that the offering of the Gentiles may be acceptable, sanctified by the Holy Spirit. (Rom 15:15-16)

For I will not venture to speak of anything except what Christ has accomplished through me to win obedience from the Gentiles. (Rom 15:18)

But we proclaim Christ crucified, a stumbling block to Jews and foolishness to Gentiles. (1 Cor 1:23)

God . . . reveal[ed] his Son in me, so that I might proclaim him among the Gentiles. (Gal 1:15-16)

Then I laid before them . . . the gospel that I proclaim among the Gentiles. (Gal 2:2)

See among the disputed Pauline letters: "a bond-servant of Christ on behalf of the Gentiles" (Eph 3:1); "This grace was given to me to preach to the Gentiles the boundless riches of Christ" (Eph 3:8); "I was appointed a herald and an apostle . . . a teacher of the Gentiles in faith and truth" (1 Tim 2:7).

Greeks

For I am not ashamed of the gospel; it is the power of God for salvation to everyone who has faith, to the Jew first and also to the Greek. (Rom 1:16)

But to those who are the called, both Jews and Greeks, Christ the power of God and the wisdom of God. (1 Cor 1:24)

Uncircumcised/Lawless

On the contrary, when they saw that I had been entrusted with the gospel for the uncircumcised, just as Peter had been entrusted with the gospel for the circumcised (for he who worked through Peter making him an apostle to the circumcised also worked through me in sending me to the Gentiles), and when James and Cephas and John, who were acknowledged pillars, recognized the grace that had been given to me, they gave to Barnabas and me the right hand of fellowship, agreeing that we should go to the Gentiles and they to the circumcised. (Gal 2:7-9)

To those outside the law I became as one outside the law. (1 Cor 9:21)

Appendix 2

NT Account of Paul's Revelation to Go to the Gentiles

1. An implication of his conversion but indeterminate as to whether he received the calling during his Christophany or discerned the reality of his calling only afterward:

    Gal 1:15-18

    15 But when God, who had set me apart before I was born and called me through his grace, was pleased 16 to reveal his Son to me, <u>so that I might proclaim him among the Gentiles,</u> I did not confer with any human being, 17 nor did I go up to Jerusalem to those who were already apostles before me, but I went away at once into Arabia, and afterward I returned to Damascus. 18 Then after three years I did go up to Jerusalem to visit Cephas and stayed with him fifteen days.

2. Given to him by Ananias in Damascus shortly after his Christophany:

    Acts 9:3-6, 13-16

    3 Now as he was going along and approaching Damascus, suddenly a light from heaven flashed around him. 4 He fell to the ground and heard a voice saying to him, "Saul, Saul, why do you persecute me?" 5 He asked, "Who are you, Lord?" The reply came, "I am Jesus, whom you are persecuting. 6 But get up and enter the city, and you will be told what you are to do." . . .

    13 But Ananias answered, "Lord, I have heard from many about this man, how much evil he has done to your saints in Jerusalem; 14 and here he has authority from the chief priests to bind all who invoke your name." 15 But the Lord said to him, "<u>Go, for he is an instrument whom I have chosen to bring my name before Gentiles and kings and before the people of Israel;</u> 16 I myself will show him how much he must suffer for the sake of my name."

3. Given to him during a revelation in the temple in Jerusalem during his first visit there after his conversion:

Acts 22:17-21

¹⁷ After I had returned to Jerusalem and while I was praying in the temple, I fell into a trance ¹⁸ and saw Jesus saying to me, "Hurry and get out of Jerusalem quickly, because they will not accept your testimony about me." ¹⁹ And I said, "Lord, they themselves know that in every synagogue I imprisoned and beat those who believed in you. ²⁰ And while the blood of your witness Stephen was shed, I myself was standing by, approving and keeping the coats of those who killed him." ²¹ Then he said to me, "<u>Go, for I will send you far away to the Gentiles.</u>"

4. Given to him during his Damascus road Christophany:

Acts 26:12-18

¹² With this in mind, I was traveling to Damascus with the authority and commission of the chief priests, ¹³ when at midday along the road, your Excellency, I saw a light from heaven, brighter than the sun, shining around me and my companions. ¹⁴ When we had all fallen to the ground, I heard a voice saying to me in the Hebrew language, "Saul, Saul, why are you persecuting me? It hurts you to kick against the goads." ¹⁵ I asked, "Who are you, Lord?" The Lord answered, "I am Jesus whom you are persecuting. ¹⁶ But get up and stand on your feet; for I have appeared to you for this purpose, to appoint you to serve and testify to the things in which you have seen me and to those in which I will appear to you. ¹⁷ <u>I will rescue you from your people and from the Gentiles—to whom I am sending you</u> ¹⁸ <u>to open their eyes so that they may turn from darkness to light and from the power of Satan to God, so that they may receive forgiveness of sins and a place among those who are sanctified by faith in me.</u>"

CHAPTER THREE

An Invasive Story: An Apocalyptic and
Salvation-Historical Rereading of Galatians

Since the mid-twentieth century a number of scholars have advanced an apocalyptic reading of Paul's letters, including Ernst Käsemann, J. C. Beker, Leander E. Keck, Marion L. Soards, J. Louis Martyn, Martinus de Boer, and Douglas Campbell.[1] On such a reading, Paul's gospel is said to be about God's liberating invasion of the cosmos, decisively revealed in the faithfulness, death, and resurrection of Jesus Christ, which wages a cosmic battle against the pow-

---

1. Ernst Käsemann, "The Beginnings of Christian Theology," 108-37; "On the Subject of Primitive Christian Apocalyptic," 138-67; and "'The Righteousness of God' in Paul," 168-82, in *New Testament Questions of Today*, trans. W. J. Montague (London: SCM, 1969); J. C. Beker, *Paul the Apostle: The Triumph of God in Life and Thought* (Philadelphia: Fortress, 1980); idem, *Paul's Apocalyptic Gospel: The Coming Triumph of God* (Philadelphia: Fortress, 1982); idem, *The Triumph of God: The Essence of Paul's Thought* (Minneapolis: Fortress, 1990); Leander Keck, "Paul and Apocalyptic Theology," *Int* 28 (1984): 229-41; Marion L. Soards, "Paul: Apostle and Apocalyptic Visionary," *BTB* 16 (1986): 148-50; J. Louis Martyn, "Apocalyptic Antinomies in Paul's Letter to the Galatians," *NTS* 31 (1985): 410-24, repr. in *Theological Issues in the Letters of Paul* (Nashville: Abingdon, 1997), 111-23; idem, "Events in Galatia: Modified Covenantal Nomism versus God's Invasion of the Cosmos in the Singular Gospel," in *Pauline Theology*, vol. 1, *Thessalonians, Philippians, Galatians, Philemon*, ed. J. M. Bassler (Minneapolis: Fortress, 1985), 160-79; idem, *Galatians: A New Translation, with Introduction and Commentary* (AB; New York: Doubleday, 1997); idem, "The Apocalyptic Gospel in Galatians," *Int* 54 (2000): 246-66; Douglas A. Campbell, *The Quest for Paul's Gospel: A Suggested Strategy* (London: T&T Clark, 2005), 56-68; idem, *The Deliverance of God: An Apocalyptic Rereading of Justification in Paul* (Grand Rapids, MI: Eerdmans, 2009), esp. 188-92; Martinus C. de Boer, "Paul and Apocalyptic Eschatology," in *Encyclopedia of Apocalypticism*, vol. 1, *The Origins of Apocalypticism in Judaism and Christianity*, ed. J. J. Collins (New York: T&T Clark, 1998), 345-83; idem, "Paul, Theologian of God's Apocalypse," *Int* 56 (2002): 21-33; idem, "Paul and Jewish Apocalyptic Eschatology," in *Apocalyptic and the New Testament: Essays in Honor of J. Louis Martyn*, ed. J. Marcus and M. L. Soards (JSNTSup 24; Sheffield: Sheffield Academic, 2003), 169-90; idem, *Galatians: A Commentary* (NTL; Louisville, KY: Westminster John Knox, 2011).

ers on the very site of Jesus' crucified body. The result is that, through Christ and the gift of the Spirit, there comes a whole new regime, a new creation. One remaining and protruding question, however, is how this "apocalyptic" Paul relates to Paul's apparent "salvation history," where Paul locates God's salvation in Jesus Christ as part of the wider story of God's saving acts in Israel's sacred history, leading up to the inclusion of the Gentiles in the people of God.[2]

This question was debated rather vigorously in a scholarly melee in the 1970s between Krister Stendahl and Ernst Käsemann over the place of salva-

---

2. We should note that English "apocalyptic" is an adjective that can describe a form of eschatology and a worldview, but generally it should not be regarded as a substantive noun, as opposed to the German *Apokalyptic*. P. D. Hanson ("Apocalypticism," in *IDBSup*, ed. K. Crim [Nashville: Abingdon, 1976], 29-30) famously distinguished apocalypse (a literary genre), apocalyptic eschatology (a religious worldview), and apocalypticism (a sociological movement). On the problem of definitions, see T. F. Glasson, "What Is Apocalyptic?," *NTS* 27 (1980): 98-105; Keck, "Paul and Apocalyptic Theology," 230-33; H. Moore, "The Problem of Apocalyptic as Evidenced in Recent Discussion," *IBS* 8 (1986): 76-91; idem, "Paul and Apocalyptic," *IBS* 9 (1987): 35-46; Robert L. Webb, "'Apocalyptic': Observations on a Slippery Term," *JNES* 49 (1990): 115-26; Scott M. Lewis, *"So That God May Be All in All": The Apocalyptic Message of 1 Corinthians 15,12-34* (Rome: Gregorian University Press, 1998), 52-123; R. E. Sturm, "Defining the Word 'Apocalyptic': A Problem in Biblical Criticism," in *Apocalyptic and the New Testament: Essays in Honor of J. Louis Martyn*, ed. J. Marcus and M. L. Soards (JSNTSup 24; Sheffield: Sheffield Academic, 2003), 17-48; Jörg Frey, "Zur Bedeutung der Qumrantexte für das Verständnis der Apokalyptik im Früh-judentum und im Urchristentum," in *Apokalyptik und Qumran,* ed. Jörg Frey and Michael Becker (Einblicke 6; Paderborn: Bonifatius, 2007), 11-62. R. Barry Matlock (*Unveiling the Apocalyptic Paul: Paul's Interpreters and the Rhetoric of Criticism* [JSNTSup 127; Sheffield: Sheffield Academic, 1996]) notes the near nebulous way that "apocalyptic" is used and how it is theologically freighted in Pauline scholarship. N. T. Wright (*Paul and His Recent Interpreters* [London: SPCK, 2015], 141) opines that often the word "apocalyptic" is "reduced to a loose, generalized, arm-waving adjective, introduced into sentences to suggest a vague atmosphere of 'cosmic' significance rather than merely private or personal relevance." On "salvation history" in relation to Pauline studies, see Robert W. Yarbrough, "Paul and Salvation History," in *Justification and Variegated Nomism,* vol. 2, *The Paradoxes of Paul*, ed. D. A. Carson, P. T. O'Brien, and M. A. Seifrid (Grand Rapids, MI: Baker Academic, 2004), 297-342; idem, "Salvation History (*Heilsgeschichte*) and Paul," in *Studies in the Pauline Epistle,* ed. M. S. Harmon and J. E. Smith (FS Douglas J. Moo; Grand Rapids, MI: Zondervan, 2014), 181-98; James Kelhoffer, "The Struggle to Define *Heilsgeschichte*: Paul on the Origins of the Christian Tradition," *BR* 48 (2003): 66-67, repr. in *Concepts of "Gospel" and Legitimacy in Early Christianity* (WUNT 324; Tübingen: Mohr Siebeck, 2014), 97-120. Robin Scroggs ("Salvation History: The Theological Structure of Paul's Thought [1 Thessalonians, Philippians, and Galatians]," in *Pauline Theology,* vol. 1, *Thessalonians, Philippians, Galatians, Philemon*, ed. J. M. Bassler [Minneapolis: Fortress, 1991], 215) defines Pauline salvation history as follows: "Paul is conscious of being a part of an ongoing story in which God, the central actor, relates to a people with an ultimate aim."

tion history in general and Israel in particular within Paul's theology. Stendahl contended that salvation history—an interlocking destiny between Israel and the Gentiles—was the core of Paul's theology, with justification by faith as no more than Paul's apologetic argument for the inclusion of Gentiles in the church.[3] In response, Käsemann identified in Paul's letters "the relics of apocalyptic theology,"[4] seen principally in his anticipation of Christ's parousia.[5] This apocalyptic theology becomes central in Käsemann's reading of Paul, for whom "apocalyptic was the mother of all Christian theology" and "apocalyptic is the driving force in Paul's theology and practice."[6]

Käsemann accepted the validity of salvation history as forming the horizon of Pauline theology, for it provided the spatial and temporal frontiers that divide off the cosmic spheres of power that led from creation to consummation by way of the Abrahamic promise and the election of Israel. But Paul was not interested in a continuous stream of history or the progress of evolutionary forces, since humanity remains trapped in a dialectic struggle between two realms: Adam and Christ, death and life, sin and salvation, law and gospel. A genuine salvation history is the story of the struggle to live with this tension, even in light of the revelation of God's eschatological saving power.[7] As

---

3. Krister Stendahl, "The Apostle Paul and the Introspective Conscience of the West," *HTR* 56 (1963): 199-215, repr. in *Paul among Jews and Gentiles* (London: SCM, 1976), 78-96; Ernst Käsemann, "Justification and Salvation History in the Epistle to the Romans," in *Perspectives on Paul* (London: SCM, 1971), 60-78. See reflections on the debate by N. T. Wright, "The Paul of History and the Apostle of Faith," *TynB* 29 (1978): 61-99, and on Stendahl in particular by Campbell, *Deliverance of God*, 172-76.

4. Käsemann, "Primitive Christian Apocalyptic," 131.

5. On what constitutes "apocalyptic," Käsemann wrote: "I speak of primitive Christian apocalyptic to denote the expectation of an imminent Parousia," and the "apocalyptic context" of the "primitive Easter kerygma" is the belief that "the return of Jesus in the role of the heavenly Son of Man is indeed the central hope which the original disciples derived from the Easter experience and constitutes, as such, their own peculiar Easter faith" ("Primitive Christian Apocalyptic," 109n1, 114 and 127, 134). Elsewhere: "The heart of primitive Christian apocalyptic, according to the Revelation and the Synoptists alike, is the accession to the throne of heaven by God and by his Christ as the eschatological Son of Man—an event which can also be characterized as proof of the righteousness of God. . . . God's justice done on and to our earth is here no longer a matter for the remote future, although it will not be universally revealed until the Parousia. . . . The central move [in New Testament apocalyptic] was in fact the hope of the manifestation of the Son of Man on his way to his enthronement" ("Beginnings of Christian Theology," 105, 107).

6. Käsemann, "Beginnings of Christian Theology," 102; idem, "Primitive Christian Apocalyptic," 137; idem, *Romans*, 136.

7. Käsemann, "Justification and Salvation History," 64, 66-68.

a result, the history of God's promise from primordial creation to Christ's parousia is not the content of theology; instead, the center of Paul's theology is the eschatological power of God breaking in upon the world in Christ and leaving humanity facing the paradoxes of life and death, liberation and slavery.[8] Furthermore, Käsemann believed that making salvation history the center of Paul's thought compromised the basis of justification, namely, the *theologia crucis,* and would lead to philosophies of history used to underwrite a triumphalistic political eschatology, as it did in Nazi Germany.[9] Viewed this way, Käsemann was consciously building on Albert Schweitzer and Karl Barth, who each argued in their own way for a "thoroughgoing eschatology" in the teaching of Jesus and as a key principle of New Testament interpretation.[10]

J. C. Beker, largely following Käsemann's lead, located Paul's apocalypticism not simply in hope for a messianic parousia, though it was part of it, as much as in the meaning of Jesus' messianic death and resurrection. Accordingly, "The coherent center of Paul's gospel is constituted by his apocalyptic interpretation of the Christ-event."[11] Beker regarded the church as the "avant-garde of the new creation in a hostile world, creating beachheads in this world of God's dawning new world and yearning for the day of God's visible lordship over creation, the resurrection of the dead."[12] Beker was also crucially aware of the danger of collapsing the apocalyptic triumph of God into Christology, a virtual Christomonism, since it would deprive the gospel of its future dimension and also spiritualize the promises given to Israel.[13] Beker was careful not to burn bridges of prophetic promises upon which his apocalyptic Paul walked.[14]

J. Louis Martyn followed Käsemann and Beker by situating Paul in apocalyptic coordinates, but Martyn also set the apocalyptic scheme in sharp antith-

---

8. N. T. Wright ("A New Perspective on Käsemann? Apocalyptic, Covenant, and the Righteousness of God," in *Studies in the Pauline Epistles,* ed. M. S. Harmon and J. E. Smith [FS Douglas J. Moo; Grand Rapids, MI: Zondervan, 2014], 243-58) attempts to show how Käsemann still regarded covenant as the backdrop to God's saving righteousness.

9. See esp. Käsemann's articles "The Beginnings of Christian Theology," "On the Subject of Primitive Christian Apocalyptic," and "'The Righteousness of God' in Paul." Note in particular the description and assessment of Käsemann's work in Matlock, *Unveiling the Apocalyptic Paul,* 186-246; Campbell, *Deliverance of God,* 189; and Wright, *Paul and His Recent Interpreters,* 145-50.

10. Note Käsemann's remarks about Schweitzer and Barth in "Primitive Christian Apocalyptic," 109n2, 113.

11. Beker, *Paul the Apostle,* 135.

12. Beker, *Apocalyptic Gospel,* 108-9.

13. Beker, *Paul the Apostle,* 355.

14. See esp. Beker, *Paul the Apostle,* 314.

esis to the entire notion of salvation history.[15] So much so that Martyn even complains that "Paul has been credited with perspectives [i.e., salvation history] proper to the theologians against whom he wages a *life-and-death battle* [i.e., the intruders in Galatia]."[16] According to Martyn, Paul's negations of pairs of opposites like circumcision and uncircumcision (Gal 3:28; 1 Cor 7:19) is an appropriation of "antinomy," which was an ancient perspective that viewed the universe as composed of a constellation of binary opposites fundamental to its structure. Paul, in Martyn's estimation, argues that these binary structures are gone, vanquished by the crucifixion of Christ, which means the death of the cosmos of religion, and the old polarity is replaced by a new unity in Christ. In the aftermath, a new polarity emerges between the old age and the coming age, with a new set of antinomies consisting of Spirit versus flesh and Christ versus law.[17] Martyn sees a salvation history as introduced by the intruding "teachers" in Galatia, who tell the Gentile believers that they can move toward God by law observance. In contrast, Paul says that God has moved, even invaded, the cosmos by sending Christ. Paul's gospel is an evangelical, cosmic, history-creating Christology that fosters an antinomy between law observance and the faithful death of Christ. For Paul, there is no linearity between salvation history and gospel because (1) Paul removes the law from the sphere of the Abrahamic promise, divorcing the law from its own narrative context; (2) although those in Christ receive Abrahamic sonship, it is secondary to receiving divine sonship; (3) by referring to the Abrahamic promise as made to the singular "seed" (i.e., Christ), Paul bypasses Israel's covenant history and places the promise in a type of "covenantal docetism"; and (4) the coming of Christ brings about the death of the cosmos, not the renewal of Israel's covenant, and Paul gives no role to

15. I think it worth noting that both Käsemann and Beker were more sympathetic to salvation history than many of their subsequent colleagues. Campbell (*Quest*, 38n16) regards Käsemann as someone who attempted to modify the salvation-historical model by taking it in an apocalyptic direction. Martyn ("Events in Galatia," 172n27; idem, *Theological Issues*, 176-81) thinks that Beker had an "admirable concentration on apocalyptic," while giving "a remarkable role to *Heilsgeschichte*." Matlock (*Unveiling the Apocalyptic Paul*, 302) considers Beker to be "something like a Käsemann who has softened considerably toward Cullmann [i.e., salvation history]." Bruce L. Longenecker (*The Triumph of Abraham's God: The Transformation of Identity in Galatians* [Edinburgh: T&T Clark, 1998], 9) notes how, in Beker's work, "Paul's apocalyptic worldview presupposes a covenant relationship between God and God's people Israel. The future triumph of God is the time in which God's covenant faithfulness to Israel will be vindicated."

16. Martyn, *Galatians*, 347 (italics added).

17. Martyn, *Theological Issues*, 111-23, 161-75; idem, *Galatians*, 570-74; idem, "Apocalyptic Gospel in Galatians," 254-59.

Israel in God's cosmic rescue. In other words, there is no *praeparatio evangelica* in the history of Israel, for Christ comes not into the context of Israel's saving history but into the epoch of Israel's slavery under the law. Martyn writes: "Indeed, one has to say that *throughout* Galatians, far from proposing a linear history that begins with Abraham, Paul stands in opposition to such a view. Given the work of the Teachers, Paul's insistence on the singularity of the gospel has necessarily to be anti-*heilsgeschichte*."[18]

More recently, Douglas Campbell has provided a further critique of the salvation-historical approach by emphasizing that salvation history is not really a soteriology but merely an account of history from a particular salvific perspective. He wishes to accommodate salvation-historical concerns, but he maintains that salvation history inevitably places the determinative emphasis on Paul's Jewish background rather than upon Paul's Christian experience, and salvation history can easily lend itself to a supersessionist view of Israel.[19] What is needed, instead, is an account of how Paul's worldview de-

18. Martyn, "Events in Galatians," 160-79 (quote from 176, italics original); idem, *Theological Issues*, 168-70; idem, *Galatians*, 302-6, 343-52. See similarly Beverly Roberts Gaventa, "The Singularity of the Gospel: A Reading of Galatians," in *Pauline Theology*, vol. 1, *Thessalonians, Philippians, Galatians, Philemon*, ed. J. M. Bassler (Minneapolis: Fortress, 1985), 147-59. John M. G. Barclay ("Paul's Story: Theology as Testimony," in *Narrative Dynamics in Paul: A Critical Assessment*, ed. B. W. Longenecker [Louisville: Westminster John Knox, 2002], 154-55), in Käsemannesque fashion, thinks that Israel's history and Paul's own story are reconstituted by "grace-shaped stories," which speak to God's justification of the ungodly. "In other words, 'justification' and 'salvation history' cannot be played off against one another: the justification of the ungodly, the gift of life to the dead, or hope to the despairing (in short grace) is what constitutes 'salvation history,' which cannot be detected other than by this criterion." Even so, Barclay adds that Paul "does not trace linear lines through historical processes of human continuities: indeed, the justification of the ungodly is more likely to proceed through paradox, surprise, and the breaking of human connection. Just as Paul sees no humanly visible line of continuity through his own life, but rather an interruption, when the 'I' is overwhelmed by the agency of God (or Christ), he finds no line linking Abraham to the present except that of the faithfulness of God."

19. Campbell (*Quest*, 37-38) says that the salvation-historical approach "tends to elevate historical Israel into something of a sacred nation or people, privileged and chosen by God. It is some variant of this sort that informs the preparatory Jewish phase in the SH [salvation history] model." While Campbell is genuinely concerned that the salvation-historical model turns Israel into a kind of vehicle for the gospel and then villain for rejecting the gospel, his own approach nonetheless explicitly denies what Scripture claims for Israel: they are an elect nation. Campbell is more positive on salvation history later (*Quest*, 133) in stating: "The fundamental *continuity* between Christianity and pre-Christian Judaism, encompassing its people, its history, and its scriptures, is a standard and non-negotiable feature of Christianity. It has been woven into the movement's warp and woof from its inception. Marcion went too far. *Some*

lineates a class of two ages cutting across space and time, incorporating both termination and reconstitution in a christological soteriology. Continuities are created by the Spirit, not the story of Israel.[20]

On the other side of the ledger, scholars such as N. T. Wright, James D. G. Dunn, Bruce Longenecker, Ben Witherington, and Richard Hays have attempted to demonstrate the unity of the apocalyptic and salvation-historical (or "covenantal," to use an alternative term) elements of Paul's theology. They proceed by drawing attention to the storied nature of Paul's theology in a way that remains married to his apocalyptic worldview rather than operating against it.[21] Such scholars contend, therefore, that there is no dichotomy between an apocalyptic and covenantal reading of Paul. Here I quote Wright in extenso:

> My opposition is not to the idea of Paul as an "apocalyptic" theologian. My objection is to the use of that word to suggest a theological position, or rather, a bewildering range of such positions, which can then be used as Procrustean beds to stop Paul saying several things which he, in line with many actual "apocalypses," really does say. I too see Paul within a historically describable "apocalyptic" framework, that of the second-

---

continuity must be affirmed. But merely affirming continuity is not enough, because the actual history of that continuity contains significant *discontinuities*" (italics original).

20. Campbell, *Quest*, 4, 27, 36-38, 62, 64, 67; idem, *Deliverance of God*, 188-92.

21. See, e.g., James D. G. Dunn, "How New Was Paul's Gospel? The Problem of Continuity and Discontinuity," in *Gospel in Paul: Studies on Corinthians, Galatians, and Romans*, ed. L. Anne Jervis and Peter Richardson (FS R. N. Longenecker; JSNTSup Sheffield: Sheffield Academic, 1994), 367-88, repr. in *The New Perspective on Paul* (rev. ed.; Grand Rapids, MI: Eerdmans, 2008), 247-64 (subsequent citations are from *New Perspective on Paul*); Bruce L. Longenecker, *The Triumph of Abraham's God: The Transformation of Identity in Galatians* (Edinburgh: T&T Clark, 1998); Ben Witherington III, *Paul's Narrative Thought World: The Tapestry of Tragedy and Triumph* (Louisville: Westminster John Knox, 1994); N. T. Wright, *The Climax of the Covenant: Christ and the Law in Pauline Theology* (Edinburgh: T&T Clark, 1991); idem, *Paul: In Fresh Perspective* (Minneapolis: Fortress, 2005), 40-58; idem, *Paul and the Faithfulness of God* (COQG 4; London: SPCK, 2013), esp. 39-40, 1071-73, 1512-13; idem, *Paul and His Recent Interpreters* (London: SPCK, 2014), 135-218; idem, *The Paul Debate* (Waco, TX: Baylor University Press, 2015), 45-64; Richard Hays, *Echoes of Scripture in the Letters of Paul* (New Haven: Yale University Press, 1989); idem, "Crucified with Christ: A Synthesis of the Theology of 1 and 2 Thessalonians, Philemon, Philippians, and Galatians," in *Pauline Theology*, vol. 1, *Thessalonians, Philippians Galatians, Philemon*, ed. J. M. Bassler (Minneapolis: Fortress, 1985), 227-46; idem, *The Faith of Jesus Christ: The Narrative Substructure of Galatians 3:1–4:11* (2nd ed.; Grand Rapids, MI: Eerdmans, 2002), esp. introduction of the second edition (pp. xxi-lii); idem, "Is Paul's Gospel Narratable?," *JSNT* 27 (2004): 217-39.

Temple Jewish world, rethought in his case around the Messiah and the spirit. I too see the heart of his gospel as the message that, in Jesus, the one God has acted dramatically and decisively to overthrow the rule of the "powers" and to liberate humans, and the world, from their grip. I, too, stress that for Paul the world's true plight is itself revealed in the gospel, and is revealed, moreover, as rendering humans, even the Jewish humans blessed by God's gift of Torah, radically incapable of initiating their own salvation and hence utterly dependent on the free gift of divine grace. I, too, stress that Paul believed that the "age to come" had been inaugurated with the death and resurrection of Jesus, and that it would be completed in the events written about in Romans 8 and 1 Corinthians 15. I, too, insist that all this generates, for Paul, a new mode of knowing (as in passages like 2 Cor 5.16-17 and Galatians 4.9), a mode which with only a slight stretch can be appropriately labelled an "apocalyptic epistemology." But these accumulated points do not work in the way that so many have supposed. This "apocalyptic" does not eliminate an emphasis on "sins," on atonement, on forgiveness; it rather embraces it. It does not rule out, but rather leads us to expect, an emphasis on the long, dark history of Israel, and on the divine purpose at work behind the scenes, not as an immanent process or progressive development but as part of the sovereignty of the creator God, bringing about the final great moment of judgment and mercy. It does not rule out, but indeed it insists upon, the larger context of the covenant: the covenant with Abraham which God has at last fulfilled, the covenant redefined around the Messiah, through whom the promises have been extended into the whole world, the covenant faithfulness of God which is both apart from Torah and yet witnessed to by Torah and prophets.[22]

In light of such responses, my aim in this chapter is to engage Martyn's apocalyptic interpretation of Paul by an examination of its claim to represent an apocalyptic perspective through a fresh reading of Galatians. My contention is that the dichotomy between salvation history and apocalyptic

---

22. Wright, *Paul and His Recent Interpreters,* 217-18 (italics original). See responses to Wright on this point by Martinus C. de Boer, "N. T. Wright's Great Story and Its Relationship to Paul's Gospel," *JSPL* 4 (2014): 49-57; Jörg Frey, "Demythologizing Apocalyptic? On N. T. Wright's 'Paul, Apocalyptic Interpretation, and the Constraints of Construction,'" in *God and the Faithfulness of Paul: A Critical Examination of the Pauline Theology of N. T. Wright,* ed. M. F. Bird, C. Heilig, and J. T. Hewitt (Tübingen: Mohr Siebeck, 2015), 334-76; and John M. G. Barclay, "Review," *SJT* 68 (2015): 235-43.

is needless. On the one hand, there can be no muting of the apocalyptic chords that play in Paul's theological symphony in Galatians.[23] The notes are played too loudly in a repertoire of motifs, including two ages, spatial and ethical dualism, determinism, angelic activity, anthropological pessimism, cosmic upheaval, anticipations of wide-scale apostasy, and ascents to heaven, found across 1 Thessalonians through to Romans.[24] On the other hand, Paul's apocalypticism does not create a cacophony of noises altogether dissonant from the story of Israel's Scriptures and its covenantal promises. The invasive action of God declared in the gospel still stands within a promise-fulfillment scheme that Paul frequently utilizes in his theological discourse. There is no requirement that we divorce Paul's apocalyptic theology from its metanarrative in the Jewish Scriptures. So, in the end, I hope to demonstrate another of the anomalous aspects of Paul's thinking, namely, how Paul's gospel both resolutely affirms and yet radically reshapes contemporary narrations of the story of Israel.

The Problem with "Apocalyptic" in the Apocalyptic Paul

The first task is to examine the understanding of "apocalyptic" that many interpreters are utilizing in their reading of Paul.[25] What emerges is that the apocalyptic reading of Paul seems to be more of a theological protest or a Barthian theological project than a contextual reading of Paul beside Jewish apocalypses.[26] While the sense of newness or even invasion in Paul's gospel

23. Campbell (*Quest*, 62) calls the apocalyptic approach a "symbolic orchestration" and an "opera."

24. See esp. Frey, "Demythologizing Apocalyptic?," 365-67. For a catalog of apocalyptic expressions and motifs in Galatians, see Martyn, *Galatians*, 97-104, and Richard B. Hays, "Apocalyptic *Poiēsis* in Galatians: Paternity, Passion, and Participation," in *Galatians and Christian Theology: Justification, the Gospel, and Ethics in Paul's Letter*, ed. M. W. Elliott, S. J. Hafemann, N. T. Wright, and J. Frederick (Grand Rapids, MI: Baker Academic, 2014), 206-9. Robert G. Hall, "Arguing Like an Apocalypse: Galatians and an Ancient *Topos* outside the Greco-Roman Rhetorical Tradition," *NTS* 42 (1996): 434-53, identifies various apocalyptic topoi in Galatians, including Paul's claim to divine inspiration, his revealing the spheres of righteousness and wickedness, urging readers to cleave to the righteous realm, and exhorting the audience to choose his perspective, all of which resonate with apocalyptic rhetoric.

25. Martyn (*Galatians*, 96n47) says: "I use the term 'apocalyptic' to refer to a theological pattern of thought, not to a literary genre."

26. For an in-house Barthian evaluation of Martyn's Barthian reading, see Bruce McCormack's "Can We Still Speak of Justification by Faith? An In-House Debate with Apocalyptic

is quite right, the precise standpoint being advocated does not seem to reflect actual Second Temple texts.[27]

The dislocation of Israel's story from the story of Paul's apocalyptic gospel first found traction with Karl Barth, who advocated a rather brutal punctiliar antihistory in his Romans commentary. Then in *Church Dogmatics*, Barth argued that believers enter into the salvation history of Jesus and not, by implication, into Israel's own covenantal history.[28] Barth sets up a duality between religion and revelation, seen most explicitly in his program labeled "The Revelation of God as the Abolition of Religion."[29] For Barth, the error of modern theology is that it is not the religion of revelation but has morphed into the revelation of religion. By such a misstep, the church risks forfeiting that which makes its own religion unique, namely, the lordship of Jesus Christ.[30] An analogous perspective was pursued in the theological exegesis of Käsemann, who relegated Israel to a living parable of religious humanity. The result was that Paul strikes against the hidden Jew inhabiting

---

Readings of Paul," in *Galatians and Christian Theology: Justification, the Gospel, and Ethics in Paul's Letter*, ed. M. W. Elliott, S. J. Hafemann, N. T. Wright, and J. Frederick (Grand Rapids, MI: Baker Academic, 2014), 158-84. McCormack believes that Barth (at one time) and Martyn have the same problem, with "no way to explain the relation of the divine action to human action, and therefore no way to explain how one man's death could be the act of God that triumphs over sin, death, and the devil" (179). Edwin Christian van Driel ("Christ in Paul's Narrative: Salvation History, Apocalyptic Invasion, and Supralapsarian Theology," in *Galatians and Christian Theology*, ed. M. W. Elliott et al. [Grand Rapids, MI: Baker Academic, 2014], 230-38) regards the "covenantal" and "apocalyptic" schemes as christologically deficient in that they both make the advent of Christ a kind of Plan B. In addition, it should be recognized that the work of Douglas Campbell (*Deliverance of God*, xxiv-xxvii) is Barthian as interpreted through a Torrancian and Trinitarian lens! On Campbell, see Wright, *Paul and His Recent Interpreters*, 187-215. To be fair, in the case of Martinus de Boer, he might have inherited a double portion of the Barthian spirit from Martyn, seen in his dogged insistence that *pistis* in Galatians almost always refers to Christ's own faithfulness (see de Boer, *Galatians*, 148-50, 192-93); to his credit, however, de Boer genuinely strives to read Paul beside other Jewish apocalypses.

27. Wright, *Paul and the Faithfulness of God*, 781.

28. See, e.g., Karl Barth, *CD*, ed. G. W. Bromiley and T. F. Torrance; trans. G. W. Bromiley et al. (4 vols.; Edinburgh: T&T Clark, 1975), 4/4:1-30. On Barth and the "apocalyptic" school of Pauline studies, see Douglas K. Harink, *Paul among the Postliberals: Pauline Theology beyond Christendom and Modernity* (Grand Rapids, MI: Brazos, 2003); idem, "Paul and Israel: An Apocalyptic Reading," *Pro Ecclesia* 16 (2007): 359-80; Benjamin Myers, "From Faithfulness to Faith in the Theology of Karl Barth," in *The Faith of Jesus Christ: Exegetical, Biblical, and Theological Studies*, ed. M. F. Bird and P. M. Sprinkle (Milton Keynes, UK: Paternoster, 2009), 291-308.

29. Barth, *CD* 1/2:280-361.

30. Barth, *CD* 1/2:284, 294.

every person who still clings to his or her religion rather than to the gift of Christ's lordship.[31]

Martyn basically takes a hybrid approach combining Barth and Käsemann, with a pinch of Beker, to claim that Paul stands over and against the religion of his proselytizing opponents, including the religion of Israel, with its Torah and covenants. Martyn's Paul "is not a covenantal theologian."[32] And this is where things get, in a manner of speaking, very interesting. In Martyn's account, the divine promises are given to Abraham but leap over Israel and forward to Abraham's seed, Christ. In the period of the law there was no seed of Abraham. Paul is driven to this position by refuting the Galatian intruders who want to add the Gentiles to Israel, and Paul's response is to deny that the covenant at Sinai was a divine act of electing a people. While Paul rescinds such a shocking view in Romans, in Galatians itself, Paul gives his readers no reason to believe in the divine election of the ancient people of Israel.[33] Martyn's claim here is controversial, since at stake is the question of whether Israel and its covenant history are in any way redemptive.[34]

The immediate problem I have is that, even if such a view of Israel's election were true, it would at best be described as christological rather than apocalyptic. It is difficult to imagine how viewing neither the Sinai covenant nor the giving of the law as part of God's electing purposes can be mapped upon Jewish apocalyptic literature and the praxis of the communities behind this literature. These writings do not deal with a human predicament and divine solution but, more properly, with Israel's plight and the divine covenantal solution.[35] In Jewish and Christian apocalypses, Israel's problem is recast and the solution redrawn, but Israel's election is never nullified and, more often than not, is intensified in opposition to pagan kingdoms and the apostate. None of the seers, as far as I can tell, deny Israel's election; but who really, truly, and rightly belongs in Israel? Well, that was another question. Moreover, much of apocalyptic literature seems to put forward a view that amounts to *extra Israel nulla salus* (without Israel there is no salvation), because Israel was central to

31. Käsemann, "The Righteousness of God in Paul," 178-81; idem, "Paul and Israel," 183-87.

32. Martyn, "Events in Galatia," 179.

33. Martyn, "Events in Galatia," 172; idem, *Galatians*, 349-52; idem, *Theological Issues*, 161-75.

34. Or as Longenecker (*Triumph of Abraham's God*, 89) asks: "What views did Paul hold in Galatians concerning the history and people of Israel, in relation to God's eschatological activity in Christ?"

35. Wright, *Paul and His Recent Interpreters*, 162-63.

God's plan. That is because apocalyptic literature is intensely intertextual; it re-tells Israel's story, affirming that story as intrinsic to the drama of redemption. The seers who wrote the apocalypses were convinced that Israel's traditions could be rehearsed and reinterpreted in such a way as to imagine, however diversely or strangely, Israel's scriptural hopes coming to a dramatic and cosmic fulfillment. The reinterpretation of prophetic visions and the reapplication of biblical types was the enduring strength of the apocalyptic tradition as it freshly imagined Israel coming safely through a sociopolitical catastrophe into a new world.[36]

An apocalypse, generically categorized, fits somewhere between mysticism and midrash as it creatively ponders Israel's experiences, hopes, and sacred literature and on that basis imagines a future redemption. For D. S. Russell, the heart of Jewish apocalyptic writings is imagining what the long story of Israel will look like when it finally reaches its climactic goal. He states: "Book after book throbs with the passionate conviction that all that God has promised would surely come to pass. The promises made to Israel by his servants the prophets must have meaning and reality and would ultimately be fulfilled. These promises declare that God would save his people and make them great among the Gentiles. . . . God would vindicate his people once and for all and bring to its consummation his purpose and plan for all the ages."[37] Though Jewish apocalypses are concerned very much with the "end," they are no less interested in "the beginning" as well. They trace back to primeval moments of creation the very inception of a salvation history, which gives indications of the nature and timing of the final acts of human history.[38] In many ways their concern is theodicy, the triumph of God over the evil empires and pagan persecution of faithful Israel.[39] The periodizing of history so typical of apocalyptic literature puts history into its proper framework and shows how the past prepares for what will be, for many, an unexpected future as a way of answering the theological problem of a dark and dismal present for God's

---

36. Gerhard von Rad, *Theologie des Alten Testaments* (2 vols.; Munich: Kaiser, 1961), 2:321: "Überhaupt wird man die geistige Leistung der Apokalyptiker ziemlich erschöpfend mit dem Begriff 'interpretation' umschreiben können."

37. D. S. Russell, *The Method and Message of Jewish Apocalyptic* (OTL; Philadelphia: Westminster, 1976), 18.

38. See, e.g., Jub. 1.26-29; 4 Ezra 3.1-36; 14.1-17.

39. See, similarly, John Anthony Dunne, "Suffering and Covenantal Hope in Galatians: A Critique of the 'Apocalyptic Reading' and Its Proponents," *SJT* 68 (2015): 1-14, who points out how Martyn and de Boer do not identify how the themes of suffering and persecution in Galatians resonate with apocalyptic literature.

faithful people.[40] As Jörg Frey notes: "Apocalyptic thought is basically a reac-

40. Ethelbert Stauffer (*New Testament Theology,* trans. J. Marsh [London: SCM, 1955], 19) writes that, in Jewish apocalyptic literature, "Salvation-history is thus the clue to human history, and human history in turn the clue to cosmic history, embracing heaven and earth and beasts and stars—'universal history' as we might put it in a word. But universal history has all the marks of a conflict. Its main theme is the dramatic conflict between the *civitas dei* and the *civitas diabolic,* from the primeval times right through to the end." Dunn ("How New Was Paul's Gospel?," 260) comments: "The point, of course, is that such Jews, in embracing an apocalyptic perspective, were not thereby abandoning a salvation-historical perspective, they were not denying their heritage as Israelites. On the contrary, an apocalypse was itself a way of reaffirming the continuity of the past with the future as both God's. To be sure, the group whose perspective came to expression in an apocalypse evidently felt itself isolated and under severe threat; it saw itself as the prey of evil powers. The characteristically dualistic pessimism of the apocalyptic perspective with regard to the present age was itself an expression of the pressure under which such groups found themselves. But fundamental to the same perspective was the claim of the apocalypticists, and those whom they represented, to embody *in themselves* the continuity of God's saving purpose from the past into the future. . . . In short, an apocalyptic perspective was a way of affirming salvation-history continuity when the faithful were suffering persecution and could see no other way for the covenant and its promises to be sustained" (italics original). Keck ("Paul and Apocalyptic Theology," 233) argues that Jewish apocalyptic theology was a "radical theology" that emerged from covenant theology to deal with the problem of theodicy. Rowland (*Open Heaven,* 30, 38) notes how apocalyptic eschatology does not depart "from the view of God's covenant" and exhibits "a view of the future which stresses the outworking of God's purposes within history." Longenecker (*Triumph of Israel's God,* 9) comments that "the expectation that God would ultimately act to set things right for Israel was rife and commonplace, as prophetic, apocalyptic, and Jewish sectarian material demonstrates well." According to David Starling (*Not My People: Gentiles as Exiles in Pauline Hermeneutics* [BZNW 184; Berlin: Walter de Gruyter, 2011], 209): "The first step to understanding the relationship between salvation history and apocalyptic in Paul's letters is the recognition that the dichotomy between them is an artificial one: apocalyptic itself is a form of salvation history. In the literature of Second Temple Judaism, apocalyptic is a particular form that salvation history takes when the blackness of the present is understood to be so thick that God's purpose can neither be perceived nor fulfilled without a new and divine intervention in both revelation and salvation." Also Frey ("Demythologizing Apocalyptic, 367-68) notes the tension between continuity and discontinuity in apocalyptic texts: "It is true that apocalyptic texts can only phrase their hope for a new saving intervention of God by an (explicit or implicit) reference to the power of the creator and heavenly king, to former experiences confirming the trust in him or at least in his power to defend his creational order against all violators and enemies. But it should likewise be considered that, in an awareness of covenant and election, a situation of suffering from foreign enemies or even wicked Israelites, or the perception of injustice and corruption in the world could become so severe that the hope for a mere restoration could appear insufficient and a much more radical, unprecedented intervention was imagined." Particularly important is Loren T. Stuckenbruck, "Overlapping Ages at Qumran and 'Apocalyptic' in Pauline Theology," in *The Dead Sea Scrolls and Pauline Literature,* ed. Jean-Sébastien Rey (STDJ 102; Leiden: Brill, 2013), 309-26; idem, "Posturing

tion to that experience of tension, related to the faithfulness of God or to the belief that God still reigns, but longing for a new act of deliverance—a purified, renewed, or even 'freshly' created world, proportional to the insight into the depth of corruption of the present world."[41]

Furthermore, the "revealed history" that permeates apocalyptic literature takes temporal events—past, present, and future—and couches them within a panoramic sociopolitical cosmology, often layered with cryptic symbolism, where heavenly realities stand behind prior and present events, and insight into this metareality is given only to a privileged few.[42] What is "new" is epistemology, an ability to perceive otherwise hidden realities thanks to otherworldly journeys, not a complete disjunction to what has preceded the new unveiling.[43] To give two examples, both Jubilees and 4 Ezra belong to the genre of apocalyptic literature, but they both rehearse the story of Israel and situate it in a cosmic history of God's triumph over the forces of evil.[44] Properly understood, an apocalypse is the climax of God's saving purpose for his people, not a whole new start, and certainly not a repudiation of the past.[45]

'Apocalyptic' in Pauline Theology: How Much Contrast with Jewish Tradition?," in *The Myth of Rebellious Angels: Studies in Second Temple Judaism and New Testament Texts* (WUNT 335; Tübingen: Mohr Siebeck, 2014), 240-56, whose work demonstrates that an understanding of time was highly complex in Jewish thought and that Second Temple Jewish authors envisioned more continuity between the ages than is often assumed (my thanks to Jason Maston for pointing to Stuckenbruck's work).

41. Frey, "Demythologizing Apocalyptic?," 371.

42. Robert G. Hall, *Revealed History: Techniques for Ancient Jewish and Christian Historiography* (JSPSup 6; Sheffield: Sheffield Academic, 1991), 246-48.

43. Here I think Martyn would agree that epistemology is the priority; see his "Epistemology at the Turn of the Ages: 2 Corinthians 5:16," in *Christian History and Interpretation: Studies Presented to John Knox*, ed. William R. Farmer et al. (Cambridge: CUP, 1967), 269-87, repr. in *Theological Issues*, 89-110.

44. In the case of Jubilees, it is a form of "Rewritten Bible" from Eden to Sinai, interspersed with many apocalyptic motifs. In the case of 4 Ezra, it is an apocalypse that looks forward to the victory of God and the Messiah over Rome as the climax of Israel's story. Dunn ("How New Was Paul's Gospel?," 260) finds a similar pattern in the Qumran scrolls, with emphasis on the covenanters as the true Israel, the new covenant people (e.g., 1QS 8.4-9), who are also constantly under threat from the spirit of wickedness (e.g., 1QS 3.13–4.26), and also preparing for the final battle between the sons of light and the sons of darkness (1QM).

45. James D. G. Dunn, *Beginning from Jerusalem* (CITM 2; Grand Rapids, MI: Eerdmans, 2009), 745n402. Elsewhere Dunn ("ΕΚ ΠΙΣΤΕΩΣ: A Key to the Meaning of ΠΙΣΤΙΣ ΧΡΙΣΤΟΥ," in *The Word Leaps the Gap*, ed. J. R. Wagner, C. K. Rowe, and A. K. Grieb [FS R. Hays; Grand Rapids, MI: Eerdmans, 2008], 354) states: "Paul could and did hold the stories of continuity and apocalyptic disruption together, as both valid and important ways of understanding the working out of God's saving purpose."

An apocalyptic eschatology is undoubtedly a crucial element in any study of Paul's theology, perhaps even the primary theological lens of Paul's theology.[46] Paul in general, and Galatians in particular, exhibits clear apocalyptic traits, as he views the saving event as a divine irruptive power that graciously liberates a captive humanity. However, apocalyptic eschatology cannot be reduced to an eschatological dualism or to a cosmic drama, and it need not require the aggravated denials of continuity and linearity with God's prior dealings with his people. Furthermore, any effort to de-story Paul's theology and to impose an absolute disconnection between him and the narrative of Israel's sacred Scriptures by appealing to the mantle of "apocalyptic" is a category mistake. That is because the apocalypticism inherited by Paul from Jewish tradition was intensely salvation-historical, even if Paul's own approach remained distinctive from other apocalyptic hopes and from other religious histories of Israel.[47] According to Gaventa, Paul's repeated reference to the Old Testament signals that "an adequate statement of the theology of this letter requires attention to the elements of continuity *and* discontinuity."[48] Paul does not so much repudiate as retrospectively revise the meaning of Israel's story in light of the revelation of Christ. As Hays comments, "God's 'apocalyptic' act in Christ does not simply shatter and sweep away creation and covenant; rather, it hermeneutically reconfigures creation and covenant, under the guidance of the Spirit, in light of the cross and resurrection."[49]

Martyn's apocalyptic reading, then, appears to be a Barthian theological enterprise dressed in a thin veil of apocalyptic motifs accompanied by overstatements about discontinuities between Israel's history and Paul's Christ-event. The attempt to divorce Israel's salvation history from the epochal saving event is not simply atypical of apocalyptic literature, it is entirely unlike apocalyptic literature, which affirms Israel's covenant story and hope. Dunn is right to claim: "In short, the degree of integration of the two perspectives

46. Edgar Krentz, "Through a Lens: Theology and Fidelity in 2 Thessalonians," in *Pauline Theology*, vol. 1, *Thessalonians, Philippians, Galatians, Philemon*, ed. J. M. Bassler (Minneapolis: Fortress, 1985), 52.

47. As Dunn (*Beginning from Jerusalem*, 744-45n402) notes, Martyn "does not do sufficient justice to the extent to which Paul sees God's saving purpose as a historical process: Abraham as progenitor of seed; the giving of the law as having a role prior to Christ; Christ coming in 'the fullness of time'; the growing up of heirs from minority (= slavery) to majority (the gift of the Spirit). In Jewish (and Paul's!) perspective, apocalypse is the climax of God's saving purpose for his people, not a whole new start."

48. Gaventa, "Singularity of the Gospel," 159 (italics original).

49. Hays, "Apocalyptic *Poiēsis* in Galatians," 205.

[salvation history and apocalyptic] within pre-Christian Judaism makes one wonder if the tendency to see the two perspectives as mutually exclusive is simply a false reading of Paul by technicians who have too much lost sight of the historical context within which Paul framed and preached his gospel."[50] Given this conclusion, we have to make a rather negative indictment of the so-called apocalyptic reading of Paul, namely, that it does not resonate with the literature ordinarily described as apocalyptic.[51] Alternatively, it appears, as many commentators have suggested, that Paul's apocalyptic worldview and his salvation-historical narrative can be welded together just as they are in Jewish apocalyptic literature.[52]

50. Dunn, "How New Was Paul's Gospel?," 262.

51. Campbell (*Quest*, 62) says that, in the apocalyptic approach, "each conceptual component is in effect a recognizable Jewish building-block paralleled in sources roughly contemporary to Paul, *but their arrangement into this particular account of salvation seems unprecedented, and even necessarily so*—at its heart is pneumatological involvement with the Christian account of Jesus" (italics added). This is a telling confession that the apocalyptic reading is a theological construct built on a select retrieval of key themes in apocalyptic literature and then applied to Paul in a somewhat ad hoc manner.

52. See Wright (*Paul*, 54): "For Paul, 'apocalyptic', the sudden, dramatic and shocking unveiling of secret truths, the sudden shining of bright heavenly light on a dark and unsuspecting world, is after all what God had always intended. One of the central tensions in Paul's thought, giving it again and again its creative edge, is the clash between the fact that God always intended what has in fact happened and the fact that not even the most devout Israelite had dreamed it would happen like this. We cannot expound Paul's covenantal theology in such a way as to make it a smooth, steady progress of historical fulfillment; but nor can we propose a kind of 'apocalyptic' view in which nothing happened before Jesus is of any value even as preparation. In the messianic events of Jesus' death and resurrection Paul believes *both* that the covenant promises were at last fulfilled *and* that this constituted a massive and dramatic irruption into the processes of world history unlike anything before or since. And at the heart of both parts of this tension stands the cross of the Messiah, at once the long-awaited fulfillment and the slap in the face for all human pride. Unless we hold on to both parts of this truth we are missing something absolutely central to Paul"; Roy E. Ciampa and Brian S. Rosner (*The First Letter to the Corinthians* [PNTC; Grand Rapids, MI: Eerdmans, 2010], 10): "The salvation-historical and apocalyptic perspectives are not, for Paul, two irreconcilable outlooks standing in unresolved tension. Instead, the two perspectives converge in Paul's thought such that he regards the history of the particular nation of Israel as finding its fulfillment, through Jesus Christ, in salvation for the entire world. The convergence of salvation-historical and apocalyptic motifs is nowhere more apparent than in the two 'bookends' to Romans: 1:1-5 and 16:25-27. The gospel of Jesus Christ, descended from David according to the flesh yet declared to be the Son of God in power according to the Spirit of holiness by his resurrection from the dead, has cosmic significance. This 'mystery' was kept secret for long ages but has now been disclosed and *through the prophetic writings* (i.e., the historical Scriptures of Israel) has been made known to all the nations, and must be proclaimed to the world and its authorities. It is

Galatians 1: The Story of Paul's Apocalyptic Gospel

Galatians is a rebuke letter, written with great pathos, to persuade the Galatians not to succumb to the designs of the Jewish Christ-believing proselytizers for them to undergo circumcision. To that end, Paul defends himself against sundry accusations about his apostleship and also contends for "the truth of the gospel" against the proselytizer's nomistic gospel by emphasizing the eschatological singularity of salvation in the crucified Messiah (see Gal 1:6; 5:2-4; 6:12-13).

Although many of the common apocalyptic motifs of Paul's theology are nowhere found in Galatians (e.g., no archangel call, no trumpet, no mention of Jesus' parousia, and no reference to a general resurrection),[53] contra Beker, in Galatians Paul does not suppress "the apocalyptic theme of the gospel."[54] In Galatians, Paul's apocalyticism is not exhibited in anticipation of the Lord's parousia, as much as it is in his particular interpretation of Jesus' death as the death of the cosmos, his own experience of the risen Lord, and the beginnings of the new creation. As de Boer comments, "The whole of God's eschatological saving activity in Jesus Christ, from beginning to end, is apocalyptic. This even involves a cosmic drama that God has begun and will bring to a conclusion

---

the eschatological 'power of God for salvation' (Rom 1:16). Paul the Jew regards himself as a herald who has been commissioned by Jesus to perform this task. Paul has been sent, through a special revelation of God's Son, to preach to the Gentiles (Gal 1:11, 16). He is one of two 'point men' in God's eschatological mission, having been entrusted with the gospel to the Gentiles just as Peter was entrusted with the gospel to the Jews (Gal 2:7)." James D. G. Dunn (*The Theology of Paul the Apostle* [Edinburgh: T&T Clark, 1998], 726): "This apocalyptic perspective, this eschatological shift, dictates much of what is most characteristic in Paul's theology. Not as a break with the past so much as a transformation of the past's relation to the present and the present's relation to the future." See also N. T. Wright, "Gospel and Theology in Galatians," in *Gospel in Paul: Studies on Corinthians, Galatians, and Romans for Richard N. Longenecker*, ed. L. Ann Jervis and P. Richardson (JSNTSup 108; Sheffield: Sheffield Academic, 1994), 237-38; idem, *Paul and the Faithfulness of God*, 1512; Mark L. Y. Chan, *Christology from within and Ahead: Hermeneutics, Contingency, and the Quest for Transcontextual Criteria in Christology* (Leiden: Brill, 2001), 291; Thomas R. Schreiner, *New Testament Theology: Magnifying God in Christ* (Grand Rapids, MI: Baker Academic, 2008), 98n11; Jason C. Meyer, *The End of the Law: Mosaic Covenant in Pauline Theology* (NACSBT; Nashville: Broadman & Holman, 2009), 3-5; Dunn, *Beginning from Jerusalem*, 547-48, 744-45n402; and Michael J. Gorman, *Reading Paul* (Eugene, OR: Cascade, 2008), 57-77.

53. Martyn, "Apocalyptic Gospel in Galatians," 252.

54. Beker, *Paul the Apostle*, x and 58; see Hays, *Faith of Jesus Christ*, 226, and his retraction in xxxviii-xxxix.

at the parousia."[55] I certainly do not deny a future eschatology present in Galatians (see Gal 4:26; 5:5, 21; 6:7-8); rather, it is an apocalyptic invasion of the future into the present.[56]

In his greeting to the recipients, Paul refers to God the Father, "who raised him [Jesus Christ] from the dead" (Gal 1:1), and to Jesus Christ, "who gave himself for our sins to set us free from the present evil age, according to the will of our God and Father, to whom be the glory forever and ever" (Gal 1:4-5).[57] Here Paul makes some passing remarks about matters that carry the utmost significance for configuring his theology and that have obvious relevance for the salvation history vs. apocalyptic debate.

First, continuity between Israel's sacred history and Paul's gospel is reinforced by the identification of God as the agent in both Israel's salvation and in Christ's resurrection. Paul's identification of God as the one who "raised the Lord Jesus from the dead"[58] parallels the Old Testament description of Israel's Lord as the "God who brought you out of the land Egypt."[59] Martyn is right that Paul believes that God identifies himself by his act of raising Jesus Christ, making the resurrection the "primal mark of his identity."[60] The only nuance we need to stress is that this is the same God as the God of Abraham and Moses. The God of the exodus has brought a new exodus through Jesus' resurrection, which is testified in Israel's sacred traditions as the long-awaited goal that God had been promising his people. To put it more concisely: the only God who has a Son and who raises the dead is the God of Israel.[61]

Second, resurrection is a divine act that invades the current order with divine life as part of a divine promise to Israel. Resurrection, the great apoca-

---

55. De Boer, "Paul," 33.

56. On the futurist eschatology in Galatians, see esp. Yon-Gyong Kwon, *Eschatology in Galatians* (WUNT 183; Tübingen: Mohr Siebeck, 2004), which is a good corrective to those who regard Paul's eschatology in Galatians as almost entirely realized, even if Kwon does overstate his point in places, especially in his reading of Galatians 3.

57. I think it noteworthy that both Galatians and Romans are bracketed by apocalyptic motifs related to revelation, rescue, wrath, the evil age, mystery, and new creation (see Gal 1:4; 6:15; Rom 1:3-4, 16-18; 16:25-26).

58. See Acts 2:24, 32; 4:10; 5:30; 10:40; 13:30; Rom 4:25; 7:4; 8:34; 10:9; 1 Cor 6:14; 15:15; Eph 1:20; Heb 13:20; 1 Pet 1:21.

59. See, e.g., Exod 20:2 and 29:46.

60. Martyn, *Galatians*, 85.

61. Wright (*Paul Debate*, 57) comments similarly: "Which 'God,' after all, are we talking about? To say that 'God has invaded the world,' or something similar, is to raise this question sharply. Is this just any 'God'? For Paul, of course, it is Israel's God, the creator of the world."

lyptic act that defeats death, set to transpire at the end of history,[62] proleptically invades in the present by the raising up of the Son of God.[63] In other words, God does for Jesus *in the middle of history* precisely what many Jews thought he would do for all Israel *at the end of history*.[64] In fact, Jesus' resurrection is a microcosm of the story of Israel, since resurrection, a metaphor for Israel's political restoration, becomes a vivid and visible affirmation of Israel's election in the resurrection of the elect Son.[65] Jesus is raised *for* Israel and raised *as* Israel. Jesus is the seed, son, and sovereign of Israel's covenantal history who embodies the deliverance of God so that alienation, corruption, curse, death, and exile would be utterly unable to carry over into the new creation. Martyn and Campbell might well agree here on Jesus' resurrection ratifying Israel's election. The qualification that needs to be made is that Jesus' resurrection affirms Israel's election only because it expresses God's faithfulness to Israel as his covenant partner. For in Jesus' resurrection God proleptically enacts what he promised to do for Israel—bring them from death to life. This perspective explains why early Christian authors believed the resurrection of Jesus to be the one great leap toward the climax of Israel's covenantal history and the fulfillment of prophetic hopes.[66] Viewed this way, Jesus' resurrection is an apocalyptic action that binds together the decisive death-defeating deed of God with God's covenantal faithfulness to Israel in order to create a resurrected world through a resurrected Israel.

Third, the eschatological dualism that Paul introduces in the opening of Galatians stresses a discontinuity between the ages, but not an absolute disconnection from Israel's story. To begin with, the precise temporal point of the rescue wrought in Jesus' atoning death is actually far more opaque than most commentators acknowledge. Paul declares that Jesus' death will bring deliverance from the cosmic powers when he writes that Jesus "gave himself for our sins *in order to* set us free from the present evil age" (Gal 1:4). Jesus' "giving of himself" for us/our sins is a recurring theme in the Pauline corpus.[67] The context of the formulations indicates that Paul conceives of Jesus' death in

---

62. On the resurrection of Israel or the "righteous" on the last day, see Dan 12:1-2; 2 Macc 7; 4Q521 2.11; 1 En. 92.3-4; Pss. Sol. 3.12; T. Jud. 25.1; Josephus, *Ag. Ap.* 2.218; Matt. 22:28 // Mark 12:23 // Luke 20:33; Luke 14:14; John 5:29; 11:24; Acts 23:6; Heb 11:35, and esp. in Paul at 1 Cor 15:51-58; Phil 3:10-11; 1 Thess 4:16-17.

63. See 1 Cor 15:20-23; Col 1:18; Rev 1:5.

64. Tom Wright, *What Saint Paul Really Said* (Oxford: Lion, 1997), 36.

65. See Ezek 37; Hos 6:2; Isa 26:19.

66. See, e.g., Acts 13:32-33; 1 Cor 15:4; 2 Cor 1:19; Heb 13:20.

67. See, e.g., Gal 2:20; 3:13; Rom 3:22-24; 5:8; 1 Cor 15:3; 2 Cor 5:14; Eph 5:2; Titus 2:14.

sacrificial and salvific terms.[68] More immediately in Galatians, Jesus' atoning death is an apocalyptic event in that it is purposed (ὅπως) for the chief end of achieving a *rescue* (ἐξαιρέω) *from the present evil age* (ἐκ τοῦ αἰῶνος τοῦ ἐνεστῶτος πονηροῦ).[69] There is, in the words of the great intergalactic theologian Optimus Prime, "no victory without sacrifice." Jesus' death for sins is the ground and condition of deliverance from the predatory powers of the present age. Ultimately the evil age and all its power will be vanquished by the Agnus Victor.[70] Yet I hasten to point out that the temporal coordinates of this "rescue" are more ambivalent than Martyn recognizes.[71] On the one hand, if the verb ἐξέληται relates back to the aorist substantive participle δόντος, then certainly the rescue can be coterminus with Jesus' act of self-giving; that is to say, Jesus' death constituted the dramatic deliverance, an apocalyptic rescue operation, a snatching away from the existing evil epoch. Alternatively, we have to remember that the aorist subjunctive ἐξέληται is aspectively perfective (i.e., it views the action from an exterior point of view), and the subjunctive mood grammaticalizes a projected state of affairs that can be either present or future.[72] Furthermore, the future indicative and the aorist subjunctive were often interchangeable,[73] and the subordinating conjunction ὅπως may also indicate a real future result. Thus, Paul could be saying that Jesus gave himself for our sins so that *one day we might* finally be set free from the present evil age.[74] Indeed, such a view is attractive because it comports with 1 Cor 15 and

---

68. See esp. Rom 3:25; 8:3; 1 Cor 5:6; Eph 5:3; 1 Tim 2:6. Martyn (*Galatians*, 97, 101, 272; idem, *Theological Issues*, 148), thinks that Christ's death does not secure the forgiveness of sins but more properly delivers people from suprahuman powers. A major problem is that this divine warfare model does not resonate with the atonement theology found in Gal 3:13 or with the wider Pauline corpus, and advocates are notoriously vague on how Jesus' death actually achieves a redemption from slavery. For a response, see Simon Gathercole, *Defending Substitution: An Essay on Atonement in Paul* (Grand Rapids, MI: Brazos, 2015), 42-54, 110.

69. The preposition ἐκ here means separation from and away from (see BDAG, 295).

70. See Henri Blocher, "*Agnus Victor:* The Atonement as Victory and Vicarious Punishment," in *What Does It Mean to Be Saved?,* ed. J. G. Stackhouse (Grand Rapids, MI: Baker Academic, 2002), 67-91.

71. Martyn, *Galatians*, 90.

72. Stanley E. Porter, *Idioms of the Greek New Testament* (2nd ed.; Sheffield: Sheffield Academic, 1994), 56-57.

73. Constantine R. Campbell, *Verbal Aspect and Non-indicative Verbs: Further Soundings in the Greek of the New Testament* (SBG; New York: Peter Lang, 2008), 57-60.

74. Kwon (*Eschatology in Galatians*, 156-57) raises similar concerns as to whether Gal 1:4 is really a lucid realized eschatology. He follows Hans Dieter Betz (*Galatians* [Hermeneia; Philadelphia: Fortress, 1979], 42) in regarding believers as saved *from the midst of* the evil age, not a change of the evil age itself. Christ's redemptive death means a continuing battle of flesh

Rom 8, where the victory of God's people remains very much future, and Galatians might not be any different.[75] Hedging my bets, I infer that Jesus' death is indeed a present victory over the powers (see 1 Cor 15:54-57; Col 2:15), but more in line with Paul's own thought, the emphasis here points decidedly toward the final victory at the consummation (see Rom 16:20; Phil 3:20; 1 Thess 1:10).[76]

In any case, with the reference to "the present evil age," we detect a tangible apocalyptic motif in Galatians, namely, an eschatological dualism.[77] Central to several apocalypses was the end of the evil age and the advent of a new age, which meant that all time could be defined as belonging to either the old epoch (the present) or to the new horizon (the future).[78] A similar scheme is implicit in the visions of Dan 2 and 7 and is also attested in the Jesus tradition (Matt 12:32; Mark 10:30; Luke 20:34-35). In this present evil age, God's authority is usurped, his glory denied, rebellion ensues from creature and creation, lawlessness reigns, and God's people await deliverance. For Paul, such a period is one of intrinsic evil (1 Cor 1:20; 2:6, 8; 2 Cor 4:4; Eph 5:16), expressed by Luke as the "times of the Gentiles" (Luke 21:24) and the "reign of darkness" (Luke 22:53), and described in the Qumran scrolls as "the time of wickedness" (CD 6.10, 14; 12.23; 15.7; 1QpHab. 5.7).[79] Paul rarely speaks of a "coming age" (only in

---

and Spirit precisely within the evil age. Similarly Sigurd Grindheim ("Not Salvation History, but Salvation Territory: The Main Subject Matter of Galatians," *NTS* 59 [2013]: 94) notes the ambiguity about whether ἐνίστημι is temporal (i.e., present time) or spatial (present place): "In Gal 1.4, we are then faced with two possibilities that are not necessarily mutually exclusive: Jesus has delivered us from the evil age that is now, or Jesus has delivered us from the evil world that is here. On either translation, Paul's language is informed by the conviction that the new creation has broken into this world (6.15). Through Jesus Christ and his resurrection, God has intervened most decisively in this world, and those who believe in Jesus Christ share in this eschatological reality. This new reality can be conceived of both as a new time, a new era, and as a new place, a new spatial realm."

75. See Kwon, *Eschatology in Galatians*, 220-21.

76. On this point Käsemann's warnings about triumphalism are very appropriate ("Primitive Christian Apocalyptic," 132-37). Note also J. R. Daniel Kirk (*Unlocking Romans: Resurrection and the Justification of God* [Grand Rapids, MI: Eerdmans, 2008], 213), who refers to a "hermeneutic of apocalyptic humility" fashioned by the observation that the redemption of the ages is not yet fully come.

77. For Paul Vielhauer ("Apocalyptic in Early Christianity," in *New Testament Apocrypha*, ed. W. Schneemelcher, trans. R. McL. Wilson [Louisville: Westminster John Knox, 1992], 542-69), eschatological dualism is the essential component of apocalypticism. But in contrast, see Wright, *Paul and His Recent Interpreters*, 139-40, 157-58.

78. See, e.g., 4 Ezra 6.9; 7.12-13, 50, 113; 8.1; 2 Bar. 14.13; 15.8; 44.11-15; 83.4-9; 1 En. 71.15.

79. James D. G. Dunn, *The Epistle to the Galatians* (BNTC; London: A&C Black, 1993), 36; idem, "How New Was Paul's Gospel?," 254.

Eph 1:21, assuming for now its authenticity) but more typically refers to a "present age" (see Rom 12:2; 1 Cor 2:6; 3:18; 2 Cor 4:4), which implies a "coming age," arguably identifiable with the future advent of "kingdom of God" (see Rom 14:17; 1 Cor 4:20; 6:9-10; 15:20; Gal 5:21; Eph 5:5; 1 Thess 2:12; 2 Thess 1:5). In apocalyptic literature the new age often arrives in a cataclysmic conflagration of the cosmos after a final judgment, and frequently the new age is essentially the old created order transformed and renewed. This is certainly analogous to what Paul refers to as the "new creation" (Gal 6:15; 2 Cor 5:17), proving that Paul definitely has a two-stage eschatology.

Yet Paul departs from this dualistic scheme in one important way. Unlike in other apocalyptic writings, God has already launched the new age in the midst of the old one in Jesus' resurrection. A cosmic war to liberate creation is underway, which calls for an attitude of resistance against the present order of things (Rom 12:2; 1 Cor 2:6-8; 10:11; Phil 2:15-16). Now, if we coordinate the "present evil age" with the "curse of the law" (Gal 3:10, 13), "slavery" to "elemental powers" (Gal 4:3, 5, 8-9), slavery in the Sinai "covenant" (Gal 4:21-31), and slavery to "circumcision" (Gal 5:1-3), then one could reasonably infer that the law and the Sinai covenant are part of the present evil age that believers are set free from because there is a nexus between law, sin, and death (1 Cor 15:56; Rom 5:12-21; 7:7-25; 8:2-3). That conclusion could suggest that the deliverance wrought by God in Christ is essentially punctiliar, rather than a continuous narrative, insofar as Israel's law and covenants compose an indelible part of the evil age, from which the Galatians need to experience redemption.

Yet what stands in the way of such a reading is not only other Pauline passages like Rom 1–11,[80] but even the argument of Galatians itself. For as we will

---

80. See Dunn (*Beginning from Jerusalem*, 548n113): "It is noticeable that the apocalyptic thesis has been based principally on Galatians since it is much harder to argue it from Romans." Wright (*Paul and His Recent Interpreters*, 184) wonders how "the Paul of this 'Galatians' could transmute into the Paul of Romans." But for an attempt to argue for an apocalyptic perspective in Romans, see briefly Martyn, *Theological Issues*, 172-75; Campbell, *Deliverance of God*, 519-832; moderately in Keck, *Romans*, esp. 32-37; and we await more fully Beverly Gaventa's Romans commentary in the NTL series. Note the objections to a salvation-historical reading of Romans by Charles Cousar, "Continuity and Discontinuity: Reflections on Romans 5–8 (in Conversation with Frank Thielman)," in *Pauline Theology*, vol. 3, *Romans*, ed. D. M. Hay and E. E. Johnson (Minneapolis: Fortress, 1995), 196-210, principally against Frank Thielman, "The Story of Israel and the Theology of Romans 5–8," in *Pauline Theology*, vol. 3, *Romans*, ed. D. M. Hay and E. E. Johnson (Minneapolis: Fortress, 1995), 169-95. More balanced are the brief summaries of Edward Adams, "Paul's Story of God and Creation," in *Narrative Dynamics in Paul: An Assessment*, ed. B. W. Longenecker (Louisville: Westminster John Knox, 2002), 37-39, and Beker, *Paul the Apostle*, 59-93. Strangely, Bruce L. Longenecker ("Sharing in Their Spiri-

see, in the wider framework of Galatians, the gospel was preached in advance to Abraham (Gal 3:8), that is, in Israel's precovenant history. Sinai did not nullify or oppose the Abrahamic promises (Gal 3:17-23):

- the law was a guardian of God's people until the Messiah, but also was intended to lead them to the Messiah (Gal 3:24-25);
- at the appointed time God sent his Son to Israel, born from a Jewish womb, and he lived as a Jew under the law (Gal 4:4-5);
- the gospel brings the blessing of Abrahamic sonship (Gal 3:29–4:7);
- the law is fulfilled in the love command as guided by the Spirit (Gal 5:13-16);
- Christians are still bound to the law of Christ (Gal 6:2); and
- all this climaxes in a benediction of peace and mercy for the Israel of God (6:16).

The invasion of God's grace into the world through Christ lays bare the temporary rather than the terminal nature of the law; it demonstrates how the law became a tool of sin, and how God determines to save through Christ rather than through the law. That said, Israel's covenant history remains affirmed throughout as summarily redemptive because it is to and through Israel that the promised "seed," the "Messiah," comes.

Fourth, Paul's account of his gospel is that its origin lay within the "apoc-

---

tual Blessings? The Stories of Israel in Galatians and Romans," in *Narrative Dynamics in Paul: A Critical Assessment*, ed. B. W. Longenecker [Louisville: Westminster John Knox, 2002], 58-84 [esp. 67-82]) thinks that Romans and Galatians share a "covenantal linearity" whereby God has elected Israel and chosen them to be in a relationship with himself, but they differ in that Romans also contains an "organic linearity" with Gentiles sharing in the story of God's elective grace upon Israel, which is said to be absent from Galatians. In response to Longenecker: (1) The differences between Romans and Galatians appear be rhetorical and reactive as Paul counters the Galatian intruders who meld Abraham and Moses together (hence his emphasis on discontinuity), and later in Romans he responds to accusations that he is antinomian and anti-Israelite (hence his emphasis of continuity). (2) Galatians provides ample evidence for an "organic linearity," since righteousness, Spirit, sonship, and inheritance are Israelite symbols of God's blessings for his people that are made available to Gentiles by faith in Jesus Christ. To be adopted into the family of Abraham the patriarch of Israel as "sons" and to be incorporated into Abraham's seed, the "Messiah," is as "organic" as you can get. And "Israel of God" is not, contra Longenecker, a "linguistic" vagary for a special relationship with God as much as it stands for incorporation into the elective grace of empirical Israel. (3) While Paul might be arguing against one particular notion of organic linearity to the effect that Gentiles must be circumcised, it does not therefore entail that he was opposed to all such organic unities.

alypse of Jesus Christ" (ἀποκαλύψεως Ἰησοῦ Χριστοῦ) and is also connected to the "will of God" (τὸ θέλημα τοῦ θεοῦ).

Paul defends himself against the allegation that his gospel was something that he was taught by others, that it was derivative of the Jerusalem church. He writes, "For I want you to know, brothers and sisters, that the gospel that was proclaimed by me is not of human origin; for I did not receive it from a human source, nor was I taught it, but I received it through a revelation of Jesus Christ" (Gal 1:11-12). Paul adds further content to his biography when he describes how his former zealous way of life in the Judean religion was dramatically ruptured at a point when God was pleased to "reveal his Son in me" (ἀποκαλύψαι τὸν υἱὸν αὐτοῦ ἐν ἐμοί). Paul's gospel and his apostolic call are attributed to God revealing the Son to him in a dramatic and arresting manner. Here, in Paul's own words, he was "apocalypsed"—he was seized and dragged into the apocalyptic drama of God's intention to renew creation through the crucified and risen Son. To describe the experience as an "apocalypse" underscores its heavenly authority and its eschatological significance.[81] Käsemann was entirely right: Paul's apostolic consciousness is comprehensible only on the basis of his apocalyptic call.[82] That conclusion would seem to directly support the apocalyptic reading, except that it needs to be nuanced by taking into account the origins of Paul's gospel, where he places its christological singularity within an ongoing salvation history.

The way Paul traces the origins of his gospel embeds inerasable elements of continuity with Israel's sacred history within his gospel. To begin with, there is an obvious tension as to whether Paul received his gospel directly from God (Gal 1:11-12) or whether it was delivered to him by early Christian tradition (1 Cor 15:3). My own suspicion is that Paul did not think that his gospel was materially different from that of the Jerusalem church (note the "we" used in Gal 2:16 and 1 Cor 15:11), only that this gospel revealed to him the identity of Jesus Christ and that it had to be heralded to be the Gentiles; this was the hub of his "revelation."[83] Importantly, it was in Israel's royal eschatological

---

81. Dunn, *Galatians*, 53.

82. Käsemann, "Primitive Christian Apocalyptic," 131.

83. Dunn, *Beginning from Jerusalem*, 354. De Boer (*Galatians*, 83-84) thinks that the issues are different between Gal 1:11-12 and 1 Cor 15:1-5. First Corinthians 15 affirms that resurrection was common to apostolic preaching from the beginning, while Galatians 1 addresses the issue of whether Gentiles need to be compelled to obey the law, beginning with circumcision. Richard B. Hays ("Letter to the Galatians," in *NIB*, ed. L. E. Keck [Nashville: Abingdon, 2000], 11:211) thinks that Galatians rebuts the accusation that Paul's gospel has a human origin, while 1 Corinthians recalls the specific terms in which the message was originally presented to them.

leader, the Messiah, that God had acted to bring Gentiles into the family of Abraham. Viewed this way, the center of gravity in Paul's revelation was not the repudiation of a salvation history but the inclusion of Gentiles within it by their inclusion in the Messiah.

Furthermore, I would hasten to point out that, in Gal 1:4, God's apocalyptic deliverance transpires "according to the will of God" (κατὰ τὸ θέλημα τοῦ θεοῦ). That will is not the isolated self-determination of God to be a savior of the cosmos; more likely, it is an extension of the divine will that Paul knows from Scripture, a will that is revealed in God's love for Israel and in God's law given to Israel. Additional proof of continuity is furnished by the way that Paul argues for the truth of his gospel. He does so fundamentally by demonstrating the conformity of his gospel to the pattern of Scripture, hence his frequent use of Gen 15:6 and Hab 2:4 (Gal 3:6-14). In addition, the story of the Galatians themselves validates this gospel, since their own pilgrimage into faith shows that God's redemptive and renewing work is accessed in the Messiah and results in receipt of the Spirit and Abrahamic sonship (Gal 3:1-5, 29; 5:1-7). Paul's testimony to the gospel thus focuses on Israel's Messiah as its subject: it accords with the will of God, it is rooted in Israel's Scriptures, and it results in redeeming the Galatian Gentiles by bringing them into the Abrahamic covenant. James Kelhoffer rightly sums up what this means when he says that "debates concerning one element of *Heilsgeschichte*—for example, the Christ-event (however construed)—cannot be separated from what came before (ancient Israel and the Jewish Scriptures) or afterward (apostolic authority and the origins of his congregations)."[84]

The preceding paragraph gives us a remit to push back against accounts that emphasize the Christ-event in such a way that separates it from Israel's salvation history. Accordingly, I conclude that Martyn's exposition of Paul's gospel as "history-creating christology" set against the law is at best a glorious half-truth.[85] Paul indeed focuses on what the gospel of Christ has done and is doing in the world. And Paul himself is the paradigm of the work of the gospel, as Beverly Gaventa has argued.[86] It is perhaps more fitting to say that Paul envisages believers as incorporated into the history of Jesus.[87] Jesus is the locus of the believers' justification (Gal 2:17) and the source of their meta-identity (Gal 2:19-20; 3:28). Yet the singularity of the gospel does not entail that all things pertaining to the law are negative. Jesus was born under the law, to redeem

---

84. Kelhoffer, "The Struggle to Define *Heilsgeschichte*," 119.

85. Martyn, "Events in Galatia," 164-66.

86. Beverly Roberts Gaventa, "Galatians 1 and 2: Autobiography as Paradigm," *NovT* 28 (1986): 310-26.

87. A Barthian theme, I might note; see *CD* 4/4.1-30!

those under the law, so that the law's own promise of Abrahamic sonship by faith would extend to those beyond the jurisdiction of the law (Gal 4:4-6). Yet this condition is not, contra Martyn, the state of all humanity, but of the Jewish people in particular. In which case, the benefit of what God does in Christ takes on universal import only as a consequent of what God has first done for the Jewish people.[88] The advent of the Messiah declared in the gospel renders the law preparatory and provisional, anticipating the moment declared in the law when God would bring Gentiles into Abraham's family. Jesus is the hinge that draws Gentile believers into Israel's election and pushes them ahead into the dawning eschaton. For Paul, Jesus is the newness of the new covenant, yet also the crucial hinge between the two eras.[89] To put it more colorfully, Paul is not marching to the tune of a covenantal nomism with a few orchestral variations (analogous to how Martyn likens salvation-history advocates), but neither does Paul see the gospel as a rock opera that interrupts and upstages a Felix Mendelssohn concerto (to which I liken Martyn).[90] Instead, we might imagine Paul's gospel as a dramatic act of God signaled in the overture of Israel's law and covenants but nonetheless still surprising its audience with its striking chords of inclusion and its singular christological motif.[91] The dialectic between salvation history and apocalyptic is resolved when we see Paul discoursing to the effect that "God always said he would act shockingly and unexpectedly, and that is precisely what he has done."[92] The upshot is that Paul's "revelation" of Jesus Christ cannot be constructed as repudiation of Israel's covenant promises and its salvation history.

To recap our discussion, in the opening greetings of Gal 1:1-4 and in his biographical narratio about his apostolic call in Gal 1:11-17, Paul theologizes out of an apocalyptic framework as he envisions God's redeeming action in Jesus'

---

88. Bruce Longenecker, "Salvation History in Galatians and the Making of Pauline Discourse," *JSPL* 2 (2012): 74.

89. Dunn, "How New Was Paul's Gospel?," 261.

90. Of course, Mendelssohn was a Jewish-born Austrian who was baptized as a Lutheran!

91. Wright (*The Paul Debate*, 56) uses Haydn as an example: "For Paul, the messianic events of Jesus' death and resurrection, and indeed the ultimate future dénouement at the *parousia*, were much more like the crashing chord a few bars from the start of the slow movement of Haydn's 'Surprise Symphony.' Haydn's trick—first lulling a postprandial audience into gentle slumber, then waking them up with a fright—does however illustrate the more subtle thing that is going on. The *sudden volume* of the chord interrupts the previous diminuendo. It brutally 'invades' it, shattering previous implicit expectations. But the chord itself belongs quite properly with the preceding *harmonic sequence*. It sums it up and prepares for what is to come" (italics original).

92. Wright, *Paul and the Faithfulness of God*, 1071-72.

death as a divine power that invades the world and redeems a people caught in the grip of sin and death. This is, as Käsemann abruptly put it, God's act to recapture the world for himself, or, as Wright memorably states, it is God's plan to put the world to rights.[93] The sending of the Son is a dramatic action that resultantly causes a virtual meltdown to competing theologies that saw Israel's Torah as somehow indelibly connected to Israel's deliverance. Nevertheless, such a radical protrusion of God's rescuing power is not a staccato act but part of an Israel-shaped narrative. It was precisely this story of God's soon-to-be-revealed covenant faithfulness that many Jews had been telling, hoping for, writing about, praying for, and imagining since the exile. Paul's apocalyptic gospel is rooted in this sacred story as apparent in Gal 1:1-4, where he stresses that (1) the God of the gospel is none other than the God of Israel;[94] (2) Jesus Christ's resurrection represents the proleptic realization of the Jewish hope for the triumph of God's power over death; (3) Paul's eschatological dualism is not a complete repudiation of the covenants, for while the Sinai covenant and its law are relativized, they are not rejected; indeed, the Christ-event fulfills precisely what was prepromised in Scripture; and (4) Paul's revelation of Jesus Christ is not a complete novum, as its key nodes are nested in Israel's salvation history, not least of all in God's will. Thus, in Paul's telling, God's dramatic act of deliverance in Messiah Jesus comes both to Israel and through Israel, as Israel's salvation history is the prism through which God's salvific light shines and so dispels the dark powers who held the world in the viselike grip of their power.

Galatians 2:15-21: Justification as Apocalyptic and Covenantal

The theological crux of Galatians is 2:15-21, with Paul's exposition of the "justification" tradition. It is preceded by Paul's narration of the Jerusalem council (2:1-10) and his recounting of the confrontation between himself and Cephas in Antioch (2:11-14), which situates Paul's response to the Galatian intruders in the wider context of the Antiochene and Jerusalemite churches' previous responses to the matter of Gentiles vis-à-vis the Torah. On the significance of

93. Käsemann, "The 'Righteousness of God' in Paul," 182; N. T. Wright argues this view in sundry places, most poignantly in *Surprised by Hope* (San Francisco: HarperOne, 2008), 72, 93, 121, 137, 145, 179, 215-16.

94. A point I think Martyn would agree with: "Paul will not allow their view [i.e., the view of the teachers] of the nomistic people of God to separate him either from the God of Israel or from Israel itself" (*Galatians*, 574).

Gal 2:15-21, those in the apocalyptic school sometimes look as if they want to force a false dichotomy. Is justification by faith Paul's apologetic for the inclusion of Gentiles in the Jewish Christ-believing assemblies without becoming proselytes, *or* is justification about a cosmic deliverance from evil, sin, and the powers that oppress God's people? I contend that the dichotomy is needless; both propositions are true, though we can haggle over where Paul's emphasis lies. In what follows, I argue that Paul's rather robust remarks about justification in Gal 2:15-21 underscore the storied character of his theology while equally affirming its apocalyptic texture. I describe in some detail the social context and apocalyptic nature of justification and provide my own sketch of the Christ/Torah antithesis.

Social Boundaries or Cosmic Conflict?

Martyn and Gaventa both note that the "Teachers" who came to Galatia were concerned with the conditions upon which Gentiles can attain full membership in the people of Israel. In contrast to these Teachers, Paul was focused not on group boundaries and rites of entry but on the singularity of the gospel and God's warlike invasion of the world to inaugurate the new creation. Paul was not, like the Teachers, concerned with a specific line of movement along which it was possible for Gentiles to shift from the sinful state into the blessed state of Abrahamic descent and merely haggling over the mechanism for their entrance. Rather, in their account, the controlling framework is the ongoing battle between Christ and the cosmos. Consequently, the antithesis between Christ and the law that emerges is governed by a more comprehensive premise of a cosmic conflict between Christ and the powers.[95]

The problem with such a reading is that Paul's theological argument in Gal 2 is absent of cosmic opponents; instead, it appears to reflect a particular social reality concerning the conditions upon which Gentiles could be admitted to Christ-believing fellowship.[96] Paul stood for the truth of gospel when certain "false brothers" entered the church in Antioch and agitated over the matter of Gentile freedom from circumcision (Gal 2:4-5). The matter was resolved at the Jerusalem meeting when Paul and Barnabas were received and recog-

---

95. Gaventa, "Singularity of the Gospel," 147-49; Martyn, "Events in Galatia," 164-65; idem, *Theological Issues*, 168-71; idem, *Galatians*, 272-73, 348n189.

96. Harink (*Paul among the Postliberals*, 16-17) sees the movement away from the socio-historical approach as a strength of the apocalyptic reading: "The stress on God's action is an important corrective to the often decidedly sociohistorical focus of the 'new perspective,' with its concomitant emphasis on human agents and the workings of human communities."

nized as authentic apostolic messengers to the Gentiles and when Titus was not compelled to be circumcised. Yet Paul had to contend again for the gospel when Peter in Antioch flip-flopped on the decision made at the Jerusalem meeting that Gentiles do not have to be circumcised (Gal 2:14). Peter's actions in Antioch suggested that Gentiles could be regarded as equal members of the community and enjoy mixed table fellowship only on the proviso that they first became Jews through circumcision (i.e., become proselytes).

Paul's response was, in effect, that a Gentile does not have to become a Jew in order to become a Christian. If we read Gal 2 synoptically with Acts 15 and Rom 3–4, the matter of rites of entry and full membership are hard to avoid. By his assertions, Paul was abruptly dissolving the category of God-fearer or adherent, someone who was "of" but not fully "in" the group. The gospel meant that all in Christ were all in one body (see Gal 3:26-28). The question of integrating non-Jews into Christ-believing social and worship space was hardly unique to the early church. Philo, Josephus, and rabbinic literature provide ample indications of how Jewish leaders had diverse perspectives on both the necessity and means of integrating proselytes into Jewish communities.[97] The social conflict of group boundaries and rites of entry for outsiders elicits Paul's argument to re-gospelize the Galatians by defending the Jewish Christian gospel and his divinely authorized apostolate.

While Paul undoubtedly believes that the advent of the new creation leads to a revised understanding of the law as temporary and salvifically ineffective, ultimately his construal of justification has a social purpose, namely, to protect the freedom and unity of believers in the new creation of Jesus Christ.[98]

Justification or Rectification?

To schematize Paul's argument in Gal 2:15-21, Paul's response to Peter beginning in Gal 2:15 merges into his first major theological argument to the Galatians about justification by faith apart from works of law. Paul appealed to a shared tradition among Jewish Christ-believers that it is by faith in Christ and not through works of law that a person is justified. To insist on any further re-

---

97. See Michael F. Bird, *Crossing Over Sea and Land: Jewish Proselytizing Activity in the Second Temple Period* (Peabody, MA: Hendrickson, 2009); on conversion in the New Testament more generally, see Beverly Roberts Gaventa, *From Darkness to Light: Aspects of Conversion in the New Testament* (Philadelphia: Fortress, 1986).

98. G. Walter Hansen, "A Paradigm of the Apocalypse," in *Gospel in Paul: Studies on Corinthians, Galatians, and Romans*, ed. L. A. Jervis and P. Richardson (JSNTSup 108; Sheffield: Sheffield Academic, 1994), 209.

quirements, even those from the law, compromises the sole demand for faith in Christ and negates the central claim of the gospel that God accepts those who believe in Jesus. Speaking largely from the well of his own experience, Paul asserts that, by seeking to be justified in Christ, Jewish Christ-believers like himself and Peter may be found to be operating outside the orbit of the law by living among and living like Gentiles. Yet it does not follow that Christ is therefore promoting Jews to become lawless Gentile sinners. On the contrary, anyone who attempts to reerect the law either as a means of separation (from sinners) or as a mode of righteousness (from sin) proves oneself a transgressor by rejecting the central claim of the gospel: faith in Christ and nothing else saves. In other words, attempting to rebuild the law as the basis for the Christian community is to sin against the completed work of Christ because it implies that the cross was insufficient to justify and define a people. Thus, Paul asserted that to retreat to the law to deal with sin/sinners is to set aside God's grace manifested in Christ. That is singularly inappropriate because Christ's death was purposed on the grounds that righteousness does not come through the law.[99] What is needed, instead, is the experience of death and resurrection. By being crucified with Christ, Paul says that he died to the law and thereafter lives to God. Evidently Christ does not quicken believers in the law so that they can apprehend righteousness there. Rather, one must die with Christ so that Christ may *live in them* and Christ may *enliven them*. The only life to be found is found in the faithfulness of the Son of God, who loved Paul and gave himself up for Paul. If that not be true, then Jesus' death was needless.[100]

The meaning of δικαιόω in Gal 2:15-21 proves to be crucial for the apocalyptic school. They adopt the translation "rectification" rather than the traditional term "justification" precisely because of the apocalyptic nature of Paul's discourse. De Boer examines the Jewish apocalypses 1 Enoch 1–36 and 2 Baruch and claims to have identified two distinct patterns of apocalyptic eschatology, one in which salvation is a cosmic drama where God rescues an enslaved cosmos from evil powers, and the other where salvation and condemnation are contingent upon human decision. The first scheme, cosmological apocalyptic eschatology, envisages humans liberated from enslavement to hostile powers. The second scheme, forensic apocalyptic eschatology, envisages salvation as

99. Ben Witherington III, *Grace in Galatia: A Commentary on Paul's Letter to the Galatians* (Grand Rapids, MI: Eerdmans, 1998), 185.

100. Michael F. Bird, "Progressive Reformed View," in *Justification: Five Views*, ed. J. K. Beilby and P. R. Eddy (Downers Grove, IL: IVP Academic, 2011), 135-36.

a matter of human responsibility and individual destiny.[101] For apocalyptic interpreters, Paul adopts the former scheme, and this divine rectification denotes God's making right what has gone wrong and emphasizes the cosmic and transformative nature of God's saving action in Jesus Christ, as opposed to the forensic and covenantal scheme of justification set forth by the intruders.[102]

On the one hand, I think that this language of "rectification" can be appreciated as a creative theological exploration of what Paul meant by δικαιόω in the gamut of his entire theology. Paul's defense of his account of δικαιόω does involve release from hostile "powers" (Gal 4:3), being crucified to the world (Gal 6:14), and participating in the new creation (Gal 6:15). In addition, a reading of Rom 1:16-17, 2:13-16, 3:21-26, and 8:32-34 indicates that God's saving power is something apocalyptically revealed in the gospel and climaxes in the eschatological vindication and cosmic vivification of believers as the people of God at the last judgment. Furthermore, this rectification can be umbilically connected to several apocalyptic motifs such as judgment and justice on the final day, fixing the problem with the pagan world, sin condemned and yet God's mercy availing for the contrite, God's covenant statues upheld, and lawbreakers forgiven. One should therefore locate justification beyond mere declarations and construe it as part of God's rectifying action in powerfully setting right all that has gone wrong in the world: in other words, justification is about cosmic liberation and justice.[103]

But even so, I have a few niggling concerns with this nomenclature. First, no lexicon lists a "cosmic" subcategory for either δικαιόω or δικαιοσύνη. Consequently, I think we might be wiser to be constrained in our exegesis by the lexis and semantics of the δικ- word group, lest we try to freight these words with too much theological baggage and fall into the fallacy of illegitimate totality transfer.

101. De Boer, "Paul and Apocalyptic Eschatology," 357-66; idem, "Paul and Jewish Apocalyptic Eschatology," 180-81.

102. Leader E. Keck, *Paul and His Letters* (Philadelphia: Fortress, 1979), 118-23; idem, *Romans* (Nashville: Abingdon, 2005); Alister E. McGrath, "Justification," in *DPL*, ed. G. F. Hawthorne, R. P. Martin, and D. G. Reid (Downers Grove, IL: InterVarsity, 1992), 518; Martyn, *Theological Issues*, 141-56; idem, *Galatians*, 249-75; Richard K. Moore, *Rectification ("Justification") in Paul, in Historical Perspective and in the English Bible: God's Gift of Right Relationship* (3 vols.; Lewiston, NY: Edwin Mellen, 2002); Martinus C. de Boer, "Paul's Use and Interpretation of a Justification Tradition in Galatians 2.15-21," *JSNT* 28 (2005): 210-15; idem, *Galatians*, 34-35; but also Hays, "Galatians," 11:187, 195, esp. 238; see more recently David A. deSilva, *Transformation: The Heart of Paul's Gospel* (Bellingham, WA: Lexham, 2014). David A. Shaw, "Apocalyptic and Covenant: Perspectives on Paul or Antinomies at War?," *JSNT* 36 (2012): 162-63, detects "an apologetic desire to distance Paul, and thereby God himself, from forensic concepts."

103. Hays, "Galatians," 11:237; Michael J. Gorman, "Justification and Justice in Paul, with Special Reference to the Corinthians," *JSPL* 1 (2011): 23-40.

Second, de Boer's "distinction between two 'tracks' of Jewish apocalyptic is essential to the reading of Galatians," and yet this turns out to be an Achilles's heel.[104] That is because de Boer's taxonomy of two types of apocalypses—cosmic and forensic—is overturned by Hefin Jones, who, after sketching the soteric patterns in 1 Enoch and 2 Baruch, concludes that "de Boer's isolation of the two patterns is overdrawn, somewhat skewed, and poses a false dilemma," on the grounds that "both apocalypses are also forensic and hold humans responsible."[105] In which case:

> The stark choice, either humanity is under the thrall of powers or it is responsible for its own actions, seems immediately reductionistic. If the evidence of these two apocalypses represent the poles of the spectrum of apocalypses then Collins' observation seems to be confirmed, "All the apocalypses, however, involve a transcendent eschatology that looks for retribution beyond the bounds of history." The presence of cosmological features such as evil powers, and God's warfare against them, does not mitigate the sense of human responsibility, even if in some apocalypses there seem to be attempts to formulate some kind of free will theodicy. The fact that de Boer can find both patterns together in numerous sources including Paul suggests that Paul and others felt less difficulty in attributing a significant role to both supra-human realities as well as human responsibility than some moderns do.[106]

Furthermore, the attempt to put the cosmic rectification of Paul over against the forensic theology of his opponents fails because, in light of Gal 2:15-21 and 6:14-15, "Paul, like the two *apocalypses,* is at home with both *forensic* and *cosmological* categories."[107]

Third, I am also concerned that the apocalyptic construal of "rectification"

<hr>

104. Martyn, *Galatians*, 97n51.

105. Hefin Jones, "Πίστις, Δικαιόω, and the Apocalyptic Paul: Assessing Key Aspects of the Apocalyptic Reading of Galatians" (PhD diss., Moore Theological College, 2015), 70. Similarly, see Wright, *Paul and His Recent Interpreters*, 160-67. Frey ("Demythologizing Apocalyptic," 354) seems to agree: "Although de Boer's study is a step forward in his detailed analysis of the Jewish texts, it basically draws on a taxonomy inspired from elsewhere and on an outdated view of Jewish apocalyptic and its basic features."

106. Jones, *Assessing Key Aspects of the Apocalyptic Reading*, 71-72 (citing Collins, *Apocalyptic Imagination*, 11). See also Shaw, "Apocalyptic and Covenant?," 164-65, who makes a similar point.

107. Jones, *Assessing Key Aspects of the Apocalyptic Reading*, 73.

is so Christocentric that it becomes virtually Christomonistic, in that we are left wondering whether there was any justification, any right relatedness with God, prior to the coming of Jesus Christ.

My own labors on justification have led to the conclusion that justification is the act whereby God creates a new people, with a new status, in a new covenant, as a foretaste of the new age. In which case, justification is forensic, apocalyptic, covenantal, and transformative.[108] To tease out this sentence: justification issues forth in a divine verdict that believers are part of God's forgiven family; the verdict of the final judgment has been proleptically declared in the present, and the verdict is one of acquittal; they are in the right before God and can't be any "righter." Gentile believers are also legitimated as full and equal members in the covenant with Jews and are part of God's people. In addition, the Spirit now works in believers to conform their status *coram Deo* to their state *en Christō*. Now, there is a clear christological center as the divine verdicts of condemnation (cross) and vindication (resurrection) are apprehended only by incorporation into and participation in the faithfulness, death, and resurrection of the Messiah. Yet this justifying act is not an unprecedented novum but occurs in conformity with the scriptural pattern reaching back from Gen 15:6, Isa 53:11-12, and Hab 2:4, the precise texts that Paul cites or alludes to in order to demonstrate the conformity of his gospel to the pattern of Scripture. Furthermore, justification is premised on Israel's election and the expansion of the covenant to include Gentiles.

Christ vs. Law?

Central to the apocalyptic approach is also postulating a very rigorous antithesis between law and Christ.[109] Here I think that Martyn is correct that the proselytizers "view God's Christ in light of God's Law, rather than the Law in light of Christ."[110] The intruders regard the Messiah as simply an add-on to Torah. On the apocalyptic reading, Paul responds by saying that the law is the enslaver and curser of all of humanity, and it is even a tyrant that believers need redemption from (esp. Gal 3:6-14; 4:3). Specifically in Gal 2:15-21, Paul is saying that the justification of believers consists of their

---

108. See Bird, *Saving Righteousness*, 3-4; idem, "Progressive Reformed."

109. Martyn, "Events in Galatia," 165-71; idem, *Theological Issues*, 149-54; idem, *Galatians*, 269-73.

110. Martyn, *Galatians*, 124.

rescue from the anti-God powers, and this comes, not through God's re-sponse to our own act of faith; rather, it occurs through the "faith of Jesus Christ" (πίστεως Ἰησοῦ Χριστοῦ). Jesus' faithfulness was his self-giving and sacrificial death on the cross as the revelation of God's rectifying power. It means that the contrast made is not between two modes of human action, believing versus doing, but between a divine action (Jesus' faithful death) and a human action (observance of the law).[111] Importantly, human faith is not entirely eclipsed; rather, its role is retained, since persons believe that they are justified precisely by the faithfulness of Christ (Gal 2:16), and Christ's faithful death even has the power to elicit faith itself (Gal 3:2).[112] Furthermore, preference for the scheme of justification by the "faithfulness of Jesus Christ" is something salvation-historical and apocalyptic interpret-ers of Paul can claim in common.[113] Even so, I think the scheme signified by the "faithfulness of Jesus Christ" might require some urgent qualifications, and the sharpness of the Christ/law antithesis needs to be blunted by other considerations.

First, on the faithfulness of Jesus Christ: this is one of the most perplexing subjects in contemporary Pauline interpretation, with a good many argu-ments both for and against the subjective genitive reading of Christ's faithful-ness.[114] Here πίστεως Ἰησοῦ Χριστοῦ is tantamount to "Christ's faithfulness as embodied in his death on the cross, which was the event through which God acted to rescue us."[115] The subjective genitive is commendable for a number of reasons: (1) law vs. Christ as an antithesis captures the theological mood of Galatians and rightly emphasizes Paul's primary contention that, for him, salvation is nothing else than the revelation of God-in-Christ and is not achieved by human efforts. (2) It is possible to translate Gal 2:19-20 as "I have been crucified with Christ, and it is no longer I who live, but Christ lives in me. So the life I now live in the body, *I live because of the faithfulness*

---

111. Martyn, *Galatians*, 270-75; Campbell, *Quest*, 178-232; idem, *Deliverance of God*, 839-40; de Boer, *Galatians*, 148-50.

112. See the excellent discussion on faith in Martyn, *Galatians*, 276-77.

113. Hays, "Galatians," 11:239-40, 246-47; Wright, *Paul*, 47; idem, *Justification*, 117; Wither-ington, *Grace in Galatia*, 179-82; Longenecker, *Triumph of Abraham's God*, 95-111; and see esp. Ardel Caneday, "The Faithfulness of Jesus Christ as a Theme in Paul's Theology in Galatians," in *The Faith of Jesus Christ: Exegetical, Biblical, and Theological Studies*, ed. M. F. Bird and P. M. Sprinkle (Milton Keynes, UK: Paternoster, 2009), 184-205.

114. See Hays, *Faith of Jesus Christ*; and see the collection of essays in Michael F. Bird and Preston M. Sprinkle, eds., *The Faith of Jesus Christ: Exegetical, Biblical, and Theological Studies* (Milton Keynes, UK: Paternoster, 2009).

115. Hays, "Galatians," 11:240.

of the Son of God, who loved me and gave himself for me." That translation is warranted if we consider that the whole sentence in Gal 2:19-20 is an explication of human faith in the context of participation in Jesus' faithful and loving act of giving himself over to death. The role of Christ is accentuated at both the beginning and the end of the sentence. Paul begins with cocrucifixion with Christ by stating, "I have been crucified with Christ"; then at the end Paul defines the crucified Son as him "who loved me and gave himself for me." The crucified Messiah who died on the cross as an act of self-giving love is the primary actor here. In addition, Paul makes two sets of contrasts between the source of human life and Christ as the agent who brings life to the believer through his death.

Believer's life	Source of that life
it is no longer I who live,	but Christ lives in me.
So the life I now live in the body,	I live in/by/because of the faithfulness of the Son of God.

In other words, the believer is alive because of the risen life, faithfulness, and self-giving death of the Son of God. (3) In Gal 3:23-25 Paul refers to the moment "when *faith* came." Here the noun πίστις is a metonym for "Christ," equivalent to the time when "God sent forth his Son" (Gal 4:4). If we coordinate Gal 2:16 ("justified . . . by the *faithfulness* of Jesus Christ") with Gal 3:23-25 ("faith" = Christ), then πίστις should be christologically conceived.

While I am convinced by the subjective genitive reading in Gal 2:19, I am not persuaded about its validity in Gal 2:16, for five reasons:

1. Paul never once makes Christ the subject of the cognate verb πιστεύω, as one might expect if Christ's own faithfulness were specifically in view.
2. From a semantic point of view, a genitive modifier restricts and defines the head term but does not fill it with additional content. So πίστεως Ἰησοῦ Χριστοῦ restricts the appropriate realm of faith to Jesus Christ rather than specifying Christ's own faith.[116]

116. Stanley E. Porter and Andrew W. Pitts, "Πίστις with a Preposition and Genitive Modifier: Lexical, Semantic, and Syntactic Considerations in the πίστις Χριστοῦ Discussion," in *The Faith of Jesus Christ*, ed. M. F. Bird and P. M. Sprinkle (Milton Keynes, UK: Paternoster, 2009), 33-53 (esp. 51).

3. The prepositions διά and ἐκ that preface πίστεως Ἰησοῦ Χριστοῦ in Gal
   2:16 are more or less abbreviations of ἐκ πίστεως from Hab 2:4 (LXX)
   and underscore human faith as the condition for "righteousness" (see
   Gal 3:8, 24; 5:5).[117]

4. The thesis stated in Gal 2:16 about a person being justified by πίστεως
   Ἰησοῦ Χριστοῦ ("faith of/in Jesus Christ") and not by ἔργων νόμου
   ("works of law") is explicated in the rest of the verse with a heavy
   emphasis on human faith. As such, justification ἐκ πίστεως Χριστοῦ
   means that ἡμεῖς εἰς Χριστὸν Ἰησοῦν ἐπιστεύσαμεν ("we have believed
   in Christ Jesus") for justification.

5. In Gal 3:1-5 Paul contrasts not Christ and law, but whether the Spirit
   was received by the Galatians through the instrument of "works of law"
   (ἔργων νόμου) or through "believing what you heard" (ἀκοῆς πίστεως).
   This latter contrast is proved further in Gal 3:6-9 with the example of
   Abraham, who "believed" (ἐπίστευσεν) and received righteousness,
   Abraham's account prefigures the gospel by promising that God would
   justify the nations by faith, and those who have faith will be blessed
   just like Abraham the man of faith. Here faith is the mechanism for
   reception of Spirit, justification, sonship, and blessing.

I suggest that a better solution to the πίστις Χριστοῦ debate lies somewhere in the middle between "faith in Christ" and the "faithfulness of
Christ." I find the traditional "faith in Christ" position, though rich in heritage and safeguarding the call for a human response to the gospel, ultimately dissatisfying because it does not capture the participationist themes
that Paul weaves into his theological discourse. However, the "faithfulness
of Christ" option, overflowing with a vat of theological new wine, doesn't
work for those of us damned with too much knowledge of Greek grammar, and it seems like a theological overread.[118] My own reading is that,
when Paul speaks of πίστις Χριστοῦ, he directs us toward human faith in the
whole apocalyptic saving reality wrought by God in the faithfulness, death,

117. Francis Watson, "By Faith (of Christ): An Exegetical Dilemma and Its Scriptural
Solution," in *The Faith of Jesus Christ*, ed. M. F. Bird and P. M. Sprinkle (Milton Keynes, UK:
Paternoster, 2009), 147-63, and Dunn, "ΕΚ ΠΙΣΤΕΩΣ," 357-66.

118. See Mark Reasoner (*Romans in Full Circle: A History of Interpretation* [Louisville:
Westminster John Knox, 2005], 39): "In the end, the best arguments for the subjective
genitive seem to be its theological utility, not the lexical or syntactical difficulties of the
objective genitive."

and resurrection of Jesus.[119] Therefore, πίστις Χριστοῦ is shorthand for the salvation-historical expression of faith, reaching back from Abraham to the Gentiles, in God's revelatory act in and through Jesus the Messiah, his death and resurrection, including its appropriation by faith and participation in the event by the Spirit.

This conclusion about πίστις Χριστοῦ in Gal 2:16 helps clarify the dense statement Paul makes in Gal 2:17-21 about dying with Christ to the law. Paul shifts without any hesitation from the community boundaries that traditionally separated Jews and Gentiles (2:1-14) to the incorporation of Jewish and Gentile believers into the revelatory event of the gospel (2:15-21). He stresses that the Jewish way of life does not open up the way for Gentiles, but through the law's own testimony, we die to the law, so that even the Gentiles might have a share in the new age (2:17-20). Paul gives himself as an example of someone who has passed beyond the jurisdiction of the law in Christ's death over into the risen life of the Son of God (2:19-20). Faith of this order means that one acts and is acted upon by God in Jesus Christ as a sign of covenantal fulfillment to what was promised to Abraham. Paul thus ties together the human responses of faith with Christ's deliberate self-giving act of loving self-sacrifice. The faithfulness of the crucified Son and faith in Christ are collapsed together in the believer's cocrucifixion. As Sam K. Williams puts it, "I live in faith—that of the Son of God who loved me."[120] There is no faith other than that which is

---

119. See Charles Cosgrove, *The Cross and the Spirit: A Study in the Argument and Theology of Galatians* (Macon, GA: Mercer University Press, 1988), 56; Francis Watson, *Paul and the Hermeneutics of Faith* (London; T&T Clark, 2004), 75-76; idem, *Paul, Judaism, and the Gentiles: Beyond the New Perspective* (Grand Rapids, MI: Eerdmans, 2007), 255; Benjamin Schließer, *Abraham's Faith in Romans 4: Paul's Concept of Faith in Light of the History of Reception of Genesis 15:6* (WUNT 224; Tübingen: Mohr Siebeck, 2007), 262; Michael F. Bird, "What if Martin Luther Had Read the Dead Sea Scrolls? Historical Particularity and Theological Interpretation in Pauline Theology: Galatians as a Test Case," *JTI* 3 (2009): 119-21; and esp. Preston M. Sprinkle, "Πίστις Χριστοῦ," in *The Faith of Jesus Christ*, ed. M. F. Bird and P. M. Sprinkle (Milton Keynes, UK: Paternoster, 2009), 165-84, with larger bibliography.

120. Sam K. Williams, "Against *Pistis Christou*," *CBQ* 49 (1987): 44; idem, *Galatians* (ANTC; Nashville: Abingdon, 1997), 67-70. Martyn (*Galatians*, 362) thinks Paul refers interchangeably to "the coming of Christ, to the coming of the Christ's Spirit, and to the coming both of Christ's faith and of the faith kindled by Christ's faith." See also arguments for Christ's faithfulness in Gal 2:20 by Hays, *Faith of Jesus Christ*, 153-56; Campbell, *Deliverance of God*, 847-49; Michael J. Gorman, *Inhabiting the Cruciform God: Kenosis, Justification, and Theosis in Paul's Narrative Soteriology* (Grand Rapids, MI: Eerdmans, 2009), 63-72.

rooted in the faithfulness of Jesus Christ.[121] By faith, one enters into Christ's state of crucifiedness, which forever changes the believer.[122]

Second, the crux about what Paul thinks about the law in Galatians is his intriguing statement about the law in Gal 2:19a: "For through the law I died to the law, so that I might live to God" (ἐγὼ γὰρ διὰ νόμου νόμῳ ἀπέθανον, ἵνα θεῷ ζήσω). What does "through the law" mean, and how has Paul "died to the law"? It would be so much easier if Paul wrote something similar to what he said in Rom 7:4: "You were put to death to the law through the body of Christ, so that you may belong to another, to him who has been raised from the dead." In Romans it is the "body of Christ" (i.e., his crucified body) that is the mechanism for dying to the law, yet in Gal 2:19a Paul says that *through the law* he died *to the law* and that this is umbilically connected to living to God and cocrucifixion with Christ in 2:19b-20. Martyn, Hays, and de Boer all take "through the law" to mean the active role that the law played in Christ's crucifixion, i.e., through the law's role in the crucifixion of Christ, Paul was separated from the law.[123] Wright, for whom Gal 2:19 exhibits a key component of Paul's theology, thinks "died to the law" must be a repudiation of the law, or else, "words have no meaning."[124] The problem is that we are at a loss to explain how the law actively engineered the death of Christ, and it is Paul, not Christ, who dies through the law and to the law.[125]

I have two observations here. First, the prepositional phrase "through the

---

121. See Barth, *CD* 2/2:559: "The fact that I live in the faith of the Son of God, in my faith in him, has its basis in the fact that He Himself, the Son of God, first believed for me . . . the great work of faith has already been done by the One whom I follow in my faith, even before I believe, even if I no longer believe, in such a way that He is always, as Heb. 12:2 puts it, the originator and completer of our faith. . . . His faith is the victory which has overcome the world." Martyn, *Galatians*, 259: "Christ's faith constitutes the space in which the one crucified with Christ can live and does live." Hays, "Galatians," 11:244: "The life that he now lives 'in the flesh' (i.e., in embodied historical existence) is both animated and determined by Jesus Christ's faithfulness."

122. Contra Dunn, *Galatians*, 144, and Hays, "Galatians," 11:243-44, the perfect participle συνεσταύρωμαι is not a past event with an going effect; rather, the perfect tense form is stative, either by aspect or by *aktionsart*, and emphasizes the state of being crucified with Christ (see Porter, *Idioms*, 21-22, 39-42).

123. Martyn, *Galatians*, 257-59n142, 278; Hays, "Galatians," 11:243; de Boer, *Galatians*, 160.

124. Wright, *Paul and the Faithfulness of God*, 1430.

125. Several scholars (Dunn, *Galatians*, 143; de Boer, *Galatians*, 160) explain this problem by way of Paul's zealous devotion to the law, which led him to persecute the church. But how was the persecution of Paul against Jewish Christians an act of the law against Christ, except in the most allegorical of senses?

law" has to mean *by way of law* or *via the instrument of the law*.[126] As strange as it sounds, the law is the means by which Paul died to the law! Second, the way in which the law instrumentally facilitated Paul's death to the law and his subsequent life in Christ should probably be coordinated what Paul says about the law elsewhere in Galatians and Romans. Galatians 3:19-25 as a whole is concerned with the role of the law as a provisional and preparatory pedagogue to lead people both to Christ and to receive justification by faith. And in Romans, Paul states that the "righteousness of God" is revealed apart from the law, while simultaneously testified by the law and the prophets (Rom 3:21). Taking all of this together, I surmise that, when Paul says, "for through the law I died to the law," he means that the law envisages its own climax in Christ, and those united to Christ die to the law in the sense of being separated from its jurisdiction. The law bears witness to God's covenant with Abraham, it points ahead to the fulfillment of God's promises in Christ, and by dying with Christ, Paul himself dies and is thus separated from the law's dominion. To paraphrase Paul, he speaks words to the effect that "the law tells me that one day I will separate from it and be bound to Christ."[127]

To recap, Paul's description of justification as a divine verdict is a clear apocalyptic motif, and yet it emerges out of an underlying narrative from Israel's Scriptures about Israel's final vindication from their own sin and the sinful world around them. Importantly, this apocalyptic imagery of God's justifying verdict is solicited to address a concrete social reality driving Paul's remarks, namely, Christ-believing Gentiles are not to be treated as would-be Jewish proselytes. Paul's explication of δικαιόω and δικαιοσύνη, while certainly capable of being placed in a wider cosmic discourse, more concretely signifies a covenant standing and a new status that avails before God. Rather than understand πίστις Χριστοῦ as the "faithfulness of Christ" in Gal 2:16, it is preferable to see it as an abbreviated way of indicating how human faith enables someone to share in a saving story reaching from Abraham to the Gentiles. Finally, the believer who is "in Christ" has been removed from the law's jurisdiction, but that act itself is something affirmed by the prophetic

---

126. See usage of διὰ νόμου: judged through the law (Rom 2:12); knowledge of sin comes through the law (Rom 3:20); Abrahamic promises not through the law (Rom 4:13); sin aroused through the law (Rom 7:5); and sin not known except through the law (Rom 7:7).

127. The next best option is probably that of Longenecker (*Triumph of Abraham's God*, 111-13), who sees Paul referring to the promise of death to covenant outsiders, so that Paul says, in effect, that through the pronouncement of the law upon covenant outsiders, he died to the obligation to observe the law, in order that he might enjoy covenant life by being crucified with Christ.

witness of the law to Christ, an observation that somewhat softens the antithesis of Christ and the law.

Galatians 3–4: Abraham, the Law, and the Messiah

In what is very much the heart of the letter, Paul constructs a series of interlocking arguments based on appeals to personal experience, Scripture, salvation history, and the theologic of his law-free gospel.[128] In order to reprove the Galatians for their willingness to indulge the designs of the intruders to be circumcised, Paul refutes the arguments of the intruders that the messianic era is really an extension of the Mosaic era. Paul undermines their approach by postulating a salvation-historical rupture between the epochs of Abraham and Moses. Paul strenuously insists that the messianic dispensation does not simply top up or round off the Mosaic dispensation nor does the journey from Abraham to the Messiah run via Moses' chosen people mover. In that sense, Beker and Martyn are right that Paul stresses discontinuities in Galatians.[129] However, I think Martyn goes too far to claim that God enters into "combat against the Law."[130] While Paul refuses to collapse the Abrahamic, Mosaic, and messianic dispensations together in a simple and continuous line, he nonetheless affirms a continuity of sorts whereby the law, despite its limitations, remains integral to the overall story of God's dealings with Israel as a conduit for the rescue of the Gentiles. Israel's covenantal life and legal constitution were limited in scope, duration, and purpose, but they were no less important for the eventual revelation of the Messiah. It is only to and through Israel and the law that the Messiah comes to bring blessings to the nations. In fact, God's plan of salvation outlined in Scripture embraces both the condemning effect of the law as well as the promise of faith.[131] So it seems that Paul's integration of Israel and the Messiah in a line of continuity stretching from Abraham to Gentile believers is a clear expression of salvation history.[132] This understanding will become evident by analysis of (1) Paul's depiction of the law as a story promising salvation, (2) Paul's description of the law as temporary yet preparatory for God's saving act, (3) the law's interim function, which negatively involved submission but positively provided protection and preparation, and (4) the

---

128. Dunn, *Galatians*, 151.
129. Beker, *Paul the Apostle*, 49-56.
130. Martyn, *Theological Issues*, 155.
131. Beker, *Paul the Apostle*, 55.
132. Dunn, "How New Was Paul's Gospel?," 252.

tension between the law as curse/slavery and promise of salvation, which is resolved by Paul's presentation of the law's curse as borne by Christ.

The Torah as Story of Salvation

Paul makes a stark contrast between the dispensations of law and of Christ as the spheres of identity and sources for salvation. Paul's reference to "those who rely on works of the law" (ὅσοι ἐξ ἔργων νόμου, Gal 3:10) and those "under law" (ὑπὸ νόμον, Gal 3:23; 4:4-5, 21; 5:18) signifies people who tie their identity and their salvation to continued observance of the law. In contrast, "those who believe" (οἱ ἐκ πίστεως, Gal 3:7-9) and those baptized and clothed "into Christ" (ὅσοι εἰς Χριστόν, Gal 3:27) refer to those who find identity and salvation through faith in Christ. The law is not a means to righteousness or life (Gal 2:21; 3:11-12, 21). Instead, it brings curses and slavery for all who submit themselves to its authority, just as it did for Israel (Gal 3:10; 4:1-7, 24-25; 5:1-3).[133] Furthermore, Paul even claims that "the law is not of faith" (ὁ δὲ νόμος οὐκ ἔστιν ἐκ πίστεως) in the sense that the law does not provide the life that is graciously given in the period of faith in Christ (Gal 3:12). Paul even compares Gentile efforts at law-observance as tantamount to a reconversion to their former slavery in pagan religion (Gal 4:8-11).[134] Paul's allegory of two mothers, two children, two Jerusalems, and two covenants regards the Sinai covenant as a period of slavery, and those enslaved attempt to persecute the free children who receive the inheritance (Gal 4:21-31). In contrast, it is faith in Christ that is a means to blessings (3:8-9, 14),

---

133. Against Martyn (*Galatians*, 311, 327), it is not the case that Paul views the curse of the law as falling on both observer and nonobserver, because (1) Paul's argument is that *if* the Gentiles get circumcised, *then* they will come under the curse of the law (Gal 5:3); and (2) Paul affirms elsewhere that the Gentiles are those not having the law and not susceptible to the judgment of the law, even if they are judged before God on the basis of conscience (Rom 2:12-16). Martyn has a profound tendency to universally apply the particular statements of the Torah to all humanity (e.g., *Galatians*, 317). Circumventing the historical and narrative context of the Torah allows Martyn to focus on Christ as the solution to an anthropological problem, but this approach overlooks the fact that Paul's own argument appears to be based on the particularity and distinctions between Jews and Gentiles.

134. Martyn (*Galatians*, 410) puts it as follows: "In short, Gentile observance of the Law is equivalent to Gentile ignorance of God." I would point out that one of the curses listed in Deut 28:58-68 is that Israel would be slaves to pagan gods. In which case, Paul is not absolutely equating the law with paganism. Instead he was pointing to the climax of the curse of the law— exile and subjugation to foreign gods—just as the Gentiles were themselves already enslaved to these gods (see Justin Hardin, *Galatians and the Imperial Cult: A Critical Analysis of the First-Century Social Context of Paul's Letter* [WUNT 2.237; Tübingen: Mohr Siebeck, 2008], 136-37).

adoption and sonship (3:7, 26, 29), righteousness (3:6, 8), and receipt of the Spirit (3:1-5, 14). Galatians 3–4 climaxes in the dramatic assertions concerning how faith in Christ and not observance of the law actualizes and accesses the Abrahamic promises for believers (Gal 3:5, 9, 14, 18, 29; 4:6, 30-31). This is prima facie evidence in favor of the apocalyptic interpretation that God enters into contention against the law. But alas, all is not so clear-cut.[135]

Paul can still postulate Israel and the law as a redemptive context for the coming of God's Son with a view to the inclusion of the Gentiles. For a start, Paul regards the law as γραφή ("Scripture") that foresaw the gospel in Abraham's call and announced the future gospel to Abraham (Gal 3:8). Such an equation of law and Scripture shows that Paul maintains a significant role for the law in the divine drama of redemptive history.[136] The law—or perhaps we should call it "Torah," to get away from purely legal connotations—is a mixture of story, promise, and command. By this citation, Paul declares that Torah proclaims and authorizes a law-free community of God's people that finds ultimate expression in Christ-believing Gentiles.[137] That is because Paul identifies the gospel as simply the working out of the promise given to Abraham, a promise in the Torah that describes Israel as divine heirs, and a promise that will lead to blessing "all" the nations. It is not hyperbolic to state that

---

135. Martyn (*Galatians*, 325, 345, 350, 354, 356-57, 366-68, 372-73; see Hans Hübner, *Law in Paul's Thought* [Edinburgh: T&T Clark, 1984], 24-36; de Boer, *Galatians*, 230: "the angels were tampering with God's *diathēkē* with Abraham, something God did not intend to happen") claims that Paul widens the gulf between the law and God by depicting the law as given by angels in God's absence and God as having no part in the genesis of the law. Martyn refers to the "angelic Law," the law and its curse constitute an "angelic parenthesis," and the law is an "enslaving parenthesis" (326, 342, 389). But this view is not convincing when we consider the following three points: (1) The divine giving of the law is also indicated by προσετέθη, which is most likely a divine passive for "added *by God*" (Gal 3:19). (2) Contra Martyn (*Galatians*, 356), the clearest reading of Gal 3:19 is that διὰ ἀγγέλων means "through angels" not "by angels," because διά plus a genitive means "through" in the specific locative sense of "through the midst of." (On the differences between the locative, instrumental, and causal uses of διά, see Porter, *Idioms*, 148-51.) Martyn's attempt to take a vague grammatical possibility and press into service a crypto-Marcionism whereby the law is not from God is simply not Paul's point, and it runs in the face of what Paul says elsewhere about the law. (3) The contrast in Gal 3 is not between the promise *given by God* and the law *given by angels;* rather, the contrast appears to be between the promise given *directly* by God to Abraham and the law given *indirectly* through angels and Moses. The promise is an unmediated blessing for everyone, whereas the law is a mediated condition for blessings for those under its jurisdiction.

136. Hays, "Galatians," 11:268.

137. Richard Hays, *Echoes of Scripture in the Letters of Paul* (New Haven: Yale University Press, 1989), 105.

Paul's mission to the Gentiles was nothing less than the fulfillment of Israel's mission to bring the blessing of Abraham to the nations.[138] It is also worth noting that the gospel being promised in the Torah mitigates the hardness of the contrast between the law and Christ. The upshot is that we can at best set Torah and its *promise* against Torah and its *commands*, rather than play off God against Torah.

Furthermore, Paul writes that the law is not "opposed" to the promise (Gal 3:21), by which he evidently means more than that the law is not "potent enough to annul it."[139] Paul is suggesting that the law does not abrogate the promise (Gal 3:17), and it genuinely accords with the promise in the senses described in Gal 3:22-25 of leading to Christ and to justification. The law and promise cannot be in opposition once their different purposes are clarified, and Scripture—the Torah narrative!—shows how the law's subjection to the power of sin ultimately served to enable the promise to be received by faith.[140] Also, in Paul's allegory of the two covenants (Gal 4:21-31), the new covenant still comes from Abraham to the Gentiles through the sacred line of Isaac and Jacob. Slavery and freedom are dual possibilities within Israel's covenant history, proving that adoption into Abraham by faith is still mediated through Israel's sacred history and cannot be bypassed in bringing the Abrahamic promise to the nations.

All in all, Gal 3–4 is situated around a particular Torah narrative that is indicated by the scriptural citations and allusions.[141] Paul's references to Abraham's faith (Gen 15:6), his blessing that extends to the nations (Gen 12:3), his singular seed (Gen 12:7), the birth of two sons (Gen 16), and the role of Isaac as his promised heir (Gen 21:10) all strongly indicate that Paul has the entire Abrahamic story in mind, so that the individual citations function as a connected series of clips through which Paul retells the Abraham story to his audience, with a particular emphasis on its applicability to them.[142] The story of Abraham, in light of God's revelation of Christ, establishes a Christotelic reading of the Torah that makes Christ the climax of Israel's covenantal history (see Rom 10:4). Hays puts it well: "The Abraham story is for Paul taken up

138. Dunn, *Galatians*, 165.
139. Martyn, *Galatians*, 326, 342.
140. See Jason Maston, "The Nature of Salvation History in Galatians," *JSPL* 2 (2012): 98-99.
141. Campbell (*Quest*, 217-19) acknowledges that Paul's use of Scripture in his argumentation here provides a platform for Christian continuity with Judaism.
142. Carol Stockhausen, "2 Corinthians and the Principles of Pauline Exegesis," in *Paul and the Scriptures of Israel*, ed. C. A. Evans and J. A. Sanders (JSNTSup 83; Sheffield: Sheffield Academic, 1993), 149.

into the Christ story, and the Christ story is understood, with the hindsight of narrative logic, as the fit sequel to the Abraham story." For Paul, then, anyone who listens to the law will see that it supports his proclamation, not that of his adversaries. For within the law itself is a single narrative that moves from the promise given to Abraham to the promised one, Christ. To quote Hays again: "Paul saw scripture not just as a repository of proof texts about Jesus as the Messiah, but as a story—a story focused on God's promise to bless and redeem all nations."[143]

The Law as Temporary Rather Than Adversary

Central to Paul's argument is the idea that the law was only temporary. Whereas many Jewish authors regarded the law as immutable and eternal,[144] Paul asserts that it was limited in its divinely intended duration.[145] This is evident in a number of Paul's statements about the temporality of the law:

The law, which came four hundred thirty years *later* [μετά], does not annul a covenant previously ratified by God. (Gal 3:17)

It [the law] was *added* [προσετέθη] because of transgressions, *until* [ἄχρι] the offspring. (Gal 3:19)

Now *before faith came* [πρὸ τοῦ δὲ ἐλθεῖν τὴν πίστιν], we were imprisoned and guarded under the law *until* [εἰς τὴν μέλλουσαν] faith would be revealed. (Gal 3:23)

The law was our disciplinarian *until* [εἰς] Christ came. (Gal 3:24)

Now that faith *has come* [ἐλθούσης δὲ τῆς πίστεως], *we are no longer* [οὐκέτι . . . ἐσμέν] subject to a disciplinarian. (Gal 3:25)

---

143. Hays, *Faith of Jesus Christ*, 226; idem, "Galatians," 190.

144. Wis 18:4; Josephus, *Ag. Ap.* 2.277; Philo, *Mos.* 2.14; Jub. 1.27; 2.23; 3.31; 6.17; 15.25.

145. Paul may be in line with a small section of Jewish thought that postulated that the law would disappear during the messianic age (1QS 9.11; CD 6.10-11; 12.23–13.1; 20.1; b. Sanh. 97a). For discussion, see Albert Schweitzer, *Quest of the Historical Jesus* (New York: Macmillan, 1968), 187-92; H. J. Schoeps, *Paul* (Philadelphia: Westminster, 1961), 171-75; W. D. Davies, *Torah in the Messianic Age and/or the Age to Come* (Philadelphia: SBL, 1952); Peter Schäfer, "Die Torah der messianischen Zeit," *ZNW* 65 (1974): 27-42; Martyn, *Galatians*, 355n203.

The heir, *as long as* [ἐφ᾽ ὅσον χρόνον] he is a child, is no different from a slave. (Gal 4:1)

He is under guardians and managers *until* [ἄχρι] the date set by his father. (Gal 4:2)

When [ὅτε] we were minors, we were enslaved to the elemental spirits of the world. (Gal 4:3)

But *when* [ὅτε] the fullness of time had come. . . . (Gal 4:4)

Rather than viewing the law as an eternal ordinance, Paul depicts it as limited in its duration to the period between its being given to Israel through angels at Sinai until the coming of Christ.[146] This temporality explains why it is the case that the law does not impart life or impute righteousness, and why the revelation of the Messiah was necessary. So, contra Martyn, Paul differs from the intruders in that he refuses to anachronistically project the Mosaic commandments back into Abraham's lifetime and make it the primary mechanism for Gentile deliverance.[147] Paul's opposition to the law is thus not premised on a cosmic antinomy but rests instead on the limited place that the law was ordained to have in salvation history. That limitation is premised on account of the punitive effects of the law upon Israel, who fell under the curse of the law by disobedience to it, which entailed Israel's temporal subjection to the law and the law's subservience to sin.[148] Israel's history, then, has moments of *unheil* in an overarching *heilsgeschichte*.[149] Or as C. H. Dodd supposed, there is a "two-beat rhythm" in salvation history from Eden to the apocalypse, from Genesis to Revelation: judgment and restoration, covenant

146. See further Longenecker, *Triumph of Abraham's God*, 117-19. D. A. Carson ("Mystery and Fulfillment: Toward a More Comprehensive Paradigm of Paul's Understanding of the Old and the New," in *Justification and Variegated Nomism*, vol. 2, *The Paradoxes of Paul*, ed. D. A. Carson, P. T. O'Brien, and M. A. Seifrid [Grand Rapids, MI: Baker Academic, 2004], 427) comments that "it is in this essentially salvation-historical reading of Genesis that enables him to come within a whisker of treating the Sinai covenant as a parenthesis." Longenecker ("Sharing in Their Spiritual Blessings?," 67-68) later refers to "Israel's reception of the law merely as a parenthesis between the primary moments of salvation history—God's promise to Abraham and the coming of Abraham's exclusive seed, Jesus Christ."

147. On Abraham keeping the law, see CD 3.2-3, Jub. 16.12-28; Sir 44:19-20; 2 Bar. 57.2.

148. Martyn wrestles with the issue of law as both promise and curse in his excursus on the two voices of the law (*Galatians*, 506-14).

149. Maston, "Salvation History in Galatians," 100-103.

curse and covenant blessing.[150] Paul thus rejects the salvation history of the intruders, which envisaged the law as the instrument for Abraham's blessing reaching the nations, in favor of his own salvation history, which saw the law, retrospectively, as both curse and custodian, as punitive and yet a preserver of the promise, as confining but still christologically oriented.

The Law as Custodian, Pedagogue, and Guardian

The temporary jurisdiction of the law means that the law cannot be a primary platform for salvation or a permanent palisade for election. The law has a different purpose. The reason for its addition to the people of God, Paul says, was to identify and restrain sin for those who are under the law (Gal 3:19, 22; see Rom 3:20; 4:15; 5:13, 20; 7:7).[151] The interim function of the law is described with a number of images in 3:22-25 and 4:1-3:

1. A protective custody: The Scripture imprisoned (συγκλείω) all things under sin (3:22), resulting in a guardianship (φρουρέω) and imprisonment (συγκλείω) under the law (Gal 3:23).
2. An educational tutor: The law became our tutor (παιδαγωγός) to lead us to Christ (Gal 3:24). After faith has come, we are no longer under the tutor (παιδαγωγός) (Gal 3:25).
3. A legal guardian: During the time of their minority, heirs remain under the guardians (ἐπίτροποι) and trustees (οἰκονόμοι) also (Gal 4:2).[152]

It is possible to take these images to the effect that "Paul goes out of his way to put the law in a very bad light," as de Boer says, given the metaphor

150. C. H. Dodd, *The Bible Today* (Cambridge: CUP, 1946), 120; Kevin J. Vanhoozer, *The Drama of Doctrine: A Canonical-Linguistic Approach to Christian Theology* (Louisville: Westminster John Knox, 2005), 387.

151. Martyn asserts that the cursing voice of the law is not the cursing voice of God, leaving us therefore with a sequence of "promissory potency and nomistic impotence," not "redemptive continuity" (*Galatians*, 326, 347n184). But that scheme deviates from what Paul says repeatedly that the cross is a divine act where God "handed over" Jesus to death and even propitiated and condemned sin on the cross (e.g., Rom 3:24; 8:3). Furthermore, the cursedness of Christ's crucifixion is a curse by God, just as Deut 21:23 explicitly announces—a point that makes some theory of penal substitution the best explanation for Jesus' accursedness (as Martyn, *Galatians*, 318n110, recognizes, though he rightly ties it to a *Christus Victor* motif as well). Maston ("Nature of Salvation History in Galatians," 99) asserts: "The anti-*heilsgeschichte* reading struggles to account for these temporal markers."

152. On the parallels between Gal 3:23-29 and 4:1-7, see Dunn, *Galatians*, 210.

of incarceration and the reputation of pedagogues for severity.[153] The law occasions imprisonment, harsh discipline, and slavery, creating what Campbell calls a "fundamentally awful scenario."[154] However, I'm convinced that these images of custody, pedagogue, and minority are meant to present the law partly positively, or perhaps benignly.

First, the image of being locked up under guard might actually intend to present the law as something that restricts sin and prevents it from being as terrible as it can be. In which case, the imprisonment might be more *preventive* than *punitive*. Dunn provides an apt image. Before the coming of Christ, Israel was "like a city garrisoned by the law within a larger territory ruled by sin."[155] There is an analogous thought in Romans, where imprisonment is actually for a positive end, since Paul remarks that "God has *bound* [συγκλείω] everyone over to disobedience *so that* he may have mercy on them all" (Rom 11:32). This arguably parallels what we find in Galatians, namely, the law imprisoned all things under sin *in order that* what has been promised through faith in Jesus Christ would come to those who believe (Gal 3:22). The temporary imprisonment under the law serves a positive purpose in God's salvation-historical plan to bring Jews and Gentiles to faith in Christ.

Second, the reputation of tutors (i.e., pedagogues) for severity is well-known, but the child-pedagogue relationship was not one-sided.[156] The intentions of the pedagogues were good, even if their manner might periodically be rough.[157] Pedagogues could also be surrogate fathers for their wards. Alexander the Great had scarcely any affection for his father, Philip of Macedon, but he risked his life to care for his pedagogue Lysimachus.[158] I also stumbled across an interesting inscription of a memorial erected by a pedagogue for his ward who was betrothed to the emperor, indicating a warm relationship between the two: "Who died on the day when the later Emperor Claudius was to have married her. . . . To Medullina, daughter of Camillus, espoused to Tiberius Claudius Nero Germanicus. The freedman of Acratus, her *paedogo-*

153. De Boer, *Galatians*, 168.

154. Campbell, *Quest*, 213. Elsewhere, however, Campbell asserts (*Deliverance of God*, 884) that the negative depictions of the law are made only retrospectively in comparison with Christ, and the negative view is relative, not absolute. Martyn (*Galatians*, 363) sees the law as a "distinctly unfriendly and confining custodian, different in no significant way from an imprisoning jailer."

155. Dunn, *Galatians*, 197.

156. See discussion of pedagogues in Witherington, *Grace in Galatia*, 263-67.

157. Campbell, *Deliverance of God*, 883.

158. Plutarch, *Alex.* 24.6.

gus.[159] The law as a pedagogue is not only to lead God's people *until* Christ but also to lead them *to Christ* (εἰς Χριστόν) and *in order that* believers might be justified by faith (Gal 3:24).[160]

Third, minors might be enslaved to the whim of their guardians and trustees, but it is undertaken at the appointment of the father; it was for the purpose of being guided into adulthood, and only for a limited time. The time of minority is constrained and submissive, but ultimately necessary and in the minor's own interest.

Put together, the law *temporarily* imprisoned Israel under sin to contain sin until Christ came; the custodianship of the law is divinely appointed by the Father to *temporarily* bring Israel to maturity; and like a pedagogue, the law leads people to Christ and to justification by faith.

I believe this shows that Paul's argument is constructed in a salvation-historical fashion, oriented around the vantage point of God's revelation in Christ, and brings Israel's law and covenants into proper perspective. Christ's act of deliverance unveils the role of the law in the redemptive story so that the law, when viewed retrospectively, is a force that hems in Israel, but is also a herald of the gospel.[161] Consequently, Christ-believing Gentiles should not strive to enter into the prior period of Israel's detention, discipline, and minority, because Christ has come to free people from its constriction and curse and to provide what the law itself promised.[162] Hence, Paul does not oppose the law because it stands in some kind of cosmic war against God; rather, he

159. *CIL* 10:6561 cited from Peter Balla, *The Child-Parent Relationship in the New Testament and Its Environment* (WUNT 155; Tübingen: Mohr Siebeck, 2003), 43n10.

160. Martyn (*Galatians*, 363; similarly de Boer, *Galatians*, 240-41) tries to explain the preposition εἰς as meaning a goal that God had in mind during the period of the law. Yet this idea flies in the face of what Paul actually says, namely, that the law was pedagogue for the purpose of tutoring believers toward Christ and toward justification by faith—no abstract intention in the divine mind can be even connoted here. Though elsewhere (*Galatians*, 366) Martyn states that "the scripture/Law played an active part in God's grand plan for humanity: It blocked every route of effective dealings between human beings and God, except the route elected by God when he sent Christ into the world." Hays ("Galatians," 11:270) rejects the idea that εἰς can be taken spatially, since Paul emphasizes the temporal nature of the law in the parallel passage in Gal 3:23, and Paul does not argue for a "progressive educative function of the Law." I demur because I think Paul's point is that, by keeping Israel in protective custody—under discipline—in minority *until* Christ, the law was in fact leading the people *to* Christ. I prefer Carson ("Mystery and Fulfillment," 427), who says that "the law's most important function is to bring Israel, *across time*, to Christ—and to bring others, too, insofar as the 'law' is found among those 'without the law'" (italics original).

161. Hays, *Faith of Jesus Christ*, xxxvi.

162. See similarly Campbell, *Deliverance of God*, 884-85.

opposes using the law as a means of salvation and source of identity because it belongs to a prior dispensation and because of its impotence to impart life or to effect righteousness. The law is no archrival to God's redemptive purposes; instead, God used the law to illuminate Israel's condition and, a fortiori, the universal condition of humanity in bondage to sin.[163]

The Law as Cause of Slavery and Promise of Salvation

Paul, in direct opposition to the teaching of the intruders, claims that perfection is not arrived at by obedience to the law, since no one properly obeys the law, as the experience of Israel well indicates. Even worse, coming under the law inevitably means coming under its curses.[164] Even so, Paul believes

163. Hays, "Galatians," 11:269.

164. That Jews were not expected to keep the law perfectly is now well-rehearsed in scholarship (see E. P. Sanders, *Paul and Palestinian Judaism: A Comparison of Patterns of Religion* [Philadelphia: Fortress, 1977], 483-84; Dunn, *Galatians*, 171; de Boer, *Galatians*, 200). The claims found in the Old Testament (e.g., Gen 6:9; 2 Sam 22:21-26; Dan 6:22; Job 1:1; Ps 18:20-26; 37:18; 119:1; Prov 11:5) and in Paul of being "innocent" or "blameless" before God (Phil 3:3-6) are more expressions of intent than forensic status (see 2 Bar. 54.5). Hays ("Galatians," 11:257) calls the view that Jews believed that perfect obedience to the law was possible "such a ridiculous caricature of Judaism." However: (1) there are many examples of figures in Jewish literature being venerated for their perfection (e.g., Pr. Man. 8; 1 En. 81.4; 82.4; Jub. 5.10; 10.3; 23.10; 27.17 [see discussion in A. Andrew Das, *Paul, the Law, and the Covenant* (Peabody, MA: Hendrickson, 2001), 12-44; idem, *Paul and the Jews* (LPS; Peabody, MA: Hendrickson, 2003), 142-48]); (2) the logic of Gal 3:10-14 still seems to work best if Paul envisages a comprehensive obedience to the law as necessary for the scheme of the intruders to work (see Das, *Paul, the Law, and the Covenant*, 145-55; idem, *Paul and the Jews*, 36-42); (3) this understanding is confirmed by Paul's reference to the intruder's apparent fixation on using law observance to achieve "fullness" (Gal 3:3) and "perfection" (Gal 5:16), and Paul also points out that even the intruders who want to circumcise the Galatians themselves do not obey the law completely (Gal 6:13); (4) While Lev 18:5 might be for Paul an "empty promise" (Hays, "Galatians," 11:259-60), nonetheless, Lev 18:5 was kind of like the "John 3:16" of Judaism (Sprinkle, *Law and Life*, vii), as many authors accentuated the link between doing the law and receiving in turn life (e.g., Bar 3:9; Pss. Sol. 14.2-3; Ps.-Philo, *Bib. Ant.* 23.10). Perhaps the intruders advocated a complete adherence to *their own way* of observing the law as the mechanism for Gentiles to be incorporated into Israel and as a means to restraining sinful desires. Also, we can grant that the "curse" in question is the Deuteronomic penalty for Israel's failure to observe the law (see Deut 27–32), as argued by Wright (*Climax*, 147) and James M. Scott ("'For as Many as Are of Works of the Law Are under a Curse' [Galatians 3:10]," in *Paul and the Scriptures of Israel*, ed. C. A. Evans and J. A. Sanders [JSNTSup 83; Sheffield: Sheffield Academic, 1993], 187-221). *But someone somewhere has not obeyed the law in order for the curses to come into effect.* It is not just the threat of a curse, not just that Israel's national way of life ended up with curses—someone disobeyed. So *relying* on the law will mean inevitably *rehearsing* Israel's disobedience and *receiving* the law's curses. The

that the law prepromises the agent through whom this curse is lifted and Gentiles are brought into the Abraham family. What is left to explain now is how Paul can simultaneously affirm the law as curse and slavery, but also as an instrumental context for the revelation of the Messiah, who actualizes the Abrahamic promises.

Part of that answer lies in Gal 3:10-14 and 4:4-5.[165] Both passages are linked by the ideas "redemption" (ἐξαγοράζω), being "under a curse [of the law]" (ὑπὸ κατάραν) or "under the law" (ὑπὸ νόμον), and presenting Jesus as the redeemer of Israel.

First, in Gal 3:13-14, the "us" is very probably Jewish Christ-believers who live under the law and therefore under its curses.[166] According to Longenecker, the argumentative logic proceeds as follows: (1) Christ took upon himself the Jewish state of being cursed by the law (Gal 3:13b), and (2) Christ redeems Israel's condition (i.e., "us") from the curse of the law (Gal 3:13a), in order that (3) a new age might dawn in which salvation is available for everyone (i.e., "we") in Christ (Gal 3:14).[167]

Second, in Gal 4:4-5 we observe that (1) the situation of Israel "under the law" is the context in which God's son was "sent"; (2) he was so sent in order that those under the law might be redeemed; and (3) then adoption into this transformed Israel would be offered beyond the boundaries of Israel.[168] Wright correctly sees a tripartite imagery at work: This an *exodus* event, with God again redeeming his people, remembering his promises to the patriarchs, and setting captives free; it is an *apocalyptic* event, with the long-awaited un-

---

crux of Paul's argument is that, if *Israel* had been unable to obey the law and so came under its curses, why would *individual Gentiles* want to rely on the law for their identity and deliverance? (see Das, *Paul, the Law, and the Covenant*, 154; idem, *Paul and the Jews*, 37-38).

165. On the shared narrative behind Gal 3:13-14 and 4:4-5, see Hays, *Faith of Jesus Christ*, 95-118; idem, "Galatians," 11:284-86; and Longenecker, *Triumph of Abraham's God*, 91-95.

166. See D. W. B. Robinson, "Distinction between Jewish and Gentile Believers in Galatians," *ABR* 13 (1965): 29-48; Linda L. Belleville, "'Under Law': Structural Analysis and the Pauline Concept of Law in Galatians 3.21–4.11," *JSNT* 26 (1986): 53-78; Hays, *Faith of Jesus Christ*, 128n19; idem, "Galatians," 11:262; Wright, *Climax*, 143; cf. Campbell, *Deliverance of God*, 883, who sees 3:24-25 as addressed "*only to Israel*, and *not* to pagans in general" (italics original). Martyn's position (*Galatians*, 334-36) is that the pronominal alternations represent a "rhetorical, psychological, and fundamentally theological language game" that Paul plays with the Galatians in order to erase rather than reinforce the distinctions between Jew and Gentile. For Martyn, Paul writes as a "former Jew" to persons who are "former Gentiles." The problem is, however, that Paul includes multiple subidentities (Jew, Greek, slave, free, male, female) in the meta-identity of being "in Christ" rather than erasing them in toto.

167. Longenecker, *Triumph of Abraham's God*, 93.

168. Longenecker, *Triumph of Abraham's God*, 92.

veiling of God's solution to Israel's problem in the "fullness of time"; and it is a *messianic* event, in the "sending" of the "Son," who achieves and actualizes deliverance.[169] Christ was born under the law and took on the curse of the law in order to redeem those cursed by the law. This action brings Israel's redemption, but it also inaugurates the eschatological salvation of the Gentiles, whereby Israel's sonship as expressed in Exod 4:22, "Israel is my firstborn son," is now possible for the Gentiles as well. God sends the messianic son for a new exodus so that a redeemed Israel is the conduit for Gentiles to share in Israel's election. Whereas it might seem that the Abrahamic covenant was interdicted by the giving of the law, with Israel cursed by their disobedience, Jesus takes upon himself the curse of the law in his death in order to redeem Israel and to open the way for Gentiles to share in the blessing of Abraham's family, Israel's sonship, a family that Genesis and Habakkuk say are characterized by faith.

A further explanation of the duality of the law as curse and promise comes in the allegory in Gal 4:21-31. This highly disputed text, committing as it does some "hermeneutical jujitsu,"[170] contests the reading of Israel's covenantal history put forward by the intruders on the grounds that it will bring Christ-believing Gentiles into a state of slavery. Paul takes up the intruder's favorite texts about the patriarchs and exposes their interpretation as fallacious and detrimental to the Galatian believers. Paul's argument, as far as one can unweave it, is that his own Gentile mission, symbolized by Sarah and her Gentile children born of the promise (i.e., the gospel), stands in opposition to the intruder's mission, symbolized by Hagar and those who are birthed by the flesh (i.e., law-observance). Consequently, the Galatian believers should throw out the intruders just as Abraham ejected Hagar and Ishmael. Paul's allegorical exegesis operates much like an apocalyptic vision that reveals the true meaning of the Torah.[171] The entire narration also builds on a well-worn apocalyptic theme: The people of God, despite undergoing suffering and adversity, are children of the heavenly Jerusalem that will be eschatologically revealed in the future.[172] The citation of Isa 54:1 accents the eschatological nature of the Abrahamic promise by linking God's restoration of Israel with God's embrace of the nations, including Paul's audience. Yet at the same time, Paul is arguing

169. Wright, *Paul and the Faithfulness of God*, 878; and *Paul and His Recent Interpreters*, 178-80.

170. Hays, *Echoes of Scripture*, 112.

171. Morna D. Hooker, "'Heirs of Abraham': The Gentiles' Role in Israel's Story; A Response to Bruce Longenecker," in *Narrative Dynamics in Paul: A Critical Assessment*, ed. B. W. Longenecker (Louisville: Westminster John Knox, 2002), 93.

172. Hays, "Galatians," 11:304.

salvation-historically by showing that the law supports a law-free mission to Gentiles by indicating that (1) law-observing Israel finds itself in slavery under foreign powers; (2) the opposition of the enslaved (Jewish Christ-believers) to the free (Gentile Christ-believers) is prefigured in the Torah; (3) the antithesis between the two strands is lessened by the fact that the "Jerusalem that is above" is the ultimate goal of the "present city of Jerusalem" (Gal 4:25); and (4) the promised children are characterized by freedom, which only Christ provides and which Abraham's son Isaac typifies.

What should be clear is that salvation history is the hub of Paul's argument, not its antithesis, since God's redemptive action in Christ moves to and through Israel and only then to the Gentiles. Paul argues much the same point in Rom 15:8-9, concerning Christ becoming a servant to Israel to confirm God's promises given to the patriarchs. Simply because the law is not necessary to inherit the promises does not warrant the deduction that the law is hostile to God or that Israel's history has been effectively detoured. Israel has always been integral to God's apocalyptic rescue plan for the world. The revelation of salvation in the Messiah means that salvation will be distinctively Israel-shaped. This is not a Christian invention but constitutes a standard Jewish hope—an eschatological promise found in prophetic literature, apocalyptic writings, and arguably even traceable in the Jesus tradition—that a transformed Israel will transform the world.[173] Belief that the Gentiles have now been incorporated into Israel through the Messiah is an essential part of Paul's story for what God purposed to achieve in the world through Israel. Bruce Longenecker puts it elegantly:

> In effecting salvation in Christ, God has not avoided, neglected, trivialized or rendered irrelevant Israel's situation. Instead, the situation of Israel is the arena wherein God's transforming power has initially been operative before extending to universal proportions. The rectification of Israel's predicament, rather than its abandonment, stands as the prerequisite for the inauguration of the new world. Israel's own situation has been the place where God had already been at work (e.g., giving the law), and it has become the inaugural locus of God's eschatological initiative (e.g.,

---

173. See exploration of this theme in T. W. Manson, *Only to the House of Israel? Jesus and the Non-Jews* (Philadelphia: Fortress, 1964); N. T. Wright, *New Testament and the People of God* (COQG 1; London: SPCK, 1992), 268; idem, *Jesus and the Victory of God* (COQG 2; London: SPCK, 1996), 306-8; Michael F. Bird, *Jesus and the Origins of the Gentile Mission* (LNTS 331; London: T&T Clark, 2006).

sending his son) in order to transform Israel's situation and consequently to inaugurate a new age.[174]

To recap, Paul's argument in Gal 3–4 is not a rejection of salvation history; rather, it is premised upon it. The law contains the threat of curses for disobedience but also the promises for salvation. The law's deficiency is its temporal limitation, not its opposition to God's purposes. The tripartite images for subjection in the law are also related to preparation for salvation. Finally, the duality of law as curse and promise is resolved by Paul's assertion that Christ bears the law's curse and thereafter emerges a people free from the law's curse, which is precisely what the law, when properly understood, intended.

Galatians 6: New Law, New Creation, and New Israel

Finally, we might consider how the "law of Christ," the "new creation," and the "Israel of God" in Gal 6 relate to the alleged dichotomy of apocalyptic versus salvation history.

In his exhortation section, Paul writes, "Carry each other's burdens, and in this way you will fulfill the *law of Christ*" (τὸν νόμον τοῦ Χριστοῦ), as stated in Gal 6:2. The only other place where Paul mentions the "law of Christ" or "Christ's law" is 1 Cor 9:20-21, where he refers to not being under the law—but instead of being lawless, he is under "Christ's law" (ἔννομος Χριστοῦ).[175] It

---

174. Longenecker, *Triumph of Abraham's God*, 94. See Terrence L. Donaldson ("The 'Curse of the Law' and the Inclusion of the Gentiles: Galatians 3.13-14," *NTS* 32 [1986]: 102-3): "This redemptive road passes through the territory of the law (and its people). . . . It was not possible to make an end run around the law and those in its domain. Rather, the way forward for both Jew and Gentile required the redemption of Israel from its plight. . . . For Paul the law was not a dead end side trail but rather something lying squarely on the path of redemptive history." Justin Hardin (*Galatians and the Imperial Cult: A Critical Analysis of the First-Century Social Context of Paul's Letter* [WUNT 2.237; Tübingen: Mohr Siebeck, 2008], 154): "Gal 4.1-7 actually contains strong apocalyptic elements within Paul's précis of salvation history, which would suggest that there is no inherent dichotomy between Paul's apocalyptic thought and his concern for the reversal of Israel's plight under the (curse of the) Law and the inclusion of Gentiles as God's people. Far from salvation history beginning from the time of God's eschatological invasion in human history through Christ, as Martyn asserts, the incarnation was rather the pinnacle (dare I saw climax?) of God's saving activity in the world."

175. See recent survey of approaches in Todd A. Wilson, "The Law of Christ and the Law of Moses: Reflections on a Recent Trend in Interpretation," *CBR* 5 (2006): 124-44, and helpful excursus in de Boer, *Galatians*, 378-81.

may well be the case that Paul intends the "law of Christ" to be contrasted with the law of Moses and denotes the example of Christ, the teaching of Christ, and life in the Spirit.[176] Yet we must remember that the renewal of the covenant in Jeremiah and Ezekiel was associated with a new power to obey God's law in the age of national restoration (e.g., Jer 31:33; Ezek 16:61). According to the Synoptic tradition and Jewish Christianity, the law featured largely in Jesus' exhortations for his followers, with an intensification of some commands and relaxation of others, as was common in Jewish renewal movements. Jesus, James, and Paul all agree that Lev 19:18 represents something of the essence of the law (Matt 5:43; 19:15; 23:29; Rom 13:9; Gal 5:15; Jas 2:8). Furthermore, despite Paul's impassioned and sometimes even polemical denial that believers are under the law, the law still seems to hold a significant place in Pauline ethical paraenesis in places like Rom 13:9-10 and 1 Cor 9:9, so that the law remains a form of wisdom for Christian behavior, even if it is not constitutive for their salvation or determinative for their way of life.[177] However, they are under the "law of Christ," so the law still figures in Paul's ethical discourse.

In addition, Paul's account of the new age is not so disjointed that it entails a complete break with ethical paradigms and patterns of Israel's covenantal past. Paul's denial of the value of circumcision and uncircumcision in favor of the value of "new creation" in Gal 6:15 is paralleled by (1) the earlier comment in Gal 5:6, where Paul also denied the importance of circumcision and uncircumcision, since what truly matters is "faith becoming effective through love," which is soon after expressed in terms of Lev 19:18 about love of neighbor in Gal 5:14; and (2) elsewhere, in 1 Cor 7:19, Paul makes a similar denial to that of Gal 6:15 about the insignificance of circumcision and uncircumcision relative to the paramount imperative of "obeying the commandments of God." In other words, Paul is saying that circumcision and uncircumcision are insignificant in the new creation, and yet the new creation requires love, which fulfills the law and keeps God's commandments. Thus, new creation and law-as-love command are not only compatible but prescribed by Paul.

Given a matrix where parts of the law are nullified and other parts are intensified in the new creation, it is likely that the "law of Christ" includes the ethical and sapiential function of the Mosaic law, since acting in love fulfills the entire Mosaic legislation (Gal 5:13-14; Rom 13:8). The law of Christ is the

---

176. See Michael F. Bird, *A Bird's-Eye View of Paul: The Man, His Mission, and His Message* (Nottingham: InterVarsity, 2008), 143-49.

177. See further Brian S. Rosner, "Paul and the Law: What He Does Not Say," *JSNT* 34 (2011): 405-19; idem, *Paul and the Law*.

law of Moses as understood through the lens of Christ's life, teachings, death, and risen life.[178] In his ethical exhortations in Galatians, Paul counters the instruction of the intruders by proposing that Jesus' example, acting in love, and life in the Spirit are the proper framework for understanding the relationship between Christ and the law. Gentiles have, then, the moral resources to live up to the strictures of the Mosaic law without being committed to actually living under it. Now if the law does retain some positive significance for the behavior of Christ-believing Gentiles, it seems impossible to identify the law as entirely in opposition to God's purposes, since it is not a bad thing done away with as much as it is a good thing that is "fulfilled" in the love that overflows from participants in the new creation.

Pressing on, the concept of "new creation" highlights the clear apocalyptic texture of Paul's theology in Galatians. Paul's remark that "neither circumcision nor uncircumcision is anything; but a new creation is everything!" (Gal 6:15) stands solidly within a Jewish apocalyptic eschatology, with God's cosmic renewal of the world (Isa 65:17-25; Ezek 47:1-12; Jub. 4.26; 1 En. 72.1; 1QS 4.25; 1QH 11.1-18; 13.5-12; 4 Ezra 7.75; 2 Bar. 32.6). Paul refers explicitly to new creation elsewhere only in 2 Cor 5:17. But new creation casts a shadow over various other remarks by Paul in Galatians, being implicit in the deliverance wrought from "the present evil age" (Gal 1:4) and felt in the transformative power of being in Christ, where circumcision and uncircumcision cease to matter (Gal 3:28; 5:6; see Col 2:13). Importantly, for Paul the new creation is not *creatio ex nihilio* but more akin to *creatura renovata*. God does not destroy and then remake the earth; instead, God renews the universe, taking it from death to rebirth. Paul is simply tapping into a scriptural story where Israel's restoration as Isaiah and Ezekiel describe it will climax in a cosmic revivification.[179] For this reason the apocalyptically infused discourse in 1 Cor 15 ends with the exhortation "Always give yourselves fully to the work of the Lord, because you know that your labor in the Lord is not in vain" (1 Cor 15:58)—

---

178. See along these lines John M. G. Barclay, *Obeying the Truth: A Study of Paul's Ethics in Galatians* (Edinburgh: T&T Clark, 1988), 131-35; Hong, *Law in Galatians*, 176-83; Dunn, *Galatians*, 322-24; Longenecker, *Triumph of Abraham's God*, 85-87; Martyn, *Galatians*, 548-49; Hays, "Galatians," 11:322-323.

179. Martyn (*Galatians*, 565 and 571) sees a "radical, uncompromising newness," and God does not intend on "repairing the old cosmos" as much as he is in the process "of replacing it." Contrast this view with that of Mark B. Stephens (*Annihilation or Renewal? The Meaning and Function of New Creation in the Book of Revelation* [WUNT 2.307; Tübingen: Mohr Siebeck, 2011]), who argues that Jewish eschatologies affirmed a mix of continuities and discontinuities between this age and any new creation.

new creation means new tasks for the people of God as vanguards of the new creation. The upshot of this is that the tendency of advocates of an apocalyptic Paul to emphasize creation and new creation is not altogether wrong, but it lacks a vital link in the chain, namely, Israel. If Eden was something of a cosmic temple and if Adam and Israel were priests of that temple, then humanity and Israel—intertwined as they are—cannot be voided or vitiated. The story of new creation moves ahead only through the prism of a new Israel and a restored humanity. Martyn I think grasps this point profoundly when he regards Israel as God's new creation in Christ.[180]

This brings us finally to Paul's reference to what can be conceptually identified as a new Israel in Gal 6:16. Paul writes in his epistolary closing, "As for those who will follow this rule, peace be upon them, and mercy, and upon the Israel of God." The identity of "the Israel of God" (τὸν Ἰσραὴλ τοῦ θεοῦ) has perplexed commentators, especially those desperate to avoid the smear of any smug supersessionism. The benediction could refer to a blessing for Jewish and Gentile Christ-believers, to Jewish Christ-believers who abide by Paul's teaching, or to ethnic Israel. Here are several factors to consider:

1. The question of who actually is Israel and debates among Jewish groups as to who are the faithful Israelites was part and parcel of Second Temple Jewish sectarianism. Philo's "Israel who sees God" and the Qumran's "sons of light" are prestige labels that invest Israel's election around an even smaller circle.

2. Romans 2 and 9 make it clear that Paul espouses a view that there can be "inward Jews" and an "Israel within Israel."

3. Paul elsewhere employs language ordinarily used to describe Israel to designate Christians such as "circumcision" and "elect" (e.g., Phil 3:3; Rom 8:33).

4. Despite Israel's inherited covenantal privileges (Rom 9:1-5) and his hope that "all Israel" will be saved (Rom 11:25-27), Paul would be unlikely to issue a blessing upon Israel irrespective of whether or not they believe in Christ, since those who do not love Christ are under a curse (1 Cor 16:22).

5. Paul has just spent the whole of Galatians arguing for the unity of Jews and Gentiles in one body, so it is highly unlikely that he would now at the end of the letter split up Jews and Gentiles and include Jews only

---

180. Martyn, *Galatians*, 575-76.

under the privileged title "the Israel of God."[181] Although the phrase "new Israel" and "true Israel" do not occur until the second century, there is a sense in which the church does pick up the baton from Israel. Paul still knows that ethnic Israel exists and holds out hope for their eventual deliverance (which is the essence of Rom 11), but it is apparent to me that Paul envisages the church, made up of Jews and Gentiles, as something like the representatives of Israel within the messianic age. They have assumed the role of Israel while waiting for the rest of empirical Israel to catch up and grow into their messianic faith.

The apocalyptic school of Pauline interpretation needs further scrutiny when it comes to Paul and Israel. The tragic irony is that the proponents of the apocalyptic school claim that they are avoiding supersessionism, while their effort to set Paul against "religion" forces them to negate Israel's election and its religious history. Martyn thinks that Paul's argument in Gal 3 focuses the covenantal promises on only two persons: Abraham and Christ. According to Martyn, Paul's point is that the plural offspring of Abraham came into existence only when human beings are incorporated into Abraham's singular seed, that is, Christ. Based on this passage alone, one may infer that, prior to Christ, there were no children of Abraham. Hence Gal 3:16 purportedly makes salvation history impossible because salvation is punctiliar and singular, not linear and gradual—in other words, it detours around Israel. Following Ulrich Luz, Martyn contends that the covenantal promise uttered by God existed in a docetic state until the advent of the singular seed, Christ. Paul implies that, in the period of the law, there was no seed of Abraham.[182] Even Bruce Longenecker is led astray by Martyn (like Barnabas led astray by Cephas in Antioch), for he remarks that the seed analogy in Gal 3:16-19 means that "Abraham and Christ are associated with each other in a manner that wholly bypasses Israel's

181. Wright (*Paul and the Faithfulness of God*, 1143-44) claims that "the noble, evocative word 'Israel' itself now denotes, however polemically, *the entire faith-family of the* Messiah, defined by 'faith working through love' (5.6) and 'new creation' (6.15)" (italics original). The best arguments for this position in my readings remain Richard N. Longenecker, *Galatians* (WBC; Dallas: Word, 1990), 296-99; Gregory K. Beale, "Peace and Mercy upon the Israel of God: The Old Testament Background to Galatians 6,16b," *Bib* 80 (1999): 204-23; Andreas Köstenberger, "The Identity of the ΙΣΡΑΗΛ ΤΟΥ ΘΕΟΥ (Israel of God) in Galatians 6:16," *Faith and Mission* 19 (2001): 3-24. Although the most cogent argument for "Israel of God" as empirical Israel is Susan G. Eastman, "Israel and the Mercy of God: A Re-reading of Galatians 6.16 and Romans 9–11," *NTS* 56 (2010): 367-95.

182. Martyn *Galatians*, 340, 345-47, 350-51.

constitutions and constituents."[183] Going further than Martyn, Longenecker even surmises that Christians are the Israel of God only in a "linguistic sense," apart from the term's traditional narrative context and denotes those who enjoy a special relationship with God in a pagan world.[184]

This reading should be resisted. We have already noted that the discontinuities posed by Gal 3:11-14, 16 must be countenanced with the continuities enumerated in Gal 3:19-25. Richard Hays asks some hard questions of what is implied by Martyn's account of Israel in his reading of Galatians: "Can Martyn really maintain at the end of the day that Galatians, as he reads it, does not lead inevitably to an anti-Jewish, supersessionist Christian theology? . . . He impressively shows that the polemic of the letter is targeted not against Jews but against rival Jewish Christian evangelists, and he argues that Galatians 'is not an anti-Judaic text.' . . . Nonetheless, the letter's slanderous statements about the Law and its radical negation (on Martyn's reading) of the election of Israel seemingly leave no room for the continuing existence of a Law-observant Jewish people."[185]

On the "seed" analogy, Christ is not so much the sole focus of the promised seed as much as he is the instrument who enables the Abrahamic promise to be shared with others.[186] Furthermore, the point of the reference to Abraham's seed is not to suggest that the promise bypasses Israel; more likely, salvation is delivered through Israel's *Christos* rather than by Israel's *nomos*. Morna Hooker points out: "In Romans 4, Abraham's seed are identified as all those who share in Abraham's faith. Yet in Gal 3:16-19 the seed is identified with Christ alone with purportedly no other seed envisaged. The link between the two texts is Gal 3:26-29 where one becomes Abraham's seed by being 'in' his seed who is Christ. Given that the link to Abraham in Galatians is by incorporation into Abraham's seed, the link with Romans is stronger than normally observed. Inclusion in Abraham's seed can hardly mean that Israel's story is excluded from salvation."[187]

If I may offer a somewhat discursive thought: the problems with the apocalyptic school go far deeper when it comes to Israel. Romans 9–11 constitutes an obvious challenge for the apocalyptic school, since it so lucidly affirms Israel's covenant status. Martyn contents himself with saying that in Romans

---

183. Longenecker, "Sharing in Their Spiritual Blessings?," 67.

184. Longenecker, "Sharing in Their Spiritual Blessings?," 71, 74.

185. Richard B. Hays, review of J. Louis Martyn, *Galatians*, *RBL* 3 (2001): 63-64.

186. Beker, *Paul the Apostle*, 50.

187. Hooker, "Heirs of Abraham," 90, 95.

Paul rescinds his earlier denial of Israel's election.[188] More theologically so-phisticated is the move by Campbell, where, reminiscent of Barth, he believes that Israel's election actually acquires a prehistory in Jesus.[189] That move is followed by Douglas Harink in his theological reading of Rom 9–11.[190] Harink calls down a pox on supersessionism but then argues that, for Paul, "Israel's history is taken up into (and therefore saved by) the apokalypsis theou in Jesus Christ—that is, it is preserved in its truth insofar as it is crucified and risen with Christ."[191] To construe Israel and Judaism in a thoroughly christological way is one thing, but it is quite another to deny Israel's God-given role in the world prior to the coming of Christ. For interpreters such as these, nothing in Israel's law or election contributes to or prepares for the revelation of Christ, which is an entirely new creative act of God. So of course this is not superses-sionism because, according to Harink and others, there wasn't really anything there worth replacing in the first place. Beker's criticism remains pointed. Neo-orthodoxy collapses apocalyptic eschatology into Christology and then defines Christology as simply God's ultimate revelatory word.[192] My suspicion is that, despite all efforts to do otherwise, the apocalyptic school of interpretation is essentially über-supersessionist, since it finds nothing redemptive in Israel's election and history.

Conclusion

Ernst Käsemann famously said that, "even when he became a Christian, Paul remained an apocalyptist."[193] I would change that to "even when Paul be-came a Christ-believer, he remained entrenched in Jewish apocalypticism and believed that, through the invasion of the gospel, God had brought about the long-awaited climax to Israel's history, and through this climax, God is recapturing the world for himself." On my reading, Galatians is about the culmination of Israel's salvation story in the apocalyptic revelation of Jesus

---

188. Martyn, *Galatians*, 351. Longenecker ("Salvation History in Galatians," 83-87) sees Paul developing an expanded-covenant model (i.e., salvation history) across the course of his apostolic ministry, based on various disputes he had with interlocutors between 50 and 57 CE.

189. Campbell, *Quest*, 143n8.

190. Douglas Harink, "Paul and Israel: An Apocalyptic Reading," *Pro Ecclesia* 16 (2007): 359-80.

191. Harink, "Paul and Israel," 368n18.

192. Beker, *Paul the Apostle*, 139, 142.

193. Käsemann "'The Righteousness of God' in Paul," 181.

Christ to include Gentiles in the family of Abraham. That claim is controversial because among recent interpreters of Galatians a chief point of contention is whether there was anything redemptive about Israel's election and the law according to Paul. I have argued that Paul does not replace salvation history with a direct and vertical apocalyptic eschatology, as much as he rejects one particular account of salvation history propounded by the intruders. Such an account merges the dispensations of Abraham, Moses, and Messiah into a single monolithic epoch that makes the inclusion of Gentiles merely an extension of Jewish proselytism with a messianic gloss. Instead, Paul sets forth a vibrant tapestry of theological instruction threaded with gospel traditions, charismatic experience, and scriptural interpretation to create a colorful montage of scriptural substories that are joined in a singular narrative that God's promise in the Torah to Abraham is made good in Gentile believers in the Messiah. The law, whether we think of it as parenthetical or preparatory, is not the hub of God's redemptive movement, but neither is the law nullified as a divinely given constitution, since the law envisages its own climax in Jesus Christ.

First, Paul's apocalyptic gospel is necessarily salvation-historical by nature of the Jewish context of his eschatology and Christology. Paul theologizes out of an apocalyptic framework, as evidenced by intense eschatological, cosmological, and ethical dualisms rooted in his own apocalyptic commission to take the gospel to the Gentiles. Whatever rupture takes place within Israel's history, Paul—just like other Jewish seers—still envisaged an event proving God's faithfulness to Israel, even if the corollaries of this deliverance meant reconfiguring Israel's Torah and Israel's election around the Messiah in an innovative way. Moreover, his testimony to Christ as crucified and risen indicates that Paul sees Christ as experiencing what Israel had to go through in order to apprehend this deliverance: accursedness and resurrection. Christ transforms Israel in himself and incorporates all persons united to himself through faith into a new Israel, a new humanity consisting of Jew and Gentile, bearing the Spirit, and adopted into God's one-world family. The rescue of creation has its proleptic beginnings in the rescue of the covenant people. Thus, the revelation of Jesus Christ combines without contradiction elements of God's covenantal faithfulness to Israel and a cosmic rescue from the powers of sin and death on the same billing. Undoubtedly, the sending of God's Son is indeed dramatic and invasive, but it transpires in accordance with God's will, a will announced and enacted in Israel's covenant history. To enter into the salvation history of Jesus is to enter the salvation history of Israel, to which the history of Jesus indelibly belongs.

Second, Paul's exposition of the justification tradition demonstrates a pattern of scriptural conformity between faith in Christ and the Abrahamic covenant. Jewish Christ-believers—both the Galatian intruders and Paul—when confronted with the issue of what to do with Gentile Christ-believers, could hardly avoid the difficult decisions about how to admit and integrate them into a Jewish movement. For Paul, the answer was justification by faith, which entailed the inclusion of Gentiles into the church as Gentiles and without circumcision. Paul attempted to scripturally reason his way to this point by his retrospective account of salvation history. In Paul's configuration, justification is wrought in God's apocalyptic act of deliverance in the faithfulness, death, and resurrection of Jesus Christ, and its basis for appropriation is faith in Christ and not in works of the law. The Christ/law antithesis applies primarily to the role of the law as a social demarcation around Israel and its limited role in salvation history as temporary and ineffectual.

Third, while Paul confutes the scriptural arguments of the intruders by postulating a distinction between the Abrahamic and Mosaic epochs, he nonetheless still maintains a form of continuity, where Israel's covenant and law are essential contexts for the revelation of Jesus Christ. Paul does not emphasize the law's opposition to the purposes of God but chiefly points to its temporal character and its impotence concerning life and righteousness. Yet the law still retains a positive role as a form of preventive detention from sin, a tutor that leads people to Christ, and a guardian appointed by God the Father. Furthermore, Gal 3:13-14 and 4:4-5 demonstrate that the law, even with its curses, is part of the story in which Jesus comes to redeem Israel, with a view to then extending salvation to the Gentiles. Jesus, born under the law and accursed by the law, redeems the nation by his coming and is the hinge between Israel's past and the inclusion of the Gentiles in Israel's future.

Fourth, continuities abound in Paul's reference to the law of Christ, the new creation, and the Israel of God. The Mosaic law is reconfigured and reapplied for Gentiles when formulated through a christological grid. The new creation will feature a renewal of creation as God's new world finally encompasses and surpasses the old order of things. The new creation itself begins with a new Israel, a renewed people of God comprising Jews and Greeks, united in the Messiah. These themes all express newness, while simultaneously incorporating continuities from Israel's covenant history. As Beker put it: "The past contains footprints of the promises of God, and these promises are taken up into the new rather than cast aside."[194]

194. Beker, *Paul the Apostle*, 150.

In all of this we still see elements of Paul's thought that make him well and truly anomalous. Paul's use of scriptural narratives and deployment of an apocalyptic worldview show him clearly embedded within a Jewish framework. But unlike other Jewish thinkers and other apocalyptic seers, Paul makes the law preparatory to salvation rather than necessary for salvation. Israel's history climaxes in the Messiah, but the story is now retold in such a way that Israel's mission, experience, and hopes are configured around a new messianic narrative. Paul fashions a new and even provocative account of what time it is, what Israel needs, what Israel must do in the present time, and what will happen to the pagan nations. His answers to such questions would be an affront to many of his contemporaries. Paul gives us a mixture of mythic storytelling (retelling the grand narrative of Israel's creation, covenant, and consummation), mystical experience (apocalyptic revelation and receipt of the Spirit), and midrashic interpretation (a christological reading of Scripture applied to the circumstances of his churches), all based on the messianic story of Jesus (the gospel). To put it simply, Paul is a servant of Israel's God and Israel's king, and he sees himself acting in a cosmic drama, an invasion story where God reaches into the world through Israel to bring deliverance to the world through his Messiah and by the gift of the Spirit, all climaxing in the revelation of a new creation.

CHAPTER FOUR

The Incident at Antioch (Gal 2:11-14): The Beginnings of Paulinism

The incident in Antioch described in Gal 2:11-14 has been an Archimedean point for criticism of Paul since F. C. Baur.[1] The short narrative is a key unit in the argumentative strategy of the epistle to the Galatians and a crucial piece of evidence about the conflict and diversity of the early church.[2] As a window into the early church, it presents us with the questions of what went wrong, why, whose fault it was,[3] and what the repercussions were for the Pauline mission.[4]

---

1. Peter Tomson, *Paul and the Jewish Law: Halakha in the Letters of the Apostle to the Gentiles* (Minneapolis: Fortress, 1990), 223.

2. On the history of interpretation, see Andreas Wechsler, *Geschichtsbild und Apostelstreit: Eine forschungsgeschichtliche und exegetische Studie über antiochenischen Zwischenfall (Gal 2,11-14)* (BZNW 62; Berlin: Walter de Gruyter, 1991); Jack J. Gibson, *Peter between Jerusalem and Antioch* (WUNT 2.345; Tübingen: Mohr Siebeck, 2013), 1-15.

3. What I find genuinely amusing is the way scholars disagree as to who is to blame for the incident. For example, C. J. den Heyer (*Paul: A Man of Two Worlds* [London: SCM, 2000], 94) notes that, although Peter is called the "rock" in Matt 16:17-19, in Antioch "he was no rock, and proved not to be capable of coming forward with authority and providing leadership for a community in confusion." In contrast, John Dominic Crossan and Jonathan L. Reed (*Excavating Jesus: Beneath the Stones, behind the Texts* [San Francisco: HarperSanFrancisco, 2001], 41) say of Paul: "Paul's position . . . was akin to machine-gunning butterflies. James, Peter, Barnabas, and all the others who agreed with him were right at Antioch. Paul was wrong at Antioch."

4. An earlier version of this essay was published as "The Incident at Antioch (Gal. 2.11-14): The Beginnings of Paulinism," in *Earliest Christian History*, ed. Michael F. Bird and Jason Maston (WUNT 2.320; Tübingen: Mohr Siebeck, 2012), 329-61.

[11] But when Cephas came to Antioch, I opposed him to his face, because he stood self-condemned; [12] for until certain men came from James, he used to eat with the Gentiles. But after they came, he drew back and kept himself separate for fear of those of circumcision. [13] And the other Jews joined him in this hypocrisy, so that even Barnabas was led astray by their playacting. [14] But when I saw that they were not walking toward the truth of the gospel, I said to Cephas before them all, "If you, though a Jew, live like a Gentile and not like a Jew, how can you compel the Gentiles to judaize?"	[11] Ὅτε δὲ ἦλθεν Κηφᾶς εἰς Ἀντιόχειαν, κατὰ πρόσωπον αὐτῷ ἀντέστην, ὅτι κατεγνωσμένος ἦν. [12] πρὸ τοῦ γὰρ ἐλθεῖν τινας ἀπὸ Ἰακώβου μετὰ τῶν ἐθνῶν συνήσθιεν· ὅτε δὲ ἦλθον, ὑπέστελλεν καὶ ἀφώριζεν ἑαυτόν φοβούμενος τοὺς ἐκ περιτομῆς. [13] καὶ συνυπεκρίθησαν αὐτῷ [καὶ] οἱ λοιποὶ Ἰουδαῖοι, ὥστε καὶ Βαρναβᾶς συναπήχθη αὐτῶν τῇ ὑποκρίσει. [14] ἀλλ᾽ ὅτε εἶδον ὅτι οὐκ ὀρθοποδοῦσιν πρὸς τὴν ἀλήθειαν τοῦ εὐαγγελίου, εἶπον τῷ Κηφᾷ ἔμπροσθεν πάντων· εἰ σὺ Ἰουδαῖος ὑπάρχων ἐθνικῶς καὶ οὐχὶ Ἰουδαϊκῶς ζῇς, πῶς τὰ ἔθνη ἀναγκάζεις ἰουδαΐζειν;

Martin Hengel's contribution to this subject is documented in his study on Peter.[5] Hengel believed that the incident led to a protracted split between Paul and the Jerusalem church that can be dated to 52/53 CE. In Hengel's reconstruction, the reason "Peter pulled back when the messengers of James came was very possibly because of a compromise to maintain the unity between the missionary communities outside of Eretz Israel and Jerusalem itself, which was under threat."[6] Peter, Barnabas, and the other Jewish Christ-believers in Antioch may not have necessarily wanted to reinstitute circumcision and the observance of purity laws for Gentile Christ-believers. Their concern was primarily the legal reputation of Jewish Christ-believers in Antioch. In Hengel's view, Paul, however, was deeply concerned that, in the aftermath of Peter's separation, Gentile Christ-believers would be asked to observe the Jewish legal prescriptions concerning circumcision, purity, and food laws as well. Furthermore, Paul worried that "works of the law" might be attributed some salvific sense for Gentiles. I think that Hengel's portrait of the incident is generally correct. The objective of this study is to probe deeper into the details of the Antioch incident and to demonstrate what it contributed to the making of Paulinism, i.e., the essence of Paul's thought concerning God, Messiah, Torah, and the salvation of the Gentiles.

5. Martin Hengel, *Der unterschätzte Petrus: Zwei Studien* (Tübingen: Mohr Siebeck, 2007), 92-106, ET: *Saint Peter: The Underestimated Apostle,* trans. Thomas Trapp (Grand Rapids, MI: Eerdmans, 2010), 57-65.

6. Hengel, *Saint Peter*, 65.

Jews and Christians in Antioch

The history of the Jews in Antioch and the arrival of Christ-believers in Antioch has been aptly documented elsewhere.[7] But in contrast to Hengel, who believed that the church in Antioch had more or less already parted from the Jewish synagogues, I want to suggest that the situation was far more fluid than that, specifically, that an overlapping membership between the Christian gatherings and Jewish synagogues in Antioch persisted for some time.[8] Indeed, it was this overlap of social space and competing perspectives that occasioned the problem in Gal 2:11-14.

During Paul's time in Antioch (ca. 37-48 CE), Christ-believing Jews and Gentiles were beginning to form their own distinct identity, worship, communal meal, and mission, while still sitting loosely within the orbit of Antiochene Judaism. A number of features point to this reality.

First, the early Christian mission in Antioch was largely synagogue-based in its initial phases. Acts 11:19-26 shows the gospel outreach of Greek-speaking Jewish Christ-believers to Gentile Greeks in the city. The Greeks who had the gospel preached to them and subsequently believed were most likely drawn from the ranks of adherents to Jewish ways ("God-fearers") and converts to Judaism ("proselytes"). The increase in the number of Greek converts (Acts 11:21, 24) probably meant that separate meetings were held for these believers for the purpose of instruction and devotion to the "Lord Jesus" and for shared meals. Yet this was supplementary rather than an alternative to involvement in Jewish synagogues, at least in the initial stages. After a period of time, however, it seems that the Jewish and Gentile devotees of Jesus were eventually labeled

7. See Wayne A. Meeks and Robert L. Wilken, *Jews and Christians in Antioch in the First Four Centuries of the Common Era* (Missoula, MT: Scholars, 1978); Richard N. Longenecker, *Galatians* (WBC; Dallas: Word, 1990), 65-71; Frank Kolb, "Antiochia in der frühen Kaiserzeit," in *Geschichte—Tradition—Reflexion*, ed. H. Cancik, H. Lichtenberger, and P. Schäfer (FS M. Hengel; Tübingen: Mohr Siebeck, 1996), 2:97-118; Martin Hengel and Anna Maria Schwemer, *Paul between Damascus and Antioch: The Unknown Years* (Louisville: Westminster John Knox, 1997), 178-204; Anna Maria Schwemer, "Paulus in Antiochien," *BZ* 42 (1998): 162-66; Markus Bockmuehl, *Jewish Law in Gentile Churches: Halakhah and the Beginning of Christian Public Ethics* (Grand Rapids, MI: Baker Academic, 2000), 51-61; Michael F. Bird, *The Saving Righteousness of God: Studies on Paul, Justification, and the New Perspective* (PBM; Milton Keynes, UK: Paternoster, 2006), 120-22; Magnus Zetterholm, *The Formation of Christianity in Antioch: A Social-Scientific Approach to the Separation between Judaism and Christianity* (London: Routledge, 2003), 18-52.

8. See Thomas A. Robinson, *Ignatius of Antioch and the Parting of the Ways* (Peabody, MA: Hendrickson, 2009), 72-88.

"Christians" (Χριστιανοί) by local Syrian officials as their faith in a crucified messianic Jewish leader brought them to public attention (Acts 11:26).[9] One can reasonably infer from other incidents in Paul's letters and in Acts that controversy in Antioch among the Jewish communities would have been aroused by questions about the legitimacy of faith in Jesus as the Messiah, competition for Gentile adherents, and division over the form and degree of Jewish Christ-believers fraternizing with Gentiles. This might have resulted in hostility toward Jewish Christ-believers and even suspicion of the ethnically mixed "Christian" gatherings by Jewish leaders. Yet nothing in Acts 11:19-26 indicates the expulsion of Christ-believers from the Antiochene synagogues or any kind of parting of the ways.[10] There is no evidence that the pogrom in Jerusalem followed believers to Antioch. Indeed, Antioch was diverse enough that it could accommodate a number of Jewish factions and a variety of Gentile "judaizers" with wide-ranging levels of commitment to Jewish theology and Jewish practices.[11]

Second, the mission of Paul and Barnabas to Cyprus, Pamphilia, and Cilicia (Gal 1:21; Acts 13–14) launched from Antioch always began with synagogues and Jewish assemblies in these territories. The approach to Jewish synagogues in the course of this mission was an extension of the participation of the Antiochene missionaries in the Antiochene synagogues. Even the later Pauline mission that was more specifically targeted toward Gentiles began with ministry in a synagogue until an exterior patron or patroness emerged. In the words of Hengel, "The way to the 'Gentiles' led through the synagogue."[12]

---

9. See Justin Taylor, "Why Were the Disciples First Called 'Christians' at Antioch? (Acts 11:26)," *RB* (1994): 75-94.

10. See Meeks and Wilken (*Jews and Christians in Antioch*, 178): "Moreover, if such a separation did take place around 70, it certainly did not mean the once-for-all isolation of the Judaeo-Christians from Gentile Christians nor of Jews from Christians. The active influence of Judaism upon Christianity in Antioch was perennial until Christian leaders succeeded at last in driving the Jews from the city in the seventh century."

11. See Josephus, *War* 2.463; 7.45; Acts 6:5, with "Nicolas of Antioch, a proselyte."

12. Hengel and Schwemer, *Paul between Damascus and Antioch*, 107; similarly James D. G. Dunn, *The Parting of the Ways: Between Christianity and Judaism and Their Significance for the Character of Christianity* (London: SCM, 1991), 125-26; Christopher Rowland, *Christian Origins* (London: SPCK, 1985), 216-17; Eckhard J. Schnabel, *Early Christian Mission,* vol. 1, *Jesus and the Twelve;* vol. 2, *Paul and the Early Church* (Downers Grove, IL: IVP Academic, 2004), 2:1300-1301; James C. Miller, "The Jewish Context of Paul's Gentile Mission," *TynB* 58 (2007): 101-15; Reidar Hvalvik, "Paul as a Jewish Believer—according to the Book of Acts," in *Jewish Believers in Jesus: The Early Centuries*, ed. O. Skarsaune and R. Hvalvik (Peabody, MA: Hendrickson, 2007), 123-35.

Third, Gal 2:4-5 and Acts 15:1-5 make it clear that the Antiochene church did not require circumcision of Gentiles at this early stage; yet this openness did not mark an immediate or necessary departure from Judaism.[13] Around the same period (ca. 44-46 CE), a certain Jewish merchant named Ananias persuaded King Izates of Adiabene to convert to the Jewish way of life (Josephus, *Ant.* 20.35). Yet later when Izates wanted to be circumcised in order to be "assuredly Jewish," Ananias persuaded him to refrain from the practice, well aware that his subjects would resent a Jewish ruler. Ananias informed Izates that "zeal for the traditions of the Jews was superior to being circumcised" (Josephus, *Ant.* 20.41). Josephus's narrative assumes the normality of circumcision for male converts, though the grounds for foregoing the ritual in Izates's case were exceptional as a matter of political expediency. Sometime later a Pharisee named Eleazar persuaded Izates to be circumcised as a matter of utmost importance.[14] Still, the incident shows that there were occasions when converts to Judaism were not circumcised. To this example we can add evidence from Philo, where the necessity of circumcision by converts seems somewhat ambivalent (Philo, *QE* 2.2; *Migr.* 92). Also Ezekiel the Tragedian (*Exag.* 152-92) does not make circumcision a requirement for sharing in the Passover, in contrast to the clear statement in Exod 12:48 that requires it.[15]

What was unique to the Greek-speaking Jewish Christ-believers in Antioch was perhaps their rationale for not circumcising Gentile Christ-believers. Paul provided a theological rationale for not circumcising Gentiles believers in Galatians, Colossians,[16] and Romans based on a particular reading of Israel's Scriptures that included affirming the priority of the Abrahamic covenant over the Mosaic covenant, appropriating the Isaianic vision of the salvation of the Gentiles, the association of the Torah with sin and death, and the absolute singularity of Jesus' death and resurrection for salvation and membership in the people of God. Yet the tenet of "righteousness by faith" appears to have been a very early Jewish-Christian tenet because Paul regarded Jewish Christ-believers like himself and Peter as custodians of the tradition of righteousness by faith (Gal 2:15-16: "We who ourselves are Jews by birth and not Gentile

---

13. On debates and practices with respect to the necessity of circumcision for conversion to Judaism, see the discussion in Michael F. Bird, *Crossing Over Sea and Land: Jewish Missionary Activity in the Second Temple Period* (Peabody, MA: Hendrickson, 2009), 24-43.

14. Josephus, *Ant.* 20.17-50.

15. See m. Pesaḥ. 8.8 on how many days a proselyte had to wait before partaking of Passover.

16. On the authenticity of Colossians as a Pauline document, see Michael F. Bird, *Colossians and Philemon* (NCCS; Eugene, OR: Cascade, 2009), 4-9.

sinners know that a person is not justified by works of law but through faith in Jesus Christ"). Perhaps the theological innovation of the Greek-speaking Jewish Christ-believers was in pressing the logic of this formulation and so denying the assumed normality of circumcising Gentiles for membership in the renewed Israel of the messianic age. Other reasons for not circumcising Gentiles could have been based on a belief that the eschatological pilgrimage of the Gentiles was already underway where the Gentiles would worship God as Gentiles without first becoming proselytes (e.g., Isa 2:2-4; 66:18-21; Mic 4:1-4; Zech 8:20-23).[17] It may have emerged out of a belief that the advent of the new age would affect the enduring significance of Torah for Jews and Gentiles. Or, if Acts is anything to go by, it was the observation that the Spirit had been poured out on Gentiles that was determinative. We do not know for sure why the requirement for the circumcision of Gentiles was dropped in Antioch. What we can say is that, although the Christian arguments for it were in some respects distinctive because of their messianology and pneumatic experience, the view that Gentiles do not have to be circumcised was not itself unprecedented within Judaism.

Fourth, the subsequent history of Antioch provides evidence of a continuous sway in the relationship between the Christian and Jewish communities from the Roman period through to the Arabic conquest of the region.[18] In the early second century Ignatius warned about the perils of learning Judaism from someone uncircumcised (*Phld.* 6.1), as well as asserting that "where there is Christianity there cannot be Judaism" (*Magn.* 10.3). Both of these remarks are probably a response to what was perceived as being too much interpermeation, theologically or socially, between Jews and Christians in Antioch.[19] Eusebius refers to a letter of Serapion of Antioch dated around the end of the second century to a certain Domnus who lapsed from the faith during a time of persecution in favor of a Jewish form of worship (Eusebius, *Hist. Eccl.* 6.12.1). Evidently, it was not all one-way traffic in terms of conversion from Judaism to Christianity; that road flowed in both directions! Even in the fourth century

---

17. See Michael F. Bird, *Jesus and the Origins of the Gentile Mission* (LNTS; London: T&T Clark, 2007), 26-38; Terence Donaldson, "Proselytes or 'Righteous Gentiles'? The Status of Gentiles in Eschatological Pilgrimage Patterns of Thought," *JSP* 7 (1990): 3-27; Paula Fredriksen, "Judaism, the Circumcision of Gentiles, and Apocalyptic Hope: Another Look at Galatians 1 and 2," *JTS* 42 (1991): 532-64; Zetterholm, *Antioch*, 134-49.

18. See Meeks and Wilken, *Jews and Christians in Antioch*; Isabella Sandwell, *Religious Identity in Late Antiquity: Greeks, Jews, and Christians in Antioch* (Cambridge: CUP, 2007).

19. See Thomas A. Robinson, *Ignatius of Antioch and the Parting of the Ways* (Peabody, MA: Hendrickson, 2009).

John Chrysostom, while serving as presbyter in Antioch, could bitterly denounce Jews and judaizing Christians in his *Adversus Judaeos* homilies (386-87 CE), most likely because of his disdain for Christian participation in Jewish rituals and gatherings.[20] By the time of Ignatius in the early second century, there were indeed two distinct and recognizable communities of "Jews" and "Christians," but there was no absolute barrier between the two groups.

Thus, there is no evidence for a "parting" between the Christians and Jews in Antioch in the 40s CE.[21] The picture we have of the Antiochene church, then, is one that is thoroughly enmeshed within Jewish communal life in the city. However, potential fracture lines are apparent, given the possibility of rivalry for Gentile adherents, controversial beliefs like faith in a crucified and risen Messiah, disputations over their partially realized eschatology, the prevalence of a Messiah-centered interpretation of Scripture, cultic veneration of Jesus, diminished concern for Gentile impurity, and a diluted zeal for the obligations of Torah for Gentiles.

What Was the Problem in Antioch?

The fracas in Antioch occurred because Cephas (i.e., Simon Peter) and a cohort of Jewish Christ-believers including Barnabas separated from table fellowship with Christ-believing Gentiles. The questions are, (1) Why did Cephas do this? and, (2) What did Paul find so objectionable? Those are the matters that I explore below, but before I do so, it is first necessary to identify the key contexts, personalities, and events of the incident at Antioch.

The Main Protagonists

It is worth considering recent events in the lives of Paul, Barnabas, Peter, and James as the background to the incident at Antioch.

---

20. See Robert L. Wilken, *John Chrysostom and the Jews: Rhetoric and Reality in the Late Fourth Century* (Eugene, OR: Wipf & Stock, 2004); Wendy Mayer and Pauline Allen, *John Chrysostom* (New York: Routledge, 2000), 148-66.

21. While I think it is legitimate to speak of a "parting of the ways" between Jews and Christians in terms of the development of two distinct self-identities, theologies, and communities in Antioch by the time of Ignatius, we are not thereby committed to the view that a parting requires absolute partition, isolation, and hostility. The ways that have parted can still have theological overlaps, experience wide-ranging socioreligious interaction, and exhibit attitudes to one another including hostility and amicability.

Paul's conversion ca. 34 CE was followed by a period of evangelistic ministry in Damascus and Arabia, most likely oriented to Jews, with a visit also to Jerusalem that probably included some preaching to Jews as well (Gal 1:17-19; 2 Cor 11:32; Rom 15:19; Acts 9:19-29; 26:16-18). Then, after a period of time in Paul's native city of Tarsus in Cilicia (Gal 1:21; Acts 9:30), Barnabas brought Paul to Antioch (Gal 1:21; Acts 11:25-26). Barnabas sought out Paul probably because Paul was a Greek-speaking Jew who was uniquely gifted to interact with Greeks on the cultural level, but also well versed in Pharisaic tradition, which was popular among many Jews. At this point, Paul's ministry shifted from being Jew-focused to being centered on mixed Jew and Gentile audiences. Paul's conversion experience poured into him the authority of the risen Lord and so implied a shift from Torah to Christ as the locus on God's saving action, which resonated with the Antiochene church's position on Torah. The Antiochene mission to Cyprus, Cilicia, and Pamphylia seems to have resulted in Paul emerging as the dominant leader in the group, given his success in recruiting Gentile converts to the faith (Acts 13–14). The intrusion of individuals from Judea into Antioch who insisted on Gentile circumcision (Gal 2:3-5; Acts 15:1-5, 24) led to the Jerusalem council (Acts 15; Gal 2:1-10). From Paul's perspective, this meeting was a success because Titus was not compelled to be circumcised, the validity of his apostolate was recognized, and the substance of his gospel to the uncircumcised was affirmed. If the apostolic decree is historical, then some form of "instruction" for Gentiles, even as a temporary via media, was agreed on that stipulated a minimal avoidance of idols, blood from a strangled animal, and sexual immorality (Acts 15:20-29).

A Cyprian Levite and Jerusalem resident named Joseph, but known to the apostles as Barnabas, along with his cousin John Mark, was a crucial link between the Greek-speaking and Aramaic-speaking Jewish Christ-believers. Barnabas was part of the Jerusalem church (Acts 4:36), but because of his Diaspora heritage he was a perfect choice as an authorized visitor to the church in Antioch when it began accepting Greek members (Acts 11:22-24). Barnabas acted as an intermediary between the newly converted Paul of Tarsus and the apostles (Acts 9:27), and he later recruited Paul's assistance for ministry in the Antiochene church (Acts 11:25). Paul appears to have regarded Barnabas as an apostle beside himself (1 Cor 9:6). Barnabas was part of the Antiochene representation to the Jerusalem pillars objecting to the intrusion by the "false brothers" (Gal 2:1; Acts 15:1-2, 24). Along with Paul, he received the right hand of fellowship from the apostles (Gal 2:9; Acts 15:25). Luke reports of a parting between Paul and Barnabas over John Mark (Acts 15:36-39), though it is very likely that this parting took place around the same time as the incident at Antioch (Gal 2:11-14). From our sources Barnabas appears as a mediating figure, a prophet and pastor to the Antiochene church, and a missionary to the churches principally in his native homeland of Cyprus. In Galatians, Paul expresses "his sorrow and embarrassment over his partner's defection."[22]

Peter was a leading disciple among Jesus' followers, the recipient of an appearance of the risen Jesus (Luke 24:34; 1 Cor 15:5), and one of the pillar apostles, along with John son of Zebedee and James the brother of Jesus (Gal 2:9). According to Acts 1–5, which need not be doubted on this point, Peter was energetically involved as a chief spokesperson for the Jerusalem church and an evangelistic preacher to fellow Jews. After a visitation to Samaria (Acts 8:14-25) and Joppa (Acts 10:5), Peter is narrated as having his own Gentile revelation in his interactions with Cornelius of Caesarea. In Joppa, Peter had a visionary experience related to the cleanness of people. He then broke Jewish halakah by entering the house of a Gentile. After presenting the gospel to his audience, he witnessed the Spirit of God fall upon Gentiles, and he consented to their baptism (Acts 10:1-48). In reporting the event to the Jerusalem church, the "circumcised believers" criticized him for eating with uncircumcised men (Acts 11:1-3). Peter's defense of his actions culminated in the claim that the Gentiles' receipt of the "same Spirit" makes it entirely inappropriate to hinder God's work among them (Acts 11:17-18). Later, at the Jerusalem council, the speech by the Lukan Peter retains the memory of Peter's defense of the Antiochene position of not imposing Torah on Gentile believers (Acts 15:7-11).[23] The speech corresponds to Peter's pro-Gentile posture in Acts 10 with Cornelius and his position summarized by Paul in Gal 2:7-9 that accepted Paul's apostolate and preaching to the Gentiles without Torah observance. The outcome was that the false brothers were reprimanded, and the Antiochene delegatation returned to Antioch having secured the freedom of their Gentile converts from Torah and circumcision. Then within a year, Peter arrived in Antioch, we do not know why—maybe he was fleeing from further persecution, or perhaps he visited as part of his missionary efforts to Syrian Jews. What we do know is that, during his time in Antioch, Peter engaged in table fellowship with Christ-believing Gentiles. In sum, during the first two decades of the early church, Peter shifted his profile from the chief disciple among the Twelve, to one of the triumvirate

---

22. Richard Bauckham, "Barnabas in Galatians," *JSNT* 2 (1979): 67.

23. Peter's remarks that "God made a choice among you, that by my mouth the Gentiles should hear the word of the gospel and believe" (Acts 15:7) and "why are you putting God to the test by placing a yoke on the neck of the disciples that neither our fathers nor we have been able to bear?" (Acts 15:10) represent a Lukan embellishment concerning Peter's effort in upholding the Antiochene church's stance concerning Gentiles and their freedom from Torah.

pillars with John and James, and then took on the role of the itinerant apostle to the circumcised.

Concerning James, the brother of Jesus, the details of his conversion are unknown to us, except that Paul counts him as an eyewitness of Jesus' resurrection (1 Cor 15:7). James's prominence in the early church first emerges with a terse statement in Acts when Peter wishes "James and the brothers" to be informed of the circumstances of his escape from prison (Acts 12:17), indicating James's heightened position within the Jerusalem church. At the Jerusalem council James affirmed Peter's testimony and supported the position by reference to Amos 9:11 about the inclusion of Gentiles in a restored Davidic kingdom. The turning of Gentiles to the Lord is a result of the widespread dissemination of the law of Moses. In fact, James makes a double affirmation of both Gentile inclusion without circumcision and the enduring validity of the Mosaic legislation. Gentiles are required to keep only elementary laws associated with idolatry, blood, and sexual immorality (Acts 15:13-29; 21:25). While it might be true that Acts 15:16-18 reflects the Septuagint rather than the Hebrew Scriptures on Amos 9:11-12, that is no firm argument against the authenticity of James's pronouncement. Richard Bauckham is correct to say that "the Jewish Christian exegete who created the text in Acts 15:16-18 [Amos 9:11] understood the eschatological temple, not as a literal building, but as the eschatological people of God composed of both Jews and Gentiles."[24] Later in Acts when Paul returned to Jerusalem, James counseled Paul about the allegations of antinomianism made against him and urged him to undertake a Nazirite vow to show that he "observes and guards the law" (Acts 21:18-24). Furthermore, around this time, there was a perception that Jewish Christ-believers in adjacent regions were acting unlawfully in their contact with Gentiles and in their own Torah observance. That state of affairs arguably led to James, along with his associates, being executed as a lawbreaker ca. 62 CE by the high priest Ananias the Younger during an interregnum of Roman governance of Judea (Josephus, *Ant.* 20.200). The drama of James's leadership of the church was his balancing act of trying to promote unity between the Hellenistic and Judean wings of the church, while striving to maintain the security of Judean Christ-believers amid allegations that members of the sect were fraternizing with Gentiles and had ceased performing important Jewish rites.

The "men from James" were key players in the incident at Antioch. We do not know exactly how this Jacobean delegation was related to the Jewish

24. Richard Bauckham, "James and the Gentiles (Acts 15:13-21)," in *History, Literature, and Society in the Book of Acts*, ed. B. Witherington III (Cambridge: CUP, 1996), 164.

Christ-believers who previously came to Antioch causing trouble. They were labeled as "false brothers" by Paul (Gal 2:4-5) and were described as "certain men" who were advocating the circumcision of Gentiles and were regarded by the Jerusalem church as acting "without our authorization," according to Luke (Acts 15:1, 24). It was their fuss that precipitated the need for the Jerusalem council, and as far as we can tell, they lost the debate. I doubt that the Jacobean delegates were the same persons as the "false brothers" because the "false brothers" were unauthorized by the Jerusalem church, whereas the "men from James" were formally authorized emissaries from James. The "false brothers" in Antioch and later the intruders in Galatia focused on Paul's Gentile converts, whereas the men from James were singularly interested in the conduct of Jewish Christ-believers. No reason for the arrival of the Jacobean delegation in Antioch is actually given. We can only speculate whether it was a general visit or whether it had some actual purpose, like passing on a message to Peter. The Jacobean messengers may have been more like an embassy making an earnest appeal than a Pharisaic inspection attempting to determine legalities.[25] Still, the Jacobean delegation might have had some sympathy with more Torah-focused Jewish Christ-believers in Antioch for reasons that will soon become clear. What is certain is that they provided the catalyst for the ensuing events by activating Peter's fear of those of the circumcision and were thus the material cause of his withdrawal from table fellowship with Gentile believers.

Exactly how much the men from James were actually speaking and acting on behalf of James has been debated. In an apologetic ploy to safeguard the unity of Paul, Peter, and James, it is often proposed that these men exceeded their remit by interfering in the common fellowship, even though James would not have approved of it.[26] But we are not told that. Indeed, we are told only that they came from James, and there is absolutely no reason to think that they did anything other than act on his terms and with his authority. Paul does not call them "so-called men from James" (οἱ λεγόμενοι ἀπὸ Ἰακώβου) or those that "seem to be from James" (οἱ δοκοῦντες ἀπὸ Ἰακώβου εἶναι). Paul never asks: "Did James really tell you to say that?" Paul recognized full well that they came with the full weight of James's authority behind them, and it was they who instigated the division in Antioch.

Concerning the identity of "those of the circumcision" (τοὺς ἐκ περιτο-

---

25. Bockmuehl, *Jewish Law*, 71.

26. See, e.g., C. K. Barrett, *A Critical and Exegetical Commentary on the Book of Acts* (2 vols.; ICC; Edinburgh: T&T Clark, 1994-98), 2:741; Don Garlington, *An Exposition of Galatians: A Reading from the New Perspective* (3rd ed.; Eugene, OR: Wipf & Stock, 2007), 126.

μῆς), I have changed my earlier view that they were a zealous Jewish Christ-believing faction in Antioch.[27] I now find it more likely that it includes, though perhaps not exclusively, non–Christ-believing Jews in Antioch, since περιτομή is most often used as a vivid descriptor for Jews in Paul's letters (Rom 3:30; 4:12; 15:8; Phil 3:3; Col 3:11; 4:11). Admittedly, account must be made of the fact that Luke twice uses οἱ ἐκ περιτομῆς to describe Jewish Christ-believers in favor of circumcising Gentiles (Acts 10:45; 11:2; see Eusebius, *Hist. Eccl.* 4.5.3-4). In addition, there were Jewish Christ-believers who believed in circumcising Gentiles and who remained hostile to Paul's view of a Torah-free gospel even into the second century.[28] However, across Gal 2, Paul appears to distinguish Jewish Christ-believers like Peter and Barnabas from the "circumcision" (πε-ριτομή), who are nonbelieving Jews (Gal 2:9). Peter became afraid of the "circumcision," and it is hard to imagine that he would be afraid of a person who recognized him as the apostle to the "circumcision" and were under his apostolic jurisdiction (Gal 2:8), whereas a mob of zealous local Jews believing that their social space was being polluted by Gentiles would be a different thing![29]

Now if there was no parting of the ways in Antioch by the mid-40s CE, then Torah-scrupulous Jewish Christ-believers may well have remained in close affinity with non–Christ-believing Jews in Antioch and shared their antipathy toward Torah-lax Jewish Christ-believers who brazenly fraternized with Gentiles and refused to require them to be circumcised.[30] Those who are identified as ἐκ περιτομῆς could have included a mixture of nonbelieving Jews and perhaps some Jewish Christ-believing dissenters who shared a disdain toward other Jewish Christ-believers with their Gentile clientele who worshiped and ate together in mixed gatherings in Antioch, even if the meals were kosher! The upshot is that the incident at Antioch was not purely an in-

27. Bird, *Saving Righteousness*, 125-26. J. Louis Martyn (*Galatians: A New Translation, with Introduction and Commentary* [AB; New York: Doubleday, 1997], 238-39) thinks it refers to a party within the early church intent on a mission to Gentiles that was at least partially law observant. He prefers to call them "Christian Jews" rather than "Jewish Christians." Gibson (*Peter*, 252) is better: "The context of Gal 2:7-9, in which περιτομή is used of non-Christian Jews, makes this the more likely alternative in Gal 2:12."

28. Acts 15:1, 5; Gal 5:2-12; 6:12-15; Justin, *Dial. Trypho* 47; Eusebius, *Hist. Eccl.* 3.4.2.

29. Zetterholm (*Formation of Christianity in Antioch*) argues for a mixture of conservative and liberal tendencies in the Jews of Antioch.

30. E. P. Sanders ("Jewish Association with Gentiles," 186; see Hays, "Galatians," 11:232; Douglas J. Moo, *Galatians* [BECNT; Grand Rapids, MI: Baker Academic, 2014], 142, 148) thinks that the problem was too much association or fraternizing with Gentiles, which might lead to contact with idolatry or transgression of the food laws. Peter's mission would be discredited if he were to engage too brazenly with Gentiles.

tramural Christian dispute but was part of the socioreligious context of Jews in Antioch concerning group boundaries, rites of entry, and acceptable limits of acculturation. According to Larry Hurtado:

> Those Jewish Christians who insisted that Gentile converts had to undergo full proselyte conversion (including circumcision of males) may well have feared that to treat Torah observance as anything less than mandatory for all could be seen as supporting the view that Torah observance was not necessary for anyone. That is, Diaspora Jews (including Jewish Christians) who were concerned to maintain solidarity in Torah observance over against other tendencies in Diaspora Jewish communities may have seen the Pauline position on the admission of Gentiles into Christian circles as implicitly supporting the sort of allegorizing Torah observance that Philo criticised. In other words, Paul's Gentile converts may be thought of as having walked into a family quarrel within Diaspora Jewish communities, unintentionally exacerbating it. If this line of inference is correct, what was at stake in the controversies over the admission of Gentiles to full Christian fellowship was not simply the terms of Gentile conversion, but was also the question of how far Diaspora Jews could allow themselves to go in negotiating their lives in non-Jewish environments.[31]

The Context for the Incident at Antioch

Consideration of the incident in Antioch must take into account several factors that shaped the formative context and recent history of the early church, including the following.

1. Because of its devotion to a crucified messianic claimant, the Jerusalem church was under scrutiny and opposition from their Jewish compatriots. The pogroms resulting in the martyrdoms of Stephen, James son of Zebedee, and James the Just show just how incendiary the church's praxis, preaching, and mission proved to be. Paul knew of Jewish persecution of the Judean churches, and he referred to specific hindrances from the Jews at sharing his message with Gentiles (1 Thess 2:14-16; Gal 6:12).

2. The period between the late 30s and the late 40s CE was a tumultuous time in Palestine. During this period Herod Antipas was exiled to Gaul for

---

31. Larry Hurtado, "Does Philo Help Explain Early Christianity?," in *Philo und das Neue Testament: Wechselseitig Wahrnehmungen*, ed. R. Deines and K.-W. Niebuhr (WUNT 172; Tübingen: Mohr Siebeck, 2004), 85-86.

stockpiling weapons.[32] There was a rise in banditry and nationalistic fervor in Judea.[33] Caligula's attempts to place a statue of himself in the Jerusalem temple prompted outrage among Jews throughout the empire.[34] The Byzantine chronicler Malalas reported an anti-Jewish riot in Antioch ca. 39-40 CE.[35] Herod Agrippa I died suddenly in 44 CE,[36] and thereafter there was a series of Roman procurators who through incompetence, ignorance, or corruption inflamed tensions with the people, which led to revolts and uprisings.[37] Around the time of the incident at Antioch (ca. 46-48 CE), the Jewish apostate and Roman procurator Tiberius Julius Alexander had the sons or grandsons of Judas the Galilean crucified.[38] On the eve of the Antioch episode was also a major riot in Jerusalem at Passover that resulted in the deaths of thousands of Jews (ca. 49 CE).[39]

3. Pharisaism was a renewal movement in Israel calling for the application of priestly codes to the general populace to hasten the dawn of national restoration. As a "dining club" of sorts, Pharisaism also concerned itself with developing and propagating the proper halakah for purity and the parameters for table fellowship. According to Acts, many Pharisees joined the Jesus movement (Acts 23:6; 26:5; Phil 3:5) and arguably brought with them some of their Pharisaic tradition concerning purity, food, and fellowship (Acts 15:5).[40]

4. The acceptance of Gentile believers without the obligation of circumcision was advocated by the Greek-speaking Jewish Christ-believers and then independently by Peter.[41] The view was by no means unanimous and prompted considerable division in the Jerusalem church.

---

32. Josephus, *Ant.* 18.240-52; *War* 2.181-83.

33. Craig A. Evans, "Revolutionary Movements, Jewish," in *DNTB*, ed. S. E. Porter and C. A. Evans (Downers Grove, IL: InterVarsity, 2000), 936-47.

34. Philo, *Flacc.* 45; *Legat.* 184-338; Josephus, *War* 2.184-203; *Ant.* 18.261-309; Tacitus, *Hist.* 5.9.

35. John Malalas, *Chron.* 10.315. Riots took place in Alexandria around the same time, according to Philo (*Flacc.* 41-55; *Legat.* 132-37).

36. Josephus, *Ant.* 19.345-50; Acts 12:20-23.

37. See, e.g., Josephus, *Ant.* 20.6, 97-99, 105-24; *War* 2.223-38.

38. Josephus, *Ant.* 20.102.

39. Josephus, *Ant.* 20.112; *War* 2.224-27.

40. See L. Ann Jervis, "Peter in the Middle: Galatians 2:11-21," in *Text and Artifact in the Religions of Mediterranean Antiquity*, ed. M. R. Desjardins and S. G. Wilson (FS Peter Richardson; Waterloo, ON; Wilfrid Laurier University Press, 2000), 45-62; E. P. Sanders "Jewish Associations with Gentiles and Galatians 2:11-14," in *The Conversation Continues: Studies in Paul and John*, ed. R. T. Fortna and B. R. Gaventa (FS J. L. Martyn; Nashville: Abingdon, 1990), 185-86.

41. Luke has probably projected the story of the Hellenist breakthrough at Antioch (Acts 11:19-21) to a later point in Acts in order to prioritize Paul's conversion (Acts 9:1-30) and

5. Peter's ministry and movements alternated between Judean, Samaritan, and Gentile settings, and his activity in these places left a question mark hanging over Peter's fidelity to the Torah for some.

6. Paul's arrival in Antioch infused theological sophistication into the Antiochene church. Paul also emerged as the leader of the Antiochene mission to the Gentiles and constituted the foremost defender of the Antiochene church's stance concerning Gentiles and circumcision.

7. The increase in the number of Gentile believers in Antioch and in Antioch's daughter churches in Cyprus, Cilicia, and Pamphylia caused alarm among the Pharisaic wing of the Jerusalem church as to what it might mean for the ethos of the church as a whole. This explains the active opposition by a constituency of the Jerusalem church to Jewish Christ-believers eating with Gentiles and forgoing the necessity of Gentile circumcision for conversion. They even took the bold initiative to try to intervene in the Antiochene church (Gal 2:4-5; Acts 15:1).

8. The Jerusalem council achieved a via media by finding in Scripture a justification for the inclusion of Gentiles within the church without requiring circumcision and placing upon Gentiles only the obligation to avoid idol food, blood in strangled animals, and sexual immorality. Paul's gospel and apostolate were affirmed by the Jerusalem pillars, but in turn they expected Paul to respect the status of the Torah in the mission to the circumcision. Yet the Jerusalem council also inadvertently permitted the existence of two parallel theologies: one theology where the Gentiles were uncircumcised equals[42] in a renewed Israel, with holiness constituted by the Spirit, and another theology where uncircumcised Gentiles were guests in a restored Israelite remnant that still defined holiness through Torah observance.[43] The Jerusalem council's decision presumed a setting where Jewish Christ-believers and Gentile Christ-believers were parallel rather than integrated, especially in relation to shared

---

Peter's conversion of Cornelius (Acts 10:1–11:18). This projection is plausible, given that Acts 9:1–11:18 appears to interrupt a continuous account of a Hellenistic mission begun at 6:1 and then resumed and completed at 11:19-30. The reason for the insertion by Luke is probably to attribute the Gentile breakthrough to Peter and give the Gentile mission apostolic precedent and to also introduce Paul prior to the Cornelius narrative.

42. Shaye J. D. Cohen (*The Beginnings of Jewishness* [Berkeley: University of California Press, 1999], 219-21) notes that there is no evidence for Jews and Gentiles being placed on an equal footing in a Jewish community.

43. See Bruce D. Chilton, "The Brother of Jesus and the Interpretation of Scripture," in *The Use of Sacred Books in the Ancient World*, ed. L. V. Rutgers, P. W. van der Horst, H. W. Havelaar, and L. Teugels (CBET 22; Leuven: Peeters, 1998), 37-40.

meals. The council did not stipulate the standard of Torah observance to be upheld for ethnically mixed table fellowship to ensue.[44]

9. At some point, we have the accession of James as the senior authority among the "elders" in Jerusalem. James stood between Paul and Barnabas on the one hand and the conservative Jewish Christ-believers on the other hand. James sought to permit the freedom of the Antiochene churches while staving off criticism from zealous Jews in Jerusalem for being insufficiently loyal to Israel, the temple, and Torah.

Why Did Peter Separate from Table Fellowship?

Peter separated from shared meals in Antioch when "certain men from James arrived" (Gal 2:12).[45] These men triggered Peter's fear of "those of the circum-

---

44. See Donald Robinson, "The Circumcision of Titus, and Paul's 'Liberty,'" *AusBR* 12 (1964): 27; Tomson, *Paul and the Jewish Law*, 227; C. K. Barrett, "Paul: Councils and Controversies," in *Conflicts and Challenges in Early Christianity*, ed. D. A. Hagner (Harrisburg, PA: TPI, 1999), 54; Vincent M. Smiles, *The Gospel and the Law in Galatia: Paul's Response to Jewish-Christian Separatism and the Threat of Galatian Apostasy* (Collegeville, MN: Liturgical, 1998), 89; Ben Witherington III, *Grace in Galatia: A Commentary on Paul's Letter to the Galatians* (Grand Rapids, MI: Eerdmans, 1998), 153; Bockmuehl, *Jewish Law*, 82; Richard Bauckham, "James and the Jerusalem Church," in *The Book of Acts in Its Palestinian Setting*, ed. R. Bauckham (Grand Rapids, MI: Eerdmans, 1995), 464; Richard B. Hays, "The Letter to the Galatians," in *NIB*, ed. L. E. Keck (12 vols.; Nashville: Abingdon, 2000), 11:232; Francis Watson, *Paul, Judaism, and the Gentiles: Beyond the New Perspective* (Grand Rapids, MI: Eerdmans, 2007), 106; James D. G. Dunn, *Jesus, Paul, and the Law: Studies in Mark and Galatians* (London: SPCK, 1990), 155-56; idem, *The Epistle to the Galatians* (BNTC; Peabody, MA: Hendrickson, 1993), 122; idem, *Beginning from Jerusalem* (CITM 2; Grand Rapids, MI: Eerdmans, 2009), 478-80; Hengel, *Saint Peter*, 57; in contrast, see Philip F. Esler, *Galatians* (NTR; London: Routledge, 1998), 133-36, who thinks that the Jerusalem consultation must have included meal-fellowship guidelines in its affirmation; Michelle Slee, *The Church in Antioch in the First Century: Communion and Conflict* (LNTS; London: T&T Clark, 2003), 42-47, believes that James changed his mind on the table-fellowship issue.

45. It is necessary to address two textual variants in Gal 2:12. First, the indefinite pronoun τινας ("certain men") is widely attested; however, τινα ("a certain man") is witnessed by 𝔓46. Donald Robinson ("Circumcision," 40-41) suggests that τινα is a neuter plural rather than masculine. If so, the neuter plural τινα could be referring to the promulgation of the decrees of the Jerusalem council that originated from James (Acts 15:19) rather than to envoys from James. Second, NA27 and UBS4 adopt the reading ἦλθον ("they came"), attested by the texts A, C, D2, H, ψ, 1739 et al., and the Vulgate, Syriac, and Coptic versions. Yet there is very strong external evidence for the alternative reading of ἦλθεν ("he came"), found in 𝔓46, ℵ, B, D*, F, G, 33, *pc*, b, d, g. If one adopts the reading ἦλθεν and regards Peter rather than the men from James as the subject of the verb, then this understanding affects both the chronology and the circumstances

cision" (Gal 2:12), which caused him to separate, and others like Barnabas joined him. What these men found objectionable with Peter's practice remains unstated. Several suggestions have been put forward, including that the food in these common meals did not conform to Jewish dietary laws,[46] the food was halakically impure,[47] or for other extenuating reasons.[48] I suggest, however,

of the incident at Antioch. The difference in meaning is whether certain men from James came (ἦλθον) *after* Peter had arrived in Antioch or whether Peter arrived (ἦλθεν) *after* the certain men from James already had entered Antioch. It would also imply Paul's rebuke of Peter was coterminus with his immediate arrival rather than after an intermittent period of time. Thus, in Robinson's reconstruction ("Circumcision," 41), Paul's clash with Peter was coterminus with Peter's immediate arrival in Antioch, when Peter applied the Jerusalem decree to the situation in Antioch, rather than Paul reacting to a Jacobean delegation that came on the scene at a later point and forced Peter to change tack. According to Metzger, the two variants τινα and ἦλθεν go together (*A Textual Commentary on the Greek New Testament* [2nd ed.; Stuttgart: Deutsche Bibelgesellschaft, 1994], 523-24). Metzger regards the alternative reading τινα as arising from "scribal oversight" and attributes the other alternative variant ἦλθεν to scribes who imitated ὅτε δὲ ἦλθεν in v. 11 or else exhibited a careless assonance with the verbs in the passage that end in -εν. I am for the most part agnostic as to the validity of ἦλθεν. Its attestation by "good and ordinarily reliable witnesses," as Metzger calls them, should give cause for thought, but it seems like it might be a stylistic repetition of the ends of the verbs ἦλθεν and συνήσθιεν from vv. 11-12. The temporal marker at the head of 2:12, πρὸ τοῦ γὰρ ἐλθεῖν τινας ("before certain men came"), would seem to place Peter in table fellowship in Antioch prior to the Jacobean delegation's arrival rather than after it. See also F. F. Bruce, *The Epistle to the Galatians* (NIGTC; Grand Rapids, MI: Eerdmans, 1982), 129-30, and, more judiciously, Stephen C. Carlson, *The Text of Galatians* (WUNT 2.385; Tübingen: Mohr Siebeck, 2015), 121-23.

46. See, e.g., E. P. Sanders, *Paul, the Law, and the Jewish People* (Minneapolis: Fortress, 1983), 20, 100-101; Traugott Holtz, "Der antiochenische Zwischenfall (Galater 2.11-14)," *NTS* 32 (1986): 344-61; Walter Schmithals, *The Theology of the First Christians* (Louisville: Westminster John Knox, 1997), 117; Martyn, *Galatians*, 232, 239, 244-45; Witherington, *Grace in Galatia*, 153n199; Smiles, *Gospel and the Law in Galatia*, 87; Barrett, "Paul," 54; Gordon D. Fee, *Galatians* (PC; Blandford Forum, UK: Deo, 2007), 78-80; Don Garlington, *An Exposition of Galatians: A Reading from the New Perspective* (3rd ed.; Eugene, OR: Wipf & Stock, 2007), 125.

47. See James D. G. Dunn, "The Incident at Antioch (Gal. 2:11-18)," *JSNT* 18 (1983): 3-57, repr. in *Jesus, Paul, and the Law*, 129-81 (esp. 138-42, 154-58), repr. in *The Galatians Debate: Contemporary Issues in Rhetorical and Historical Interpretation*, ed. M. D. Nanos (Peabody, MA: Hendrickson, 2002), 199-234; idem, *Galatians*, 121-24; idem, *The New Perspective on Paul* (2nd ed.; Grand Rapids, MI: Eerdmans, 2007), 27-28, 31-34, 36-41; idem, *Beginning from Jerusalem*, 470-82; Frank J. Matera, *Galatians* (SP; Collegeville, MN: Liturgical, 2007), 89.

48. The suggestion of Markus Bockmuehl (*Jewish Law*, 61-70) is interesting that geography plays an important role in the incident, namely, because Antioch was within Eretz Israel and therefore some Jewish Christ-believers believed that they were committed to a form of halakah that made commensality with Gentiles inappropriate because they were still within the sacred space of Israel (see also Holtz, "Antiochenische Zwischenfall," 354-55, who thinks that James expected Gentiles to obey the laws expected of resident aliens living in the land of Israel). The

that the problem was not the food itself but the company in which the food was consumed.

Many Jews were suspicious of food prepared by Gentiles.[49] Avoidance of Gentile food became symbolic for covenant loyalty in some circles.[50] Josephus describes how persons who were expelled from the Essenic order starved to death because they would not eat food that was considered impure.[51] The food laws of Lev 11:1-23 and Deut 14:3-21 meant that a faithful Jew had to avoid food that was "impure" (ἀκάθαρτος) and "profane" (κοινός).[52] Consequently, Jews of the Diaspora imported food that was ceremonially clean.[53] It seems for the most part that the food laws and circumcision were closely observed in the Diaspora. The distinctive Jewish diet, especially the abstinence from pork, was well-known and even provoked ridicule from pagan authors. Juvenal wrote: "They see no difference between eating swine's flesh, from which their father abstained, and human flesh."[54] In light of this, E. P. Sanders rightly notes:

> If we bring together the facts that pious groups in Palestine had some special food laws and interpreted all the laws strictly, and that the food laws of Lev. 11 were observed in the Diaspora, where it was more difficult to keep them than in Palestine, we must conclude that the biblical food laws were in general kept very strictly throughout Jewish Palestine. In terms of day-in and day-out Jewish practice, both in Palestine and in the Diaspora, the food laws stood out, along with observance of the Sabbath, as being a central and defining aspect of Judaism.[55]

---

geopolitical dimension has something going for it, particularly if one regarded Syria as the gateway for the return from exile of a renewed Israel in a restored kingdom. The problem is that the Torah makes ample provisions for Jews to interact and eat with resident aliens within the land of Israel. So a redrawn geopolitical mind-map would not necessarily require Jewish separation from Gentiles.

49. Gentile food could be regarded as unclean (Ezek 4:13; Hos 9:3-4) for a variety of reasons: if the food had been contaminated by some association with idolatry (Exod 34:15; 1 Cor 10:28), came from an unclean animal (Lev 11:1-20), or was improperly prepared (Exod 23:19).

50. Dan 1:8-16; Tob 1:10-11; Jdt 10:5; 12:1-2; Add Esth 14:17; 1 Macc 1:62-63; 2 Macc 5:27; 11:31; 3 Macc 3:4; 4 Macc 5:1-38; 6:16-22; 8:2, 12, 29; 13:2; Ep. Arist. 142; Josephus, *Life* 13-16; Philo, *Flacc.* 95-96; Jos. and Asen. 7.1.

51. Josephus, *War* 2.143.

52. 1 Macc 1:47, 62; Mark 7:2, 5, 18; Rom 14:14; Rev 21:27; Josephus, *Ant.* 11.346; and note the collocation of ἀκάθαρτος and κοινός in Acts 10:14, 28; 11:8.

53. Josephus, *Ant.* 14.261; Philo, *Spec.* 2.25-36; 4.105, 110, 114.

54. Juvenal, *Sat.* 14.98-99; cf. Philo, *Leg.* 361; Plutarch, *Quaest. Conv.* 4.5.

55. Sanders, *Jewish Law*, 27.

Other Jews took the issue of food and purity to a further halakic level by refusing to share meals with Gentiles for fear of contracting impurity because of Gentile association with idolatry. The author of Jubilees urges, "Separate yourself from the Gentiles, and do not eat with them, and do not perform deeds like theirs. And do not become associates of theirs."[56] According to Acts, some Palestinian Jews considered it unlawful for a Jew to enter a Gentile's house and eat with the residents there, a view that persisted in the Jerusalem church.[57] The Qumran scrolls strictly forbid a member of the community from accepting food from a Gentile.[58] Tacitus writes about the Jews, with his usual contempt for them, that "they sit apart at meals."[59] Several passages in the Mishnah assume the uncleanness of Gentiles and their living quarters.[60]

Now that is not to say that a refusal to share meals with non-Jews was uniform and unanimous. Many Jews believed that they were still able to participate in the social fabric of the Greco-Roman world without necessarily compromising their religious beliefs. Jews did dine with Gentiles under certain conditions.[61] The Mishanic tractate 'Abodah Zarah (idolatry) assumes interaction with Gentiles and seeks to define the legitimate context for such association.[62] Furthermore, proselytes did not appear in Jewish communities ex nihilo but were drawn in through an extended period of socialization and interaction, which in the ancient world required sharing meals together. So Tessa Rajak is corrected to conclude, "It is not inevitable that special dietary laws compel people to eat away from others. . . . All sorts of arrangements are feasible, where there is a social reason to make them."[63]

Markus Bockmuehl lists the primary options open to Torah-observant Jews regarding table fellowship with Gentiles:

56. Jub. 22.16; cf. Josephus, *Ant.* 13.245; Ep. Arist. 142.

57. Acts 10:28; 11:1-3.

58. 4Q394 frags. 3-7.

59. Tacitus, *Hist.* 5.5.2; cf. Diodorus, *Bib. Hist.* 34.1.1-2; Philostratus, *Vit. Ap.* 33.

60. m. Mak. 2.3; m. 'Ohal. 18.7.

61. Tob 1:11; Dan 1:3-17; Jdt 10:5; 12:17-19; Ep. Arist. 172-86; Josephus, *Ag. Ap.* 2.174, 282; *War* 2.461-63; Jos. and Asen. 20.8; Cf. Sanders, "Jewish Association with Gentiles," 170-88; Dunn, *Jesus, Paul, and the Law,* 137-48; Alan Segal, *Paul the Convert: The Apostolate and Apostasy of Saul the Pharisee* (New Haven: Yale University Press, 1990), 230-33; Tomson, *Paul and the Jewish Law,* 230-36; Bockmuehl, *Jewish Law,* 56-61; Zetterholm, *Antioch,* 151-56.

62. See m. 'Abod. Zar. 4.6; 5.5; m. Ber. 7.1.

63. Tess Rajak, "The Jewish Community and Its Boundaries," in *The Jews among Pagans and Christians in the Roman Empire,* ed. J. Lieu, J. North, and T. Rajak (London: Routledge, 1992), 18.

1.   Refuse all table fellowship with Gentiles and refuse to enter a Gentile house.
2.   Invite Gentiles to their house and prepare a Jewish meal.
3.   Take their own food to a Gentile's house.
4.   Dine with Gentiles on the explicit or implicit understanding that food they would eat was neither prohibited in the Torah nor tainted with idolatry.

Bockmuehl notes that options 2-4 would all be compatible with a shared eucharistic meal involving bread and wine.[64] Part of the problem is that New Testament scholars assume an all-or-nothing approach to the Jewish food laws when there was a broad spectrum of opinion and practice, in both Palestine and the Diaspora, when it came to food, fellowship, and Gentiles. If we loosen the Antioch incident from this legal dichotomy, it is possible to envisage the shared meals as remaining Jewish in character.[65]

Importantly, the Jacobean delegates placed pressure on Peter and not on the Gentiles to change their behavior. Unlike the intruders in Galatia, the "men from James" in Antioch are not immediately concerned with the status of Gentiles vis-à-vis the Torah. Rather, the Jacobeans are formally concerned with the praxis and piety of the Jewish Christ-believing chapter in the socioreligious context of association with Gentiles, particularly with Peter. That Gentiles are being forced to "judaize" (the meaning of which is explored below) is an inference that Paul draws from Peter's withdrawal from table fellowship, not the purpose of the Jacobean intervention itself.[66] Their objective was to change Peter's behavior, not necessarily that of the Gentile believers. To put it differently, the Jacobean delegation wanted to insist on a particular view of

64. Bockmuehl, *Jewish Law*, 57-59. On the "Eucharistic" nature of these meals, see Dieter Lührmann, "Abendmahlsgemeinschaft? Gal. 2:11ff.," in *Kirche*, ed. D. Lührmann and G. Strecker (FS G. Bornkamm; Tübingen: Mohr Siebeck, 1980), 271-86; Heinrich Schlier, *Der Brief an die Galater* (KEK 7; Göttingen: Vandenhoeck & Ruprecht, 1989), 83-84; Robert Jewett, "Gospel and Commensality: Social and Theological Implications of Galatians 2:14," in *Gospel in Paul: Studies on Corinthians, Galatians, and Romans for Richard N. Longenecker*, ed. L. A. Jervis and P. Richardson (Sheffield: Sheffield Academic, 1994), 248; Hengel, *Saint Peter*, 59.

65. Bockmuehl, *Jewish Law*, 60; Mark D. Nanos, "What Was at Stake in Peter's 'Eating with Gentiles' at Antioch?," in *The Galatians Debate: Contemporary Issues in Rhetorical and Historical Interpretation*, ed. M. D. Nanos (Peabody, MA: Hendrickson, 2002), 295.

66. See Stephen A. Cummins, *Paul and the Crucified Christ in Antioch: Maccabean Martyrdom and Galatians 1 and 2* (SNTSMS 114; Cambridge: CUP, 2007), 168-69; Bockmuehl, *Jewish Law*, 73; Gibson, *Peter*, 260.

sacred space and ethnic purity as normative for all Christ-believing Jews, even in the Diaspora.[67]

To repeat our earlier question, if the presenting issue to the Jacobean delegates (i.e., "certain men from James") and local Jews (i.e., "the circumcision") was the proximity of Jewish Christ-believers to Gentile Christ-believers in the context of a shared table fellowship, what precisely was the root of their objection? Did they object to the nonobservance or relaxed adherence to the Jewish food laws by Antiochene Jewish Christ-believers caused by the inclusion of Gentiles at communal meals? Was the problem too much association between Jews and Gentiles that endangered the reputation of the Jewish Christ-believers? Our options are multiple!

Received scholarly wisdom suggests that Paul did not observe the Jewish food laws when among Gentiles and that he expected Jewish Christ-believers to do the same, which, in the case of Peter and Barnabas, they did.[68] However, a few things may be noted. First, Paul was willing to order the Gentile churches to hold to the apostolic decree when he urged them to abstain from food sacrificed to idols if it caused offense, even when he and the Corinthians knew that food was just food and idols were nothing (1 Cor 8–10). Second, Paul urged the Roman Gentile believers to show respect to the convictions of "weaker brothers," who undoubtedly included Jewish Christ-believers, when it came to matters of food and drink—a clear act of ecumenical deferment toward those with sensitive consciences (Rom 14:1-23). Third, Paul's Torah-free mission to the Gentiles was founded on his respect for the Torah-observant mission of Peter to the Jews, as per the Jerusalem agreement (Gal 2:8-9). If Paul had abandoned the Jewish dietary laws in toto and induced Jewish Christ-believers like Peter, Barnabas, and Antiochene Jews to do the same when in Gentile company, then it was he who had violated the apostolic decree, it would mean that the rumors about him teaching Jews to turn away from Moses were true, and the men from James were simply calling him to account (Acts 15:20; 21:21).[69]

I want to suggest that Paul's jibe about Peter that he "lives as a Gentile and not as a Jew" does not require an abandonment or even a relaxed adherence to Torah. There is no indication that the food in the communal meals was impure or simply the lowest common denominator, i.e., Noachide food. Paul is not accusing Peter of abandoning the Jewish lifestyle when it came to table

67. Ronald Charles, *Paul and the Politics of Diaspora* (Minneapolis: Fortress, 2014), 142-43.

68. See, e.g., E. P. Sanders, *Paul, the Law, and the Jewish People* (Minneapolis: Fortress, 1983), 100-101, 177, 185.

69. Tomson, *Paul and the Jewish Law*, 227-28.

fellowship with Gentiles and then reneging on his position. Indeed, the meals in Antioch were probably sensitive to Jewish aversions to impurity and idolatry precisely because of the social proximity of other Jews who were still objects of missionary work—hence Peter's presence in Antioch—and because of a geographic proximity to Jerusalem as well. But even if the food was not kosher or if entering a Gentile's dwelling was the point of contention, the problem could be easily rectified by a change of menu or a change of venue. It would not require outright withdrawal and separation. A solution to this kind of problem would not require segregating Jews from Gentiles. Yet the men from James did not advocate a stricter observance of Jewish dietary laws but something far more radical: the complete withdrawal of Jewish Christ-believers from ethnically mixed table fellowship.

There are several reasons why the Gentiles in Antioch, Paul, Peter, or even James would have no problem with Gentiles adhering to Jewish food laws for the sake of unity. First, the Gentile Christ-believers were probably still in a minority. The Gentiles were the guests of Jewish Christ-believers and were thus obligated to follow Jewish specifications about food at shared meals. In addition, if these Gentile converts to Christianity were brought over from God-fearer and proselyte ranks, then they were probably well used to accommodating themselves to Jewish culinary scruples. A request to change the menu in order to permit Jewish Christ-believers to eat their special food, even a meal in parallel, could easily be accommodated and might be thought of as a gesture of unity.[70]

Second, at the Jerusalem council the question of Gentile adherence to the Torah was finally settled. Although it was decided that Gentiles did not have to adhere to the Torah, there was a qualification added when it came to food. In order to appease a certain Jewish Christ-believing faction, James sought a working compromise whereby Gentiles would abide by certain commandments in order to make sure that they abstained from idolatry and so that Jewish scruples would not be offended (Acts 15:20, 29).[71] We should take into account that the apostolic decree and the Jacobean embassy were not really about food per se. The former was concerned with minimal standards of Gentile behavior vis-à-vis idolatry, and the latter with maintaining the fidelity of Jews to their covenantal way of life vis-à-vis the pressure of persecution.

---

70. See similarly Gibson, *Peter*, 246-47.

71. On the decrees as mandating Noachide laws, see Justin Taylor, "The Jerusalem Decrees (Acts 15:20, 29 and 21:25) and the Incident at Antioch (Gal 2:11-14)," *NTS* 47 (2001): 372-80; Bockmuehl, *Jewish Law*, 145-73.

The apostolic decree presupposed that Gentiles did not have to be circumcised, which was a major victory for the Antiochene church. The dietary requirements of the decree were soft concessions and hardly onerous burdens. Furthermore, such observances may have already been taking place, and the decree was an affirmation of the status quo lest it be liberalized, rather than the imposition of a new dietary code in Antioch. In which case, the promulgation of the apostolic decree in Antioch, before or after Peter's arrival, would not have caused a disruption to table fellowship.[72]

Third, I do not think that Paul's impassioned characterization of Peter's action as "pretense" and "not keeping in step with the gospel" would arise out of Gentiles being asked to follow Jewish food laws. Let us not forget that in Rom 14:1–15:7 and 1 Cor 8:1-13 that Paul pleads with the "strong" (i.e., Gentiles or Jewish Christ-believers such as himself) to exercise their convictions about food for the benefit of others so as to promote unity in the house churches, where Jewish scruples about purity and idolatry were still followed. The same principle could have been applied to Antioch so that the Gentiles, by what they ate, would not cause Jewish Christ-believers to stumble (Rom 14:15). Larry Hurtado states:

> Although some Jews refused any meal with Gentiles under any circumstances, for many, probably most religious Jews in the Hellenistic-Roman period, eating ordinary meals with Gentiles was not an insuperable problem; any claims by scholars to the contrary are simply misinformed. In principle, so long as the food on the table fell within what was permitted for Jews to eat under Torah (e.g., no pork), and so long as eating did not implicate a Jew in participating in a feast in honor of a god (e.g., no libation of wine or consecration of meat to a god), there was no major problem. Second, Jewish Christians' objections to eating with Gentile Christians in Acts (11:1-18) and Galatians (2:11-21) were not about what food was served, but about having meal fellowship with Gentiles whom they regarded as incompletely converted. This issue was not "purity laws," but the requirements for treating Gentiles as fully converted to the God of Israel.[73]

---

72. Bauckham, "James and the Jerusalem Church," 462-64. Slee (*Antioch*, 48-49) thinks the decree was promulgated in response to the incident at Antioch. Bruce (*Galatians*, 129-30) supposes that the decree was promulgated in order to facilitate social fellowship between Jewish and Gentile Christians.

73. Larry Hurtado, *Lord Jesus Christ: Devotion to Jesus in Earliest Christianity* (Grand Rapids, MI: Eerdmans, 2003), 162n18. See T. L. Carter (*Paul and the Power of Sin: Redefining*

If that is the case, then the incident *did not* consist of Paul abandoning the food laws, with Peter and Barnabas following suit, then afterward Peter and Barnabas got into trouble with men from James for not eating kosher. So it goes that Peter and Barnabas consequently returned to their Torah-compliant Jewish lifestyles and were forcing Gentiles to eat kosher food by separating from fellowship. Far more probably the heart of the matter was whether Jews and Gentiles could eat together without endangering either the Torah observance of the Jewish Christ-believers or compromising the freedom of Gentile Christ-believers from the Torah. Paul, Barnabas, and Peter said yes, while the men from James said no. Peter, Barnabas, and other Antiochene Jewish Christ-believers then capitulated on this point and adopted the halakic logic of the Jacobeans.[74] Paul saw this step as a betrayal of the Jerusalem agreement, a rebuke to his own apostolic authority, and an affront to the truth of the gospel itself.[75]

This leads to the conclusion that the problem was not with the food but with the company in which the food was consumed, i.e., the uncircumcised Gentiles.[76] The common fellowship meals ignited halakic debates about the limits of acceptable table fellowship between Jews and Gentiles. What was so reprehensible to "certain men from James" and "those of the circumcision" was not the nature of the food in these shared meals but the implication that the meals identified Gentiles as equals with Jews without making them

---

"*Beyond the Pale*" [SNTSMS 115; Cambridge: CUP, 2002], 95): "On the basis of the evidence available, it is not possible to draw definitive conclusions as to the nature of the table fellowship at Antioch. Esler is right to argue that Jewish food laws did reinforce Jewish isolationism, but such social boundaries were constantly subject to erosion as a result of pressure to conform to the surrounding Gentile world." Zetterholm (*Antioch*, 159-60) thinks that the joint meals in Antioch had nothing to do with Paul's theology or that of Jewish Christians in Antioch but were "part of a local Antiochean halakah prevalent among Hellenized Jews in general."

74. Robinson, "Circumcision," 27; Tomson, *Paul and the Jewish Law*, 227; Bockmuehl, *Jewish Law*, 82; see Dunn, *Jesus, Paul, and the Law*, 155-56; idem, *Galatians*, 122.

75. See Charles (*Paul and Politics of Diaspora*, 161), who sees wider issues at play, including "inclusion and equality, home and diaspora, center and periphery, native and stranger, diaspora and interethnic identifies, solidarity and tensions between people of the same group occupying the same diaspora space, and over how far Diaspora Judeans could allow themselves to go in negotiating their lives in non-Jewish environments."

76. See Peter Richardson, "Pauline Inconsistency: 1 Corinthians 9:19-23 and Galatians 2:11-14," *NTS* 26 (1980): 351-55; Pierre-Antoine Bernheim, *James, Brother of Jesus*, trans. J. Bowden (London: SCM, 1997), 177; Esler, *Galatians*, 137; Bockmuehl, *Jewish Law*, 73; Jervis, "Peter in the Middle," 57; Hays, "Galatians," 11:232; Watson, *Paul, Judaism, and the Gentiles*, 64; Slee, *Antioch*, 46-47; Zetterholm, *Antioch*, 135-36; Moo, *Galatians*, 141-52.

come via the route of proselytization.[77] The presenting issue was not that Peter ate *with* Gentiles but the *way* that he ate with Gentiles, i.e., as if they were covenantally faithful Jews.[78] This was not what was envisaged at the Jerusalem council, where uncircumcised Gentiles seem to have been joyfully embraced because of their faith, but their integration into a single "church" was perhaps not considered.[79] In the very least, the Jerusalem council gave no forethought as to the terms that would permit mixed table fellowship to occur when it was tacitly assumed that the Jewish and Gentile missions would remain *somewhat* independent. The offense was that to include Gentiles as equal participants in communal meals was to lower the currency of Israel's election and to deny the superiority or the advantage of the Jew.[80] This was the very kind of behavior that would invoke umbrage and action from Judean zealots and furnish them with further proof that Jewish Christ-believers were antinomian.

77. See David Garland ("Paul's Defense of the Truth of the Gospel regarding Gentiles [Galatians 2:15-3:22]," *RevExp* 91 [1994]: 170-71): "If there had been a church bus in Antioch, the Gentiles would always have had to move to the back. In the church building, one might find a Gentile water fountain and a Jewish water fountain; and the Gentiles would have had to sit in a special Gentile balcony section. Signs in various areas of the church might warn, 'Jews Only, No Gentiles Allowed,' and the bulletin logo might announce 'Separate but Equal in Christ.' In practice, however, the Gentile Christians were considered unfit for full equality. The compulsion was subtle but real. If Gentiles wanted to eat the Lord's Supper with Cephas and the other Jewish Christians, they would have to do something to make themselves fit. They would have to become Jews, submit to circumcision and abide by Jewish dietary regulations. The truth of the gospel, as far as Paul was concerned, does not mix with his kind of compulsion."

78. Nanos, "What Was at Stake," 283, 301; see Moo, *Galatians*, 148.

79. Note Sanders (*Paul, the Law, and the Jewish People*, 177): "If Jewish and Gentile Christians were to eat together, one would have to decide whether to live as a Jew or as a Gentile. Paul might conceivably act one way in Jerusalem and another in Asia Minor and Greece, or one way in the Jewish section of a city and another way in the remainder of it, but even he, artful though he was, could not do both simultaneously. And neither could Peter. When the issue was pressed in Antioch, Peter decided that he had better live like a Jew 'in order to win Jews' (I presume that such was his motive, and Paul accused him of not being true to the gospel (Gal. 2:11-14)." According to Moo (*Galatians*, 143): "The Jerusalem consultation focused on what should be required of Gentile converts. In Antioch, on the other hand, the issue had to do with how Jewish converts should relate to Gentile converts. On this matter, apparently, Peter and Paul drew different conclusions from the Jerusalem decisions. Peter perhaps thought that the Jerusalem agreement simply did not cover the kind of situation he encountered in Antioch."

80. This view could more readily reflect the position of Palestinian Jews than necessarily that of James or the Jewish Christians in general. Nevertheless, in order to avoid persecution, they thought that it was a position they had to advocate, at least for the moment.

Antioch and the "Zealot" Hypothesis

In light of the foregoing argument, what motivated James to send the delegation to Antioch and what energized the agitators in Galatia to urge a more rigorous form of Torah observance was probably the rising tide of anti-Gentile zealotry in Palestine and the desire to avoid persecution from zealous Judeans.[81] According to Robert Jewett, "Jewish Christians in Judea were stimulated by Zealot pressure into a nomistic campaign among their fellow Christians in the late forties and early fifties. Their goal was to avert the suspicion that they were in communion with lawless Gentiles. It appears that the Judean Christians convinced themselves that circumcision of Gentile Christians would thwart Zealot reprisals."[82]

Christians were evidently on the receiving end of this zealotry, given outbreaks of persecution against them. The reason for the persecution was probably the perception that the Christians were "lawbreakers," an accusation going back to Jesus' own ministry (see Mark 2:24; 3:4; Luke 13:14; 14:1-6), the Hellenistic circle associated with Stephen (Acts 6:13-14), and now exacerbated by the breaking down of the Jew-Gentile divide in Antioch (see Josephus, *Ant.* 20.200, where James was accused of being a lawbreaker as well). It is notable that, during the Maccabean rebellion, several Hellenized Jews were sallied upon because they were said to have made a covenant with the Gentiles and removed the marks of circumcision (1 Macc 1:11-15). Perhaps Christ-believers, especially the Greek-speaking Jewish Christ-believers in Antioch, were accused of making similar compromises with covenant, circumcision, and Gentiles and became susceptible to zealous violence as a result. So in order to avoid further persecution of the Jerusalem church, James sent a message to Peter in Antioch to adopt a stricter approach to Gentiles and meals. In order to prevent further persecutions, James required the Jewish Christ-believers in Antioch to undertake a stricter halakah of Torah-keeping when it came to contact with Gentiles. I take this to mean that they

---

81. Robert Jewett, "The Agitators and the Galatian Congregation," *NTS* 17 (1971): 198-212; Dunn, *Jesus, Paul, and the Law*, 133-36; Bruce, *Galatians*, 130; Longenecker, *Galatians*, 74-75; Hengel and Schwemer, *Paul between Damascus and Antioch*, 244-51; Witherington, *Grace in Galatia*, 155-56; Bockmuehl, *Jewish Law*, 73-75; Hays, "Galatians," 11:232-33; Hengel, *Saint Peter*, 61-65; Charles, *Paul and Politics of Diaspora*, 148-49; Moo, *Galatians*, 148-49; D. A. Carson, "Mirror-Reading with Paul and against Paul: Galatians 2:11-14 as a Test Case," in *Studies in the Pauline Epistles*, ed. M. S. Harmon and J. E. Smith (FS Douglas Moo; Grand Rapids, MI: Zondervan, 2014), 108-12; Gibson, *Peter*, 262-75.

82. Jewett, "Agitators," 205.

were to foster a Jewish social space conducive for intimate social intercourse with other Jews but not necessarily commensurable to open fellowship with Gentiles. The delegation sent to Antioch inferred that this meant withdrawing from contact with Gentiles at meals, unless of course the Gentiles were circumcised and perhaps observed regulations pertinent to resident aliens (e.g., Gen 15:18; Exod 23:31; Lev 17–18; Num 13:21-22; 34:7-9; Deut 1:7-8; 11:24; Josh 1:4; Ezek 47:15-17; 48:1).

Thus, if Jewish Christ-believers were to deflect suspicions of being legally lax or consorting with Gentiles, that would necessitate certain constraints on the fellowship between Jewish and Gentile Christ-believers. Either table fellowship would have to completely cease, or else the Gentiles would have to be circumcised. It is this implication that Peter, Barnabas, and others follow by withdrawing from fellowship. They were keeping the Jerusalem agreement by not forcing the Gentiles to be circumcised, but they were abandoning fellowship unless they were otherwise circumcised. They had kept the letter of the agreement, but in Paul's eyes they had violated the spirit in which the agreement was made.[83] Richard Longenecker contends that Peter committed a "misguided tactical maneuver made under pressure—the action of one whose convictions were proper, but who became confused under pressure, could not bring himself to express his true convictions, and so found himself retreating from what he knew to be right."[84]

The Real Issue: Gentile Circumcision

There are indications from Gal 2:11-14 and the wider context of Galatians that circumcision was the unstated but underlying issue in the incident at Antioch. First, part of the debate rides on the meaning of the word ἰουδαΐζειν ("to judaize"). The meaning of ἰουδαΐζειν varies from following the Jewish way of life in general, to politically supporting the Jewish people, to signifying full conversion to Judaism.[85] Dunn regards judaizing in Gal 2:14 as denoting the effort to force Gentiles to follow the Jewish dietary practices, and he cites a number of parallel texts to that end.[86] The problem is that, while "judaizing"

---

83. See Garlington, *Galatians*, 124.

84. Longenecker, *Galatians*, 75, while Moo (*Galatians*, 143) thinks Peter viewed his action as a "tactically wise accommodation to the concerns of stricter Jewish Christians."

85. Esth 8:17; Josephus, *War* 2.454, 463; *Acts of Pilate* 2.1; Plutarch, *Cic.* 7.5-6; Ignatius, *Magn.* 10.3; Eusebius, *Praep. Ev.* 9.22.5; *Hist. Eccl.* 6.17.

86. Dunn, *Jesus, Paul, and the Law*, 149-50, 153-54; idem, *Beginning from Jerusalem*, 473-74 (esp. n. 258).

does not always entail circumcision, the texts that Dunn cites show that, when compulsion was involved, judaizing was *always* connected with circumcision. Although "judaize" can mean to generally adopt the Jewish way of life, the terminus of judaizing was always circumcision.[87] It is clear from our sources that circumcision was the final threshold to be crossed in judaizing. Forced circumcisions were well-known and constituted a visible way of expressing Israel's triumph over pagan religion and pagan kingdoms.[88] A compulsion to judaize has to mean a compulsion to be circumcised because ἰουδαΐζειν most usually appears in a context involving circumcision under duress. Thus, if the issue was the equality of Gentiles in the Antioch congregation, then "judaize" probably carries this fuller meaning of conversion to Judaism via the ritual of circumcision. In this environment compelling Gentiles to "judaize" meant compelling them to become Ἰουδαῖοι ("Jews").[89]

Second, forcing Gentiles to judaize (i.e., to be circumcised) connects the incident at Antioch with Paul's report of the prior meeting with the "pillar" apostles in Gal 2:1-10 and with the situation arising in Galatia. The phrase "you compel to judaize" (ἀναγκάζεις ἰουδαΐζειν) in Gal 2:14 is similar in language to the compulsions for Gentiles to be circumcised in Gal 2:3 and 6:12. Narrating the Jerusalem meeting, Paul recalls that Titus was not "compelled to be circumcised" (ἠναγκάσθη περιτμηθῆναι) by the Jerusalem pillars (Gal 2:3), and this concession was inadvertently reneged upon, given the machinations by the Jacobeans in Antioch. Similarly, in the final section of Galatians, Paul says about the intruders that "they compel you to be circumcised" (ἀναγκάζουσιν ὑμᾶς περιτέμνεσθαι) as a symbol of Judean nationalism (Gal 6:12). The compulsions to judaize (Gal 2:14) and to be circumcised (Gal 2:3; 6:12) are parallel and equivalent. Thus, compulsion to be circumcised is the theme that links together the Jerusalem council, the incident at Antioch, and the problem in Galatia caused by the intruders.[90]

---

87. Josephus (*War* 2.454) refers to a certain Roman Metilius, who, when captured by Judean rebels, offered to "judaize to the point of circumcision" (μέχρι περιτομῆς ἰουδαΐσειν).

88. 1 Sam 18:25-27; Esth 8:17; Jdt 14:10; 1 Macc 2:46; Strabo, *Geog.* 16.2.34; Josephus, *Life* 112-13, 149-54; *Ant.* 13.257-58, 318-19, 397; 15.254-55; *War* 2.454.

89. Esler, *Galatians*, 137; Nanos, "What Was at Stake," 306-12; Moo, *Galatians*, 151; Caroline Johnson Hodge, *If Sons, Then Heirs: A Study of Kinship and Ethnicity in the Letters of Paul* (Oxford: OUP, 2007), 56.

90. See Betz, *Galatians*, 112; Tomson, *Paul and the Jewish Law*, 226; Barrett, "Paul," 54; Philip F. Esler, *The First Christians in Their Social Worlds: Social-Scientific Approaches to New Testament Interpretation* (London: Routledge, 1994), 58-62; Cummins, *Antioch*, 185; Zetterholm, *Antioch*, 135-36; Martinus C. de Boer, *Galatians: A Commentary* (NTL; Louisville: Westminster John Knox, 2011), 136-38.

Third, in Gal 2:14, that Peter lives ἐθνικῶς ("in the manner of a Gentile") cannot mean that Peter abandoned the food laws or that he lived a double life as a Torah-observant Jew when in Jerusalem and then as a Torah-free Jew elsewhere.[91] It is most unlikely that Peter, the apostle to the circumcision, could successfully conduct his mission to the Jews if he was known to be nonobservant on the food laws that Jews in Palestine and the Diaspora meticulously followed.[92] We should note as well that, even in Peter's vision in Caesarea, his conclusion was not that all food was now clean for him to eat; rather, it was that no person is unclean—the vision was parabolic for the cleanness of persons that God has made clean (Acts 10:15, 34-35; 11:9, 12).

More likely ἐθνικῶς is a rhetorical jibe that Peter has chosen not live in accordance with Jewish halakah concerning separation from Gentile impurities, but instead has been willing to live beside and among Gentile Christ-believers.[93] Furthermore, ἐθνικῶς stands in contradistinction to ἰουδαΐζειν ("to judaize"). When it is said that Peter "lives as a Gentile," this is the opposite of forcing Gentiles to follow a Jewish lifestyle or to become Jewish (i.e., judaize). Thus, that Peter lived *as a Gentile* means that he lived *in accord with and in proximity to* Gentiles, accepting them and eating with them, and without the imposition of any constraints upon Gentiles for fellowship.[94] That inclusive attitude toward Gentiles is confirmed by the reports of Peter's actions by Luke concerning Peter's ministry in Caesarea, with its defense before the Jerusalem elders (Acts 10–11), and Paul's report about Peter's stance in the Jerusalem agreement, where Gentiles were accepted as believers without circumcision (Gal 2:6-9). In other words, Paul was urging Peter to stay consistent with a Jewish lifestyle and a messianic missional ethos that did not force Gentiles to judaize and become proselytes.

Fourth, the group called "those of the circumcision" (τοὺς ἐκ περιτομῆς) are to be identified as Jews in Antioch who advocated the circumcision of Gentiles. This faction of Antiochene Jews was strenuously objecting to Jewish Christ-believing laxity in this area, and Peter feared violent reprisals from them. That makes sense, given that there was an established tradition of proselytism in Antioch, even if it was spasmodic (see Josephus, *War* 7.45; Acts 6:5).

91. Schlier, *Galaterbrief*, 86; Dunn, *Galatians*, 128.
92. See Richardson, "Pauline Inconsistency," 360-61. And note Dunn's defense of Peter's actions in *Beginning from Jerusalem*, 481-82.
93. Sanders, "Jewish Association with Gentiles," 186-87.
94. See Tomson, *Paul and the Jewish Law*, 230.

The designation οἱ ἐκ περιτομῆς is used in Acts to describe Jewish Christ-believers in favor of circumcising Christ-believing Gentiles (Acts 10:45; 11:2). As such, we need to integrate into our reconstruction the fact that one of the opposing parties in Antioch was not called "those of the clean food" but "those of the circumcision."[95]

In sum, the presupposition for the shared meals between Jewish and Gentile believers in Antioch was that Messiah and Spirit were determinative for their identity and unity, not Torah. The delegation from James observed the open fellowship between Christ-believing Jews and Gentiles, understood its implication for the perceptions of Jewish Christ-believers before other Jews, and argued that Jewish Christ-believers must withdraw from fellowship unless the Gentiles completely judaized, that is, converted to Judaism and followed the Torah.[96] Mark Nanos comments, "The ones advocating proselyte conversion of these Gentiles thus objected to circumventing the place of this rite to identify these Gentiles *as full and equal members* of this Jewish subgroup— which was how they were being identified at these meals, rather than as merely pagan guests."[97] Bauckham is similar: "If it is because the Gentile Christians are *Gentiles* that the men from James have persuaded Peter not to eat with them, then eating with them would only be possible if they became Jews."[98] Thus, Peter's separation signified a denial of the equal status of Gentiles in the messianic community and represented a demand (implied or verbalized) that Gentiles would have to judaize (i.e., undergo circumcision) in order to attain that status.[99]

---

95. See Martyn (*Galatians*, 234): "In the context one might have expected to hear that Peter was afraid of 'the food party'"; Nanos ("What Was at Stake," 303): "It should be noted that in this text Paul never mentions the food itself, and he does not identify those whom Peter fears as 'the ones for Jewish diet' or 'for a more rigorous diet,' not even, per Dunn, for example, for what might be described as 'a more rigorous Noachide diet.'"

96. See Esler, *First Christians*, 58-62; idem, *Galatians*, 137-38; Tomson, *Paul and the Jewish Law*, 227-30; Watson, *Paul, Judaism, and the Gentiles*, 107; de Boer, *Galatians*, 136; Moo, *Galatians*, 151.

97. Nanos, "What Was at Stake," 301 (italics original).

98. Richard Bauckham, "James, Peter, and the Gentiles," in *The Missions of James, Peter, and Paul: Tensions in Early Christianity*, ed. B. Chilton and C. Evans (Leiden: Brill, 2004), 126 (italics original).

99. See Zetterholm (*Antioch*, 162): "In practice, the explicit demand for separation of the community would soon, of course, function as an *implicit* demand on the Jesus-believing Gentiles formally to become Jews" (italics original).

Why Did Paul Object to Cephas's Actions?

Paul, it seems, did not agree with this Realpolitik of James and with Peter's compliance with it. In Galatians, Paul decried the efforts of those who wanted to compel Gentiles to be circumcised in order to "avoid being persecuted for the cross of Christ" (Gal 6:12). Paul would not adhere to the demand of anyone who wanted to use the foreskins of Gentile converts to save their own skins from the sword. Paul himself knew full well the ferocious violence of zealous Judeans because he had been part of it prior to his Damascus Christophany (Gal 1:13-14, 23; Phil 3:6; Acts 8:3; 9:1-2). Yet he would not relent in the face of violent opposition, and if his own testimony is to be believed, he was willing to risk his own safety from his compatriots in order to announce the gospel to Gentiles (Gal 5:11; 2 Cor 11:21-33). Peter's actions meant that the original "false brothers" who came to Antioch had found another means of getting their way. The freedom of Gentiles from circumcision was not upheld in the context of mixed Jew-Gentile fellowship.

Paul opposed Peter in public "to his face," which reflects a Jewish idiom (Deut 9:2; Num 27:17, 19, 21-22?; Josh. 1:5; 7:2 [LXX]). The substance of Paul's response to Peter, at least his account of it to the Galatians, is that Peter was condemned (καταγινώσκω) by his actions (perhaps κατεγνωσμένος is a divine passive for "condemned by God"). Paul also accused Peter of playacting and leading others into the same pretense (ὑπόκρισις, συνυποκρίνομαι). Peter's actions become a form of pretense for the sake of fostering a positive public persona when his real convictions are known to be otherwise. If the logic of Paul's accusation is correct, Peter's pretense is not his playing the part of a pro-Gentile Jewish Christ-believer in Antioch, but his playing the part of a zealous Jew to placate those of the circumcision party. Finally, the willingness of Peter and his consorts to embrace the "walk" (i.e., the halakah) of zealous Jews concerning the circumcision of Gentiles and separation from Gentiles meant that they were not "walking toward the truth of the gospel" (οὐκ ὀρθο-ποδοῦσιν πρὸς τὴν ἀλήθειαν τοῦ εὐαγγελίου). In other words, by their actions, they had trampled upon the "walk of the gospel" by adopting the "walk" of Judean zealotry. The "truth of the gospel" refers to the prior practice of the Antiochene church in sharing table fellowship with Jews and Gentiles without requiring the latter to take on circumcision and the yoke of the Torah.[100] As Ben Witherington put it, "They chose Jewish purity over body unity."[101] Hans

---

100. Esler, *Galatians*, 131-32.
101. Witherington, *Grace in Galatia*, 158.

Dieter Betz comments similarly, "By attempting to preserve the integrity of the Jewish Christians as Jews, Cephas destroyed the integrity of Gentile Christians as believers in Christ."[102] The Gentiles become little more than pawns in the quest to further the victory of Israel over the pagan world.

Conclusion: The Making of Paulinism

In sum, the "incident at Antioch" seems to have transpired as follows: The Antiochene church—with Peter, Barnabas, and Paul—included Jewish and Gentile Christ-believers worshiping together and eating kosher meals together, while still within the orbit, or at least on the fringes, of the Antiochene Jewish community. However, a surge in Judean zealotry led James in Jerusalem to dispatch a delegation to Antioch to urge Peter to separate from Gentiles on account of their inherent impurity unless the Gentiles judaized and become circumcised proselytes. This played right into the hands of the "circumcision" party in Antioch, local Jews and a small faction of Christ-believing Jewish sympathizers, who were affronted by Peter and Paul's blatant fraternizing with Gentiles. This faction applied pressure on Peter to comply with the Jacobean embassy's request, which Peter reluctantly did. Paul saw this pragmatic move as a betrayal of the truth of the gospel that God accepts Gentiles as Gentiles on the basis of faith. He publicly called Peter to account, but it seems that the majority sided with Peter.

On the significance of this event, according to Hengel, the "account of the catastrophe in Gal 2:11 shows a deep hurt which was not fully healed even years afterwards."[103] I want to suggest that Gal 2:11-14 signifies a "parting *in the ways*" between Paul and the Jerusalem church. If Paul had won the argument at Antioch, that is, had he won the support of the majority of Jewish Christ-believers there, he presumably would have said so to the Galatians.[104] Instead, he became an outsider to the very assemblies that he had helped to establish, grow, and defend. He had to seek another base of mission operations and was left with only the support of Gentile-majority churches in Galatia and Cilicia. As time passed, even his foothold there proved to be tenuous, and some ground may have been lost in Galatia, even while Paul succeeded in his letter

---

102. Betz, *Galatians*, 112.

103. Hengel and Schwemer, *Paul between Damascus and Antioch*, 215.

104. Bruce, *Galatians*, 134; Holtz, "Der Antiochenische Zwischenfall," 124; Longenecker, *Galatians*, 79; Hill, *Hellenists and Hebrews*, 126; Watson, *Paul, Judaism, and the Gentiles*, 56; Dunn, *Beginning from Jerusalem*, 489-94.

to the Galatians in preventing a wholesale defection to the nomistic gospel of the intruding proselytizers.

This parting "in" the ways rather than "of" the ways meant that the break with the Jerusalem church was not absolute. There seems to have remained a genuine but uneasy relationship between the two parties. Paul's only genuine adversaries were the false brothers who caused divisions in Antioch and who finally found a way to gain a concession from the Jerusalem church for their circumcision view by playing on the fears that Jewish fraternizing with uncircumcised Gentiles would lead to further pogroms in Jerusalem. It was most likely persons from this faction who entered Galatia, but as far as can be ascertained from Galatians, they were not authorized by the Jerusalem church. The enduring but cagey relationship that Paul had with the Jerusalem church is evidenced by Paul's affirmation of Barnabas's and Peter's ministry (1 Cor 1:12; 9:6), Paul's affirmation of a common gospel shared with the Jerusalem church (1 Cor 15:1-8), his sense of continuing solidarity with the Judean churches in their persecution (1 Thess 2:15-16), at least one visit to Antioch after the hurtful incident sometime around 52 CE (Acts 18:22), Paul's reconciliation with John Mark probably during his time in Ephesus (Phlm 24; Col 4:11), and his collection for the needy saints in Jerusalem, which was an olive branch in search of cordial relations (1 Cor 16:1-7; Rom 15:25-28). Paul's fear in going to Jerusalem was primarily from unbelieving Jews (Rom 15:31), and James's response to Paul's visit to Jerusalem in Acts 21:20-25 is realistic by affirming Paul's ministry to Gentiles, urging Paul to address the matter of his antinomian reputation, and reaffirming the requirement of the apostolic decree as a minimal law for Gentiles.

Paul was ultimately trying to stay true to the revelation that he had received on the Damascus road, and he was endeavoring to stand firm on the principles agreed on at the Jerusalem council. As Hengel wrote, "If the community in Jerusalem now—contrary to an earlier attitude—called for the circumcision of the 'Gentiles,' Paul's whole proclamation of the gospel to the 'Gentiles' since his call, i.e., since Damascus, would have been in vain, as his message and the faith brought about by it would be 'nothing' if Christ had not risen from the dead (I Cor. 15:14). For Paul, a separated Gentile Christian Church which alone was 'orthodox,' i.e., a divided body of Christ, was an impossible idea."[105] Paul remained an activist for the "old Antioch" position on Christ, Torah, and Gentiles before the Jerusalem church apparently caved in to political pressure from zealous Judeans. James and Peter probably saw their position as fair in that it did not strictly advocate the circumcision of Gentiles (unless they wanted to

---

105. Hengel and Schwemer, *Paul between Damascus and Antioch*, 208.

be part of table fellowship) and necessary in the politically volatile climate of Judea (which it had become).

The incident at Antioch demonstrates Paul's uncompromising commitment to the gospel of Jesus Christ as the single and supreme instrument of salvation for Jews and Gentiles. He could not accept the compromise of "equal but separate" or "accepted but more acceptable if circumcised." The same unyielding stance was manifested in the letter to the Galatians, where Paul's insistence on Gentile Christ-believers remaining free from proselytism resulted in his most polemical argumentation and his most freighted rhetoric. While Romans might be the mature distillation of his thought toward the end of his life, with appropriate qualifications and apologetic motifs, Galatians exhibits Paul in his most raw and radical state.

In the incident at Antioch we confront the first public expression of Paulinism, understood as the antithesis between Christ and Torah when the salvation and equal status of Gentiles is on the line. This paradigmatic shift from Torah to Christ as the locus of God's saving actions was impregnated in Paul's Damascus road experience, publicly debuted in Antioch, unleashed with the fury of a radical iconoclast in Galatians, clinically applied in 2 Cor 3, given its mature and prudent form in Romans, and eventually lent itself toward the genesis of two competing theologies of proto-orthodoxy and Marcionism in the second century, which both claimed ancestry from Paul. This Paulinism is aptly captured by Martin Hengel:

> For him, the encounter with the Resurrected One near Damascus set before him the question of the law or Christ in the form of a soteriological alternative. For Judaism of that time the Torah was in manifold expression the essence of salvation, and could be identified with the fundamental religious metaphor, "life." . . . Since the opposition between Torah and Jesus of Nazareth had made him into a persecutor, now the relationship between Christ and Torah had to become a fundamental issue, in which the inversion of the opposition immediately became apparent: he, the Resurrected One, is ζωή for those who believe (2 Cor. 4:11-12; cf. 2:16).[106]

I think that Hengel has tapped in to the nerve of Paul's thought and demonstrated the radical stance of Paul toward the Torah that made him the contro-

---

106. Martin Hengel, "The Stance of the Apostle Paul toward the Law in the Unknown Years between Damascus and Antioch," in *Justification and Variegated Nomism*, vol. 2, *The Paradoxes of Paul*, ed. D. A. Carson, P. T. O'Brien, and M. A. Seifrid (Grand Rapids, MI: Baker Academic, 2004), 84.

versial figure that he was. Yet this Christ-Torah antithesis needs some qualifications, as I suspect that it does not mean what many Protestant commentators think it means. It does not mean that Jewish Christ-believers should cease observing the Torah, nor does it mean that the Torah has nothing relevant for the ethical life of Gentile Christians. Rather, the advent of Christ means that his death and resurrection has effected the end of ages and broken the link between law, sin, and death. Christ turns the condemnation of the law into justification; Christ made the curse of the law into redemption. Faith in Christ is the testimony of the law, and yet faith in Christ places believers beyond the jurisdiction of the law. Christ terminates the Mosaic dispensation in order to fulfill the Abrahamic hopes. Christ serves the circumcision by making Gentiles heirs of the patriarchs. Christ and not Torah is what now defines and saves the people of God.

The anomaly that is Paul first appeared in the incident at Antioch, where a Hebrew of Hebrews argued for the dissolution of the category "God-fearer" and, as a corollary, refused to entertain the idea of two classes of insiders in the churches of Christ or consent to the notion of two separate churches of Jews and Gentiles segregated by their stance to the Torah.[107] That became the presupposition for what would be his most enduring contribution to Christian thought, and what was perhaps the most peculiar belief of any Jew in the first century, namely, that both Jews and Gentiles can stand righteous before the God of the covenant on the basis of faith in the Lord Jesus Christ.

107. See Segal (*Paul the Convert*, 265): "A God-fearer would have welcomed Paul's message with excitement, because it removed the status-ambiguity, the double alienation of being no longer gentile but not yet Jewish. Instead of being neither pagans nor Jews, God-fearers entered gentile Christianity community as true equals, without having to undergo the seemingly irrelevant ritual conversion to Judaism."

CHAPTER FIVE

The Apostle Paul and the Roman Empire

Paul, like many Jews, had to daily negotiate his way through the socio-political and cultural challenges that the Roman Empire posed for the Jewish people.[1] Those challenges were manifold and included things like maintaining certain standards of purity amid the contaminants of Greco-Roman cities, the ubiquity of polytheism and idolatry with the many temples and family shrines, the reality of Roman political and military hegemony, the worship of Rome's deities and emperor as a mark of civil loyalty, and widespread prejudice against the Jews for their distinctive practices. These challenges were experienced in varied ways depending on one's geographic location (Palestine, Asia Minor, Greece, Africa, or Rome), social status (Roman citizen, parentage, patronage), and socioeconomic position (elite, merchant, artisan, freedman, laborer, slave). These challenges could be negotiated in a host of ways ranging from collaboration to indifference to resistance.[2] One has only to compare Tiberius Alexander, Herod the Great, Philo, Josephus, and the Qumran sectarians to observe the range of possibilities for practicing Jewish religious devotion in the Roman Empire. For a case in point, in the Jerusalem temple the Judeans made sacrifices not to the emperor but on the emperor's behalf, a familiar enough stance in the

---

1. An earlier and much shorter version of this essay was published as Michael F. Bird, "'One Who Will Arise to Rule over the Nations': Paul's Letter to the Romans and the Roman Empire," in *Jesus Is Lord, Caesar Is Not: Evaluating Empire in New Testament Studies*, ed. S. McKnight and J. B. Modica (Downers Grove, IL: IVP Academic, 2013), 146-65. Used by permission of InterVarsity Press, P. O. Box 1400, Downers Grove, IL 60515, USA, www.ivpress.com.

2. See H.-G. Gradl, "Kaisertum und Kaiserkult: Ein Vergleich zwischen Philos *Legatio ad Gaium* und Offenbarugen des Johannes," *NTS* 56 (2010): 116-38.

ancient world,[3] which allowed for Jewish sensibilities, yet still expressed subjugation to Rome.[4]

Where was Paul in this cultural matrix of divided loyalties? Was Paul a zealot, a political conformist, or something altogether different? The issue of Paul's stance vis-à-vis the Roman Empire has been a well-studied topic in the last ten or so years of biblical scholarship.[5] Some see Paul as a political radical, and others suppose that Paul was rather uninterested in the affairs of the Roman political apparatus. My thesis in this chapter is that, although Paul's thought and praxis do not suggest a militant anti-Roman activism, he nonetheless engages in a not-so-subtle critique of the Roman socioreligious edifice because it stands opposed to the ultimate manifestation of the kingdom of God and the lordship of Jesus Christ. An examination of Paul's letter to the Romans will be utilized to demonstrate such a point. It will be shown that Paul's anomaly here is that he is a Roman citizen who looks forward to the supersession of the Roman empire by the new empire of Israel's God.

---

3. Simon R. F. Price, *Rituals and Power: The Roman Imperial Cult in Asia Minor* (New York: CUP, 1984), 209-14, 232-33. Ittai Gradel (*Emperor Worship and Roman Religion* [Oxford: OUP, 2002], 20-22) reports that a college of priests, the Arval brothers, routinely offered sacrifices to mark imperial anniversaries and victories: "The Arvals offer striking and detailed evidence of the extent to which the emperor and his house quickly came to dominate the state cult in Rome, without, however, receiving direct worship in this sphere, and without supplanting the more traditional cults and celebrations" (22).

4. Josephus, *War* 2.409-10. Although Philo (*Legat.* 357) reports Caligula saying that the current arrangement was not to his satisfaction.

5. For surveys of Paul and the Roman Empire, see Christian Strecker, "Taktiken der Aneignung: Politische Implikationen der paulinischen Botschaft im Kontext der römischer imperialen Wirklichkeit," in *Das Neue Testament und politische Theorie: Interdisziplinäre Beiträge zur Zukunft des Politischen*, ed. E. Reinmuth (Stuttgart: Kohlhammer, 2001), 114-48; Wiard Popkes, "Zum Thema 'Anti-imperiale Deutung neutestamentlicher Schriften,'" *ThLZ* 127 (2002): 850-62; J. J. Meggitt, "Taking the Emperor's Clothes Seriously: The New Testament and the Roman Empire," in *The Quest for Wisdom: Essays in Honour of Philip Budd*, ed. C. E. Joynes (Cambridge: Orchard Academic Press, 2002), 143-69; Warren Carter, "Paul and the Roman Empire: Recent Perspectives," in *Paul Unbound: Other Perspectives on the Apostle*, ed. M. D. Given (Peabody, MA: Hendrickson, 2010), 7-26; idem, *The Roman Empire and the New Testament: An Essential Guide* (Nashville: Abingdon, 2006); P. J. J. Botha, "Assessing Representations of the Imperial Cult in New Testament Studies," *VerbEccl* 25 (2004): 14-25; Judith A. Diehl, "Empires and Epistles: Anti-Roman Rhetoric in the New Testament Epistles," *CBR* 10 (2012): 217-52; idem, "Anti-imperial Rhetoric in the New Testament," in *Jesus Is Lord, Caesar Is Not: Evaluating Empire in New Testament Studies*, ed. S. McKnight and J. B. Modica (Downers Grove, IL: IVP Academic, 2013), 38-81.

Situating the Debate about the Anti-imperial Paul

There is good reason to be positively disposed toward the thesis that Paul possessed, at least on some level, an anti-imperial perspective.

First, a prima facie case for the anti-imperial nature of Paul's theology can be found in a comparison of Paul's linguistic register with that of the imperial cults and its sociopolitical expressions.[6] As many have pointed out, words like "gospel" (εὐαγγέλιον), "Lord" (κύριος) "Savior" (σωτήρ) "Son of God" (υἱὸς θεοῦ), "fidelity" (πίστις), "parousia" (παρουσία), and "peace" (εἰρήνη) were not technical Christian religious terms but shared a linguistic background in the politics, propaganda, and pantheon of the Roman Empire.[7] The various media of coins, inscriptions, temples, and building dedications saturated the landscape with claims about and for the imperium. Roman power was propagated to the provinces, as evidenced by three copies of Augustus's *Res Gestae* ("Achievements") that were found in Asia Minor, specifically, Ancyra, Apollonia, and Pisidian Antioch.[8] Imperial images in particular were enfaced all over the empire, in banks, booths, baths, gymnasia, graffiti, shops, markets, taverns, parades, placards, porches, festivals, windows, and temples.[9] Urban life, especially in Rome but also elsewhere, was literally crammed with political imagery that heralded imperial power and was designed to simultaneously unite and Romanize the diverse peoples of the Mediterranean under a single

---

6. Importantly, the imperial cults were diversified in content, medium, and participants. The imperial cults encompassed a range of practices oriented to deceased emperors, the living emperor, his heirs and family; often integrated with the goddess Roma and other gods; with devotion exhibited in speeches, poetry, inscriptions, coinage, festivals, shrines, temples, and sacrifices; and variably practiced in private homes, in neighborhood shrines, in clubs and associations, and among public festivals and temples. On imperial cults in the plural, see Steven J. Friesen, "Normal Religion; or, Words Fail Us: A Response to Karl Galinsky's 'The Cult of the Roman Emperor: Uniter or Divider?,'" in *Rome and Religion: A Cross-Disciplinary Dialogue on the Imperial Cult*, ed. J. Brodd and J. L. Reed (Atlanta: SBL, 2011), 24. For a good description of the emergence and development of the imperial cults, see Christoph Heilig, *Hidden Criticism? The Methodology and Plausibility of the Search for a Counter-Imperial Subtext in Paul* (WUNT 2.392; Tübingen: Mohr Siebeck, 2015), 73-78.

7. See the helpful chart in Michael J. Gorman, *Apostle of the Crucified Lord: A Theological Introduction to Paul and His Letters* (Grand Rapids, MI: Eerdmans, 2004), 108-9; the similarities were noted earlier by Dieter Georgi, *Theocracy in Paul's Praxis and Theology*, trans. D. E. Green (Minneapolis: Fortress, 1991), 82.

8. David Nystrom, "We Have No King but Caesar: Roman Imperial Ideology and the Imperial Cult," in *Jesus Is Lord, Caesar Is Not: Evaluating Empire in New Testament Studies*, ed. S. McKnight and J. B. Modica (Downers Grove, IL: IVP Academic, 2013), 31.

9. Marcus Cornelius Fronto, *Ep.* 4.12.6.

and supreme imperial polity.[10] Paul's language for the gospel, Christ's lordship, and salvation parallels imperial terminology. So much so that Harry O. Maier comments that "the Pauline corpus singles itself out as the body of New Testament writings most heavily steeped in imperial language, metaphor and ideas."[11] Similar is Christian Strecker, who identifies "throughout Paul's letters and assertions many ideas that can be understood as a messianic appropriation of important elements of the imperial political-religious discourse and its corresponding performances."[12]

As to what this means, Adolf Deissman identified a "polemical parallelism between the cult of the emperor and the cult of Christ, which makes itself felt where ancient words derived by Christianity from the treasury of the Septuagint and the Gospels happen to coincide with solemn concepts of the imperial cult which sounded the same or similar."[13] Yet for Deissman these parallels between imperial language and Pauline vocabulary amounted to little more than a "silent protest" against Roman power, albeit an "intended" one.[14] Wilhelm Bousset said that, despite the "factual and linguistic analogies," it would be mistaken to think that the "worship of Jesus as the Lord has developed in conscious opposition to" the imperial cult.[15] Yet for other researchers these parallels suggest a deliberate and provocative challenge to the supremacy of Roman imperial power by mimicking the language of the imperial cults in order to undermine them.[16] Accordingly, several scholars believe that Paul's

10. Harry O. Maier, *Picturing Paul in Empire: Imperial Image, Text, and Persuasion in Colossians, Ephesians, and the Pastoral Epistles* (London: Bloomsbury, 2013), 2-3. See also Paul Zanker, *The Power of Images in the Age of Augustus,* trans. A. Shapiro (Ann Arbor: University of Michigan Press, 1988). No less than thirteen altars dedicated to Augustus have been found in the lower city of Athens; see Anna Benjamin and Antony E. Bautischek, "Arae Augusti," *Hesperia* 28 (1959): 65-85.

11. Maier, *Picturing Paul in Empire,* 6.

12. Strecker, "Taktiken der Aneignung," 161: "In der Tat finden sich namentlich in den Paulusbriefen zahlreiche Aussagen und Vorstellungen, die sich als messianische Aneignung wichtiger Elemente des kaiserzeitlichen politisch-religiösen Diskurses und entsprechender Performanzen begreifen lassen."

13. Adolf Deissmann, *Light from the Ancient East: The New Testament Illustrated by Recently Discovered Texts of the Graeco-Roman World,* trans. L. R. M. Strachan (2nd ed.; London: Hodder & Stoughton, 1927), 346.

14. Deissmann, *LAE,* 355.

15. Wilhelm Bousset, *Kyrios Christos: A History of the Belief in Christ from the Beginnings of Christianity to Irenaeus,* trans. J. E. Steely, ed. L. Hurtado (Waco, TX: Baylor University Press, 1970), 141.

16. Dieter Georgi ("God Turned Upside Down," in *Paul and Empire: Religion and Power in Roman Imperial Society,* ed. R. Horsley [Valley Forge, PA: TPI, 1997], 152): "If the terms chosen

gospel has a clear sociopolitical texture and arguably a counterimperial posture by parodying the imperial rhetoric in his gospel about Jesus as Son of God and Lord, who brings salvation and peace to the world. Paul's letters exhibit a tacit anti-Roman rhetoric that is encoded in his discourse. This sets the claims of Christ and the claims of Caesar on a collision course. John Dominic Crossan and Jonathan L. Reed aver that "to proclaim Jesus as Son of God was deliberately denying Caesar his highest title."[17] The similarity in language is judged by many to be highly antithetical, as N. T. Wright puts it: "At every point, therefore, we should expect what we in fact find: that for Paul, Jesus is Lord and Caesar is not."[18] Joseph Fantin concludes his study of κύριος language in the Greco-Roman world and in Paul's letters with the following claim: "Given the relational nature of κύριος and the exclusive nature of supreme lord, using the title for Christ with explicit features such as unique modifiers, creedal formulas, praise hymns would be viewed by the original readers as challenging the default supreme lord."[19]

Second, we can note Luke's report that, during Paul's time in Thessalonica, the local Jews stirred up violent opposition against Paul's converts by claiming that "these men who have caused trouble all over the world have now come here, and Jason has welcomed them into his house. They are all defying Caesar's decrees, saying that there is another king, one called Jesus" (Acts 17:6-7). In Luke's telling, the Christian declaration that Jesus was king stood in apparent defiance against the kingship of Caesar, a point confirmed by an anecdote related from Suetonius about Caligula's unwillingness to concede the idea of there being other kings: "Upon hearing some kings, who came to the city to pay him court, conversing together at supper, about their illustrious descent, he exclaimed 'Let there be but one prince, one king' [εἷς κοίρανος ἔστω, εἷς βασιλεύς]."[20] It is significant that someone connected to the Pauline circle regarded Paul's claim about Jesus as incommensurate with the exclusive authority claimed for the emperor.[21]

---

by Paul for his Roman readers have associations with the slogans of Caesar religion, then Paul's gospel must be understood as competing with the gospel of the Caesars."

17. John Dominic Crossan and Jonathan L. Reed, *In Search of Paul: How Jesus's Apostle Opposed Rome's Empire with God's Kingdom* (San Francisco: HarperSanFrancisco, 2004), 11.

18. N. T. Wright, *Paul: In Fresh Perspective* (Minneapolis: Fortress, 2009), 69.

19. Joseph D. Fantin, *Lord of the Entire World: Lord Jesus, a Challenge to Lord Caesar?* (NTM 31; Sheffield: Sheffield Phoenix, 2011), 266.

20. Suetonius, *Caligula* 22.

21. See C. Kavin Rowe (*World Upside Down: Reading Acts in the Graeco-Roman Age* [Oxford: OUP, 2009], 99-102), who sees the claim in Acts 17:6 as false, since Jesus is not in a

Third, Roman attitudes toward Christ-believers highlight the perceived incommensurability between Christ-devotion and Roman religion, especially the imperial cults. The Christ-believers who were persecuted under Nero in the mid-60s CE, including the probable executions of Peter and Paul,[22] were probably motivated by complex local factors relating to religious scruples and social competition. It is certainly true that abstention from the imperial cult is not treated as the reason for the Neronian persecution in our sources. What we do know from Tacitus is that Christ-believers were despised for their "abominations," as a "mischievous superstition"; they were typical of things "hideous and shameful" that make their way to Rome and scorned for their "hatred of mankind."[23] Of course, similar criticisms were said of many Eastern rites that had come to Rome, both Judaism and the Bacchus cultus,[24] so why the focus on the Christ-believers in the Neronian persecution?

Most likely, Christ-believers were singled out because they were regarded as committing national apostasy. By abandoning and critiquing Roman religion, they were perceived as religiously impious and politically disloyal.[25] Although

---

competitive relationship to Caesar that would lead to revolt, but true in the sense that the Christian mission entails a call to another way of life, which will turn the world upside down.

22. Eusebius, *Hist. Eccl.* 2.25.5-8.

23. Tacitus, *Ann.* 15.44.

24. Compare Livy, *Hist.* 39.8-19, and Tacitus, *Hist.* 5.5. See discussion in Mikael Tellbe, *Paul between Synagogue and State: Christians, Jews, and Civic Authorities in 1 Thessalonians, Romans, and Philippians* (ConBNT 34; Stockholm: Almqvist & Wiksell, 2001), 26-35.

25. See Pliny, *Ep.* 10.96.2; *Mart. Pol.* 9.2; Tertullian, *Apol.* 24.1; 28.2. Note that Trajan's reply to Pliny reveals a "don't ask, don't tell" policy about Christ-believers; if they are found, however, then they must be punished unless they recant by "worshiping our gods." See John Granger Cook, *Roman Attitudes toward the Christians* (WUNT 261; Tübingen: Mohr Siebeck, 2010), 89-92, 290-93. Barclay (*Pauline Churches*, 359-61) notes that refusing to worship the Roman gods was the point of contention, and he regards failure to participate in the imperial cult as only one facet of the "atheism" of Christians. The problem I have is that the imperial cult—not the cults of Roma, the Capitoline triad, or local cults like Artemis, Serapis, or Diana—was always *the* litmus test of loyalty. So while the imperial cult might not necessarily have been the primary mode of idolatry critiqued by Paul, even so, Roman officials always insisted on devotion to the imperial cult as a way of unmasking the atheism of Christians, which implies the imperial cult's prominence within Roman religion and its prominence among those critical of Roman religion. As N. T. Wright (*Paul and the Faithfulness of God* [COQG 4; London: SPCK, 2013], 1313-14) puts it: "Yes, the Christian refusal to worship the gods in general mattered; but Caesar was always the particular case." Similar is Dorothea H. Bertschmann (*Bowing before Christ—Nodding to the State? Reading Paul Politically with Oliver O'Donovan and John Howard Yoder* [LNTS 502; London: T&T Clark, 2014], 88n39), who accepts Barclay's point that imagining a Christ vs. Caesar slam-fest is misleading but notes: "Still, I suggest that when the head of political powers orders his Christian subjects to commit compromising actions it can be

Roman religion was pluralistic, it was not necessarily tolerant toward foreign cults, especially if they were thought to promote debauchery and disorder.[26] For a Roman resident to profess faith in Jesus as an alternative to Roman religion lent itself to accusations of atheism and hatred of the human race and was interpreted as a rejection of the *mos maiorum* (ancestral customs) and committing *maiestas* (affronting the majesty of Caesar). Neglect of local deities and civic religious duties, especially those sponsored by imperial patronage, amounted to a charge of atheism. This lack of devotion could hardly go unnoticed because it would be conspicuous by its absence from family shrines, from nonparticipation in religious rites in associations, and from nonattendance at public festivals.[27] Certainly by the early second century, the profession by believers that "Jesus is Lord" carried with it the seeming impossibility of Christ-believers ascribing the same title to Caesar and worshiping his image, even upon the threat of death, as famously demonstrated in Pliny's persecution of Christians in Bithynia and in the martyrdom story of Bishop Polycarp.[28] Similarly, Tertullian wrote how Christians faced "the accusation of treason

---

easily imagined how the confession 'Christ is Lord' takes a sharp, polemical ring over against 'Caesar is Lord.' Caesar then usurps God's prerogatives not just by virtue of presenting himself as divine but claiming the ultimate power to tell people how to live."

26. Cicero (*Leg.* 2.19) said that, in his ideal state, "no one will separately have gods, either new or alien, unless accepted by the state." Cassius Dio (52.36.1-2) presents a speech where Maecenas counsels a young Octavian with the charge: "Those who attempt to distort our religion with strange rites, you should abhor and punish not merely for the sake of the gods (since if a man despises these he will not pay honour to any other divine being) but because such men, by bringing new divinities in place of old, persuade many to adopt foreign practices from which spring up conspiracies, factions and cabals which are far from profitable to monarchy. Do not, therefore, permit anybody to be an atheist or sorcerer."

27. A similar analogy can be found with an inscription testifying to the prosecution of Calpurnius Piso in 20 CE on the grounds that "it was also the opinion of the senate that the *numen* of the divine Augustus was violated by him [i.e., Piso] in that he withheld every honour that had been accorded to his memory or to those portraits which were [granted] to him before he was included in the number of the gods" (cited in Michael Koortbojian, *The Divinization of Caesar and Augustus* [Cambridge: CUP, 2013], 156). Evidently, nonparticipation in civic rights was civic disloyalty. There was room for leniency, given Tiberius's famous remark that "wrongs done to the gods are the gods' concern," reported in Tacitus, *Ann.* 1.73.

28. Pliny, *Ep.* 10.96.1-10; *Mart. Pol.* 8.1–12.2. We should note that saying "X is Lord" (e.g., "Serapis is Lord"), as we find in the papyri, does not necessarily imply "Caesar is not." Tertullian (*Apol.* 34.1) could say, "For my part, I am willing to give the emperor this designation ['Lord'], but in the common acceptation of the word, and when I am not forced to call him Lord as in God's place." The polemic emerges only when a rivalry develops between two apparent Lords, each described with superlative status and ascribed with unsurpassed authority.

most of all against Roman religion."[29] Failure to offer sacrifices and respect imperial images is precisely the accusation brought against Christians by the pagan critics Caecilius and Celsus.[30]

Although much of the evidence discussed derives from the second century, Christian antipathy to the imperial cults most probably goes back to the first century. It was impossible to ignore the imperial cults, since Herod the Great had ringed Judea with temples to Augustus before the time of Christ,[31] and Caligula and Nero were abnormally active in cultivating divine honors during the time of Paul. Yes, the imperial cult was merely one facet of Roman religion, enmeshed beside and within other cults in the first century. Yet Donald Jones comments: "From the perspective of early Christianity, the worst abuse in the Roman Empire was the imperial cult. Honors which should be reserved for God alone could not be bestowed on men."[32] The exclusive Christ-devotion of the early church could not absorb veneration of the emperor; by refusing to participate, Christians were perceived to cut the cords that held politics, pantheon, and people together as the fabric of social cohesion.

Viewed this way, Christ-believers were persecuted because they neglected what some thought necessary (worship of the gods), their meetings broke down the social orders between the classes (hierarchies of power and privilege), they promoted controversy and clashes among Jewish communities (a threat to peace), and they abhorred precisely what many adored (Roman power and its benefactions). Certain Christ-believers refused to place themselves within the matrix of relationships between the gods, emperor, civic elites, and people and thus, in the Roman understanding, displaced them-

---

29. Tertullian, *Apol.* 24.1; Pliny, *Ep.* 10.96-97.

30. Minucius Felix, *Octavius* 5-10; Origen, *Contra Celsus* 8.55-67.

31. On the imperial cult in Palestine, see James S. McLaren, "Jews and the Imperial Cult: From Augustus to Domitian," *JSNT* 27 (2005): 257-78; idem, "Searching for Rome and the Imperial Cult in Galilee: Reassessing Galilee-Rome Relations (63 B. C.E to 70 C. E.)," in *Rome and Religion: A Cross-Disciplinary Dialogue on the Imperial Cult*, ed. J. Brodd and J. L. Reed (Atlanta: SBL, 2011), 111-36; Monika Bernett, "Der Kaiserkult in Judäa unter herodischer und römischer Herschaft: Zu Herausbildung und Herausfoderung neuer Konzepte Jüdischer Herrschaftslegitimation," in *Jewish Identity in the Greco-Roman World*, ed. J. Frey, D. R. Schwartz, and S. Gripentrog (AJEC 71; Leiden: Brill, 2007), 219-51; Werner Eck, ed., *Judäa— Syria Palästina: Ein Euseinandersetzung ein Provinz mit römischer Politik und Kultur* (TSAJ 340; Tübingen: Mohr Siebeck, 2014).

32. Donald L. Jones, "Christianity and the Roman Imperial Cult," in *ANRW* 2.23.2, ed. H. Temporini and W. Haase (Berlin: Walter de Gruyter, 1980), 1023. See Tertullian, *Apol.* 27; *De Idol.* 15; Minucius Felix, *Oct.* 10.2.

selves from humanity's place in the world.[33] Thus, Christ-believers were not randomly chosen for Nero's scapegoating among many superstitious cults that had blown in from the East; rather, the non-Roman nature of their devotion, the counterimperial nature of their discourse, and the antisocial nature of their meetings probably brought them to the attention of authorities.

Fourth, we have tangible evidence from the late second century, in the *Acts of Paul,* that Paul was undoubtedly being read as a counterimperial agent. In this fictitious narrative, the emperor Nero finds out that his servant Patroclus has been raised from the dead by Paul. Nero warmly greets his servant but becomes enraged at Patroclus's new faith that has spread even to his advisers:

> But when he came in and saw Patroclus he cried out, "Patroclus, are you alive?" he answered, "I am alive, Caesar." But he said, "Who is he who made you alive?" And the boy, uplifted by the confidence of faith, said, "Christ Jesus, the king of the ages." The emperor asked in dismay, "Is he to be king of ages and destroy all kingdoms?" Patroclus said to him, "Yes, he destroys all kingdoms under heaven, and he alone shall remain in all eternity, and there will be no kingdom which escapes him." And he struck his face and cried out, "Patroclus, are you also fighting for that king?" He answered, "Yes, my lord and Caesar, for he has raised me from the dead." And Barsabas Justus the flat-footed and Urion the Cappadocian and Festus of Galatia, the chief men of Nero, said, "And we, too, fight for him, the king of the ages." After having tortured those men whom he used to love, he imprisoned them and ordered that the soldiers of the great king be sought, and he issued an edict that all Christians and soldiers of Christ that were found should be executed.[34]

This document, though admittedly late second century, is far more than dramatic fiction. It seems to indicate that faith in Christ and allegiance to Cae-

---

33. According to Simon R. F. Price ("Ritual and Power," in *Paul and Empire: Religion and Power in Roman Imperial Society*, ed. R. A. Horsley [Harrisburg, PA: TPI, 1997], 71), the imperial cult was "a major part of the web of power that formed the fabric of society"; and for Barclay (*Pauline Churches*, 355-56), "The worship of the divine Augustus (and Roma) indicated the recognition that the imperial order was the guarantor and mediator of the favor of the gods, and that Roman emperors, with their unique and superhuman capacities, were endowed with divine powers to benefit society. . . . One did not choose between worshipping 'the gods' and worshipping the imperial house; one worshipped the imperial house because of its central role within the cosmic order sponsored and sustained by the whole panoply of gods."

34. *Acts of Paul* 11.2, trans. M. R. James.

sar, when viewed as absolute authorities, were regarded as mutual exclusives and that Christians were thought to be potentially destabilizing to the religious and social fabric of the imperium.

There are, however, a few lingering problems with reading anti-imperial rhetoric into Paul's letters.[35] First, Paul's letters indicate that he was hardly consumed with political activism, and his focus pertained to establishing churches with harmonious relations between Jewish and Gentile believers. In fact, much of Paul's letters concern themselves with urging Christ-believers to live at peace with those outside their community (see Rom 12:14-21; 1 Cor 10:32-33). That does not necessarily make him apolitical, but he was hardly a political-change agent. That should be unsurprising because in the New Testament the ratio of θεός to Καῖσαρ is 30:1.[36]

Second, a further problem is that many of these so-called anti-imperial readings look suspiciously like a coded critique of American foreign and economic policy under GOP presidents. One is left wondering, then, if scholarly reconstructions of Paul's critique of Roman power are really a veiled critique of American policy by left-leaning academics. To be honest, there is no question about it, since Richard Horsley is quite explicit in this regard.[37] The word "empire" carries negative connotations of hegemonic and tyrannical power,[38]

---

35. See criticisms in Christopher Bryan, *Render to Caesar: Jesus, the Early Church, and the Roman Superpower* (New York: OUP, 2005), 9-10, 91-93; A. Standhartinger, "Die paulinische Theologie im Spannungsfeld römisch-imperialer Machtpolitk: Eine neue Perspecktive auf Paulus, kritisch geprüft anhand des Philippersbriefs," in *Religion, Politik und Gewalt*, ed. F. Schweitzer (Gütersloh: Gütersloher Verlag, 2006), 364-82; Denny Burk, "Is Paul's Gospel Counterimperial? Evaluating the Prospects of the 'Fresh Perspective' for Evangelical Theology," *JETS* 51 (2008): 309-37; Seyoon Kim, *Christ and Caesar: The Gospel and the Roman Empire in the Writings of Paul and Luke* (Grand Rapids, MI: Eerdmans, 2008); Joel White, "Anti-imperial Subtexts in Paul: An Attempt at Building a Firmer Foundation," *Bib* 90 (2009): 305-33; Colin Miller, "The Imperial Cult in the Pauline Cities of Asia Minor and Greece," *CBQ* 72 (2010): 314-31; John M. G. Barclay, *Pauline Churches and Diaspora Jews* (WUNT 1.275; Tübingen: Mohr Siebeck, 2011), chs. 18-19. Negative also are most of the essays in Scot McKnight and Joseph B. Modica, eds., *Jesus Is Lord, Caesar Is Not: Evaluating Empire in New Testament Studies* (Downers Grove, IL: IVP Academic, 2013).

36. Dale C. Allison, *Resurrecting Jesus* (London: T&T Clark, 2005), 23.

37. Richard Horsley, *Jesus and Empire: The Kingdom of God and the New World Order* (Minneapolis: Fortress, 2002), 1-14. Scot McKnight and Joseph B. Modica ("Introduction," in *Jesus Is Lord, Caesar Is Not: Evaluating Empire in New Testament Studies*, ed. S. McKnight and J. B. Modica [Downers Grove, IL: IVP Academic, 2013], 19) comment that "empire criticism sounds too much like one's personal progressive, left-leaning, neo-Marxist, or whatever, politics." See also Barclay, *Pauline Churches*, 367.

38. I'm reminded of the John le Carré character Connie Sachs, who remembers "the days

and by pitting Paul against "empire," one is thereby casting Paul as a type of Christianized Che Guevara. In other words, this anti-imperial Paul might be more about modern politics than ancient politics.[39]

Third, it also needs to be noted that the experience and expression of the Roman Empire varied around the Mediterranean according to local circumstances. The visibility of empire diverged in rural Judea, Greek cities in Asia Minor, Romanized cities in Greece, and in Rome itself. [40] On the Jewish side, perspectives toward Rome were not singularly critical but were determined by one's own citizenship, patronage, and social status. Philo and Josephus are obviously examples of two Jewish leaders embedded in the Roman political world who can advocate for Jews within that world. Let us not forget either that it was the Judeans who took the initiative to make an alliance with Rome, it was the Romans who assisted Herod the Great to defeat the Parthian-sponsored leadership of Antigonus, and Rome proposed to avenge Herod Antipas against Aretas IV before the death of Tiberius prevented it.[41] Across the Jewish Diaspora one finds synagogue inscriptions praising local Roman leaders as benefactor of their assemblies.[42] Similarly, Christ-believing groups, who were socially stratified and geographically diverse, would have often had ambivalent rather than necessarily negative relations with Roman authorities. Most Christ-believers rarely had direct contact with Roman officials; instead, as Acts shows, when they found themselves in trouble, it was ordinarily with resident synagogues and local civic leaders, not with imperial authorities.[43] This is buttressed by the absence of any official list of accredited religions that civil officials could enforce, the so-called *religio licita*. Rather, decisions about

---

before 'Empire' became a dirty word." After the Second World War, Britain renamed the "British Empire" the "British Commonwealth," precisely because it wanted to avoid the connotations of the old colonialism. In addition, as I write this, my son is watching *Star Wars: The Empire Strikes Back*, which has probably shaped conceptions of "empire" more than any other media in the last generation.

39. See N. T. Wright, "A Fresh Perspective on Paul?," *BJRL* 83 (2001): 28, who makes a similar criticism.

40. See Simon R. F. Price, "Response," in *Paul and the Roman Imperial Order*, ed. R. A. Horsley (Harrisburg, PA: TPI, 2004), 175-83.

41. See 1 Macc 8:1-29; 12:1-4; 14:24, 40; 15:16-24 (Maccabean alliance with Rome); Josephus, *Ant.* 14.384–15.10; *War* 1.282-303 (Roman support for Herod against the Parthians); Josephus, *Ant.* 18.111-26 (Antipas vs. Aretas).

42. The Aphrodisias inscriptions are a case in point.

43. Matthew V. Novenson, "What the Apostles Did Not See," in *Reactions to Empire: Sacred Texts in Their Socio-political Contexts,* ed. J. A. Dunne and D. Batovici (WUNT 2.372; Tübingen: Mohr Siebeck, 2014), 70.

migrating cults were based on local circumstances, including their antiquity, capacity to provoke social discord, and set criteria for adding new gods to a local pantheon.[44] In other instances, though probably limited instances, the Christ-believers in prominent Roman households (Rom 16:10-11), even in Caesar's household (Phil 4:22), who held public offices like "director of public works" (Rom 16:23) may not have regarded all of the imperial system as deliberately oppressing them all of the time. The Roman Empire fostered a period of relative justice, peace, and prosperity, which facilitated the spread of the gospel and the migration of Christ-believers across territories. Given the relative stability of the empire, it is no wonder that Christ-believers in the apostolic and postapostolic period could offers prayers for the emperor and urge submission to political authorities as a common good.[45] Tertullian can even say, "I might say Caesar is more ours than yours, for our God has appointed him"[46] and "A Christian is enemy to none, least of all to the Emperor of Rome, whom he knows to be appointed by his God, and so cannot but love and honour; and whose well-being moreover, he must needs desire, with that of the empire over which he reigns so long as the world shall stand—for so long as that shall Rome continue."[47] It is possible to imagine Paul, then, not simply living in resistance to the imperium but trying to shrewdly navigate his way through it and making use of its benefits where possible, like his "appeal to Caesar" to escape imprisonment (Acts 25:11). Bruno Blumenfeld is not unlike many who infer that, since Paul relied on the Roman Empire for his missionary success, therefore "Paul must not upset—and, more important, does not wish to upset—the Roman political establishment."[48] Viewed this way, Price is right to complain against the claim that "inflates the importance of the imperial cult and posits a stark choice between Christ and the Caesars."[49]

Fourth, much of Paul's language of "gospel" and "salvation" and Jesus' lordship seems to be inherited from Septuagintal vocabulary and not imported directly from Roman socioreligious language; it therefore cannot be regarded as derivation for the purpose of refutation.[50]

44. See Jörg Rüpke, Religion of the Romans, trans. R. Gordon (Cambridge: Polity, 2007), 35.
45. 1 Tim 2:1-2; Titus 3:1; 1 Pet 2:13-17; 1 Clem. 61.1; Mart. Pol. 10.2; Tertullian, Apol. 30-32.
46. Tertullian, Apol. 33.1.
47. Tertullian, Ad Scap. 2.
48. Bruno Blomenfeld, The Political Paul: Justice, Democracy, and Kingship in a Hellenistic Framework (JSNTSup 210; London: T&T Clark, 2003), 289.
49. Price, Rituals and Power, 15.
50. Burk, "Gospel," 317; White, "Subtexts," 309-10. Although, as Peter Oakes argues (Philippians: From People to Letter [SNTSMS 110; Cambridge: CUP, 2001], 172), a shared Septuagintal

Fifth, however one spins the details, Rom 13:1-7 gives a clear affirmation of Paul's belief in the submission of Christ-believers to state authorities, not a call for revolution. What Paul says here looks more like political quietism, an affirmation of the status quo, than a script for sociopolitical resistance. Granted, one might wonder whether Paul would have written the same exhortations if he knew about Nero's impending pogrom against Christ-believers, but the fact of the matter is that the one explicit thing said about the state in Romans affirms Christian submission to ruling authorities.[51]

The evidence offered so far seems finely balanced. It is hoped that the stalemate can be broken through a close reading of Paul's letter to the Romans.

Paul, Romans, and Empire in Recent Scholarship

The place to begin is with the state of scholarship on Paul, Romans, and empire. Paul's engagement with Roman imperial ideology has been mapped onto Romans in several ways.

Dieter Georgi paved the way for anti-imperial readings of Paul by highlighting the collision of Paul's eschatology with the propaganda of the Julio-Claudian dynasty. He emphasized several points of contrast, including Christ's resurrection over and against the apotheosis of the emperors (Rom 1:3-4), the solidarity of Christ as *princeps* with his enemies (Rom 5:6-10), and the preeminence of Christ as benefactor over the age of Augustus and Nero (Rom 5:6-21). Paul, in Romans, portrays God as sovereignly entering into solidarity with subjugated masses of the empire in his appointed *princeps,* Jesus Christ. Georgi concludes that Paul was advocating an "alternative social utopia" in a way that represented a veiled critique of the empire and emperor.[52]

Richard A. Horsley has perhaps done more than anyone else in the last

---

and imperial context and connotation for the language is not impossible; it does not have to be an either/or. Heilig (*Hidden Criticism?,* 145) also adds: "Many critics jump too easily from establishing a septuagintal background to rejecting a Roman foreground. We always have to keep in mind what the explanandum really is: Is it the *source* of the wording or the *intention* lying behind its use?" (italics original).

51. Worth consulting here is S. Krauter, *Studien zu Röm 13,1-7: Paulus und der politische Diskurs der neronischen Zeit* (Tübingen: Mohr Siebeck, 2009), and J. Botha, *Subject to Whose Authority? Multiple Readings of Romans 13* (Atlanta: Scholars, 1994).

52. Georgi, *Theocracy in Paul's Praxis and Theology.*

decade to publicize political readings of Paul.[53] His concern has been to re-capture the biblical legitimacy of resistance and to demonstrate how Jesus and Paul both represent models of defiance against imperial power. In Romans, Horsley detects Paul's attempt to convince the Roman Christians that at the heart of their apocalyptic battle was their struggle against patronage, power, and privilege as it was symbolically manifested in the rites of idolatry prac-ticed in Rome. Horsley's Paul is asking the Romans to financially support an underground movement with subversive anti-imperial beliefs.[54]

John Dominic Crossan and Jonathan L. Reed see Paul in Romans advocat-ing one world under the aegis of divine justice. Paul propounds the "righteous-ness of God," understood as a global distributive justice where God's earthly administration matches God's heavenly character. The gospel of Paul, which advocates equality in Christ and covenantal justice, stands at loggerheads with the violent imperialism of the gospel of Rome.[55]

N. T. Wright describes how the Roman emperors, starting with Augustus, had touted themselves as bringing justice and peace to lands caught in dis-array. Roman military power established a new world order in which Caesar was revered as *Kyrios*, or "Lord."[56] Wright sees a sharp contrast between the cult of the goddess *Iustitia* ("Justice") created by Augustus and the dominating theme of Romans as the revelation of God's δικαιοσύνη ("righteousness" or "justice"). In Romans, Paul identifies "King Jesus" with the revelation of God's redemptive *iustitia* in a way that laid down a direct challenge to Roman claims that its empire was the divine harbinger of *iustitia* through its punitive military

53. Richard A. Horsley and Neil Asher Silberman, *The Message and the Kingdom: How Jesus and Paul Ignited a Revolution and Transformed the Ancient World* (New York: Penguin Putnam, 1997); Richard A. Horsley, ed., *Paul and Empire: Religion and Power in Roman Imperial Society* (Harrisburg, PA: TPI, 1997); Horsley, ed., *Paul and Politics: Ekklesia, Imperium, Interpretation* (FS Krister Stendahl; Harrisburg, PA: TPI, 2000); Horsley, *Paul and the Roman Imperial Order* (Harrisburg, PA: TPI, 2004); Horsley, ed., *In the Shadow of Empire: Reclaiming the Bible as a History of Faithful Resistance* (Louisville: Westminster John Knox, 2008).

54. Horsley and Silberman, *Message and the Kingdom*, 189-90.

55. Crossan and Reed, *In Search of Paul*, 290, 379-403.

56. N. T. Wright, "Paul's Gospel and Caesar's Empire," in *Paul and Politics: Ekklesia, Israel, Imperium, Interpretation: Essays in Honor of Krister Stendahl*, ed. R. A. Horsley (Har-risburg, PA: TPI, 2000), 160-83; idem, "A Fresh Perspective on Paul?," *BJRL* 83 (2001): 21-39; idem, "Paul and Caesar: A New Reading of Romans," in *A Royal Priesthood: The Use of the Bible Ethically and Politically*, ed. C. Bartholomew, J. Chaplin, R. Song, and A. Walters (Carlisle, UK: Paternoster, 2002), 173-93; idem, "Romans," in *NIB*, ed. L. E. Keck (12 vols.; Nashville: Abingdon, 2002), 10:404-5; idem, *Paul*, 59-79; idem, *Paul and the Faithfulness of God*, 1271-1319.

campaigns. In Wright's reading of Paul, Rome is one of the malevolent powers that needs to be dealt with. Wright suggests that Paul was not "a traveling evangelist offering people a new religious experience" but "an ambassador for a king-in-waiting, establishing cells of people loyal to this new king, and ordering their lives according to his story, his symbols, and his praxis, and their minds according to his truth. This could only be construed as deeply counterimperial, as subversive to the whole edifice of the Roman Empire; and there is in fact plenty of evidence that Paul intended it to be so construed, and that when he ended up in prison as a result of his work he took it as a sign that he had been doing his job properly."[57]

Ekkehard W. Steggemann maintains that Paul's central claim in Romans is that Jesus Christ is the "Son of God" and "Lord." Such a claim orchestrates a challenge between two competing eschatologies: that between Rome and Israel's God. While Paul's gospel is *euangelion* for believers, it is *dysangelion* for Rome because Paul looks forward to the removal of all authorities at the return of Christ. In addition, Jesus is designated by God as the universal ruler, in striking counterpoint to the similar claims made for Roman emperors. The boundary marker of imperial *fides*, namely, the trustworthiness of the emperor, which is reciprocated with loyalty to him, is replaced by Paul with the faithfulness of God that is reciprocated with human faithfulness to Jesus Christ. Furthermore, Christ rather than Caesar ascends to rule a kingdom in heaven.[58]

Ian Rock situates Romans in the aftermath of the Claudius edict in 49 CE expelling the Jews from Rome. This was at a time when Claudius was presenting himself as the guardian of Rome's ancient rituals and continued propagating the Aeneidian mythology of Rome as a divinely created military power. In Romans, Paul offers a subcultural response to the Aeneidian mythology by reference to the kingship of David, the universal covenant with Abraham, the cosmic character of the law of Moses, the history of Israel as God's chosen people, and the articulation of Jesus as Messiah and Lord. Paul inscribes this letter, directly at points, with the Song of Moses (Deut 32), where nations like Rome are to be objects of God's vengeance. Consequently, Paul's Roman letter was critiquing Gentile Christians who attempted to shame and exclude the returning Jewish Christians from their exile after

---

57. Wright, "Paul's Gospel and Caesar's Empire," 161-62.

58. Ekkehard Stegemann, "Coexistence and Transformation: Reading the Politics of Identity in Romans in an Imperial Context," in *Reading Paul in Context: Explorations in Identity Formation*, ed. K. Ehrensperger and B. J. Tucker (FS W. S. Campbell; LNTS 428, London: T&T Clark, 2010), 2-23.

Claudius died (54 CE). For Paul, an affirmation of Jesus Christ requires an affirmation of the election of Israel and the primacy of the Jewish people in God's purposes.[59]

Stanley E. Porter describes the significance of the various public inscriptions around the Roman Empire that venerated the emperors and their achievements as forming the background to Paul's gospel ministry. He notes the near-ubiquitous number of inscriptions erected by a certain Paulus Fabius Maximus, who heralded an imperial gospel through these inscriptions about the good news of Caesar's advent. In contrast, Porter sees Paul's styling himself as the new erector of a new inscription to the true Lord, Jesus Christ. Comparing Romans with the calendrical inscriptions from Priene, Apamea, Kobotos, Maiomia, and Eumeneia, Porter points to a sharp distinction between the Lord Jesus and Caesar in the areas of fulfilled order, natural birth, good fortune, divine benefit, worship, and obedience. Porter comments: "Thus, from start to nearly finish, the book of Romans is Paul's attempt to indicate in the face of Roman imperialism the nature of the true Lord, Jesus Christ, and what the good news of his lordship might indicate for those who wish to follow him in the obedience of faith."[60]

One of the most concerted advocates of a political reading of Romans has come from Neil Elliott.[61] Elliott argues that Romans is "Paul's attempt to counteract the effects of imperial ideology within the Roman congregation," partly because of anti-Jewish tendencies among the Roman cultural elites that have been imbibed into the Roman congregations.[62] The heart of Paul's mission is to create a new society, one that diametrically opposed the Roman

---

59. Ian E. Rock, "Another Reason for Romans—a Pastoral Response to Augustan Imperial Theology: Paul's Use of the Song of Moses in Romans 9–11 and 14–15," in *Reading Paul in Context: Explorations in Identity Formation*, ed. K. Ehrensperger and B. J. Tucker (FS W. S. Campbell; LNTS 428; London: T&T Clark, 2010), 74-89.

60. Stanley E. Porter, "Paul Confronts Caesar with the Good News," in *Empire in the New Testament*, ed. S. E. Porter and C. L. Westfall (Eugene, OR: Cascade, 2011), 189.

61. Neil Elliott, *Liberating Paul: The Justice of God and the Politics of the Apostle* (2nd ed.; Minneapolis: Fortress, 2006); idem, "The Letter to the Romans," in *A Postcolonial Commentary on the New Testament Writings*, ed. F. F. Segovia and R. S. Sugirtharajah (New York: T&T Clark, 2007), 194-219; idem, *The Arrogance of Nations: Reading Romans in the Shadow of Empire* (Minneapolis: Fortress, 2008); idem, "'Blasphemed among the Nations': Pursuing an Anti-imperial 'Intertextuality' in Romans," in *As It Is Written: Studying Paul's Use of Scripture*, ed. S. E. Porter and C. D. Stanley (SBLSS 50; Leiden: Brill, 2008), 213-33; idem, "Paul's Political Christology: Samples from Romans," in *Reading Paul in Context: Explorations in Identity Formation*, ed. K. Ehrensperger and J. B. Tucker (FS W. S. Campbell; LNTS 428; London: T&T Clark, 2010), 39-51.

62. Elliott, *Arrogance of Nations*, 158.

vision for its colonies.[63] He even calls Romans an "ideological intifada" against imperial thought.[64]

James Harrison believes that Paul's gospel constitutes an ideological collision with the Julio-Claudian conception of rule. In relation to Paul's letter to the Romans, he thinks Paul engages the Roman cyclic view of time, the ideology of the *forum Augustum*, the republican quest for glory, the portrayal of the ruler as the divinely elected bestower of grace and victory, the celebration of divine providence in the ruler's reign, and the ruler as the embodiment of *virtus*.[65] Harrison contends that "Paul's counterimperial benefaction communities, established through the soteriological obedience of a dishonoured and vindicated benefactor, embraced a radically different narrative of power and grace that would empower and transform the weak and marginalized of all nations. Paul depicts Christ as simultaneously the fulfillment of universal world history and Jewish covenantal history in a rhetorical strategy designed to dismantle the ideology of rule articulated through the Roman 'founder' narratives."[66]

Robert Jewett argues in his magisterial commentary that Romans is an "anti-imperialist letter" that represents "the antithesis of official propaganda about Rome's superior piety, justice, and honor." Paul presents himself in this letter as the "king's official," who works for the gospel of his king, and this gospel has a program for "global pacifificicaton and unification."[67]

David Wallace asserts that Paul's gospel explicated in Romans counteracts significant themes from Virgil's *Aeneid*, a prophetic-poetic work heavily embedded with religious themes, complete with a political eschatology and a "messianic" Augustus. Wallace sees Paul as following a similar pattern to the *Aeneid,* so that Romans can be read as Paul countervailing many of the socioreligious themes in Virgil's *Aeneid*.[68]

In contrast, classics scholar and Augustus guru Karl Galinski offers several salient qualifications and criticism of anti-imperial readings of Paul by New Testament scholars.[69] He celebrates the "Columbus-like discovery of the

63. Elliott, "Apostle Paul and Empire," 108-9.

64. Elliott, *Liberating Paul*, 215.

65. James R. Harrison, *Paul and the Imperial Authorities at Thessalonica and Rome* (WUNT 273; Tübingen: Mohr Siebeck, 2011).

66. Harrison, *Paul and the Imperial Authorities*, 335.

67. Robert Jewett, *Romans* (Hermeneia; Minneapolis: Fortress, 2007), 2, 49, 100-101.

68. David R. Wallace, *The Gospel of God: Romans as Paul's Aeneid* (Eugene, OR: Pickwick, 2008).

69. Karl Galinsky, "The Cult of the Roman Emperor: Uniter or Divider?," in *Rome and Re-*

historical context of the New Testament by biblical scholars" when it comes to the relevance of the imperial cults.[70] However, two of his major points are as follows: (1) the need for greater recognition of the cult of the emperor as intertwined with that of other gods. Some imperial temples such as those in Aphrodisias and Ephesus were freestanding and dominated their religious environments, while others were less conspicuous and often subordinated to existing cults. In which case, he cautions against "looking at the imperial cult as if it were the overwhelming, let alone only culture or religious phenomenon in town whose presence early Christianity had to negotiate."[71] (2) When it comes to the parallel language between Paul and the Roman Empire, Galinski notes the similarities between imperial claims with texts like 1 Thess 5:3 ("peace and security") and Phil 2:6 ("equal with God"). Yet he wonders whether what we have here is not rejection of Roman concepts but more akin to a form of mimicry, with "their more perfect fashioning in the realm of God," so that the imperium is "surpassed, in a far more perfect way, by God and the kingdom of heaven."[72] In the end, Galinski warns that to identify Paul as "anti-imperial" may be "convenient," but it is "too heavy-handed and imprecise."[73]

The scholarly melee between John Barclay and N. T. Wright indicates the divide in the debate.[74] According to Barclay, the imperial cult was merely one manifestation of the idolatry and demonic forces in the world, and Paul himself paid scant attention to it. In regard to the similar vocabulary of devotion,

---

ligion: A Cross-Disciplinary Dialogue on the Imperial Cult, ed. J. Brodd and J. L. Reed (Atlanta: SBL, 2011), 1-21; idem, "In the Shadow (or Not) of the Imperial Cult: A Cooperative Agenda," in *Rome and Religion: A Cross-Disciplinary Dialogue on the Imperial Cult*, ed. J. Brodd and J. L. Reed (Atlanta: SBL, 2011), 215-25.

70. Galinsky, "The Cult of the Roman Emperor," 1.

71. Galinsky, "The Cult of the Roman Emperor," 6.

72. Galinsky, "The Cult of the Roman Emperor," 13; idem, "In the Shadow of the Imperial Cult," 222. See also James Constantine Hanges ("To Complicate Encounters: A Response to Karl Galinksy's 'The Cult of the Roman Emperor: Uniter or Divider?,'" in *Rome and Religion: A Cross-Disciplinary Dialogue on the Imperial Cult*, ed. J. Brodd and J. L. Reed [Atlanta: SBL, 2011], 35), who notes that juxtaposition is not necessarily tantamount to opposition. But Heilig (*Hidden Criticism?*, 133-34, 136) rightly observes that "a kingdom surpassing the Roman Empire would have been regarded as nothing less than anti-imperial from a *Roman* perspective" (italics original), and when a larger context is evoked, the potential conflict can be "much *bigger* than the one of bare juxtaposition" (italics original).

73. Galinsky, "In the Shadow of the Imperial Cult," 222.

74. Barclay, *Pauline Churches*, 345-87; Wright, *Paul and the Faithfulness of God*, 1271-1330. According to Heilig (*Hidden Criticism?*, 114), the point of contention between Barclay and Wright is, "What is the real frontline in God's *heilsgeschichtlichem* drama?"

Barclay thinks such overlaps need not imply a competitive relationship unless rhetorical clues are suitably provided. In conclusion, Barclay reasons that

> Paul's gospel is subversive of Roman imperial claims precisely by not opposing them within their own terms, but by reducing Rome's agency and historical significance to just one more entity in a much greater drama. To oppose the Roman empire as such would be take its claims all too seriously; to upstage or outdo Rome would be to accept its terms of reference, even in surpassing them. . . . Paul, more radically, reframes reality, including political reality, mapping the world in ways that reduced the claims of the imperial cult and of the Roman empire to comparative insignificance.[75]

Wright responds to Barclay that Paul was living out a Jewish paradox, one heightened by his eschatology, whereby believers lived in submission to authorities and practiced civic virtues, even while waiting for the current round of rulers to be held to account. Therefore, "For someone such as Paul steeped in the Jewish apocalyptic tradition, as Paul was, it would have been impossible to imagine that Rome was 'insignificant.'"[76] The emperor, in giving himself "divine" status, might be just another one of the powers that are relativized in light of the reign of God, but even more, the imperium is also outflanked, upstaged, and delegitimized by Paul's gospel taking root. Wright agrees that Paul saw Rome as ultimately just one of the "powers," but he adds that "Paul nevertheless saw these powers coming together and doing their worst precisely in and through Rome itself."[77]

Finding a Counterimperial Apostle

Before beginning, a few comments are in order about the purpose of Romans and the precise way in which counterimperial motifs can be detected. First, Paul wrote Romans to a cluster of house churches in the capital of the Roman Empire, but it is not about empire. I take Paul's letter to the Romans chiefly as a letter-essay concerned with gaining support for the Pauline mission to Spain, healing fractious divisions in the Roman house churches, and seeking

75. Barclay, *Pauline Churches*, 386.
76. Wright, *Paul and the Faithfulness of God*, 1281.
77. Wright, *Paul and the Faithfulness of God*, 1311.

to win over the Romans to his version of the gospel as he prepares to travel to Jerusalem.[78] The Roman Empire, at most, is on the margins of Paul's concern in the letter, even if Paul's thought mimics facets of imperial ideology or rehearses imperial claims, and even if Paul has a counterimperial disposition that is apparent at some points. The imperial cults are but one, albeit a highly prominent, manifestation of the idolatry that Paul critiques.[79]

Second, on the methodology for finding traces of counterimperial motifs in Romans, something needs to be said about parallelomania, potential echoes, and hidden transcripts. To begin with, I'm all too aware that a study that compares Pauline honorific language for Christ with acclamations about the emperor from papyri and inscriptions lends itself to a criticism of "parallelomania."[80] Endlessly listing parallel texts or similar words does not amount to Paul's intention or equate to how the first readers of Romans necessarily understood the letter. That qualification should not lead us to deny, however, the value of exploring wider cultural influences, textual and nontextual, and showing how they highlight features of Paul's discourse like polemics in relation to the imperium.[81] We might find that shared terminology does not necessitate a polemical ideology; however, it is also true that mimicry is an effective form of mockery, and replication can envisage replacement.

---

78. See Michael F. Bird, "Letter to the Romans," in *All Things to All Cultures: Paul among Jews, Greeks, and Romans*, ed. M. Harding and A. Knobbs (Grand Rapids, MI: Eerdmans, 2012), 190-92.

79. Harrison, *Paul and the Imperial Authorities*, 2. See also Fantin's sober remarks (*Lord of the Entire World*, 40, 43): "Where the Paul and Politics movement suggests that Paul's message was *primarily* anti-imperial, I maintain that it is only a *part* of the message, and in many (or even most) cases it is not his primary concern. . . . I reject the notion that Paul's message was *primarily* anti-imperial. The anti-imperial message was part of the package but was not the only or even necessarily the most important aspect of Paul's thought" (italics original).

80. See Samuel Sandmel, "Parallelomania," *JBL* 81 (1962): 1-13.

81. See similar critiques by Burk, "Is Paul's Gospel Counter-Imperial?," 315-22; Kim, *Christ and Caesar*, 28-30; Bryan, *Render to Caesar*, 90-91. Several anti-imperial proponents are indeed aware of the charge of parallelomania (e.g., N. T. Wright, "Paul's Gospel and Caesar's Empire," 162), but note the nuanced comments of Harrison (*Paul and the Imperial Authorities*, 2), who thinks that "a nuanced understanding of the Julio-Claudian world can contribute riches to exegetical method," especially when it comes to mining "local evidence." He also points out that "precisely because of Paul's familiarity with the LXX and the wider currents of Second Temple Judaism, Paul must have given some thought to how his Jewish soteriological and messianic language intersected with similar motifs in the imperial cult, if only to distinguish his eschatological understanding of Christ's rule from the propaganda of the Julio-Claudian dynasty" (*Paul and the Imperial Authorities*, 25).

In addition, I remain unsure whether we should try to detect "echoes" of imperial texts in Paul's letters. I hesitate because the imperium was not a text but a culture, with its own literature to be sure, but it also contained nonverbal communication in the form of temples, statues, and images that spoke louder than any text. In any case, how does one detect echoes of a festival honoring the emperor, a culture of fear within an illegal association, a triumphal procession, or feigned fealty to political overlords?[82] In terms of understanding how Paul and his readers experienced and negotiated the imperium, we have to look beyond intertextuality, probing more broadly the sociopolitical *Wirklichkeit* of the entire empire as the context to Paul's letters.[83] In other words, we are pursuing a background plausibility against which Paul's letter becomes increasingly coherent; intertextual echoes are merely one facet of that background.

I think the notion of "hidden transcripts"[84] that encode forms of protest does have some merit in limited instances in Paul's letters (e.g., Rom 13:1-7).[85] These hidden transcripts are veiled critiques that are deliberately ambiguous and undermine the ruling elite.[86] The problem I have, however, is that sometimes these hidden transcripts are so effectively hidden in the literary code that one starts to wonder whether they are even there in the first place.[87] Although

82. See further Heilig, *Hidden Criticism?*, 104-8 (and 159) on "other expressions of imperial ideology," against Miller, "Cult," 317, who needlessly restricts the imperial cult to sacrificial cults.

83. The notion of "echoes" is borrowed from Richard Hays's work on the use of the OT in the NT (*Echoes of Scripture in the Letters of Paul* [New Haven: Yale University Press, 1989]) and adopted by Wright, *Paul*, 61-62; Elliott, *Arrogance of Nations*, 22. Noteworthy is Christoph Heilig ("Methodological Considerations for the Search of Counter-Imperial 'Echoes' in Pauline Literature," in *Reactions to Empire: Sacred Texts in Their Socio-political Contexts*, ed. J. A. Dunne and D. Batovici [WUNT 2.372; Tübingen: Mohr Siebeck, 2014], 73-92; idem, *Hidden Criticism?*, 35-49), who uses Bayes's theorem to refine the methodology of echoes. Finally, I hasten to add that Hays's methodology is predicated on the notion of an "ideal reader" who has maximal access and maximal ability to detect these intertextual echoes. Such a reader might remain heuristically valuable for plotting intertextual echoes, but he or she is somewhat artificial and should not be correlated with a first or real reader.

84. James C. Scott, *Domination and the Arts of Resistance: Hidden Transcripts* (New Haven: Yale University Press, 1990); Richard A. Horsley, ed., *Hidden Transcripts and the Arts of Resistance: Applying the Work of James C. Scott to Jesus and Paul* (Atlanta: SBL, 2004). See esp. the summary in Carter, *Roman Empire*, 12-13.

85. See Harrison, *Paul and the Imperial Authorities*, 32; Wright, *Paul and the Faithfulness of God*, 1315.

86. Applied by Elliott, *Arrogance of Nations*, 27-40; Wright, *Paul*, 60.

87. See similarly Kim, *Christ and Caesar*, 32-33, 68; Harrison, *Paul and the Imperial Authorities*, 30-33.

some Jewish and Christian authors could use code words to refer to Rome like "Babylon" (1 Pet 5:13; Rev 14:8; 16:19; 17:5; 18:2, 10, 21), "kittim" (1QM), and "eagle" (4 Ezra 11–12), we find no such code words used in Paul's letters.[88] Let us not forget either that some Jewish authors, like Philo and Josephus, did not feel the need to hide their protest and revulsion at the imposition of the imperial cult in Jerusalem.[89] Indeed, it would seem that Paul also did not hide his protest against idolatry and other "lords" in his correspondences with his churches (1 Cor 2:6-10; 8:5-8; 1 Thess 1:9; Rom 1:23). Paul can be so explicit in his criticism because he is writing to "insiders" for private consumption, providing what James Scott calls "offstage" comments about the powers to fellow believers, so he need not hide his protest.[90]

By way of an alternative to the pursuit of parallel texts, the search for echoes, and the detection of hidden transcripts, we are on firmer ground if we examine the claims exhibited in various artifacts—such as literature, papyrus, statues, coins, and inscriptions—which Paul's letter might call to the mind of readers familiar with the imperial context of Rome and other cities of the empire. I favor, then, the notion of a range of reasonable resonances, whereby one sets forth a text, coin, or inscription as indicative of a widespread cache of ideas and influences with which readers could be expected to have a reasonable prospect of familiarity.[91] I don't think we can assume that this church for sure knew that text, used this coin, or saw those inscriptions. We shall have to be content with relating texts and artifacts to a wider cultural span that undoubtedly shaped the world of the recipients of Paul's letter. At the end of the day, reading is a matter of context. If one's context is the first-century Roman Empire, then, from the Palatine Hill in Rome to the temple to

88. Barclay, *Pauline Churches*, 380.

89. See Josephus, *Ant.* 18.256-309; *Ag. Ap.* 2.75; Philo, *Legat.* 118, 198, 218, 347-48. Among Roman "hidden" critiques of Roman power, see Tacitus's speech attributed to Calgacus in *Agricola* 30.3–31.2. See further Barclay, *Pauline Churches*, 381.

90. Barclay, *Pauline Churches*, 381-83. In response, Heilig (*Hidden Criticism?*, 64) believes that Paul encouraged circulation of his letters, so that a private form of correspondence was affected by concerns of public scrutiny and rules of public discourse, though I suspect that this claim is far from demonstrable.

91. Note Galinsky ("The Cult of the Roman Emperor," 8), who says: "I would put the impact of the [imperial] cult most in terms of *resonance*—not hard power, but soft power" (italics original). Heilig (*Hidden Criticism?*, 134, 157) provides a good example: "If the apostle [Paul] was aware of the inevitable resonances the term 'lord' would evoke, one could construe the underlying semantic structure of such a statement as follows: 'You know these claims of Caesar to be 'Lord'—*that is what Jesus is!*" and "we are dealing with a *resonance* of Roman concepts that are in conflict with Christian ideas" (italics original).

Augustus in Petra, among Roman literature and Roman *lares*, upon images and inscriptions, imperial claims were made through this media and constantly imposed itself on the populace. It is not hard to imagine such images and texts influencing Paul's composition of the letter and resonating with real readers who received the letter. I'm aware that such broad contextual evidence can be overread, but neither should it be underestimated.[92] Unless we think Paul and other Christ-believers walked around the Mediterranean blindfolded, then we have reason to suspect that imperial motifs are a plausible background to his letters.[93]

In what follows, I briefly exposit the parts of Romans that, when read against the backdrop of Roman imperial culture, illustrate something of Paul's stance toward the Roman Empire.

Paulus versus Roma:
Paul and Imperial Rome in the Letter to the Romans

Yahweh versus the "Gods" as Background to Romans

We should note that Israel's sacred traditions always included an explicit contest between Yahweh and the pagan gods. The people of Israel and Israel's king relied on Israel's God to deliver them from the peril of the pagan kings, who looked to their own gods for victory. The exodus is the story of God rescuing the Israelites from Pharaoh and from Egypt's gods (Exod 7–12). The Shema—the bedrock confession of Israel's faith—contained a forthright denunciation of idolatry and called for steadfast devotion in the one true God of Israel (Deut 6:4-6). In the confrontation story about Elijah the prophet versus the Baal prophets on Mount Carmel, Yahweh proves overwhelmingly superior (1 Kgs 18). In Isaiah a prophecy concerning the destruction of the nations with their pantheon occurs along with a mocking treatment of idol worship (e.g., Isa 13–24; 44:9-20). In addition, in Jewish apocalyptic literature there is a strong focus on God's eschatological act, his kingdom, eclipsing the Babylonian, Persian, Greek, and Roman kingdoms (e.g., Dan 2; 4; 7). Some Jewish authors could even identify Rome as the ultimate enemy of God's people (e.g.,

92. If Paul wrote his letters to people who were part of "Caesar's household" (Phil 4:22) and in prominent Roman households (Rom 16:10-11), then their familiarity with Roman imperial rhetoric seems beyond question.

93. See Deissmann, *LAE*, 340; Heilig, "Counter-Imperial 'Echoes' in Pauline Literature," 91; idem, *Hidden Criticism?*, 28-33, 158-59.

1QM; 1QpHab 2.10-13; 6.1-8; 4 Ezra 11.1-14). More specifically, the memory of Pompey's seizure of Jerusalem did not fade,[94] and Caligula's attempt to have a statue of himself placed in the temple highlighted the intrusive and predatory nature of imperial religion.[95] Josephus noted how constant banditry in Judea was caused in part by anti-Roman sentiment.[96] The Israelite religion, when faced with invading empires with ruler cults and idol-worship, was always anti-imperial.[97] We should not be surprised, then, if a Christ-believing Jewish author like Paul—invested with a strong theocentric, apocalyptic, and messianic theology—shared a similar worldview that believed in the eventual downfall of pagan power and the victory of the God of Israel through his Messiah.[98]

Romans 1:1-4

Jewish sociologist of religion Jacob Taubes saw in Rom 1:3-4 a subversive and anti-Caesar gambit by Paul in his opening words. Taubes declares, "I want to stress that this is a political declaration of war, when a letter introducing using these words, and not others, is sent to the congregation in Rome to be read aloud. One doesn't know into whose hands it will fall, and the censors weren't idiots. One could, after all, have introduced it pietistically quietistically, neutrally, or however else; but there is none of that here. That is why my thesis is that in this sense the Epistle to the Romans is a political theology, a *political*

---

94. See Pss. Sol. 2.1-2; 8.19-21; 17.11-14.

95. Josephus, *Ant.* 18.261-309; 19.300-312; Philo, *Legat.*, esp. 188, 208, 238, 265, 292.

96. Josephus, *War* 2.264-65; *Ant.* 17.285.

97. See Norman K. Gottwald, "Early Israel as an Anti-imperial Community," in *Paul and Empire: Religion and Power in Roman Imperial Society*, ed. R. A. Horsley (Harrisburg, PA: TPI, 1997), 9-24; Bryan, *Render to Caesar*, 11-37; White, "Anti-imperial Subtexts in Paul," 316-26; Mark J. Boda, "Walking in the Light of Yahweh: Zion and the Empire," in *Empire in the New Testament*, ed. S. E. Porter and C. L. Westfall (Eugene, OR: Cascade, 2011), 54-89; Anthea E. Portier-Young, *Apocalypse against Empire: Theologies of Resistance in Early Judaism* (Grand Rapids, MI: Eerdmans, 2011); Andrew T. Abernethy et al., eds., *Isaiah and Imperial Context: The Book of Isaiah in the Times of Empire* (Eugene, OR: Pickwick, 2013); Amanda M. Davis Bledsoe, "Attitudes towards Seleucid Imperial Hegemony in the Book of Daniel," in *Reactions to Empire: Sacred Texts in Their Socio-Political Contexts*, ed. J. A. Dunne and D. Batovici (WUNT 2.372; Tübingen: Mohr Siebeck, 2014), 23-40.

98. See White, "Subtexts," 325-33; Heilig, *Hidden Criticism?*, 114-19, 145; and Wright (*Paul and the Faithfulness of God*, 1281): "Either the history of Rome provides the true story, with Christian faith content to shelter, as a 'permitted religion,' under its banner. Or the history of Israel, climaxing in the crucified and risen Messiah, must be seen as the true story, with that of Rome, however much under the overarching divine providence, as at best a distorted parody of the truth."

declaration of war on the Caesar."[99] I agree, and the failure to see this tension is attributable to failing to see Christ's lordship as political and the religious dimension of the imperial cults.[100] So I think Taubes is correct; Rom 1:3-4 has political teeth, as long as the Messiah is envisaged as the ruler of the world, benefactor of the nations, and a high priest for his people, over and against the currently recognized ruler of the world, the offer of his patronage, and his role as the highest priest of the empire.

Paul opens his letter to the Romans by weaving together a standard epistolary greeting with some tradition material about the "gospel of God" and "Messiah Jesus." The gospel of God is the good news from God and also about God. The background of this "gospel" lies, on the one hand, in the Jewish world, with the promise of the coming reign of Yahweh to bring an end to Israel's exile (Isa 52:7; 61:1; Pss. Sol. 11.1). Yet on the other, it also fits within the Greco-Roman context about news of political victory, specifically, the news of the triumph and accession of the emperor. For instance, a calendrical inscription from Priene published by the Asian League in 9 BCE refers to the birthday of Augustus as the "beginning of good news [εὐαγγελία] for the world."[101] An inscription at Amphiaraia on the Oropos around 1 CE mentions the "good news of Rome's victory [εὐαγγελία τῆς Ῥωμαίων νίκης]" and situates "gospel" into the political rhetoric of empire. In another inscription it is said that the day when a son of Augustus takes on the toga (i.e., comes of age into manhood) is "good news for the city [εὐαγγελίσθη ἡ πόλις]."[102] Contemporary with Paul is an extant papyrus claiming that Nero was "the good god of the inhabited world, the beginning of all good things [Ἀγαθὸς Δαίμων τῆς οἰκουμένης ἀρχὴ ὤν τε πάντων ἀγαθῶν]."[103] Josephus provides a report about Vespasian's accession to the imperial throne, narrating how "every city celebrated the good news [εὐαγγελία] and offered sacrifices on his behalf."[104] Then, later, Josephus adds, "On reaching Alexandria, Vespasian was greeted by the good news

---

99. Jacob Taubes, *The Political Theology of Paul*, trans. D. Hollander (Stanford, CA: Stanford University Press, 2004), 16 (italics original). Contrast this view with that of Bruno Blumenfeld (*The Political Paul*, 292), who supposes that Paul's argument in Romans is so indebted to the terms of imperial rule that "one could fancy it as a contribution to a *Festschrift* for Nero, to celebrate the emperor's *quinquennium aureum*" (italics original).

100. John L. White, *The Apostle of God: Paul and the Promise of Abraham* (Peabody, MA: Hendrickson, 1999), 126.

101. *OGIS* 458.

102. *NDIEC* 3:12.

103. P.Oxy. 1021.

104. Josephus, *War* 4.618.

[εὐαγγελία] from Rome and embassies of congratulation from every quarter of the world now his own."[105] This is more than pleasant news of Vespasian's rise to imperial power through a political coup d'état; it is part of a political eschatology going back to the time of Augustus, whereby a period of turmoil is followed with a golden age through the advent of an unrivaled political master. That is, Vespasian's accession was regarded as no mere happenstance but the sociopolitical salvation of the Roman Empire from the disastrous year of 68-69 CE, which had seen three emperors (Galba, Otho, and Vitellius) all quickly rise and fall in the wake of Nero's suicide. An Egyptian papyrus from the early third century CE describes the author's joy at hearing "the good news [εὐαγγελία] concerning the proclaiming of Caesar [i.e., Gaius Julius Verus Maximus Augustus]," which the author thinks should be celebrated with a procession for the gods.[106] Immediately we have to say that Paul's gospel is conveyed in language normally used for the celebration of Rome's emperors, their universal reign, and its worship in popular discourse.[107]

The title Χριστός ("Messiah") in Pauline usage has routinely been de-judaized and depoliticized in scholarship by those who want to show that Paul did not have a messianic or political faith. Yet the evidence overwhelmingly points in the other direction, with messianism forming the hub of Paul's Christology (see Rom 9:5; 1 Cor 10:4; 15:22; 2 Cor 5:10; 11:2-3; Eph 1:10, 12, 20; 5:14; Phil 1:15, 17; 3:7).[108] Importantly, "Messiah" implies kingship in Jewish tradition (2 Sam 7:14; Pss 2:2, 7; 89:19-21, 26-27; Pss. Sol. 17.32). N. T. Wright goes so far as to translate Rom 1:1 as "Paul, a slave of King Jesus, called to be an apostle, set apart for God's good news."[109] The Jewish Messiah was a triumphant king who subdued the nations, and the Romans knew it. Tacitus referred to a prediction from Israel's sacred traditions about how "at this very time the East was to grow powerful, and rulers, coming from Judea, were to acquire a universal empire."[110] Suetonius writes how "there had spread over all the Ori-

105. Josephus, *War* 4.656-57.

106. Deissmann, *LAE* 367; *NDIEC* 3:12.

107. Ernst Käsemann (*Commentary on Romans,* trans. G. W. Bromiley [Grand Rapids, MI: Eerdmans, 1980], 7) objects on the grounds that "the antithesis between the worship of Christ and the emperor worship does not play in the primitive Church the role presupposed for such a derivation [of gospel]."

108. On Paul's messianic Christology, see Michael F. Bird, *Jesus Is the Christ: The Messianic Testimony of the Gospels* (Carlisle, UK: Paternoster, 2012), 15-22; Matthew V. Novenson, *Christ among the Messiahs: Christ Language in Paul and Messiah Language in Ancient Judaism* (New York: OUP, 2012); Wright, *Paul and the Faithfulness of God,* 815-911.

109. N. T. Wright, *The New Testament for Everyone* (London: SPCK, 2011), 337.

110. Tacitus, *Hist.* 5.13.

ent an old and established belief, that it was fated at that time for men coming from Judaea to rule the world."[111] Most likely, such views were acquired from Jewish authors who mentioned Jewish messianic hopes in passing.[112] Paul was identifying Jesus with the scriptural hopes for a messianic ruler to come from the East, and the Romans were well acquainted with the story.

Paul explicates this gospel "regarding his Son, who as to his earthly life was a descendant of David, and who through the Spirit of holiness was appointed the Son of God in power by his resurrection from the dead" (Rom 1:3-4). We must remember that lineage meant legitimation. Claims to divine lineage, ancient roots to a city, and honorable family origins were common in the biographies of the emperors. Suetonius wrote that Julius Caesar was a descendant of the goddess Venus.[113] Virgil narrated that Augustus was a descendant of Aeneas, the founder of Rome, himself descended from the goddess Venus.[114] Jesus is linked to the line of David, from whom Israel's rightful king would come, and declared by resurrection to be Son of God, in the sense of acclaiming him as the highest human authority on earth and in heaven.[115]

Behind such language stands a contrast between two kinds of divine sonship. After Julius Caesar was deified by the Roman Senate, Octavius became by adoption a son of the divine Julius. During Octavius's (i.e., Augustus's) reign, coins were minted in Philippi for "Augustus, son of the Divine, for the Divine Julius [Augustus Divi Filius Divo Iulio]," accompanied with the image of a statue of Augustus on a pedestal being crowned by Julius Caesar.[116] The advent of his sonship was declared to have ushered in a golden age with prosperity and peace for Rome. Virgil wrote about Augustus, "This is he whom you have so often heard promised to you, Augustus Caesar, son of a god [*divi genus*], who shall again set up the Golden Age."[117] In a marble pedestal in Pergamum one finds, "The Emperor, Caesar, son of a god, the god Augustus, of every land and sea, the overseer."[118] More contemporary with Paul, some inscriptions describe Nero as "son of the divine Claudius," "son of the divine Augustus," and even

111. Suetonius, *Vespasian* 4.5.

112. See Josephus, *War* 6.312-13; Philo, *Mos.* 1.290.

113. Suetonius, *Julius* 6.1.

114. Virgil, *Aeneid* 1.286-90.

115. See Michael F. Bird, *Are You the One Who Is to Come? The Historical Jesus and the Messianic Question* (Grand Rapids, MI: Baker Academic, 2009), 31-62.

116. Lukas Bormann, *Philippi—Stadt und Christgemeinde zur Zeit des Paulus* (Leiden: Brill, 1995), 34-35.

117. Virgil, *Aeneid* 6.791-93.

118. Deissmann, *LAE*, 347.

"son of the greatest of the gods, Tiberius Claudius."[119] Evidently Augustus and those emperors after him flooded their provinces with media and artwork designed to herald their divinity and accomplishments.

In addition, the designation of Jesus as the "Son of God" does not follow on from the deification of his adopted father, nor is divinity granted as an honorific title for some military achievement, not even granted by postmortem apotheosis. Jesus was designated the "Son of God" by resurrection from the dead. This is all the more significant because, while Roman mythology could imagine journeys to the underworld, in general, Romans did not believe in resurrection.[120] For instance, the poet Horace lamented that the late Quintilius "sleeps the sleep [from] which men never recover."[121] We might consider also that resurrection was politically threatening, as it constituted a mythology about the vindication, victory, vivification of those killed for opposing imperial rule, as it is in Dan 12, 2 Macc 7, and Rev 20. Resurrection implies the supernatural return of those slaughtered for their resistance to pagan idolatry and power. Rock asserts that resurrection is "positive evidence that Rome's power was not final"[122]—a valid point, since resurrection implies the apocalyptic upheaval of the inhabited world, a radical reordering of power, an inversion of the pyramid of privilege, reversing the tyrant's ultimate weapon, so that those killed in brutality and disgrace are raised to reign in divine glory. The significance of this is well spelled out by Wright: "To come to Rome with the gospel of Jesus, to announce someone else's accession to the world's throne, therefore, was to put on a red coat and walk into a field with a potentially angry bull."[123]

To sum up, we can trace in Rom 1:3-4 a dense compilation of terms for competing ideas of the recipient of divine kingship.[124] N. T. Wright is probably on to something when he says that Rom 1:3-4 "was a royal proclamation aimed at challenging other royal proclamations."[125] Paul announced a "gospel" about an anointed Jewish king from the Davidic line who carries the title "Son of God,"

119. Elliott, *Arrogance of Nations*, 71-72; Deissmann, *LAE*, 347.
120. N. T. Wright, *Resurrection of the Son of God* (COQG 3; London: SPCK, 2003), 32-84.
121. Horace, *Odes* 1.24.
122. Ian E. Rock, *Paul's Letter to the Romans and Roman Imperialism: An Ideological Analysis of the Exordium (Romans 1:1–17)* (Eugene, OR: Pickwick, 2012), 118.
123. Wright, "Romans," 10:423.
124. John Pairman Brown ("Divine Kingship, Civic Institutions, Imperial Rule," in *Israel and Hellas* [2 vols.; BZAW 231; Berlin: Walter de Gruyter, 1995], 2:83) puts it: "The opposition between Christ and Caesar arose from the fact that they fell heir to opposite aspects of the old divine kingship."
125. Wright, "Paul's Gospel and Caesar's Empire," 168.

a person who was put to death by Roman authorities as a royal pretender and who had been brought back to life by Israel's God and had been installed as Lord. Read in light of a matrix of possible resonances, the alternatives could hardly be starker. When it comes to who rules the world, it is not the Son of Augustus, but the Son of David! When it comes to divine sonship, it is Jesus, not the Julio-Claudian line. In the stakes of divine kingship and arbitration over divine sonship, Paul has only one candidate in mind: "Lord Jesus Messiah" (Rom 1:7), a title that might even stand in counterpoint to "Imperator Caesar Augustus."[126]

Romans 1:16-17

In Rom 1:16-17, the central thesis of Romans, Paul declares that the righteousness of God is revealed in the gospel: "I am not ashamed of the gospel, because it is the power of God that brings salvation to everyone who believes: first to the Jew, then to the Gentile. For in the gospel the righteousness of God is revealed—a righteousness that is by faith from first to last, just as it is written: 'The righteous will live by faith.'"

The "righteousness of God" is the righteous character of God enacted and embodied in his saving actions. Its background is primarily in Israel's Scriptures, given the close association of "salvation" and "righteousness" with connotations of God's faithfulness to his covenant promises and his intent to establish justice throughout all of creation (e.g., Isa 51; Ps 98). Yet many of Paul's readers/hearers might well have been aware of the connotations that "righteousness" (δικαιοσύνη/*iustitia*) had with the imperial household. The *Res Gestae* honors Augustus for his "mercy and righteousness" (ἐπείκειαν καὶ δικαιοσύνην/*clementiae iustitiae*).[127] Ovid refers to *iustitia* being enshrined in Augustus's heart as a god.[128] Tiberius dedicated a statue in Rome to the Iustitia Augusta, the divine representative of justice.[129] In addition, Latin speakers in Rome may have thought of justice *(iustitia)* in terms of fairness *(aequitas).* The primary image of Aequitas in Roman coinage was that of a woman holding a balance in her outstretched right hand. Some Alexandrian coins, stemming from the third year of Nero's reign (ca. 56-57 CE), show a picture of Nero on one side and on the other side a young woman holding the balance, and the accompanying inscription reads in Greek letters δικαιοσύνη. It seems that

---

126. Earl J. Richard, *Jesus, One and Many: The Christological Concept of New Testament Authors* (Wilmington, DE: Glazier, 1988), 326; Novenson, *Christ among the Messiahs*, 94-97.

127. *Acts of Augustus* 34.

128. Ovid, *Pont.* 3.6.23-24.

129. Tellbe, *Paul between Synagogue and State*, 204.

those familiar with Roman coinage and imperial claims may well have associated ideas of righteousness along the lines of impartiality, equality, and fairness in association with the emperor as the embodiment and bestower of divine justice. In counterpoint, Paul emphasizes exactly the same qualities of God as just and equitable when he refers to salvation as coming equally to both Jews and Gentiles (Rom 1:16), his persistent focus on God's impartiality (Rom 2–3), the lack of "difference" between Jews and Gentiles in either condemnation or justification (Rom 3:22; 10:12), and God's repaying back to all as they deserve (Rom 2:6; 12:19). If so, the righteousness of God brings vindication for the faithful, as well as fairness and equity to all.[130]

The righteousness of God revealed in the gospel also results in "salvation" for Jews and Gentiles. The meaning of "salvation" *(sōtēria)* is deliverance and rescue from danger (see Rom 5:9-10; 10:9-13; 11:11, 14, 26; 13:11). Interestingly enough, the Romans had a cult of "the salvation of the people of Rome [*salus populi Romani*]," which was restored by Augustus after a period of neglect.[131] Salvation was secured through the emperor executing his duties as *princeps* ("first among equals") and *pontifex maximus* ("high priest") over the empire, mediating between the people and the gods, and so bringing blessings, benefits, fortune, favor, prosperity, and provision to Rome and her clients and colonies. Horace wrote in his typical sycophantic prose in praise of Augustus as defender of Rome: "As long as Caesar is safe, who would fear the Parthian, who [would fear] the frozen Scythian, who [would fear] the swarms which savage Germany breeds? Who would worry about war with fierce Spain?"[132] In addition, Roman literature often extolled the "salvation" that Rome and the Roman emperor brought to the world. Josephus describes how Vespasian, on his elevation to the principate, received embassies of celebration with "the whole empire being now secured and the Roman state saved beyond expectation."[133] Dieter Georgi infers that "the *sōtēria* represented by Caesar and his empire is challenged by the *sōtēria* brought about by Jesus. Like that of Caesar, the *sōtēria* of the God Jesus is worldwide."[134] That is perhaps pushing the analogy too far. Paul does not directly polemicize against the Roman *salus;* however, his gospel of salvation delivers from sin and death, is superior to

130. Frank Thielman, "God's Righteousness as God's Fairness in Romans 1:17: An Ancient Perspective on a Significant Phrase," *JETS* 54 (2011): 35-48 (esp. 41-44).

131. *Acts of Augustus* 19-21; Horace, *Odes* 3.6.1; Virgil, *Aeneid* 6.716; Ovid, *Fasti* 2.63; Suetonius, *Augustus* 30.

132. Horace, *Odes* 4.5.

133. Josephus, *War* 4.656-57.

134. Georgi, "God Turned Upside Down," 152.

Roman salvation in quality, and is naturally contrasted with what the imperial cult and its political benefactors had to offer. For Paul it is certainly true that "evangelical persuasion rather than political and military power is thus the means whereby the salvation of the world is now occurring."[135]

The gospel that reveals God's righteousness calls for the response of faith and faithfulness. Both trust and trustworthiness can be implied by the noun *pistis* and by the wider context of Hab 2:4, which Paul cites. This entails faith in God and fidelity to God. This evangelical "faith" can be naturally contrasted with Roman *fides*. The goddess Fides, the deity of loyalty and fidelity, was understood to operate through Rome's emperors. The emperor personified Roman faithfulness to its treaties and subjects but in return demanded reciprocal faithfulness from those over whom he ruled. The *Res Gestae* state that those subjugated by Rome have "discovered the good faith [*fides*/πίστις] of the Roman people."[136] The Roman governor of Egypt, Tiberius Alexander (an apostate Jew), ordered "the legions and the multitude to take the oath of fidelity to Vespasian."[137] The "faith" of Roman subjects was somewhere between fealty and slavery. Roman emperors kept faith with their subjects as long as the latter were obedient and subservient. For Paul, faith is not fealty but a believing in and belonging to the God who calls people to himself (Rom 9:25-26). Paul will go on to say that pagan Romans have "no fidelity, no love, no mercy" (Rom 1:31), yet these are the very qualities that the God of the Messiah possesses (Rom 5:8; 8:28-39; 9:15-18, 23; 11:30-32; 12:1; 15:9).

Furthermore, the idolatry that Paul trenchantly criticizes in Rom 1:21-23 undoubtedly would include the imperial cults. The imperial cults were not stand-alone entities, being normally embedded within or beside local temples and shrines across the eastern Mediterranean. It is no surprise, then, that Paul can often present Christ as an alternative "Lord" to the general religious pluralism of the Roman age, with its many lords and gods (see 1 Cor 8:5-6, 10; 10:7, 14-22; Gal 4:8-10; 1 Thess 1:9). It was the "rulers of this age," the wicked false gods, who crucified the Lord (1 Cor 2:8).

In a nutshell, in Rom 1 we have a natural juxtaposition between two competing reigns, the house of Caesar and the house of David, with two competing eschatologies: "Rome offered a long and powerful story of a divinely appointed city, nation and culture from which had emerged the *divi filius* himself, bringing peace and justice and world domination. Paul told the long and evocative

---

135. Jewett, *Romans*, 141.
136. *Acts of Augustus* 31-33.
137. Josephus, *War* 4.617.

story of a divinely appointed people from whom, despite their many failures and tragedies, there had emerged the *theou huios* himself, bringing peace and justice and claiming worldwide allegiance."[138] This is more than an *allusion* by Paul to political propaganda that is laden with religious language. The juxtaposition is more like a *collision* of two gospels, a confrontation between two Lords, the good news of Roman military victory versus the good news of redemption through the Lord Jesus Christ.

Romans 2–4

In Romans, Paul strives to establish a foothold among the Roman Christians, desiring their support for his apostolate to the Gentiles. So we should not expect political themes to dominate in the letter, though the main body does touch upon themes that have sociopolitical connotations.

The reference to God's "kindness, forbearance and patience" (Rom 2:4) perhaps echoes the Roman trait of clemency *(clementia)* that emperors from Julius Caesar to Nero exercised toward their opponents. Such clemency was not motivated purely by compassion but was for political advantage. It eventually featured in Roman propaganda, and the Roman senate vowed to erect a temple to the deified spirit of Julius Caesar's *clementia*. The discriminate clemency of Rome also contrasts with the indiscriminate mercy of God (Rom 11:32). The mercy of Israel's God leads the nations to worship him for his mercy, rather than offer sacrifices to Caesar for his clemency, which would be idolatry (Rom 15:9).[139]

For Paul, "works of law" (Rom 3:20, 27-28) means the Jewish way of life as codified in the Torah. Paul's assertion is that the performance and possession of the Jewish law is no talisman for salvation, since Israel's law did not fix the sin problem, and God's intention was always to reach the world beyond the jurisdiction of ethnic Israel. In addition, the Romans prided themselves on their legal traditions. So "works of law" might carry a connotation of Roman law for Roman readers.[140] Viewed this way, Paul is rejecting the view that any law is a means to salvation or the vehicle to construct a privileged cultural identity.

In Rom 4 Paul writes that "it was not through the law that Abraham and his offspring received the promise that he would be *heir of the world*, but through

---

138. Wright, *Paul and the Faithfulness of God*, 1281.

139. See Melissa B. Dowling, *Clemency and Cruelty in the Roman World* (Ann Arbor: University of Michigan Press, 2006), esp. 26-28; and Elliott, *Arrogance of Nations*, 87-119.

140. Crossan and Reed, *In Search of Paul*, 387-88; Jewett, *Romans*, 266; Elliott, *Arrogance of Nations*, 138-41.

the righteousness that comes by faith" (Rom 4:13). Virgil put into the mouth of Jupiter the claim that the toga-wearing Romans were "heirs of heaven" and the "Lords of the world."[141] In contrast, Paul here rehearses the Jewish story that it is Abraham's family, now defined around the Messiah, who will inherit and bless the world. For the Roman Christians, many of whom were among the poor and had no inheritance, their blessing came not from Rome but from the Messiah's kingdom. For Paul, contra Virgil, it is the descendant of Abraham (i.e., Jesus) and not the descendant of Aeneas (i.e., Augustus) whom God elects to bring into the world an everlasting kingdom typified by peace and justice.[142]

Romans 5

Rom 5:1-11 is a transition section between 3:21–4:25 and 5:12–8:39. This short section contrasts quite naturally with much imperial propaganda of the Augustan age. When Paul mentions that those justified by faith "have peace with God," this Pax Christi stands in contrast to the Pax Romana.[143] The Pax Romana, or "Peace of Rome," is a period used by historians to designate the time extending from 27 BCE to 180 CE, when Rome was at its highest glory. For Roman rulers, peace was both a virtue and a strategic empire-wide goal. Peace meant the absence of civil wars and success in subduing foreign territories. There was a symbiotic relationship between *pax* and *imperium*, peace and victory. Romans celebrated their "peace" in coinage; devotion to Pax, the Roman goddess of peace, the erection of the Ara Pacis, the "Altar of Augustan Peace," and the achievement of peace figure prominently in the Priene inscription and in the *Res Gestae*. Ironically, this period of peace was a time of unprecedented Roman military expansion. According to Virgil, the Roman mission was to conquer the world and "crown peace with justice."[144] Augustus's acts included "peace secured through victories."[145] Tacitus puts into the mouth of the Caledonian king Calgacus a stunning critique about the Romans: "To robbery, slaughter, plunder, they give the lying name of empire; they make a solitude and call it peace."[146] The contrast here is noted by Maier, who points out that "the peace that Jesus offers is not then the violent peace of Rome, but

---

141. Virgil, *Aeneid* 1.359.

142. Wallace, *Gospel of God*, 131, 163; Elliott, *Arrogance of Nations*, 136-38.

143. See Klaus Wengst, *Pax Romana and the Peace of Jesus Christ,* trans. J. Bowden (Philadelphia: Fortress, 1987); Georgi, "God Turned Upside Down," 154n17.

144. Virgil, *Aeneid* 6.851-53; *Acts of Augustus* 34.

145. *Acts of Augustus* 13.

146. Tacitus, *Agricola* 30.

a peace based on grace and divine self-giving."[147] A similar sentiment is given by David Odell-Scott: "Unlike the reconciling unity and peace of Rome successfully wrought at the hands of the legions to subdue peoples of the world, Paul's Christ occasions a reconciling unity in his own death."[148]

Paul's claim that "Christ died for the ungodly" (Rom 5:6) and "Christ died for us" (Rom 5:8) assumes the sacrificial nature of Jesus' death in light of Rom 3:24-25 and 8:3. The benefits of Jesus' death accrued to believers undoubtedly *resources* various traditions from Israel's sacrificial cultus and Isaianic imagery (see, e.g., Lev 17:11; Isa 53:5, 11-12), as well as Jewish martyrdom traditions (see 2 Macc 7:32-38; 4 Macc 6:28-29; 17:21-22). However, Jesus' death also *resonates* with Hellenistic traditions of kings surrendering their lives for the sake of their subjects.[149] In addition, sacrifice was common in Roman religion; indeed, death, sacrifice, and religion were central to the founding of Rome, according to Ovid.[150] Sacrifice was expected and routine in the imperial cults and took many forms, ranging from libations offered to the genius of the emperor to sacrifices offered on behalf of the emperor in the Jerusalem temple. Augustus is very important in this regard, in that he placed shrines dedicated to the Lares Augusti at important crossroads where bloodless sacrifices of cake, incense, and wine could be offered. In other words, what were once public neighborhood cults were now extensions of the private cults of Augustus and his family. Household images and statues were also so common that Tacitus reports that "worshipers of Augustus" could be found "in all Roman households."[151] According to George Heyman:

> Through sacrificial practices, the emperor became present on almost every street corner. While religious in nature, such sacrifices, usually in the form of incense altars, were formative of a Roman sacrificial discourse in which political control was established without the physical presence of the ruling monarch. Cults to Augustus and the Sebastoi (the imperial

147. Maier, *Picturing Paul in Empire*, 57.
148. David Odell-Scott, *Paul's Critique of Theocracy: A/theocracy in Corinthians and Galatians* (JSNTSup 250; London: T&T Clark, 2003), 161.
149. See David Seeley, *The Noble Death: Graeco-Roman Martyrology and Paul's Concept of Salvation* (JSNTSup 28; Sheffield: JSOT Press, 1990), 83-112; Christina Eschner, *Gestorben und hingegeben "für" die Sünder: Die griechische Konzepten des Unheil abwendenden Sterbens und deren paulinischen Aufnahme für die Deutung des Todes Jesu Christi* (2 vols.; WMANT 122; Berlin: Neukirchener Verlag, 2010), 1:274-360.
150. Ovid, *Fasti* 4.833-48.
151. Tacitus, *Ann.* 1.73. See Gradel, *Emperor Worship*, 198-212.

line) were easily welcomed in the Greek provinces previously accustomed
to similar "divine-like" honors accorded the former Hellenistic rulers.
A sacrifice of unmixed wine was poured at each official Roman banquet
in honor of the emperor after the death of Augustus in 14 CE. The Latin
west also saw altars inscribed to the numen Augusti (the "divine spirit"
of Augustus) from Spain to Gaul and North Africa.[152]

And there was the problem: Christ-believers looked not to Roman religion or to the emperor but to Christ as the one sacrifice that counted, and
which saved them. Christ was the ideal king, who surrendered his life on
behalf of others, and his subjects offered their lives as "living sacrifices" to
the God of Israel and regarded the offering of sacrifices to divinized humans
as blasphemous (see Rom 1:21-23; 1 Thess 1:9). This was subversive—again, as
Heyman observes:

> The hostility between Rome and early Christianity arose from Christian
> refusal to become fully identified with Roman religio-political rule. The
> idea of sacrifice functioned as a rhetorical marker for creating political
> power and social identity. . . . The clash between Christians and Romans
> was a clash within discourses. If "sacrifice," as either a ritual act or a rhe-
> torical tool, can unite a group by creating identity and social power, then
> it can be used as an ideological or ritual weapon when identity and social
> power are contested. Simply put, because sacrifice was such a symbolic
> focal point for the expression of both religious and social power, it was
> natural that it became the lightning rod for social conflict. This Christian
> expectation of a "kingdom of God" quite naturally made the "kingdom
> of Caesar" nervous. This is not simply to impute crass political motives
> to the rhetoric of early Christianity, but to suggest a rationale for why
> such a highly ritualized form of religious behavior, like sacrifice, became
> so contentious.[153]

In addition, Paul's argument in Rom 5:12-21 explicates what he has asserted
elsewhere about the nexus of Law-Sin-Death in the old Adam being broken by

152. George Heyman, *The Power of Sacrifice: Roman and Christian Discourses in Conflict* (Washington, DC: Catholic University of American Press, 2007), 226-27. See too Tellbe, *Paul between Synagogue and State*, 146: "Augustus thus received worship with the gods of the house-hold, and it was this form of cult at public and private banquets that prepared the way for a more formal state worship of the emperor and his family."

153. Heyman, *The Power of Sacrifice*, 219, 222.

the obedience-righteousness-life of the New Adam (see Phil 2:5-11; 1 Cor 15:56). The biographical claim of the Julio-Claudian dynasty to trace its heritage all the way back through Romulus to Aeneas becomes a hollow claim.[154] Paul's narrative assumes a different genealogical epic in terms of Adam, Abraham, and Christ, which meets a deeper need. What the world needs is not more empire, not even bread and circuses, but someone to break the power of death and corruption. The figure who does this is not a new Aeneas but a new Adam. For Paul, Jesus is this new Adam, who brokers peace, righteousness, reconciliation, and life to all people. Jesus' defeat of death and the gift of eternal life stand in contrast to the "culture of arbitrary violence and death," which so often characterized imperial power.[155] The emperor is most definitely not, as Seneca said of Nero, "the arbiter of life and death for the nations."[156] The risen Christ and his followers reign over death, while the apotheosized rulers still belong to the Adamic age and remain captive to death and cannot help their clients (Rom 5:17, 21; 6:9).[157] For in the Messiah, God has chosen to identify with his rebellious subjects rather than to simply crush them. Jesus has done more than sheathed the sword by clemency; he has conquered death by resurrection life. The gracious benefaction of the emperors is surpassed by the superabounding gracious gift of the Lord Jesus Christ.[158] In the end, for Paul, Jesus is what the *princeps* claimed to be: the representative, reconciler, and ruler of the human race.[159]

Romans 8-11

Paul also writes that, by receiving the Spirit of adoption, the Roman Christians are God's children and therefore *"heirs of God and joint heirs with Christ"* (Rom 8:17). Their inheritance is not lands given by a conquering Rome to surviving veterans but the glory of God in a new creation (Rom 8:18-21). Whereas Roman authors associated the reign of the emperors with prosperity, fecundity, restoring the idyllic qualities of Mother Earth, and the fruitfulness of nature,[160] Paul tells the struggling churches in Rome a counterstory where

154. On Augustus as a "new Aeneas," see Horace, *Carmen Saeculare* 41-46; Virgil, *Aeneid* 8.720-28; Ara Pacis in the Augustan forum.

155. Harrison, *Paul and the Imperial Authorities*, 113-14.

156. Seneca, *Clem.* 1.19.8.

157. Harrison, *Paul and the Imperial Authorities*, 115.

158. James R. Harrison, "Paul, Eschatology, and the Augustan Age of Grace," *TynB* 40 (1999): 79-91.

159. Georgi, "God Turned Upside Down," 154.

160. Virgil, *Eclogues* 4.11-41; Horace, *Carmen Seculare* 29-32.

they are the heirs of a forthcoming renewed creation over which Messiah Jesus is Lord. The *saeculum Augustum* is part of the "evil age" upon which God's kingdom already imposes itself. The golden Augustan age is supplanted with a messianic kingdom.[161]

Later in the same chapter, Paul writes: "Who then is the one who condemns? No one. Christ Jesus who died—more than that, who was raised to life—is at the right hand of God and is also interceding for us" (Rom 8:34). The notion of Christ as seated at the right hand of God obviously represents an allusion to Ps 110. Interestingly enough, numismatic evidence depicts an apotheosized Claudius sitting at the right hand of the divine Augustus on the top of a chariot drawn by four elephants. Harrison infers: "Over and against the symbolic universe of the Caesars—with its apotheosized rulers (Caesar, Augustus, Claudius) and Son of god (Nero) answering petitions of their clients—Jesus ruled as the risen Son of God in power on behalf of his church within the empire."[162] Jesus, then, is the real deputy of heavenly powers, and it is him, not the emperors as commonly thought, who could be consulted in prayer.[163]

In Rom 9–11 Jesus is called "God over all" (ὁ ὢν ἐπὶ πάντων θεός, 9:5),[164] "Lord Jesus" (κύριον Ἰησοῦν, 10:9), and "the Rescuer" (ὁ ῥυόμενος, 11:26). This comports with the tradition of Hellenistic rulers acclaimed in such language, as found in many inscriptions and writings in the eastern Mediterranean.

Celebration and acclamation of the emperor as a θεός ("god") are not hard to find. For instance, an inscription from Myra of Lycia labels Emperor Augustus as the "Divine Augustus, son of a god, Caesar, emperor of land and sea, the benefactor and savior of the whole world."[165] In an inscription from Ephesus, Julius Caesar is described as "the manifested god from Ares and Aphrodite and universal savior of human life."[166] Even in Rome the title "god" could flow. Virgil wrote that the Augustus was "a god who wrought for us this peace—for

---

161. See Mark Forman, *The Politics of Promise* (SNTSMS 148; Cambridge: CUP, 2011); Robert Jewett, "The Corruption and Redemption of Creation: Reading Rom. 8:18-23 within the Imperial Context," in *Paul and the Roman Imperial Order*, ed. R. A. Horsley (Harrisburg, PA: TPI, 2004), 25-46; Wallace, *Gospel of God*, 158-60.

162. Harrison, *Paul and the Imperial Authorities*, 116.

163. Virgil, *Aeneid* 1.286-91; Ovid, *Metamorphoses* 15.888-90.

164. See Hans-Christian Kammler, "Die Prädikation of Jesu Christi als 'Gott' und die paulinische Christologie: Erwägungen zur Exegese von Röm 9,5b," *ZNW* 92 (2003): 164-80.

165. David C. Braund, *Augustus to Nero: A Sourcebook on Romans History, 31 BC–AD 68* (London: Crook Helm, 1985), § 66.

166. SIG 76.

a god he shall ever be to me; often shall a tender lamb from our folds stain his altar."[167] Not to be outdone, Horace said of Augustus: "Thunder in heaven confirms our faith—Jove rules there; but here on earth Augustus shall be hailed as god also, when he makes new subjects of the Britons and the dour Parthians."[168] It is hard to determine precisely what type of ontological claim this god language carries. The emperors, living or dead, possessed relative rather than absolute divinity. The emperor's divinity was associated with the Roman gods, but it did not replace them or obscure their place in Roman religion.[169] For the most part, divine honors simply represent the highest accolade available in an ascending scale of honors that could be heaped upon a ruler, by offering sacrifices to them in altars and worship of the ruler's *genius, numen,* image, family, and person.[170]

Examples abound of the first-century emperors designated as κύριος ("Lord") in papyri, literature, and inscriptions (although often varied in their geographic distribution, with concentrations in places like Egypt and Asia Minor, and spiking during Nero's reign). One notable inscription offers prestige honors to "Nero, the lord of the entire world" (ὁ τοῦ παντὸς κόσμου κύριος Νέρων).[171] The title κύριος indicates that the emperor, as *princeps* ("first citizen") and σεβαστός ("venerable one"), held a unique and

---

167. Virgil, *Eclogues* 1.6-8.

168. Horace, *Odes* 3.5.

169. Part of the debate pertains to whether there is a difference between the meaning of *divus* and *deus* and whether there is a difference between being worshiped as "a god" or "as to a god." See discussion in Simon R. F. Price, "Gods and Emperors: The Greek Language of the Roman Imperial Cult," *Journal of Hellenic Studies* 104 (1984): 79-95; Gradel, *Emperor Worship,* 261-371; Koortbojian, *Divinization of Caesar and Augustus,* 1-8, 21-24, 156-58, 177-81. On the one hand, even the established gods like Jupiter were thought by some to be former men who were elevated to divine status (Ennius, *Sacra Historia* 11.132-37V), and Cicero claims that brave and powerful men have been deified after death and are worthy objects of worship, prayers, and adoration (*Leg.* 2.7.19). On the other hand, some claimed that there were two classes of gods, the eternal and the imperishable (i.e., celestial), and others who were made gods (i.e., terrestrial) (Diodorus 6.1-2 from Eusebius, *Praep. Ev.* 2.2.53); some mocked the notion of apotheosis, like Cicero's philosopher Cotta and Seneca the Younger lampooning the deification of Claudius (*Natura Deorum* 1.119; Seneca, *Apocolocyntosis*); and even Alexander the Great's demands that Greece recognize him as a god were met with derisive complicity, with the Spartan Damis laconically stating, "Since Alexander wants to be a god, let him be a god" (Plutarch, *Moralia* 219).

170. See Philo, *Legat.* 146-50; Nicolaus of Damascus, *FGrH* 90 F 125. See Gradel, *Emperor Worship and Roman Religion.* John L. White (*The Apostle of God,* 99) sums it up well: "Good rulers were divinized for the same reason that gods were worshipped: they were acknowledged as saviors of the social order."

171. Fantin, *Lord of the Entire World,* 221.

superlative position as a "supreme lord" over all hierarchies in the realm. It was a supremacy covering a cross-section of military, political, social, and religious domains. This supremacy, argues Fantin, is *relational* in that the emperor provides patronage and benefaction to all inferiors in the empire, and *exclusive* in that only one figure was able to exert unrivaled control; for another claimant to rise would lead to certain civil war.[172] Furthermore, if the confession of Jesus as Lord in Rom 10:9-11 was analogous to an oath of loyalty with the demand for exclusive devotion to one master—ancient Near Eastern and Greco-Roman loyalty oaths are similar in this regard[173]—then Christ-believers were expressing a loyalty toward Jesus as the superlative authority over and against the same claim made for the emperor. Oaths to the emperor were common in the provinces, exemplified by those found in inscriptions at Paphlagonia and Cyprus.[174]

In addition, Clifford Ando warns that we should not "underestimate the eagerness of individuals to demonstrate loyalty . . . to placate, persuade, or dupe their Roman overlords."[175] The imperial cult was not purely imposed but enthusiastically consumed as well.[176] Making such oaths and offering accolades to the emperor was fundamentally a way of ingratiating oneself to imperial patronage by showing steadfast loyalty and bestowing divine honors on the emperor as a preeminent master, which is precisely why so many provincial cities did it so frequently. Provincial subjects embraced the imperial cults as it gave them a piece and partnership in the empire. That qualification is important because it shows that the imperial cults were not simply forced upon populaces from the top down, yet it does not deny that a certain top-down pressure was applied for Roman and imperial cults to be planted in Eastern cities. As a case in point, Cassius Dio records how Augustus required Roman citizens in Asia and Bithynia to venerate the cult Divus Iulius, and local inhabitants were required to pay honor to the cult of Augustus and Roma.[177] Tacitus sneers among the turmoil of Augustus's family, "No honor was left for the gods, when Augustus chose to be himself worshiped with temples and statues, like those of the deities, and with flamens

---

172. Fantin, *Lord of the Entire World*, 209-15.

173. Moshe Weinfeld, *Normative and Sectarian Judaism in the Second Temple Period* (LSTS 54; London: T&T Clark, 2005), 11-12, 30-34.

174. Clifford Ando, *Imperial Ideology and Provincial Loyalty in the Roman Empire* (Berkeley: University of California Press, 2000), 359-60.

175. Ando, *Imperial Ideology*, 231.

176. Friesen, "Normal Religion," 24.

177. Dio Cassius 51.20.6-8.

and priests."[178] During Tiberius's reign, the city of Cyzicus was deprived of its freedom for a series of assaults on Roman citizens and for its failure to complete a temple to Augustus.[179] While the imperial cults were undoubtedly shaped by local coloring, they also intentionally propagated a utopian vision for the Romanization of the world and "helped to bind the inhabitants of the empire together in a religious community that could be shared anywhere in the empire."[180]

More generally, emperors could be eulogized as saviors, benefactors, and rescuers of cities, peoples, and the whole empire. Philo lauds Augustus: "The whole race exhausted by mutual slaughter was on the verge of utter destruction had it not been for one man and leader, Augustus, whom men fitly call the averter of evil."[181] Velleius Paterculus, an official chronicler of Rome, heaped accolades on Augustus by claiming that there "is nothing that man can desire from the gods, nothing that the gods can grant to a man, nothing that wish can conceive or good fortune bring to pass, which Augustus on his return to the city did not bestow upon the republic, the Roman people, and the world."[182] Even Caligula, Philo says, is the "Saviour and Benefactor who was expected to rain down fresh and everlasting springs of blessings upon all of Asia and Europe."[183]

The veneration of non-Roman religious deities and political figures would not have been perceived to be a threat to Roman power as long as these figures were integrated within the imperium. One reason why the imperial cults were so powerful is because they were able to integrate with family shrines, neighborhood festivals, and city cults. The worship of the emperor's genius besides the Lares and the construction of imperial temples besides existing ones involved slaves, freedmen, artisans, magistrates, and elites, all of whom were given a stake in the interlocking socioreligious life of the state.[184] Augustus, like his republican forebears, was able to assuage the conquered by blending power with service and reward, and by incorporating local elites and their clients into a wider sphere of power.[185] But outside of the imperium, beyond the

---

178. Tacitus, *Ann.* 1.10.

179. Tacitus, *Ann.* 4.36.2; Suetonius, *Tiberius* 37.3.

180. Eric M. Orlin, "Augustan Religion: From Locative to Utopian," in *Rome and Religion: A Cross-Disciplinary Dialogue on the Imperial Cult*, ed. J. Brodd and J. L. Reed (Atlanta: SBL, 2011), 57.

181. Philo, *Leg.* 144.

182. Velleius Paterculus, *Hist.* 2.89.2-3.

183. Philo, *Leg.* 22.

184. White, *The Apostle of God*, 124-27.

185. Nystrom, "We Have No King but Caesar," 24.

standard lines of sociopolitical hierarchy, external to the domain of approved temples and cults, claims to superlative authority could be problematic. So, for the Roman political apparatus, in a letter addressed to Rome's Jewish minority and its Christ-believing chapter, there could be something objectionable, even treasonous, about ascribing such honorific titles to a man who was executed by Rome, who was venerated as a messianic king, said to have been invested with heavenly power and superlative divine honors. While there was often a restrained usage of divine language for emperors in the state cult, even so, worship of the living emperor was widespread in private cults and provincial towns in Italy. In any case, Christ-devotion to Jesus as God, Lord, and Savior seems to compete with Caesar-devotion, since we have here rival accounts of who possesses the most divine honors, who is the source of salvation and deliverance, who is the recipient of loyalty, and who is the supreme lord, right in the very capital of Rome. To call Jesus "God," "Savior," and "Lord," then, was to offer him the same honors and loyalty that political masters thought they were due from their subjects. Harrison's comment is quite apt: "At its soteriological core, Paul's gospel of God's triumphant grace in Christ invisibly undermined the boasting in the benefits dispensed by the ruler and the idolatry of power that had now become vested by perpetuity, in the minds of the rule's clients at least, in the Julio-Claudian house."[186]

Romans 13:1-14

The one text in Romans that says the most about the Roman governing authorities is Rom 13:1-7. Yet this passage is arguably benign in its remarks concerning Roman power. If anything, this text promotes submission to the state and complicity with its requirements by Christians. Would such a text have elicited Nero's enthusiasm if it had been brought to his attention?[187] No surprise that this text has been controversial in its history of reception concerning church and state relationships, and various provenances have been proposed for its occasion.[188] It may also be the case that Paul's apparent subjection of Christians to Roman political power is not meant to be unchecked or unqualified.

---

186. Harrison, *Paul and the Imperial Authorities*, 164.

187. Richard J. Cassidy, *Christians and Roman Rule in the New Testament: New Perspectives* (New York: Crossroad, 2001), 72.

188. See survey in Krauter, *Studien zu Röm 13,1-7*, 4-38; Gillian Clark, "Let Every Soul Be Subject: The Fathers and the Empire," in *Images of Empire*, ed. L. Alexander (JSOTSup 122; Sheffield: JSOT Press, 1991), 251-75.

Ernst Käsemann popularized the position that Paul was calling certain enthusiasts back to an earthly order and resisting the attitude that heavenly citizenship meant treating political authorities with indifference. To forgo obedience to the state would lead to anarchy, which would destroy love and peace in the community and discredit Christianity in the eyes of the world. Precisely because the political sphere is provisional, Paul makes such exhortations to his audience.[189]

Neil Elliott situates Rom 13:1-7 in Paul's effort to stem emergent supersessionism among Gentile Christians. Romans 8–1 and 12–15 function as paraenetic sections designed to quell Gentile arrogance and to protect the vulnerable Jewish community from political attacks. As such, Rom 13:1-7 is designed to head off any sort of public unrest that could jeopardize the vulnerable situation of beleaguered Jewish communities in Rome.[190] Elsewhere Elliott maintains that Rom 13:1-7 is a standard prophetic-apocalyptic affirmation that empires rise and fall at God's command. So church members must be prevented from causing trouble in the streets, not only for their own benefit, but because, as the previous context of Rom 12:19-21 states, judgment and retribution are ultimately prerogatives of God.[191]

According to Carter, Paul employs a rhetoric of flattery in Rom 13:1-7, clearly out of sync with the rest of the letter, but necessary because of circumstances for which now we can only speculate. He maintains, "These verses do not comprise a political treatise that presents a fixed ethic of submission for every situation." It is about creating the illusion of loyalty to the state for the sake of personal survival.[192]

Crossan and Reed think that Rom 13:1-7 is not a universal and abstract command but "prudent advice" specific to the Roman context, where the Christians in Rome could suffer political punishments like those suffered under Claudius if they appear disloyal. In a "hierarchy of the negative" one must choose when to obey and when to disobey. Crossan and Reed, however, also believe in the "primacy of the positive," where Paul is set on establishing an alternative to the Roman Empire, where there emerges a "positively incarnated global justice on the local, ordinary, and everyday level."[193]

---

189. Käsemann, *Commentary on Romans*, 350-59.

190. Neil Elliott, "Romans 13:1-7 in the Context of Imperial Propaganda," in *Paul and Empire: Religion and Power in Roman Imperial Society*, ed. R. A. Horsley (Harrisburg, PA: TPI, 1997), 184-204.

191. Neil Elliott, *Liberating Paul: The Justice of God and the Politics of the Apostle* (Sheffield: Sheffield Academic, 1995), 223-24.

192. Carter, *Roman Empire*, 133-36 (136 for quotation).

193. Crossan and Reed, *In Search of Paul*, 394, 409-12.

Porter believes that Rom 13:1-7 should not be seen as teaching "unqualified obedience to the state." Paul calls authorities to account because they are exercising divinely given powers, and there are situations when disobedience is warranted when this power is misused. Furthermore, when Paul refers to "governing authorities" (ἐξουσίαις ὑπερεχούσαις), he does not mean any authority; rather, ὑπερέχω can have a qualitative sense of superiority in quality (e.g., Dan 5:11; Sir 33:7 [LXX]; Phil 2:3; 3:8; 4:7). According to Porter, Paul expects Christians to obey only authorities who are qualitatively superior, that is, authorities who are just.[194]

Wright maintains that this passage is about establishing a community right under Caesar's nose in Rome that witnesses to the work of the one true God but avoids the view that loyalty to Jesus would mean civil disobedience or political revolution in a way that would just reshuffle the cards of political order. The church is not to become a Christian version of the Jewish "fourth philosophy."[195] Yet here is still an anti-imperial vision, as Wright sees Paul demoting the political authorities from divine powers to subordinate servants of God. The political authorities, much like Cyrus in Isaiah (Isa 45:1), have appointed tasks and bring a measure of God's order and justice to the world. So believers in the Messiah do not have a carte blanche to ignore governing authorities. The church lives under authority until Jesus abolishes all authorities hostile to himself.[196]

Dorothea H. Bertschmann tries to bring Rom 13:1-7 into dialogue with theologians Oliver O'Donovan and John Howard Yoder.[197] On Paul and empire in general (esp. the Christ-poem of Phil 2), Bertschmann contends that (1) Paul does not exploit any potential paths for directly or indirectly critiquing the idolatry of political rulers like the imperial cults; (2) Paul does not follow up the ethical potential for criticizing malevolent rulers; (3) Paul does not exploit any potential for challenging rulers on theocratic grounds;[198] and (4) Paul does not offer up any missional potential to integrate rulers into Christ's hierarchy. She argues, on Rom 13:1-7 in particular, that Paul is far from counterimperial because:

---

194. Porter, "Paul Confronts Caesar," 184-89; idem, "Romans 13:1-7 as Pauline Political Rhetoric," *FilNT* 3 (1990): 115-39.

195. Wright, "Romans," 10:716-20; idem, "Paul's Gospel and Caesar's Empire," 168.

196. Wright, "Romans," 10:716-23; idem, *Paul*, 78-79.

197. Bertschmann, *Bowing before Christ*.

198. Bertschmann, *Bowing before Christ*, 122-25, 173.

1. Paul never juxtaposes or contrasts Christ as ruler with present political rulers; that is, parallel language does not amount to polemic.
2. The church, although it lives in a sociopolitical sphere, does not seek to be politicized, since it is a community under the authority of Jesus.
3. The church respects political authorities as they mirror God's judging work and are deserving of support and respect.
4. Appropriation of Paul in a post-Christendom age means (a) learning to get beyond the dichotomy of political powers as either enemies or deputies of the church and (b) living in hope for Christ's eventual dominion and in the meantime supporting the rulers' attempts to promote human flourishing and to exercise a prophetic, pastoral, and polemic voice from the margins of society.[199]

The occasion calling for Paul to write Rom 13:1-7 is hard to discern because it was undoubtedly complex. My own view is that Rom 13:1-7 must be informed by four things.

First, Paul stands in the enduring Jewish tradition of seeing Gentile rulers and their kingdoms as divine servants.[200] In Israel's sacred traditions, God raises up rulers and tears them down in accordance with his sovereign plans. Josephus sums up this sentiment by saying, "No ruler attains his office save by the will of God."[201] This is precisely why obedience is entirely appropriate, even to Gentile rulers, on occasions.[202]

Second, we must remember that Paul's terse remarks about submission to authorities are saturated with God-language, with six references to θεός ("God") in the space of seven verses. For Paul there is no authority *except from God*; the powers are *appointed by God*; those who resist his appointed political authorities oppose the *authority of God*; political authorities preserving social order with the sword are in effect the *agents of God*; and political

199. Bertschmann, *Bowing before Christ,* 174-87.
200. 2 Sam 12:8; 2 Chr 20:6; Prov 8:15-16; Isa 45:1; Dan 2:21, 37-38; 4:17, 25, 31; 5:21; Sir 10:4; Wis 6:1-5; Ep. Arist. 219, 224; 1 En. 46.5; 2 Bar. 82.9; 4 Macc 12:11.
201. Josephus, *War* 2.140.
202. Loren Stuckenbruck ("A Place for Socio-political Oppressors at the End of History? Eschatological Perspectives from *1 Enoch,*" in *Reactions to Empire: Sacred Texts in Their Sociopolitical Contexts,* ed. J. A. Dunne and D. Batovici [WUNT 2.372; Tübingen: Mohr Siebeck, 2014], 21) gives a good example from Enochic literature: "The Enoch writers and those for whom they wrote were convinced that no matter how bad conditions become in the created world, God will have God's way and those regarded as agents of evil are eventually going to acknowledge and submit to it."

authorities are even *servants of God*. This is perhaps the closest we get to a "hidden transcript" because imperial authority is affirmed but at the same time subordinated by those who know the Jewish tradition about YHWH raising up and deposing Gentile rulers.[203] This is not a capitulation to pagan power but a fervent affirmation of divine authority over earthly powers, as inherited from the prophetic and apocalyptic tradition.[204]

Third, we have to read Rom 13:1-7 in light of Paul's apocalyptic narrative about the overthrow of all authorities at the return of Jesus and the certainty of a final judgment (see Rom 13:11-14; 16:20; 1 Cor 15:24-28; Col 2:15; 2 Thess 2:1-12). Paul elsewhere declares that the "powers," whether political or spiritual (the two were intertwined), have been disarmed and are impotent before Jesus' lordship (see Rom 8:38; 1 Cor 2:8; 15:25-26; Col 2:15).[205] Paul's remarks about obedience to governing authorities in Rom 13:1-7 are relativized by his subsequent exhortation in Rom 13:11-14. Paul urges his hearers/readers with "you know what time it is, how it is now the moment for you to wake from sleep" and "for salvation is nearer to us now than when we became believers; the night is far gone, the day is near," so that salvation is at least near and impending and will bring with it the judgment and dissolution of these very same authorities. Paul acquiesces to political submission for the sake of respecting God's appointed servants who genuinely benefit the city. However, he is certain that Rome is not the *Roma aeterna* ("eternal Rome") because "time is short" (1 Cor 7:29), the "day is near" (Rom 13:12), and all stand before the "judgment seat of Christ" (Rom 14:10).[206] As Harrison surmises, "The ruler's propaganda, with its claim about the 'eternal' rule of the imperial house over its subjects, embodied an idolatry of power that conflicted with Paul's proclamation of the reign of the crucified, risen and returning Son of God over his world. The 'symbolic universe' of the Julio-Claudian rulers stood at odds with the eschatological

203. Elliott, "Strategies of Resistance," 119-22; Harrison, *Paul and the Imperial Authorities*, 307-8.

204. Elliott, *Liberating Paul*, 224; Stegemann, "Coexistence and Transformation," 13-14; Tellbe, *Paul between Synagogue and State*, 200.

205. A problem I have with Kim's (*Christ and Caesar*, 67) critique of counterimperial readings of Paul is that he splits up political and spiritual powers, which is foreign to the biblical worldview.

206. See similarly Bryan, *Render to Caesar*, 81-82; White, "Anti-imperial Subtexts in Paul," 329-30; Bruce W. Winter, "Roman Law and Society in Romans 12–15," in *Rome in the Bible and the Early Church*, ed. P. Oakes (Carlisle, UK: Paternoster, 2002), 88-89.

denouement of world history, which, in Paul's view, culminated in the arrival of God's new creation upon Christ's return as Lord of all."[207]

Fourth, I hasten to add that Rom 13:1-7 is part of the complex process of negotiating the realities of living in an urban Greco-Roman context by a new "cult" that is migrating into a new territory, where it would not necessarily be warmly received. In Rome, Christians were, as Mike Duncan colorfully puts it, "capital O 'other' in every sense of the word."[208] Most Christians were noncitizen resident aliens, Eastern in origin, speaking Greek rather than Latin, and usually from the lower echelons of society; they looked different, spoke different, belonged to a cult or association that caused tumult within Jewish communities, and venerated as a divine king a man who was crucified by Rome and was supposed one day to return to conquer the world. The Christians were socially marginal, with several grounds for suspicion against them, and were therefore highly vulnerable. Courting controversy and pursuing active resistance would not be prudent advice for a group in this position. Praying for Rome's defeat or disempowerment while simultaneously trying to live at peace with one's Roman neighbors makes life a little complicated. The sociopolitical reality is such that it is never a total dualism of Christ versus Caesar, for resistance, acculturation, and survival are all simultaneously engaged.[209] Even with a disposition toward opposition, there are still "contingencies" that often need to be deployed in order to just get by,[210] much like how Tertullian said that Christians did not worship the gods or "offer sacrifices for the emperor"; but he could still declare that all men owed the emperor "their piety and religious devotion and loyalty."[211] Paul, like most Jews most of the time in the Roman world, hovered between assimilation and resistance.[212] The pragmatic reality is that Paul would not be comfortable singing *laudes imperii*, but neither was he likely to lead a mob charging up the Palatine Hill chanting *sic semper tyrannis*.

For a better word, Paul does not want Christians trying to effect a temporary revolution that effectively replaces one divinized dictator with another one, or believing that they transcend obligations to the state regarding either taxes or respect, or throwing their lot in with the increasingly violent anti-Roman sentiment

---

207. Harrison, *Paul and the Imperial Authorities*, 1.

208. Mike Duncan, *The History of Rome*, podcast, Episode 66, "666," 15:00-57 mins.

209. Hanges, "To Complicate Encounters," 29-31.

210. Galinsky, "The Cult of the Roman Emperor," 15.

211. Tertullian, *Apol.* 10.1; 36.2.

212. L. Michael White, "Capitalizing on the Imperial Cult: Some Jewish Perspectives," in *Rome and Religion: A Cross-Disciplinary Dialogue on the Imperial Cult*, ed. J. Brodd and J. L. Reed (Atlanta: SBL, 2011), 174.

festering in Palestine at the time. They are in a position of vulnerability as a sect or superstition without official recognition, hence they are liable to shame, suffering, sword, accusation, and persecution (Rom 5:3-5; 8:18, 31-39; 12:14, 17). The wise thing to do is, to use modern images, stay under the radar and keep one's head below the parapet. This should not be read as a watered-down compromise because, for those on the margins of the empire, survival is one of the best forms of defiance. So Paul wants believers to respect the authorities and do good because pagan authorities from Cyrus to Caesar serve an ordained role in God's purposes. They can do so because they know something that the Gentile rulers don't know, namely, that the rulers themselves are "servants" of the "only wise God" (Rom 13:4; 16:27), to whom they will be held to account when they stand before the judgment seat of Christ (Rom 2:16; 14:10); furthermore, vengeance belongs to God (Rom 12:19). In the fullness of time the Roman Empire will be removed and even crushed by the kingdom of Christ (Rom 13:11-12; 16:20). Therefore, as Martin Hengel concludes, "The significance of governmental authorities is limited and relativized. They are instituted by God and surely necessary, and salutary, but their days are numbered, their significance is only transitory."[213]

Romans 15

The climax to Romans arguably comes in Rom 15:5-13, with exhortations to unity in Messiah Jesus. Paul reiterates that the Gentiles join God's people only through Israel, not despite Israel (see Rom 1:16; 2:9-10; 3:1-2; 9:4-5; 11:1-31). The coming of Jesus confirms God's saving purposes to both Jews and Gentiles in unison. Thereafter, Paul inserts a catena of scriptural citations to reinforce an ethic of mutual inclusion, with the Gentiles glorifying and praising Israel's God by faith in Israel's Messiah (Ps 17:50; 2 Sam 22:50 [Rom 15:9]; Deut 32:45 [Rom 15:10]; Ps 117:1 [Rom 15:11]; and Isa 11:10 [Rom 15:12]).

The most pertinent element for our study is Rom 15:12, with the citation of Isa 11:10: "Isaiah says, 'The Root of Jesse will spring up, one who will arise to rule over the nations; in him the Gentiles will hope.'" "Root of Jesse" is a messianic designation for a royal eschatological deliverer, equivalent to "Root of David" (1QSb 5.26; 4QFlor 1.11; Pss. Sol. 17.21-46; Sir 47:22; Rev 5:5; 22:16). Paul taps into Israel's prophetic script that Israel's kingdom will rise from its humiliating subjugation under foreign powers like Rome, which will be achieved through Messiah Jesus. Jewett thinks that Paul eliminates the "toxic residues of chauvinism and imperialism from the context of Isaiah 11." The problem is

213. Martin Hengel, *Christ and Power* (Philadelphia: Fortress, 1977), 36.

that Paul's messianic discourse here mimics the imperial transcript, where the world is ruled by a Jewish monarch in an eschatological future.[214] Paul sets forth the rule of the Messiah over the nations as benign and beneficial, since Jesus is the object of the Gentiles' hope.[215] Jesus' reign is not a this-worldly militarism, but it certainly dethrones all powers and authorities hostile to God's kingdom, chiefly Satan (Rom 16:20), in a historical future.

If Jesus is the appointed ruler over the nations and the source of their hope, then he is precisely what many believed Rome's empire to be. The *Aeneid* asserts that Rome could achieve "sovereignty without limit." There was even a "gift of the nations" brought to Caesar.[216] Virgil used his poetry to teach that the Romans will "rule earth's peoples."[217] The universal reach of Rome's power in bringing other nations under its patronage is celebrated in the *Res Gestae*, with emphasis on the pacification of peoples, colonization of territories, and the extension of Rome's empire into northern Europe, Africa, and Asia.[218] Augustus even arranged for a statue of himself to be erected next to the speaker's rostrum, depicting him in the nude with his foot resting on a globe.[219] But this unchallengeable Roman power is challenged by this simple citation from Isa 11 concerning the Root of Jesse, who will regather the exiles from the "four quarters of the earth," and "Judah's enemies will be destroyed" (Isa 11:11-12). For Paul, this is a reality already in the messianic community, consisting of Jews and Gentiles praising God for his mercy demonstrated in the Messiah. Furthermore, Rom 1:3-4 and 15:12 indicate that Romans is constructed with a counterimperial bookend, so that it is the Son of David, not the Son of Augustus, who is the ruler of the nations.[220]

Conclusion

So where does that leave us? In general, I think Maier is right that Paul exhibits neither "relentless opposition to the Roman Empire" nor "a kind of spiritual quietism or political conservatism for the sake of larger theological

214. Ronald Charles, *Paul and the Politics of Diaspora* (Minneapolis: Fortress, 2014), 195-200.

215. Contra Jewett, *Romans*, 897.

216. Virgil, *Aeneid* 8.715-28.

217. Virgil, *Aeneid* 6.1151-52.

218. *Acts of Augustus* 26-33.

219. Jewett, *Romans*, 48.

220. Wright, *Paul*, 76; Tellbe, *Paul between Synagogue and State*, 202.

formulations"; he focuses more on a "negotiation of the cultural and social arrangements of his urban contexts to make his Gospel persuasive to his listeners."[221] Paul's letter to the Romans is not a political manifesto conceived for social protest or militant resistance. It is pastoral theology, albeit not a theology divorced from the sociopolitical realities of the Roman Mediterranean. Romans is Paul's argument for his trans-ethnic gospel, one that unites Jews, Romans, Greeks, and Barbarians under the lordship of Jesus Christ. Rehearsing this gospel to the Romans was part of his effort to prevent the Roman house churches from fracturing along halakic lines pertaining to how and whether one need observe the Jewish way of life. Yet the totalizing vision of Paul's gospel clearly competes with the Roman vision, with its preeminence of the emperor and the unchallenged hegemony of the empire over the eastern Mediterranean. The kingdom of Paul's Messiah did not constitute a military threat to the Roman Empire, however; it was a social threat by establishing alternative modes of patronage and devotion, as well as expressions of family and kinship that competed with existing hierarchies, and it regarded Rome's religious tradition as blasphemous and dehumanizing. Paul's theology could not be baptized into the Roman imperium, but Rome could genuinely face the threat of being Christianized if Paul's theopolitical vision, with all its subversive social tendencies, ever took root—which is precisely what it did! The result is that, as William Ramsay wrote, "A universal Paulinism and a universal Empire must either coalesce, or the one must destroy the other."[222] History has shown that this was indeed the case.

Our survey of Romans has demonstrated that Paul's gospel has a sociopolitical texture because Israel's religion was always sociopolitical. Paul clearly evokes and revises imperial concepts in his theological discourse. Paul was en-

---

221. Maier, *Picturing Paul in Empire*, 38. Similarly for Strecker ("Taktiken der Aneignung," 161): "Paulus war, wie hier zu zeigen versucht wurde, kein polemischer Opponent des Imperium Romanum und der Macht der Caesaren, sondern ein Taktiker, in dessen komplexer Theologie sich viele messianische Verwertungen römisch-imperialer Machtstrukturen ausmachen lassen . . . Sie bewegt sich mithin in einer nur schwer fixierbaren Weise zwischen Widerstand und Anpassung" ("Paul was not a polemical opponent of the Roman Empire and the power of the Caesars, but a tactician with a complex theology that made a deliberate messianic exploitation of Roman imperial power structures . . . [a theology that] moves in a difficult and fixed manner between resistance and negotiation"). In many ways Wright (*Paul and the Faithfulness of God*, 1298-99) moves in a similar direction, with Paul being neither "pro-Roman" nor "anti-Roman."

222. William Ramsay, *The Cities of St. Paul: Their Influence on His Life and Thought* (Grand Rapids, MI: Baker, 1979), 70. See further Barclay, *Pauline Churches*, 361-62, on the radical and totalizing ideology that made Christianity a threat to the Roman Empire.

gaging in something analogous to what postcolonial interpreters have termed "mimicry," whereby a suppressed minority imitates the rhetoric and claims of the dominating power in order to define themselves apart from it and to mark themselves in opposition to it.[223] To be sure, Paul's principal source for his theologizing is the Septuagint and Christian traditions, yet he simultaneously echoes themes, language, and symbols ubiquitous in the Roman imperial context.

Paul's εὐαγγέλιον is the royal announcement that God's δικαιοσύνη avails for believing Jews and Greeks (Rom 1:2-4, 16-17), but this is bad news for the powers because of the concurrent revelation of God's wrath against idolatry and wickedness (Rom 1:18-23). In addition, the violence of Roman military power and the foolishness of Roman religion will all collapse under the weight of the parousia of Christ (Rom 13:11-14; 16:20) because Rome and Rome's rulers will face recompense for their wickedness at the divine tribunal (Rom 3:24-26; 5:1; 8:1; 10:9-11).[224] In addition, we see that Romans is bracketed by reference to the reign of Jesus the Messiah and Lord, who rules over the nations and brings them to obedience to Israel's God (Rom 1:1-5; 15:12; 16:26). What we find here is, as Wright says, "God's gospel; God's son; supreme power; worldwide allegiance from all nations; the ancient Israelite dream of all nations coming to worship the one God, and the more focused ancient vision of a coming king from David's line who would 'rise up to rule the nations.'"[225] Paul's letter to the Romans is thus delivered to the heart of the empire with a bold thesis that there is only one true God, the Father, and one true Lord, Jesus Christ.[226]

Anyone vaguely familiar with the Roman imperium could see Paul articulating the vision of an alternative empire. It is not simply the parallel terminology that Paul uses like κύριος or εὐαγγέλιον, but the apocalyptic and messianic narrative that such language is couched in that makes it tacitly counterimperial. There is room for only one Lord to subjugate the nations at any one time.[227] Should a Roman official have read Paul's letter to the Romans, it

---

223. See Catherine Keller, Michael Nausner, and Mayra Rivera, eds., *Postcolonial Theologies: Divinity and Empire* (St. Louis: Chalice, 2004); Jeremy Punt, *Postcolonial Biblical Interpretation: Reframing Paul* (Leiden: Brill, 2015), 40-41.

224. Stegemann, "Coexistence and Transformation," 8.

225. Wright, *Paul and the Faithfulness of God*, 1300-1301.

226. Porter, "Paul Confronts Caesar," 184.

227. See similarly Wright, *Paul*, 69, and idem, *Paul and the Faithfulness of God*, 1293 (about the narrative in Philippians 2); and Heilig, *Hidden Transcripts?*, 103, 136, 154 (on the importance of christological discourse and apocalyptic narratives that challenge the Roman perspective on power). Note the conclusion of Tellbe (*Paul between Synagogue and State*, 205-6 and 291):

would have appeared highly anomalous. Here was a letter heralding a dead Judean man as a potential rival, in some sense, to Caesar. The letter would have appeared to be the ravings of a fanatical Eastern superstition, religiously malicious at best, and politically seditious at worst.[228]

"It should, however, be pointed out here that in highlighting particular theological terms in Romans as having their counterpart in Roman imperial ideology, it is not the terms themselves that contrast or oppose this ideology. *It is only when these terms are taken together with the over-arching theme of the universal and political claims of the justice of God and the lordship of Christ that the contrast with Roman imperial ideology is strongly implied*" (italics original).

228. See Novenson ("What the Apostles Did Not See," 70), who notes that only rarely were Christ-believers brought to the attention of magistrates. However, "when they [Christ-believers] caught the attention of Roman magistrates, they looked like and were treated like treasonous Jews."

Bibliography

Translation of ancient sources come from the pertinent volumes of the Loeb Classical Library, except Philo and the *Acts of Augustus*, which are the author's own, and Tertullian, which comes from the *Ante-Nicene Fathers*.

Abernethy, Andrew T., et al., eds. *Isaiah and Imperial Context: The Book of Isaiah in the Times of Empire*. Eugene, OR: Pickwick, 2013.

Adams, Edward. "Paul's Story of God and Creation: The Story of How God Fulfills His Purpose in Creation." In *Narrative Dynamics in Paul: An Assessment*, edited by B. W. Longenecker, pp. 19-43. Louisville: Westminster John Knox, 2002.

Allison, Dale C. *Resurrecting Jesus*. London: T&T Clark, 2005.

Ando, Clifford. *Imperial Ideology and Provincial Loyalty in the Roman Empire*. Berkley: University of California Press, 2000.

Bachmann, Michael. *Anti-Judaism in Galatians? Exegetical Studies on a Polemical Letter and on Paul's Theology*. Translated by R. L. Brawley. Grand Rapids, MI: Eerdmans, 2008.

Bachmann, Michael, and Johannes Woyke, eds. *Lutherische und neue Paulusperspektive: Beiträge zu einem Schlüsselproblem der gegenwärtigen exegetischen Diskussion*. WUNT 182. Tübingen: Mohr Siebeck, 2005.

Baker, Cynthia. "A 'Jew' by Any Other Name?" *JAJ* 2 (2011): 153-80.

Balla, Peter. *The Child-Parent Relationship in the New Testament and Its Environment*. WUNT 155. Tübingen: Mohr Siebeck, 2003.

Barclay, John M. G. *Obeying the Truth: A Study of Paul's Ethics in Galatians*. Edinburgh: T&T Clark, 1988.

———. "Paul among Diaspora Jews: Anomaly or Apostate?" *JSNT* 60 (1995): 89-120.

———. *Jews in the Mediterranean Diaspora: From Alexander to Trajan (323 BCE–117 CE)*. Berkeley: University of California Press, 1996.

———. "Paul's Story: Theology as Testimony." In *Narrative Dynamics in Paul: A Critical*

Assessment, edited by B. W. Longenecker, pp. 133-56. Louisville: Westminster John Knox, 2002.

———. "Who Was Considered an Apostate in the Jewish Diaspora?" In *Pauline Churches and Diaspora* Jews, pp. 141-55. WUNT 275. Tübingen: Mohr Siebeck, 2011.

Barclay, John M. G., and Simon J. Gathercole, eds. *Divine and Human Agency in Paul and His Cultural Environment*. LNTS 335. London: T&T Clark, 2007.

Barnett, Paul. *Jesus and the Rise of Early Christianity: A History of New Testament Times*. Downers Grove, IL: InterVarsity, 1999.

Barrett, C. K. *A Critical and Exegetical Commentary on the Book of Acts*. ICC. 2 vols. Edinburgh: T&T Clark, 1994-98.

———. "Paul: Councils and Controversies." In *Conflicts and Challenges in Early Christianity*, edited by D. A. Hagner, pp. 42-74. Harrisburg, PA: Trinity Press International, 1999.

Barth, Karl. *Church Dogmatics*. 4 vols. Edited by Geoffrey W. Bromiley and T. F. Torrance. Translated by Geoffrey W. Bromiley et al. Edinburgh: T&T Clark, 1956-75.

Barth, Markus. "Jews and Gentiles: The Social Character of Justification in Paul." *JES* 5 (1968): 241-67.

———. "Der gute Jude Paulus." In *Richte unsere Füsse auf den Weg des Friedens*, edited by A. Baudis, D. Clausert, V. Schliski, and B. Wegener, pp. 107-37. Munich: Christian Kaiser, 1979.

Bauckham, Richard. "Barnabas in Galatians." *JSNT* 2 (1979): 61-70.

———. "James and the Jerusalem Church." In *The Book of Acts in Its Palestinian Setting*, edited by R. Bauckham, pp. 415-80. Grand Rapids, MI: Eerdmans, 1995.

———. "James and the Gentiles (Acts 15.13-21)." In *History, Literature and Society in the Book of Acts*, edited by B. Witherington, pp. 154-84. Cambridge: Cambridge University Press, 1996.

———. "Apocalypses." In *Justification and Variegated Nomism*. Vol. 1, *The Complexities of Second Temple Judaism*, edited by D. A. Carson, P. T. O'Brien, and M. A. Seifrid, pp. 135-87. Grand Rapids, MI: Baker Academic, 2001.

———. "James, Peter and the Gentiles." In *The Missions of James, Peter and Paul: Tensions in Early Christianity*, edited by B. Chilton and C. Evans, pp. 91-142. Leiden: Brill, 2004.

Beale, Gregory K. "Peace and Mercy upon the Israel of God: The Old Testament Background to Galatians 6, 16b." *Bib* 80 (1999): 204-23.

Beker, J. C. *Paul the Apostle: The Triumph of God in Life and Thought*. Philadelphia: Fortress, 1980.

———. *Paul's Apocalyptic Gospel: The Coming Triumph of God*. Philadelphia: Fortress, 1982.

———. *The Triumph of God: The Essence of Paul's Thought*. Minneapolis: Fortress, 1990.

Bell, Richard H. *Provoked to Jealousy: The Origin and Purpose of the Jealousy Motif in Romans 9–11*. WUNT 2.63. Tübingen: Mohr Siebeck, 1994.

———. *The Irrevocable Call of God*. WUNT 184. Tübingen: Mohr Siebeck, 2005.

Belleville, Linda L. "'Under Law': Structural Analysis and the Pauline Concept of Law in Galatians 3.21–4.11." *JSNT* 26 (1986): 53-78.

Benjamin, Anna, and Antony E. Raubitschek. "Arae Augusti." *Hesperia* 28 (1959): 65-85.

Bernett, Monika. "Der Kaiserkult in Judäa unter herodischer und römischer Herschaft: Zu Herausbildung und Herausfoderung neuer Konzepte Jüdischer Herrschaftslegitimation." In *Jewish Identity in the Greco-Roman World*, edited by J. Frey, D. R. Schwartz, and S. Gripentrog, pp. 219-51. AJEC 711. Leiden: Brill, 2007.

Bernheim, Pierre-Antoine. *James, Brother of Jesus.* Translated by J. Bowden. London: SCM, 1997.

Bertschmann, Dorothea H. *Bowing before Christ—Nodding to the State? Reading Paul Politically with Oliver O'Donovan and John Howard Yoder.* LNTS 502. London: T&T Clark, 2014.

Betz, Hans Dieter. *Galatians.* Hermeneia. Philadelphia: Fortress, 1979.

Birnbaum, Ellen. *The Place of Judaism in Philo's Thought: Israel, Jews, and Proselytes.* Providence, RI: Brown University Press, 1996.

Bird, Michael F. "'Light to the Nations' (Isaiah 42:6 and 49:6): Intertextuality and Mission Theology in the Early Church." *RTR* 65 (2006): 122-31.

———. *The Saving Righteousness of God: Studies on Paul, Justification, and the New Perspective.* PBM. Milton Keynes, UK: Paternoster, 2006.

———. *Jesus and the Origins of the Gentile Mission.* LNTS 331. London: T&T Clark, 2007.

———. "Jesus as Law-Breaker." In *Who Do My Opponents Say That I Am? An Investigation of the Accusations against the Historical Jesus*, edited by S. McKnight and J. B. Modica, pp. 3-26. LNTS 358. London: T&T Clark, 2008.

———. *Are You the One Who Is to Come? The Historical Jesus and the Messianic Question.* Grand Rapids, MI: Baker, 2009.

———. *Colossians and Philemon.* NCCS. Eugene, OR: Wipf & Stock, 2009.

———. *Crossing Over Sea and Land: Jewish Missionary Activity in the Second Temple Period.* Peabody, MA: Hendrickson, 2009.

———. "What if Martin Luther Had Read the Dead Sea Scrolls? Historical Particularity and Theological Interpretation in Pauline Theology: Galatians as a Test Case." *JTI* 3 (2009): 107-25.

———. "Progressive Reformed View." In *Justification: Five Views*, edited by J. K. Beilby and P. R. Eddy, pp. 131-57. Downers Grove, IL: IVP Academic, 2011.

———. "The Incident at Antioch (Gal. 2.11-14): The Beginnings of Paulinism." In *Earliest Christian History*, edited by M. F. Bird and J. Maston, pp. 329-61. WUNT 2.320. Tübingen: Mohr Siebeck, 2012.

———. *Jesus Is the Christ: The Messianic Testimony of the Gospels.* Carlisle, UK: Paternoster, 2012.

———. "Letter to the Romans." In *All Things to All Cultures: Paul among Jews, Greeks and Romans*, edited by M. Harding and A. Knobbs, pp. 177-204. Grand Rapids, MI: Eerdmans, 2012.

———. "Salvation in Paul's Judaism." In *Paul and Judaism: Crosscurrents in Pauline Ex-*

egesis and the Study of Jewish-Christian Relations, edited by R. Bieringer and D. Pollefeyt, pp. 15-40. LNTS 463. London: T&T Clark, 2012.

———. "'One Who Will Arise to Rule over the Nations': Paul's Letter to the Romans and the Roman Empire." In *Jesus Is Lord, Caesar Is Not: Evaluating Empire in New Testament Studies*, edited by S. McKnight and J. B. Modica, pp. 146-65. Downers Grove, IL: IVP Academic, 2013.

Bird, Michael F., ed. *The Apostle Paul: Four Views*. Grand Rapids, MI: Zondervan, 2012.

Bird, Michael F., C. Heilig, and J. T. Hewitt, eds. *God and the Faithfulness of Paul*. WUNT 2.320. Tübingen: Mohr Siebeck, 2016.

Bird, Michael F., and Preston Sprinkle. "Jewish Interpretation of Paul in the Last Thirty Years." *CBR* 6 (2008): 355-76.

Bird, Michael F., and Preston M. Sprinkle, eds. *The Faith of Jesus Christ: Exegetical, Biblical, and Theological Studies*. Milton Keynes, UK: Paternoster, 2009.

Blaschke, Andreas. *Beschneidung: Zeugnisse der Bible und verwandter Text*. TANZ 28. Tübingen: Francke, 1998.

Blocher, Henri. "*Agnus Victor*: The Atonement as Victory and Vicarious Punishment." In *What Does It Mean to Be Saved?* edited by J. G. Stackhouse, pp. 67-91. Grand Rapids, MI: Baker Academic, 2002.

Blomenfeld, Bruno. *The Political Paul: Justice, Democracy and Kingship in a Hellenistic Framework*. JSNTSup 210. London: T&T Clark, 2003.

Boccaccini, Gabriele. *Roots of Rabbinic Judaism: An Intellectual History, from Ezekiel to Daniel*. Grand Rapids, MI: Eerdmans, 2002.

———. "Inner-Jewish Debate on the Tension between Divine and Human Agency in Second Temple Judaism." In *Divine and Human Agency in Paul and His Cultural Development*, edited by J. M. G. Barclay and S. J. Gathercole, pp. 9-26. London: T&T Clark, 2007.

Bockmuehl, Markus. *Jewish Law in Gentile Churches: Halakhah and the Beginning of Christian Public Ethics*. Grand Rapids, MI: Baker, 2000.

———. "1 Thessalonians 2:14-16 and the Church in Jerusalem." *TynB* 52 (2001): 1-31.

Boda, Mark J. "Walking in the Light of Yahweh: Zion and the Empire." In *Empire in the New Testament*, edited by S. E. Porter and C. L. Westfall, pp. 54-89. Eugene, OR: Cascade, 2011.

Boer, Martinus C. de. "Paul and Apocalyptic Eschatology." In *The Origins of Apocalypticism in Judaism and Christianity*, edited by J. J. Collins, pp. 345-83. New York: T&T Clark, 1998.

———. "Paul, Theologian of God's Apocalypse." *Int* 56 (2002): 21-33.

———. "Paul and Jewish Apocalyptic Eschatology." In *Apocalyptic and the New Testament: Essays in Honor of J. Louis Martyn*, edited by J. Marcus and M. L. Soards, pp. 169-90. JSNTSup 24. Sheffield: Sheffield Academic, 2003.

———. "Paul's Use and Interpretation of a Justification Tradition in Galatians 2.15-21." *JSNT* 28 (2005): 189-216.

———. *Galatians: A Commentary*. NTL. Louisville: Westminster John Knox, 2011.

———. "N. T. Wright's Great Story and Its Relationship to Paul's Gospel." *JSPL* 4 (2014): 49-57.

Bornkamm, Günther. *Paul.* Translated by D. M. G. Stalker. New York: Harper & Row, 1971.

Botha, Jan. *Subject to Whose Authority? Multiple Readings of Romans 13.* Atlanta: Scholars, 1994.

Botha, Peter J. J. "Assessing Representations of the Imperial Cult in New Testament Studies." *VerbEccl* 25 (2004): 14-25.

Bousset, Wilhelm. *Kyrios Christos: A History of the Belief in Christ from the Beginnings of Christianity to Irenaeus.* Translated by J. E. Steely. Edited by L. Hurtado. Waco, TX: Baylor University Press, 2013.

Boyarin, Daniel. *A Radical Jew: Paul and the Politics of Identity.* Berkeley: University of California Press, 1994.

Braund, David C. *Augustus to Nero: A Sourcebook on Romans History, 31 BC–AD 68.* London: Crook Helm, 1985.

Brown, John Pairman. "Divine Kingship, Civic Institutions, Imperial Rule." In *Israel and Hellas,* 2:81-118. 2 vols. BZAW 231. Berlin: Walter de Gruyter, 1995.

Bruce, F. F. *The Acts of the Apostles: The Greek Text with Introduction and Commentary.* Grand Rapids, MI: Eerdmans, 1951.

———. *Paul: Apostle of the Free Spirit.* Carlisle, UK: Paternoster, 1980.

———. *The Epistle to the Galatians.* NIGTC. Grand Rapids, MI: Eerdmans, 1982.

———. *Romans.* TNTC. Rev. ed. Leicester, UK: InterVarsity, 1985.

Bryan, Christopher. *Render to Caesar: Jesus, the Early Church, and the Roman Superpower.* New York: Oxford University Press, 2005.

Buell, Denise Kimber. *Why This New Race: Ethnic Reasoning in Early Christianity.* New York: Columbia University Press, 2005.

Bultmann, Rudolf. *Primitive Christianity in Its Contemporary Setting.* Translated by R. H. Fuller. London: Thames & Hudson, 1956.

Burk, Denny. "Is Paul's Gospel Counterimperial? Evaluating the Prospects of the 'Fresh Perspective' for Evangelical Theology." *JETS* 51 (2008): 309-37.

Byrne, Brendan. "Interpreting Romans: The New Perspective and Beyond." *Int* 58 (2004): 241-52.

Campbell, Constantine R. *Verbal Aspect and Non-indicative Verbs: Further Soundings in the Greek of the New Testament.* SBG. New York: Peter Lang, 2008.

Campbell, Douglas A. *The Quest for Paul's Gospel: A Suggested Strategy.* London: T&T Clark, 2005.

———. *The Deliverance of God: An Apocalyptic Rereading of Justification in Paul.* Grand Rapids, MI: Eerdmans, 2009.

———. "Christ and the Church in Paul: A 'Post–New Perspective' Account." In *The Apostle Paul: Four Views,* edited by M. F. Bird, pp. 113-43. Grand Rapids, MI: Zondervan, 2012.

Campbell, William S. "Perceptions of Compatibility Between Christianity and Judaism in Pauline Interpretation." *BI* 13 (2005): 298-316.

———. *Paul and the Creation of Christian Identity*. London: T&T Clark, 2006.

———. "Religion, Identity and Ethnicity: The Contribution of Paul the Apostle." *Journal of Beliefs and Values* 29 (2008): 139-50.

Caneday, Ardel. "The Faithfulness of Jesus Christ as a Theme in Paul's Theology in Galatians." In *The Faith of Jesus Christ: Exegetical, Biblical, and Theological Studies*, edited by M. F. Bird and P. M. Sprinkle, pp. 185-205. Milton Keynes, UK: Paternoster, 2009.

Carlson, Stephen C. *The Text of Galatians*. WUNT 2.385. Tübingen: Mohr Siebeck, 2015.

Carson, D. A. "Summaries and Conclusions." In *Justification and Variegated Nomism.* Vol. 1, *The Complexities of Second Temple Judaism*, edited by D. A. Carson, P. T. O'Brien, and M. A. Seifrid, pp. 543-48. Grand Rapids, MI: Baker Academic, 2001.

———. "Mystery and Fulfillment: Toward a More Comprehensive Paradigm of Paul's Understanding of the Old and the New." In *Justification and Variegated Nomism.* Vol. 2, *The Paradoxes of Paul*, edited by D. A. Carson, P. T. O'Brien, and M. A. Seifrid, pp. 393-436. Grand Rapids, MI: Baker Academic, 2004.

———. "Mirror-Reading with Paul and against Paul: Galatians 2:11-14 as a Test Case." In *Studies in the Pauline Epistles*, edited by M. S. Harmon and J. E. Smith, pp. 99-112. Grand Rapids, MI: Zondervan, 2014.

Carson, D. A., Peter T. O'Brien, and Mark A. Seifrid, eds. *Justification and Variegated Nomism.* Vol. 1, *The Complexities of Second Temple Judaism*. Grand Rapids, MI: Baker Academic, 2001.

———. *Justification and Variegated Nomism.* Vol. 2, *The Paradoxes of Paul*. Grand Rapids, MI: Baker Academic, 2004.

Carter, T. L. *Paul and the Power of Sin: Redefining "Beyond the Pale."* SNTSMS 115. Cambridge: Cambridge University Press, 2002.

Carter, Warren. *The Roman Empire and the New Testament: An Essential Guide*. Nashville: Abingdon, 2006.

———. "Paul and the Roman Empire: Recent Perspectives." In *Paul Unbound: Other Perspectives on the Apostle*, edited by M. D. Given, pp. 7-26. Peabody, MA: Hendrickson, 2010.

Cassidy, Richard J. *Christians and Roman Rule in the New Testament: New Perspectives.* New York: Crossroad, 2001.

Chan, Mark L. Y. *Christology from within and Ahead: Hermeneutics, Contingency, and the Quest for Transcontextual Criteria in Christology*. Leiden: Brill, 2001.

Charles, Ronald. *Paul and the Politics of Diaspora*. Minneapolis: Fortress, 2014.

Chilton, Bruce D. "The Brother of Jesus and the Interpretation of Scripture." In *The Use of Sacred Books in the Ancient World*, edited by L.V. Rutgers, P. W. van der Horst, H. W. Havelaar, and L. Teugels, pp. 29-48. CBET 22. Leuven: Peeters, 1998.

Ciampa, Roy E., and Brian S. Rosner. *The First Letter to the Corinthians*. PNTC. Grand Rapids, MI: Eerdmans, 2010.

Clark, Gillian. "Let Every Soul Be Subject: The Fathers and the Empire." In *Images of Empire*, edited by L. Alexander, pp. 251-75. JSOTSup 122. Sheffield: JSOT Press, 1991.

Cohen, Shaye J. D. *The Beginnings of Jewishness*. Berkeley: University of California Press, 1999.

———. *Why Aren't Jewish Women Circumcised: Gender and Covenant in Judaism*. Berkeley: University of California Press, 2005.

Cook, John Granger. *Roman Attitudes toward the Christians*. WUNT 261. Tübingen: Mohr Siebeck, 2010.

Cosgrove, Charles. *The Cross and the Spirit: A Study in the Argument and Theology of Galatians*. Macon, GA: Mercer University Press, 1988.

Cosgrove, Charles, Herold Weiss, and Khiok-Khng Yeo. *Cross-Cultural Paul: Journeys to Others, Journeys to Ourselves*. Grand Rapids, MI: Eerdmans, 2005.

Cousar, Charles. "Continuity and Discontinuity: Reflections on Romans 5–8 (in Conversation with Frank Thielman)." In *Pauline Theology*. Vol. 3, *Romans*, edited by D. M. Hay and E. E. Johnson, pp. 196-210. Minneapolis: Fortress, 1995.

Cranfield, C. E. B. *Epistle to the Romans*. 2 vols. ICC. Edinburgh: T&T Clark, 1975-79.

Crossan, John Dominic, and Jonathan L. Reed. *Excavating Jesus: Beneath the Stones, behind the Texts*. San Francisco: HarperSanFrancisco, 2001.

———. *In Search of Paul: How Jesus's Apostle Opposed Rome's Empire with God's Kingdom*. San Francisco: HarperSanFrancisco, 2004.

Crossley, James G. *Why Christianity Happened: A Sociohistorical Account of Christian Origins (26-50 CE)*. Louisville: Westminster John Knox, 2006.

Cummins, Stephen A. *Paul and the Crucified Christ in Antioch: Maccabean Martyrdom and Galatians 1 and 2*. SNTSMS 114. Cambridge: Cambridge University Press, 2007.

Dahl, N. A. "The Doctrine of Justification: Its Social Function and Implications." In *Studies in Paul*, pp. 95-120. Minneapolis: Augsburg, 1977.

———. "The One God of Jews and Gentiles (Rom. 3:29-30)." In *Studies in Paul*, pp. 178-91. Minneapolis: Augsburg, 1977.

Das, A. Andrew. *Paul and the Jews*. LPS. Peabody, MA: Hendrickson, 2003.

———. *Paul, the Law, and the Covenant*. Peabody, MA: Hendrickson, 2004.

———. "Paul and the Law: Pressure Points in the Debate." In *Paul Unbound: Other Perspectives on the Apostle*, edited by M. D. Given, pp. 99-116. Peabody, MA: Hendrickson, 2010.

Davies, W. D. *Torah in the Messianic Age and/or the Age to Come*. Philadelphia: SBL, 1952.

———. *Paul and Rabbinic Judaism: Some Rabbinic Elements in Paul's Theology*. London: SPCK, 1955.

———. "Paul: From the Jewish Point of View." In *The Cambridge History of Judaism*. Vol. 3, *The Early Roman Period*, edited by W. Horbury, W. D. Davies, and J. Sturdy, pp. 678-730. Cambridge: Cambridge University Press, 1999.

Davis Bledsoe, Amanda M. "Attitudes towards Seleucid Imperial Hegemony in the Book of Daniel." In *Reactions to Empire: Sacred Texts in Their Socio-Political Contexts*, edited by J. A. Dunne and D. Batovici, pp. 23-40. WUNT 2.372. Tübingen: Mohr Siebeck, 2014.

Deines, Roland. "The Pharisees between 'Judaisms' and 'Common Judaism.'" In *Justification and Variegated Nomism*. Vol. 1, *The Complexities of Second Temple Judaism*, edited by D. A. Carson, P. T. O'Brien, and M. A. Seifrid, pp. 443-504. Grand Rapids, MI: Baker Academic, 2001.

Deissmann, Adolf. *Light from the Ancient East: The New Testament Illustrated by Recently Discovered Texts of the Graeco-Roman World*. Translated by L. R. M. Strachan. 2nd ed. London: Hodder & Stoughton, 1927.

deSilva, David A. *Transformation: The Heart of Paul's Gospel*. Bellingham, WA: Lexham, 2014.

Diehl, Judith A. "Empires and Epistles: Anti-Roman Rhetoric in the New Testament Epistles." *CBR* 10 (2012): 217-52.

———. "Anti-imperial Rhetoric in the New Testament." In *Jesus Is Lord, Caesar Is Not: Evaluating Empire in New Testament Studies*, edited by S. McKnight and J. B. Modica, pp. 38-81. Downers Grove, IL: IVP Academic, 2013.

Dodd, C. H. *The Bible Today*. Cambridge: Cambridge University Press, 1946.

Donaldson, Terence L. "The 'Curse of the Law' and the Inclusion of the Gentiles: Galatians 3.13-14." *NTS* 32 (1986): 94-112.

———. "Proselytes or 'Righteous Gentiles'? The Status of Gentiles in Eschatological Pilgrimage Patterns of Thought." *JSP* 7 (1990): 3-27.

———. *Paul and the Gentiles: Remapping the Apostle's Convictional World*. Minneapolis: Fortress, 1997.

———. "Jewish Christianity, Israel's Stumbling and the *Sonderweg* Reading of Paul." *JSNT* 29 (2006): 27-54.

———. *Judaism and the Gentiles: Jewish Patterns of Universalism (to 135 CE)*. Waco, TX: Baylor University Press, 2007.

———. *Jews and Anti-Judaism in the New Testament: Decision Points and Divergent Interpretations*. London: SPCK, 2010.

———. "Paul within Judaism: A Critical Evaluation from a 'New Perspective' Perspective." In *Paul within Judaism: Restoring the First-Century Context to the Apostle*, edited by M. Nanos and M. Zetterholm, pp. 277-302. Minneapolis: Fortress, 2015.

Dowling, Melissa B. *Clemency and Cruelty in the Roman World*. Ann Arbor: University of Michigan Press, 2006.

Driel, Edwin Christian van. "Christ in Paul's Narrative: Salvation History, Apocalyptic Invasion, and Supralapsarian Theology." In *Galatians and Christian Theology*, edited by M. W. Elliott, S. J. Hafemann, N. T. Wright, and J. Frederick, pp. 230-38. Grand Rapids, MI: Baker Academic, 2014.

———. "Climax of the Covenant vs Apocalyptic Invasion: A Theological Analysis of a Contemporary Debate in Pauline Exegesis." *IJST* 17 (2015): 6-25.

Dunn, James D. G. "The Incident at Antioch (Gal. 2:11-18)." *JSNT* 18 (1983): 3-57.

———. *Romans 1–8*. WBC. Dallas, TX: Word, 1988.

―――――. *Jesus, Paul and the Law: Studies in Mark and Galatians*. London: SPCK, 1990.

―――――. *The Parting of the Ways: Between Christianity and Judaism and Their Significance for the Character of Christianity*. London: SCM, 1991.

―――――. *The Epistle to the Galatians*. BNTC. Peabody, MA: Hendrickson, 1993.

―――――. "Paul: Apostate or Apostle of Israel." *ZNW* 89 (1998): 256-71.

―――――. *The Theology of Paul the Apostle*. Edinburgh: T&T Clark, 1998.

―――――. "Who Did Paul Think He Was? A Study of Jewish Christian Identity." *NTS* 45 (1999): 174-93.

―――――. *The New Perspective on Paul*. 2nd ed. Grand Rapids, MI: Eerdmans, 2007.

―――――. "ΕΚ ΠΙΣΤΕΩΣ: A Key to the Meaning of ΠΙΣΤΙΣ ΧΡΙΣΤΟΥ." In *The Word Leaps the Gap*, edited by J. R. Wagner, C. K. Rowe, and A. K. Grieb, pp. 351-66. Grand Rapids, MI: Eerdmans, 2008.

―――――. "How New Was Paul's Gospel? The Problem of Continuity and Discontinuity." In *Gospel in Paul: Studies on Corinthians, Galatians, and Romans*, edited by L. A. Jervis and P. Richardson, pp. 367-88. JSNTSup. Sheffield: Sheffield Academic, 1994. Reprinted in *The New Perspective on Paul*, pp. 247-64. Rev. ed. Grand Rapids, MI: Eerdmans, 2008.

―――――. *Beginning from Jerusalem*. CITM 2. Grand Rapids, MI: Eerdmans, 2009.

Dunne, John Anthony. "Suffering and Covenantal Hope in Galatians: A Critique of the 'Apocalyptic Reading' and Its Proponents." *SJT* 68 (2015): 1-14.

Eastman, Susan G. "Israel and the Mercy of God: A Re-reading of Galatians 6.16 and Romans 9–11." *NTS* 56 (2010): 367-95.

Eck, Werner, ed. *Judäa—Syria Palästina: Ein Euseinandersetzung ein Provinz mit römischer Politik und Kultur*. TSAJ 340. Tübingen: Mohr Siebeck, 2014.

Ehrensperger, Kathy. *That We May Be Mutually Encouraged: Feminism and the New Perspective in Pauline Studies*. London: T&T Clark, 2004.

Eisenbaum, Pamela M. "Is Paul the Father of Misogyny and Antisemitism?" *Crosscurrents* 50, no. 4 (2000-2001): 506-24.

―――――. "Following in the Footnotes of the Apostle Paul." In *Identity and the Politics of Scholarship in the Study of Religion*, edited by S. Davaney and J. Cabezon, pp. 77-97. New York: Routledge, 2004.

―――――. "A Remedy for Having Been Born of Woman: Jesus, Gentiles, and Genealogy in Romans." *JBL* 123 (2004): 671-702.

―――――. "Paul, Polemics, and the Problem of Essentialism." *BI* 13 (2005): 224-38.

―――――. *Paul Was Not a Christian: The Original Message of a Misunderstood Apostle*. New York: HarperCollins, 2009.

Elliott, John H. "Jesus the Israelite Was Neither a 'Jew' Nor a 'Christian': On Correcting Misleading Nomenclature." *JSHJ* 5 (2007): 119-54.

Elliott, Mark Adam. *The Survivors of Israel: A Reconsideration of the Theology of Pre-Christian Judaism*. Grand Rapids, MI: Eerdmans, 2000.

Elliott, Neil. *Liberating Paul: The Justice of God and the Politics of the Apostle*. Sheffield: Sheffield Academic, 1995.

————. "Romans 13:1-7 in the Context of Imperial Propaganda." In *Paul and Empire: Religion and Power in Roman Imperial Society*, edited by R. A. Horsley, pp. 184-204. Harrisburg, PA: Trinity Press International, 1997.

————. *Liberating Paul: The Justice of God and the Politics of the Apostle*. 2nd ed. Minneapolis: Fortress, 2006.

————. "The Letter to the Romans." In *A Postcolonial Commentary on the New Testament Writings*, edited by F. F. Segovia and R. S. Sugirtharajah, pp. 194-219. New York: T&T Clark, 2007.

————. *The Arrogance of Nations: Reading Romans in the Shadow of Empire*. Minneapolis: Fortress, 2008.

————. "'Blasphemed among the Nations': Pursuing an Anti-imperial 'Intertextuality' in Romans." In *As It is Written: Studying Paul's Use of Scripture*, edited by S. E. Porter and C. D. Stanley, pp. 213-33. SBLSS 50. Leiden: Brill, 2008.

————. "Paul's Political Christology: Samples from Romans." In *Reading Paul in Context: Explorations in Identity Formation*, edited by K. Ehrensperger and J. B. Tucker, pp. 39-50. LNTS 428. London: T&T Clark, 2010.

Engberg-Pedersen, Troels, ed. *Paul beyond the Judaism/Hellenism Divide*. Louisville: Westminster John Knox, 2001.

Enns, Peter. "Expansions of Scripture." In *Justification and Variegated Nomism*. Vol. 1, *The Complexities of Second Temple Judaism*, edited by D. A. Carson, P. T. O'Brien, and M. A. Seifrid, pp. 73-98. Grand Rapids, MI: Baker Academic, 2001.

Eriksen, Thomas Hylland. *Ethnicity and Nationalism: Anthropological Perspectives*. 2nd ed. London: Pluto, 2002.

Eschner, Christina. *Gestorben und hingegeben "für" die Sünder: Die griechische Konzepten des Unheil abwendenden Sterbens und deren paulinischen Aufnahme für die Deutung des Todes Jesu Christi*. 2 vols. WMANT 122. Berlin: Neukirchener Verlag, 2010.

Eskola, Timo. "Paul, Predestination and 'Covenantal Nomism'—Re-assessing Paul and Palestinian Judaism." *JSJ* 29 (1997): 390-412.

————. *Theodicy and Predestination in Pauline Theology*. WUNT 2.100. Tübingen: Mohr Siebeck, 1998.

Esler, Philip F. *The First Christians in Their Social Worlds: Social-Scientific Approaches to New Testament Interpretation*. London: Routledge, 1994.

————. *Galatians*. NTR. London: Routledge, 1998.

Evans, Craig A. "Revolutionary Movements, Jewish." In *DNTB*, edited by S. E. Porter and C. A. Evans, pp. 936-47. Downers Grove, IL: InterVarsity, 2000.

————. "Paul and 'Works of Law' Language in Late Antiquity." In *Paul and His Opponents*, edited by S. E. Porter, pp. 201-26. Leiden: Brill, 2005.

Fantin, Joseph D. *Lord of the Entire World: Lord Jesus, a Challenge to Lord Caesar?* NTM 31. Sheffield: Sheffield Phoenix, 2011.

Fee, Gordon D. *Galatians*. PC. Blandford Forum, UK: Deo, 2007.

Feldmeier, Ronald, Ulrich Heckel, and Martin Hengel, eds. *Heiden: Juden, Christen und das Problem des Fremden*. WUNT 70. Tübingen: Mohr Siebeck, 1994.

Forman, Mark. *The Politics of Promise*. SNTSMS 148. Cambridge: Cambridge University Press, 2011.

Fredriksen, Paula. "Judaism, the Circumcision of Gentiles, and Apocalyptic Hope: Another Look at Galatians 1 and 2." *JTS* 42 (1991): 532-64.

———. "Judaizing the Nations: The Ritual Demands of Paul's Gospel." In *Paul's Jewish Matrix*, edited by T. G. Casey and J. Taylor, pp. 327-54. Rome: Gregorian & Biblical Press, 2011.

Freeman, Charles. *A New History of Early Christianity*. New Haven: Yale University Press, 2009.

Frey, Jörg. "Paul's Jewish Identity." In *Jewish Identity in the Greco-Roman World*, edited by J. Frey, D. R. Schwartz, and S. Gripentrog, pp. 285-321. AGJU 71. Leiden: Brill, 2007.

———."Zur Bedeutung der Qumrantexte für das Verständnis der Apokalyptik im Früh-judentum und im Urchristentum." In *Apokalyptik und Qumran*, edited by J. Frey and M. Becker, pp. 11-62. Paderborn: Bonifatius, 2007.

———. "Demythologizing Apocalyptic? On N. T. Wright's Paul, Apocalyptic Interpretation, and the Constraints of Construction." In *God and the Faithfulness of Paul*, edited by M. F. Bird, C. Heilig, and J. T. Hewitt, pp. 334-76. WUNT 2. Tübingen: Mohr Siebeck, 2016.

Frey, Jörg, Daniel R. Schwartz, and Stephanie Gripentrog, eds. *Jewish Identity in the Greco-Roman World*. AGJU 71. Leiden: Brill, 2007.

Friesen, Steve J. "Normal Religion, or, Words Fail Us: A Response to Karl Galinsky's 'The Cult of the Roman Emperor: Uniter or Divider?'" In *Rome and Religion: A Cross-Disciplinary Dialogue on the Imperial Cult*, edited by J. Brodd and J. L. Reed, pp. 23-26. Atlanta: SBL, 2011.

Fuller, Daniel. *Gospel and Law: Contrast or Continuum?* Grand Rapids, MI: Eerdmans, 1980.

Gager, John G. *Reinventing Paul*. Oxford: Oxford University Press, 2000.

———. "The Rehabilitation of Paul in Jewish Tradition." In *"The One Who Sows Bountifully": Essays in Honor of Stanley K. Stowers*, edited by C. Hodge, S. Olyan, D. Ullicci, and E. Wasserman, pp. 29-41. Providence, RI: Brown Judaic Studies, 2013.

Galinsky, Karl. "The Cult of the Roman Emperor: Uniter or Divider?" In *Rome and Religion: A Cross-Disciplinary Dialogue on the Imperial Cult*, edited by J. Brodd and J. L. Reed, pp. 1-21. Atlanta: SBL, 2011.

———. "In the Shadow (or Not) of the Imperial Cult: A Cooperative Agenda." In *Rome and Religion: A Cross-Disciplinary Dialogue on the Imperial Cult*, edited by J. Brodd and J. L. Reed, pp. 215-25. Atlanta: SBL, 2011.

Garland, David. "Paul's Defense of the Truth of the Gospel regarding Gentiles (Galatians 2:15-3:22)." *RevExp* 91 (1994): 166-81.

Bibliography

Garlington, Donald B. *"The Obedience of Faith": A Pauline Phrase in Historical Context.* WUNT 2.38. Tübingen: Mohr Siebeck, 1991.

————. *In Defense of the New Perspective on Paul: Essays and Reviews.* Eugene, OR: Wipf & Stock, 2004.

————. *An Exposition of Galatians: A Reading from the New Perspective.* 3rd ed. Eugene, OR: Wipf & Stock, 2007.

Garroway, Joshua D. *Paul's Gentile-Jews: Neither Jew nor Gentile, But Both.* New York: Palgrave Macmillan, 2012.

Gaston, Lloyd. *Paul and the Torah.* Vancouver: University of British Columbia Press, 1987.

Gathercole, Simon J. *Where Is the Boasting? Early Jewish Soteriology and Paul's Response in Romans 1–5.* Grand Rapids, MI: Eerdmans, 2002.

Gaventa, Beverly Roberts. "The Singularity of the Gospel: A Reading of Galatians." In *Pauline Theology.* Vol. 1, *Thessalonians, Philippians, Galatians, Philemon*, edited by J. M. Bassler, pp. 147-59. Minneapolis: Fortress, 1985.

————. *From Darkness to Light: Aspects of Conversion in the New Testament.* Philadelphia: Fortress, 1986.

————. "Galatians 1 and 2: Autobiography as Paradigm." *NovT* 28 (1986): 310-26.

Georgi, Dieter. *Theocracy in Paul's Praxis and Theology.* Translated by D. E. Green. Minneapolis: Fortress, 1991.

————. "God Turned Upside Down." In *Paul and Empire: Religion and Power in Roman Imperial Society*, edited by R. Horsley, pp. 148-57. Valley Forge, PA: Trinity Press International, 1997.

Gerdmar, Anders. *Rethinking the Judaism-Hellenism Dichotomy: A Historiographical Case Study of Second Peter and Jude.* ConBNT 36. Stockholm: Almqvist & Wiksell, 2001.

————. *Roots of Theological Anti-Semitism: German Biblical Interpretation and the Jews, from Herder and Semler to Kittel and Bultmann.* Leiden: Brill, 2009.

Gibson, Jack J. *Peter between Jerusalem and Antioch.* WUNT 2.345. Tübingen: Mohr Siebeck, 2013.

Given, Mark D., ed. *Paul Unbound: Other Perspectives on the Apostle Paul.* Peabody, MA: Hendrickson, 2010.

Glasson, T. F. "What Is Apocalyptic?" *NTS* 27 (1980): 98-105.

Gorman, Michael J. *Apostle of the Crucified Lord: A Theological Introduction to Paul and His Letters.* Grand Rapids, MI: Eerdmans, 2004.

————. *Reading Paul.* Eugene, OR: Cascade, 2008.

————. *Inhabiting the Cruciform God: Kenosis, Justification, and Theosis in Paul's Narrative Soteriology.* Grand Rapids, MI: Eerdmans, 2009.

————. "Justification and Justice in Paul, with Special Reference to the Corinthians." *JSPL* 1 (2011): 23-40.

Gottwald, Norman K. "Early Israel as an Anti-imperial Community." In *Paul and Empire: Religion and Power in Roman Imperial Society*, edited by R. A. Horsley, pp. 9-24. Harrisburg, PA: Trinity Press International, 1997.

Gradel, Ittai. *Emperor Worship and Roman Religion*. Oxford: Clarendon, 2002.

Gradl, Hans-Georg. "Kaisertum und Kaiserkult: Ein Vergleich zwischen Philos *Legatio ad Gaium* und Offenbarung des Johannes." *NTS* 56 (2010): 116-38.

Graf, David. "Nabateans." In *ABD* 4:972-73. New Haven: Yale University Press, 1992.

Grindheim, Sigurd. "Not Salvation History, but Salvation Territory: The Main Subject Matter of Galatians." *NTS* 59 (2013): 91-108.

Gruen, Eric. *Diaspora: Jews amidst Greeks and Romans*. Cambridge, MA: Harvard University Press, 2002.

Gurtner, Daniel M., ed. *This World and the World to Come: Soteriology in Early Judaism*. LSTS 74. London: T&T Clark, 2011.

Haacker, Klaus. "Das Evangelium Gottes und die Erwählung Israels: Zum Beitrag des Römerbriefs zur Erneuerung des Verhältnisses zwischen Christen und Juden." *TBei* 13 (1982): 59-72.

Haenchen, Ernst. *Acts of the Apostles: A Commentary*. Oxford: Blackwell, 1971.

Hagner, D. A. "Paul in Modern Jewish Thought." In *Pauline Studies*, edited by D. A. Hagner and M. J. Harris, pp. 143-65. Exeter, UK: Paternoster, 1980.

————. "Paul and Judaism, the Jewish Matrix of Early Christianity: Issues in the Current Debate." *BBR* 3 (1993): 111-30.

————. "Paul as a Jewish Believer—according to His Letters." In *Jewish Believers in Jesus: The Early Centuries*, edited by O. Skarsaune and R. Hvalvik, pp. 96-120. Peabody, MA: Hendrickson, 2007.

Hahn, Ferdinand. *Mission in the New Testament*. SBT 37. London: SCM, 1965.

Hall, Robert G. *Revealed History: Techniques for Ancient Jewish and Christian Historiography*. JSPSup 6. Sheffield: Sheffield Academic, 1991.

————. "Arguing Like an Apocalypse: Galatians and an Ancient *Topos* outside the Greco-Roman Rhetorical Tradition." *NTS* 42 (1996): 434-53.

Hanges, James Constantine. "To Complicate Encounters: A Response to Karl Galinsky's 'The Cult of the Roman Emperor: Uniter or Divider?'" In *Rome and Religion: A Cross-Disciplinary Dialogue on the Imperial Cult*, edited by J. Brodd and J. L. Reed, pp. 27-34. Atlanta: SBL, 2011.

Hansen, Bruce. *All of You Are One: The Social Vision of Galatians 3.28, 1 Corinthians 12.13 and Colossians 3.11*. LNTS 409. London: T&T Clark, 2010.

Hansen, G. Walter. "A Paradigm of the Apocalypse." In *Gospel in Paul: Studies on Corinthians, Galatians and Romans*, edited by L. A. Jervis and P. Richardson, pp. 194-209. JSNTSup 108. Sheffield: Sheffield Academic, 1994.

Hanson, P. D. "Apocalypticism." In *IDBSup*, edited by K. Crim, pp. 27-34. Nashville: Abingdon, 1976.

Hardin, Justin. *Galatians and the Imperial Cult: A Critical Analysis of the First-Century Social Context of Paul's Letter*. WUNT 2.237. Tübingen: Mohr Siebeck, 2008.

Harink, Douglas. *Paul among the Postliberals: Pauline Theology beyond Christendom and Modernity*. Grand Rapids, MI: Brazos, 2003.

————. "Paul and Israel: An Apocalyptic Reading." *Pro Ecclesia* 16 (2007): 359-80.

Harnack, Adolf von. *What Is Christianity?* New York: Harper & Row, 1957.

Harrison, James R. "Paul, Eschatology and the Augustan Age of Grace." *TynB* 40 (1999): 79-91.

———. *Paul the Imperial Authorities at Thessalonica and Rome.* WUNT 273. Tübingen: Mohr Siebeck, 2011.

Hays, Richard. "Crucified with Christ: A Synthesis of the Theology of 1 and 2 Thessalonians, Philemon, Philippians, and Galatians." In *Pauline Theology.* Vol. 1, *Thessalonians, Philippians, Galatians, Philemon,* edited by J. M. Bassler, pp. 227-46. Minneapolis: Fortress, 1985.

———. *Echoes of Scripture in the Letters of Paul.* New Haven: Yale University Press, 1989.

———. *First Corinthians.* Interpretation. Louisville: Westminster John Knox, 1997.

———. "The Letter to the Galatians." In *NIB,* edited by L. E. Keck, 11:183-348. 12 vols. Nashville: Abingdon, 2000.

———. *The Faith of Jesus Christ: The Narrative Substructure of Galatians 3:1–4:11.* 2nd ed. Grand Rapids, MI: Eerdmans, 2002.

———. "Is Paul's Gospel Narratable?" *JSNT* 27 (2004): 217-39.

———. "Apocalyptic *Poiēsis* in Galatians: Paternity, Passion, and Participation." In *Galatians and Christian Theology: Justification, the Gospel, and Ethics in Paul's Letter,* edited by M. W. Elliott, S. J. Hafemann, N. T. Wright, and J. Frederick, pp. 200-219. Grand Rapids, MI: Baker Academic, 2014.

Heilig, Christoph. "Methodological Considerations for Search of Counter-Imperial 'Echoes' in Pauline Literature." In *Reactions to Empire: Sacred Texts in Their Sociopolitical Contexts,* edited by J. A. Dunne and D. Batovici, pp. 73-92. WUNT 2.372. Tübingen: Mohr Siebeck, 2014.

———. *Hidden Criticism? The Methodology and Plausibility of the Search for a Counter-Imperial Subtext in Paul.* WUNT 2.392. Tübingen: Mohr Siebeck, 2015.

Hengel, Martin. *Judaism and Hellenism.* Translated by J. Bowden. 2 vols. London: SCM, 1974.

———. *Christ and Power.* Philadelphia: Fortress, 1977.

———. *Acts and the History of Earliest Christianity.* Translated by J. Bowden. Philadelphia: Fortress, 1979.

———. *Jews, Greeks, and Barbarians.* Translated by J. Bowden. Philadelphia: Fortress, 1980.

———. *Between Jesus and Paul.* London: SCM, 1983.

———. *The Four Gospels and the One Gospel of Jesus Christ.* London: Bloomsbury/T&T Clark, 2000.

———. "The Stance of the Apostle Paul toward the Law in the Unknown Years between Damascus and Antioch." In *Justification and Variegated Nomism.* Vol. 2, *The Paradoxes of Paul,* edited by D. A. Carson, P. T. O'Brien, and M. A. Seifrid, pp. 75-103. Grand Rapids, MI: Baker Academic, 2004.

———. *Der unterschätzte Petrus: Zwei Studien.* Tübingen: Mohr Siebeck, 2007.

————. *Saint Peter: The Underestimated Apostle*. Translated by Thomas Trapp. Grand Rapids, MI: Eerdmans, 2010.

Hengel, Martin, and Anna Maria Schwemer. *Paul between Damascus and Antioch: The Unknown Years*. Louisville: Westminster John Knox, 1997.

Heyer, C. J. den. *Paul: A Man of Two Worlds*. London: SCM, 2000.

Heyman, George. *The Power of Sacrifice: Roman and Christian Discourses in Conflict*. Washington, DC: Catholic University of America Press, 2007.

Hill, Craig. *Hellenists and Hebrews: Reappraising Division within the Earliest Church*. Minneapolis: Fortress, 1994.

Hock, Ronald. *The Social Context of Paul's Ministry: Tentmaking and Apostleship*. Philadelphia: Fortress, 1980.

Hodge, Caroline Johnson. "Apostle to the Gentiles: Constructions of Paul's Identity." *BI* 13 (2005): 270-88.

————. *If Sons, Then Heirs: A Study of Kinship and Ethnicity in the Letters of Paul*. Oxford: Oxford University Press, 2007.

Hofius, Otfried. "Gesetz und Evangelium nach 2. Korinther 3." In *Paulusstudien*, pp. 75-120. WUNT 51. Tübingen: Mohr Siebeck, 1994.

Hogan, Pauline Nigh. *"No Longer Male and Female": Interpreting Galatians 3:28 in Early Christianity*. LNTS 380. London: T&T Clark, 2008.

Holmberg, Bengt. *Exploring Early Christian Identity*. Tübingen: Mohr Siebeck, 2008.

Holtz, Traugott. "Der antiochenische Zwischenfall (Galater 2.11-14)." *NTS* 32 (1986): 344-61.

Hooker, Morna D. *From Adam to Christ*. Cambridge: Cambridge University Press, 1990.

————. "'Heirs of Abraham': The Gentiles' Role in Israel's Story: A Response to Bruce Longenecker." In *Narrative Dynamics in Paul: A Critical Assessment*, edited by B. W. Longenecker, pp. 85-96. Louisville: Westminster John Knox, 2002.

Horsley, Richard A., ed. *Paul and Empire: Religion and Power in Roman Imperial Society*. Harrisburg, PA: Trinity Press International, 1997.

————. *Paul and Politics: Ekklesia, Imperium, Interpretation*. Harrisburg, PA: Trinity Press International, 2000.

————. *Jesus and Empire: The Kingdom of God and the New World Order*. Minneapolis: Fortress, 2002.

————. *Hidden Transcripts and the Arts of Resistance: Applying the Work of James C. Scott to Jesus and Paul*. Atlanta: SBL, 2004.

————. *Paul and the Roman Imperial Order*. Harrisburg, PA: Trinity Press International, 2004.

————. *In the Shadow of Empire: Reclaiming the Bible as a History of Faithful Resistance*. Louisville: Westminster John Knox, 2008.

Horsley, Richard A., and Neil Asher Silberman. *The Message and the Kingdom: How Jesus and Paul Ignited a Revolution and Transformed the Ancient World*. New York: Penguin Putnam, 1997.

Hübner, Hans. *Law in Paul's Thought*. Edinburgh: T&T Clark, 1984.

———. "Zur gegenwärtigen Diskussion über die Theologie des Paulus." *JBTh* 7 (1992): 399-413.

Hurtado, Larry. *Lord Jesus Christ: Devotion to Jesus in Earliest Christianity*. Grand Rapids, MI: Eerdmans, 2003.

———. "Does Philo Help Explain Early Christianity?" In *Philo und das Neue Testament: Wechselseitig Wahrnehmungen*, edited by R. Deines and K.-W. Niebuhr, pp. 73-92. WUNT 172. Tübingen: Mohr Siebeck, 2004.

Hvalvik, Reidar. "A 'Sonderweg' for Israel: A Critical Examination of a Current Interpretation of Romans 11:25-27." *JSNT* 38 (1990): 87-107.

———. "Paul as a Jewish Believer—according to the Book of Acts." In *Jewish Believers in Jesus: The Early Centuries*, edited by O. Skarsaune and R. Hvalvik, pp. 123-35. Peabody, MA: Hendrickson, 2007.

Jervis, L. Anne. "Peter in the Middle: Galatians 2:11-21." In *Text and Artifact in the Religions of Mediterranean Antiquity*, edited by M. R. Desjardins and S. G. Wilson, pp. 45-62. Waterloo, ON: Wilfrid Laurier University Press, 2000.

Jewett, Robert. "The Agitators and the Galatian Congregation." *NTS* 17 (1971): 198-212.

———. "Gospel and Commensality: Social and Theological Implications of Galatians 2.14." In *Gospel in Paul: Studies on Corinthians, Galatians and Romans*, edited by L. A. Jervis and P. Richardson, pp. 240-52. Sheffield: Sheffield Academic, 1994.

———. "The Corruption and Redemption of Creation: Reading Rom. 8:18-23 within the Imperial Context." In *Paul and the Roman Imperial Order*, edited by R. A. Horsley, pp. 25-46. Harrisburg, PA: Trinity Press International, 2004.

———. *Romans*. Hermeneia. Minneapolis: Fortress, 2007.

Jones, Donald L. "Christianity and the Roman Imperial Cult." In *ANRW* II.23.2, edited by H. Temporini-Gräfin Vitzthum and W. Haase, pp. 1023-54. Berlin: Walter de Gruyter, 1980.

Jones, Hefin. Πίστις, Δικαιόω and the Apocalyptic Paul: Assessing Key Aspects of the Apocalyptic Reading of Galatians. PhD diss. Moore Theological College, 2015.

Jossa, Giorgio. *Jews or Christians?* WUNT 202. Tübingen: Mohr Siebeck, 2006.

Kammler, Hans-Christian. "Die Prädikation of Jesu Christi als "Gott" und die paulinische Christologie: Erwägungen zur Exegese von Röm 9,5b." *ZNW* 92 (2003): 164-80.

Käsemann, Ernst. "The Beginnings of Christian Theology." In *New Testament Questions of Today*, pp. 108-37. Translated by W. J. Montague. London: SCM, 1969.

———. "On the Subject of Primitive Christian Apocalyptic." In *New Testament Questions of Today*, pp. 138-67. Translated by W. J. Montague. London: SCM, 1969.

———. "Paul and Israel." In *New Testament Questions of Today*, pp. 183-87. Philadelphia: Fortress, 1969.

———. "'The Righteousness of God' in Paul." In *New Testament Questions of Today*, pp. 168-82. Translated by W. J. Montague. London: SCM, 1969.

———. "Justification and Salvation History in the Epistle to the Romans." In *Perspectives on Paul*, pp. 60-78. London: SCM, 1971.

————. *Commentary on Romans*. Translated by G. W. Bromiley. Grand Rapids, MI: Eerdmans, 1980.

Keck, Leander E. *Paul and His Letters*. Philadelphia: Fortress, 1979.

————. "Paul and Apocalyptic Theology." *Int* 28 (1984): 229-41.

————. "The Jewish Paul among the Gentiles: Two Portraits." In *Early Christianity and Classical Culture: Comparative Studies in Honor of Abraham J. Malherbe*, edited by J. T. Fitzgerald, T. H. Olbricht, and L. M. White, pp. 461-81. NovTSup 110. Leiden: Brill, 2003.

————. *Romans*. ANTC. Abingdon: Nashville, 2005.

Kelhoffer, James A. "The Struggle to Define *Heilsgeschichte*: Paul on the Origins of the Christian Tradition." *BR* 48 (2003): 45-67. Reprinted in *Concepts of "Gospel" and Legitimacy in Early Christianity*, pp. 97-120. WUNT 324. Tübingen: Mohr Siebeck, 2014.

Keller, Catherine, Michael Nausner, and Mayra Rivera, eds. *Postcolonial Theologies: Divinity and Empire*. St. Louis: Chalice, 2004.

Kim, Seyoon. *Paul and the New Perspective: Second Thoughts on the Origin of Paul's Gospel*. Grand Rapids, MI: Eerdmans, 2002.

————. *Christ and Caesar: The Gospel and the Roman Empire in the Writings of Paul and Luke*. Grand Rapids, MI: Eerdmans, 2008.

Kirk, J. R. Daniel. *Unlocking Romans: Resurrection and the Justification of God*. Grand Rapids, MI: Eerdmans, 2008.

Klausner, Joseph. *From Jesus to Paul*. Boston: Beacon, 1939.

Knox, John, and Douglas R. A. Hare. *Chapters in a Life of Paul*. Edited by Douglas R. A. Hare. Rev. ed. Macon, GA: Mercer University Press, 1987.

Kolb, Frank. "Antiochia in der frühen Kaiserzeit." In *Geschichte—Tradition—Reflexion*, edited by H. Cancik, H. Lichtenberger, and P. Schäfer, 2:97-118. Tübingen: Mohr Siebeck, 1996.

Koortbojian, Michael. *The Divinization of Caesar and Augustus*. Cambridge: Cambridge University Press, 2013.

Köstenberger, Andreas. "The Identity of ΊΣΡΑΗΛ ΤΟΥ ΘΕΟΥ (Israel of God) in Galatians 6:16." *Faith and Mission* 19 (2001): 3-24.

Krauter, Stefan. *Studien zu Röm 13,1-7. Paulus und der politische Diskurs der neronischen Zeit*. Tübingen: Mohr Siebeck, 2009.

Krentz, Edgar "Through a Lens: Theology and Fidelity in 2 Thessalonians." In *Pauline Theology*. Vol. 1, *Thessalonians, Philippians, Galatians, Philemon*, edited by J. M. Bassler, pp. 52-62. Minneapolis: Fortress, 1985.

Kroeker, P. Travis. "Recent Continental Philosophers." In *The Blackwell Companion to Paul*, edited by S. Westerholm, pp. 440-55. Oxford, MA: Wiley-Blackwell, 2011.

Kuula, Kari. *The Law, the Covenant and God's Plan: Paul's Treatment of the Law and Israel in Romans*. FES 85. Göttingen: Vandenhoeck & Ruprecht, 2002.

Kwon, Yon-Gyong. *Eschatology in Galatians*. WUNT 183. Tübingen: Mohr Siebeck, 2004.

Laato, Timo. *Paul and Judaism: An Anthropological Approach*. Atlanta: Scholars, 1995.

Manson, T. W. *Only to the House of Israel? Jesus and the Non-Jews*. Philadelphia: Fortress, 1964.

Marshall, I. Howard. "Palestinian and Hellenistic Christian: Some Critical Comments." *NTS* 19 (1973): 271-87.

Martin, T. W. "Hellenists." In *ABD* 3:135-36. New Haven: Yale University Press, 1992.

Martyn, J. Louis. "Apocalyptic Antinomies in Paul's Letter to the Galatians." *NTS* 31 (1985): 410-24.

———. "Events in Galatia: Modified Covenantal Nomism versus God's Invasion of the Cosmos in the Singular Gospel." In *Pauline Theology*. Vol. 1, *Thessalonians, Philippians, Galatians, Philemon*, edited by J. M. Bassler, pp. 160-79. Minneapolis: Fortress, 1985.

———. "Epistemology at the Turn of the Ages: 2 Corinthians 5:16." In *Christian History and Interpretation: Studies Presented to John Knox*, edited by W. R. Farmer et al., pp. 269-87. Cambridge: Cambridge University Press, 1967. Reprinted in *Theological Issues in the Letters of Paul*, pp. 89-110. London: T&T Clark, 1997.

———. *Theological Issues in the Letters of Paul*. Nashville: Abingdon, 1997.

———. *Galatians: A New Translation with Introduction and Commentary*. AB. New York: Doubleday, 1997.

———. "The Apocalyptic Gospel in Galatians." *Int* 54 (2000): 246-66.

Mason, Steve. "Jews, Judaeans, Judaizing, Judaism: Problems of Categorization in Ancient History." *JSJ* 38 (2007): 457-512.

Maston, Jason. *Divine and Human Agency in Second Temple Judaism and Paul: A Comparative Study*. WUNT 2.297. Tübingen: Mohr Siebeck, 2010.

———. "The Nature of Salvation History in Galatians." *JSPL* 2 (2012): 89-103.

Matera, Frank J. *Galatians*. SP. Collegeville, MN: Liturgical, 2007.

Matlock, R. Barry. *Unveiling the Apocalyptic Paul: Paul's Interpreters and the Rhetoric of Criticism*. JSNTSup 127. Sheffield: Sheffield Academic, 1996.

Mayer, Bernhard. *Unter Gott Heilsratschluss. Prädestinationaussagen bei Paulus*. Würzburg: Echter, 1974.

Mayer, Wendy, and Pauline Allen. *John Chrysostom*. New York: Routledge, 2000.

McCormack, Bruce. "Can We Still Speak of Justification by Faith? An In-House Debate with Apocalyptic Readings of Paul." In *Galatians and Christian Theology: Justification, the Gospel, and Ethics in Paul's Letter*, edited by M. W. Elliott, S. J. Hafemann, N. T. Wright, and J. Frederick, pp. 159-84. Grand Rapids, MI: Baker Academic, 2014.

McCready, Wayne O., and Adele Reinhartz, eds. *Common Judaism: Explorations in Second-Temple Judaism*. Minneapolis: Fortress, 2008.

McGrath, A. E. "Justification." In *DPL*, edited by G. F. Hawthorne, R. P. Martin, and D. G. Reid, pp. 517-23. Downers Grove, IL: InterVarsity, 1992.

McKnight, Scot, and Joseph B. Modica. "Introduction." In *Jesus Is Lord, Caesar Is Not: Evaluating Empire in New Testament Studies*, edited by S. McKnight and J. B. Modica, pp. 15-21. Downers Grove, IL: IVP Academic, 2013.

McKnight, Scot, and Joseph B. Modica, eds. *Jesus Is Lord, Caesar Is Not: Evaluating Empire in New Testament Studies*. Downers Grove, IL: IVP Academic, 2013.

McLaren, James S. "Jews and the Imperial Cult: From Augustus to Domitian." *JSNT* 27 (2005): 257-78.

———. "Searching for Rome and the Imperial Cult in Galilee: Reassessing Galilee-Rome Relations (63 B.C.E to 70 C.E.)." In *Rome and Religion: A Cross-Disciplinary Dialogue on the Imperial Cult*, edited by J. Brodd and J. L. Reed, pp. 111-36. Atlanta: SBL, 2011.

Meeks, Wayne A. *The First Urban Christians: The Social World of the Apostle Paul*. New Haven: Yale University Press, 1983.

———. "Breaking Away: Three New Testament Pictures of Christianity's Separation from Jewish Communities." In *"To See Ourselves as Others See Us": Christians, Jews, and "Others" in Late Antiquity*, edited by J. Neusner and E. S. Frerichs, pp. 93-115. Chico, CA: Scholars, 1985.

Meeks, Wayne A., and Robert L. Wilken. *Jews and Christians in Antioch in the First Four Centuries of the Common Era*. Missoula, MT: Scholars, 1978.

Meggitt, J. J. "Taking the Emperor's Clothes Seriously: The New Testament and the Roman Empire." In *The Quest for Wisdom: Essays in Honour of Philip Budd*, edited by C. E. Joynes, pp. 143-69. Cambridge: Orchard Academic Press, 2002.

Meißner, Stefan. *Die Heimholung des Ketzers: Studien zur jüdischen Auseindandersetzung mit Paulus*. WUNT 2.87. Tübingen: Mohr Siebeck, 1996.

Metzger, Bruce M. *A Textual Commentary on the Greek New Testament*. 2nd ed. Stuttgart: Deutsche Bibelgesellsschaft, 1994.

Meyer, Jason C. *The End of the Law: Mosaic Covenant in Pauline Theology*. NACSBT. Nashville: Broadman & Holman, 2009.

Mijoga, H. B. P. *The Pauline Notion of Deeds of the Law*. San Francisco: International Scholars Publications, 1999.

Miller, Colin. "The Imperial Cult in the Pauline Cities of Asia Minor and Greece." *CBQ* 72 (2010): 314-31.

Miller, David M. "Ethnicity, Religion and the Meaning of *Ioudaios* in Ancient 'Judaism.'" *CBR* 12 (2014): 216-65.

Miller, James C. "The Jewish Context of Paul's Gentile Mission." *TynB* 58 (2007): 101-15.

———. "Paul and His Ethnicity: Reframing the Categories." In *Paul as Missionary: Identity, Activity, Theology, and Practice*, edited by T. J. Burke and B. S. Rosner, pp. 37-50. LNTS 420. London: T&T Clark, 2011.

Montefiore, C. G. *Judaism and St. Paul: Two Essays*. New York: Dutton, 1915.

Moo, Douglas J. *The Epistle to the Romans*. NICNT. Grand Rapids, MI: Eerdmans, 1996.

———. *Galatians*. BECNT. Grand Rapids, MI: Baker Academic, 2014.

Moore, H. "The Problem of Apocalyptic as Evidenced in Recent Discussion." *IBS* 8 (1986): 76-91.

———. "Paul and Apocalyptic." *IBS* 9 (1987): 35-46.

Moore, Richard K. *Rectification ("Justification") in Paul, in Historical Perspective and in the English Bible: God's Gift of Right Relationship*. 3 vols. Lewiston, NY: Edwin Mellen, 2002.

Moule, C. F. D. "Jesus, Judaism, and Paul." In *Tradition and Interpretation in the New Testament*, edited by G. F. Hawthorne and O. Betz, pp. 43-52. Grand Rapids, MI: Eerdmans, 1987.

Munck, Johannes. *Paul and the Salvation of Mankind*. London: SCM, 1959.

Murphy-O'Connor, Jerome. *Paul: A Critical Life*. Oxford: Oxford University Press, 1997.

Myers, Benjamin. "From Faithfulness to Faith in the Theology of Karl Barth." In *The Faith of Jesus Christ: Exegetical, Biblical, and Theological Studies*, edited by M. F. Bird and P. M. Sprinkle, pp. 291-308. Milton Keynes, UK: Paternoster, 2009.

Nanos, Mark D. *The Mystery of Romans: The Jewish Context of Paul's Letter*. Minneapolis: Fortress, 1996.

———. "The Jewish Context of the Gentile Audience Addressed in Paul's Letter to the Romans." *CBQ* 61 (1999): 283-304.

———. *The Irony of Galatians: Paul's Letter in First-Century Context*. Minneapolis: Fortress, 2002.

———. "What Was at Stake in Peter's 'Eating with Gentiles' at Antioch?" In *The Galatians Debate: Contemporary Issues in Rhetorical and Historical Interpretation*, edited by M. D. Nanos, pp. 272-318. Peabody, MA: Hendrickson, 2002.

———. "How Inter-Christian Approaches to Paul's Rhetoric Can Perpetuate Negative Valuations of Jewishness—although Proposing to Avoid That Outcome." *BI* 13 (2005): 255-69.

———. "Paul between Jews and Christians." *BI* 13 (2005): 221-316.

———. "Paul and Judaism: Why Not Paul's Judaism?" In *Paul Unbound: Other Perspectives on the Apostle*, edited by M. D. Given, pp. 117-60. Peabody, MA: Hendrickson, 2010.

———. "A Jewish View." In *Four Views on the Apostle Paul*, edited by M. F. Bird, pp. 159-93. Grand Rapids, MI: Zondervan, 2012.

———. "Paul's Relationship to Torah in Light of His Strategy 'to Become Everything to Everyone' (1 Corinthians 9.19-23)." In *Paul and Judaism: Cross-Currents in Pauline Exegesis and the Study of Jewish-Christian Relations*, edited by R. Bieringer and D. Pollefeyt, pp. 106-40. LNTS 463. London: T&T Clark, 2012.

———. "To the Churches within the Synagogues of Rome." In *Reading Paul's Letter to the Romans*, edited by J. L. Sumney, pp. 11-28. Atlanta: SBL, 2012.

———. "Paul's Polemic in Philippians 3 as Jewish-Subgroup Vilification of Local Non-Jewish Cultic and Philosophical Alternatives." *JSPL* 3 (2013): 47-92.

———. "Was Paul a 'Liar' for the Gospel?: The Case for a New Interpretation of Paul's 'Becoming Everything to Everyone' in 1 Corinthians 9:19-23." *RevExp* 110 (2013): 591-608.

———. "Paul's Non-Jews Do Not Become 'Jews,' But Do They Become 'Jewish'? Reading Romans 2:25-29 within Judaism, alongside Josephus." *Journal of the Jesus Movement in Its Jewish Setting* 1 (2014): 26-53.

————. "The Question of Conceptualization: Qualifying Paul's Position on Circumcision in Dialogue with Josephus's Advisors to King Izates." In *Paul within Judaism: Restoring the First-Century Context to the Apostle*, edited by M. D. Nanos and M. Zetterholm, pp. 105-52. Minneapolis: Fortress, 2015.

Nanos, Mark D., and Magnus Zetterholm, eds. *Paul within Judaism*. Minneapolis: Fortress, 2015.

Neusner, Jacob. *The Emergence of Judaism*. Louisville: Westminster John Knox, 2004.

Nickelsburg, George W. E. *Ancient Judaism and Christian Origins: Diversity, Continuity, and Transformation*. Minneapolis: Fortress, 2003.

Niebuhr, K.-W. *Heidenapostel aus Israel: Die jüdische Identität des Paulus nach ihrer Darstellung in seinen Briefen*. WUNT 62. Tübingen: Mohr Siebeck, 1992.

Novenson, Matthew V. *Christ among the Messiahs: Christ Language in Paul and Messiah Language in Ancient Judaism*. New York: Oxford University Press, 2012.

————. "Paul's Former Occupation in *Ioudaismos*." In *Galatians and Christian Theology: Justification, the Gospel, and Ethics in Paul's Letter*, edited by M. W. Elliott, S. J. Hafemann, N. T. Wright, and J. Frederick, pp. 24-39. Grand Rapids, MI: Baker Academic, 2014.

————. "What the Apostles Did Not See." In *Reactions to Empire: Sacred Texts in Their Socio-political Contexts*, edited by J. A. Dunne and D. Batovici, pp. 55-72. WUNT 2.372. Tübingen: Mohr Siebeck, 2014.

Nystrom, David. "We Have No King but Caesar: Roman Imperial Ideology and the Imperial Cult." In *Jesus Is Lord, Caesar Is Not: Evaluating Empire in New Testament Studies*, edited by S. McKnight and J. B. Modica, pp. 23-37. Downers Grove, IL: IVP Academic, 2013.

Oakes, Peter. *Philippians: From People to Letter*. SNTSMS 110. Cambridge: Cambridge University Press, 2001.

O'Brien, Peter T. "Was Paul a Covenantal Nomist?" In *Justification and Variegated Nomism*. Vol. 2, *The Paradoxes of Paul*, edited by D. A. Carson, P. T. O'Brien, and M. A. Seifrid, pp. 249-96. Grand Rapids, MI: Baker Academic, 2004.

Odell-Scott, David. *Paul's Critique of Theocracy: A Theocracy in Corinthians and Galatians*. JSNTSup 250. London: T&T Clark, 2003.

Orlin, Eric M. "Augustan Religion: From Locative to Utopian." In *Rome and Religion: A Cross-Disciplinary Dialogue on the Imperial Cult*, edited by J. Brodd and J. L. Reed, pp. 49-59. Atlanta: SBL, 2011.

Overman, J. Andrew. *Church and Community in Crisis: The Gospel according to Matthew*. Valley Forge, PA: Trinity Press International, 1996.

Park, Eung Chun. *Either Jew or Gentile: Paul's Unfolding Theology of Inclusivity*. Louisville: Westminster John Knox, 2003.

Popkes, Wiard. "Zum Thema 'Anti-imperiale Deutung neutestamentlicher Schriften.'" *ThLZ* 127 (2002): 850-62.

Porter, Stanley E. "Romans 13:1-7 as Pauline Political Rhetoric." *FilNT* 3 (1990): 115-39.

————. *Idioms of the Greek New Testament*. 2nd ed. Sheffield: Sheffield Academic, 1994.

————. "Was Paul a Good Jew? Fundamental Issues in a Current Debate." In *Christian-Jewish Relations through the Centuries*, edited by S. E. Porter and B. W. R. Pearson, pp. 148-74. JSNTSup 192. Sheffield: Sheffield Academic, 2000.

————. "Paul Confronts Caesar with the Good News." In *Empire in the New Testament*, edited by S. E. Porter and C. L. Westfall, pp. 164-96. Eugene, OR: Cascade, 2011.

Porter, Stanley E., and Andrew W. Pitts. "Πίστις with a Preposition and Genitive Modifier: Lexical, Semantic, and Syntactic Considerations in the Πίστις Χριστοῦ Discussion." In *The Faith of Jesus Christ*, edited by M. F. Bird and P. M. Sprinkle, pp. 33-53. Milton Keynes, UK: Paternoster, 2009.

Portier-Young, Anthea E. *Apocalypse against Empire: Theologies of Resistance in Early Judaism*. Grand Rapids, MI: Eerdmans, 2011.

Price, Simon R. F. "Gods and Emperors: The Greek Language of the Roman Imperial Cult." *Journal of Hellenic Studies* 104 (1984): 79-95.

————. *Rituals and Power: The Roman Imperial Cult in Asia Minor*. New York: Cambridge University Press, 1984.

————. "Ritual and Power." In *Paul and Empire: Religion and Power in Roman Imperial Society*, edited by R. A. Horsley, pp. 47-71. Harrisburg, PA: Trinity Press International, 1997.

————. "Response." In *Paul and the Roman Imperial Order*, edited by R. A. Horsley, pp. 175-83. Harrisburg, PA: Trinity Press International, 2004.

Punt, Jeremy. *Postcolonial Biblical Interpretation: Reframing Paul*. Leiden: Brill, 2015.

Rad, Gerhard von. *Theologie des Alten Testaments*. 2 vols. Munich: Kaiser, 1961.

Rajak, Tess. "The Jewish Community and Its Boundaries." In *The Jews among Pagans and Christians in the Roman Empire*, edited by J. Lieu, J. North, and T. Rajak, pp. 9-28. London: Routledge, 1992.

Ramsay, William. *The Cities of St. Paul: Their Influence on His Life and Thought*. Grand Rapids, MI: Baker, 1979.

Reasoner, Mark. *Romans in Full Circle: A History of Interpretation*. Louisville: Westminster John Knox, 2005.

Richard, Earl J. *Jesus, One and Many: The Christological Concept of New Testament Authors*. Wilmington, DE: Glazier, 1988.

Richardson, Peter. "Pauline Inconsistency: 1 Corinthians 9:19-23 and Galatians 2:11-14." *NTS* 26 (1980): 347-62.

Riesenfeld, Harald. *The Gospel Tradition*. Oxford: Blackwell, 1970.

Riesner, Rainer. *Paul's Early Period: Chronology, Mission Strategy, Theology*. Translated by Doug Stott. Grand Rapids, MI: Eerdmans, 1998.

Robinson, Donald. "The Circumcision of Titus, and Paul's 'Liberty.'" *AusBR* 12 (1964): 24-42.

————. "Distinction between Jewish and Gentile Believers in Galatians." *AusBR* 13 (1965): 29-48.

Robinson, Thomas A. *Ignatius of Antioch and the Parting of the Ways*. Peabody, MA: Hendrickson, 2009.

Rock, Ian E. "Another Reason for Romans—A Pastoral Response to Augustan Imperial Theology: Paul's Use of the Song of Moses in Romans 9–11 and 14–15." In *Reading Paul in Context: Explorations in Identity Formation*, edited by K. Ehrensperger and B. J. Tucker, pp. 74-89. LNTS 428. London: T&T Clark, 2010.

———. *Paul's Letter to the Romans and Roman Imperialism: An Ideological Analysis of the Exordium (Romans 1:1–17)*. Eugene, OR: Pickwick, 2012.

Roetzel, Calvin. *Paul, a Jew on the Margins*. Louisville: Westminster John Knox, 2003.

Rosner, Brian R. "Paul and the Law: What He Does Not Say." *JSNT* 34 (2011): 405-19.

———. *Paul and the Law*. NSBT. Downers Grove, IL: IVP Academic, 2013.

Rowe, C. Kavin. *World Upside Down: Reading Acts in the Graeco-Roman Age*. Oxford: Oxford University Press, 2009.

Rowland, Christopher. *Christian Origins*. London: SPCK, 1985.

Rudolph, David J. *A Jew to the Jews: Jewish Contours of Pauline Flexibility in 1 Corinthians 9:19-23*. WUNT 2.304. Tübingen: Mohr Siebeck, 2011.

Runesson, Anders. "Particularistic Judaism and Universalistic Christianity? Some Critical Remarks on Terminology and Theology." *ST* 54 (2000): 55-75.

Rüpke, Jörg. *Religion of the Romans*. Translated by R. Gordon. Cambridge: Polity, 2007.

Russell, D. S. *The Method and Message of Jewish Apocalyptic*. OTL. Philadelphia: Westminster, 1976.

Russell, Peter J. *Heterodoxy within Second-Temple Judaism and Sectarian Diversity within the Early Church: A Correlative Study*. Lewiston, NY: Edwin Mellen, 2008.

Sandnes, Karl Olav. "A Missionary Strategy in 1 Corinthians 9.19-23?" In *Paul as Missionary: Identity, Activity, Theology, and Practice*, edited by T. J. Burke and B. S. Rosner, pp. 128-41. LNTS 420. London: T&T Clark, 2011.

Sanders, E. P. *Paul and Palestinian Judaism: A Comparison of Patterns of Religion*. Philadelphia: Fortress, 1977.

———. *Paul, the Law, and the Jewish People*. Minneapolis: Fortress, 1983.

———. "Jewish Associations with Gentiles and Galatians 2:11-14." In *The Conversation Continues: Studies in Paul and John*, edited by R. T. Fortna and B. Roberts Gaventa, pp. 170-88. Nashville: Abingdon, 1990.

———. *Judaism: Practice and Belief, 63 BCE–66 CE*. London: SCM, 1992.

———. "Common Judaism Explored." In *Common Judaism: Explorations in Second-Temple Judaism*, edited by W. O. McCready and A. Reinhartz, pp. 11-23. Minneapolis: Fortress, 2008.

———. "Covenantal Nomism Revisited." *JSQ* 16 (2009): 23-55.

———. "Paul's Jewishness." In *Paul's Jewish Matrix*, edited by T. G. Casey and J. Taylor, pp. 51-73. Rome: Gregorian & Biblical Press, 2011.

Sanders, E. P., et al., eds. *Jewish and Christian Self-Definition*. Vol. 2, *Aspects of Judaism in the Graeco-Roman Period*. London: SCM, 1981.

Sandmel, Samuel. "Parallelomania." *JBL* 81 (1962): 1-13.

———. *Judaism and Christian Beginnings*. Oxford: Oxford University Press, 1978.

———. *The Genius of Paul*. Philadelphia: Fortress, 1979.

Sandwell, Isabella. *Religious Identity in Late Antiquity: Greeks, Jews, and Christians in Antioch*. Cambridge: Cambridge University Press, 2007.

Satlow, Michael. "Jew or Judaean?" In *"The One Who Sows Bountifully": Essays in Honor of Stanley K. Stowers*, edited by C. Johnson Hodge et al., pp. 165-75. Providence, RI: Brown Judaic Studies, 2013.

Schäfer, Peter. "Die Torah der messianischen Zeit." *ZNW* 65 (1974): 27-42.

Schlier, Heinrich. *Der Brief an die Galater*. KEK. Göttingen: Vandenhoeck & Ruprecht, 1989.

Schließer, Benjamin. *Abraham's Faith in Romans 4: Paul's Concept of Faith in Light of the History of Reception of Genesis 15:6*. WUNT 224. Tübingen: Mohr Siebeck, 2007.

Schmithals, Walter. *The Theology of the First Christians*. Louisville: Westminster John Knox, 1997.

Schnabel, Eckhard. *Early Christian Mission*. 2 vols. Downers Grove, IL: IVP Academic, 2004.

Schnelle, Udo. *Apostle Paul: His Life and Theology*. Translated by M. Eugene Boring. Grand Rapids, MI: Baker Academic, 2005.

Schoeps, H. J. *Paul: The Theology of the Apostle in the Light of Jewish Religious History*. Philadelphia: Westminster, 1961.

Schrage, Wolfgang. *Der erste Brief an die Korinther*. 3 vols. Neukirchen-Vluyn: Neukirchener Verlag, 1991-99.

Schreiner, Thomas R. *Paul: Apostles of God's Glory in Christ: A Pauline Theology*. Downers Grove, IL: InterVarsity, 2001.

———. *New Testament Theology: Magnifying God in Christ*. Grand Rapids, MI: Baker Academic, 2008.

Schwartz, Seth. "How Many Judaisms Were There? A Critique of Neusner and Smith on Definition and Mason and Boyarin on Categorization." *Journal of Ancient Judaism* 2 (2011): 221-38.

Schweitzer, Albert. *Quest of the Historical Jesus*. New York: Macmillan, 1968.

Schwemer, Anna Maria. "Paulus in Antiochien." *BZ* 42 (1998): 162-66.

Scott, J. C. *Domination and the Arts of Resistance: Hidden Transcripts*. New Haven: Yale University Press, 1990.

Scott, James M. "'For as Many as Are of Works of the Law Are under a Curse' (Galatians 3:10)." In *Paul and the Scriptures of Israel*, edited by C. A. Evans and J. A. Sanders, pp. 187-221. JSNTSup 83. Sheffield: Sheffield Academic, 1993.

———. *Paul and the Nations: The Old Testament and Jewish Background on Paul's Mission to the Nations with Special Reference to the Destination of Galatians*. WUNT 84. Tübingen: Mohr Siebeck, 1995.

Scroggs, Robin. "Salvation History: The Theological Structure of Paul's Thought (1 Thessalonians, Philippians, and Galatians)." In *Pauline Theology*. Vol. 1, *Thessalonians, Philippians, Galatians, Philemon*, edited by J. M. Bassler, pp. 212-26. Minneapolis: Fortress, 1991.

Sechrest, Love L. *A Former Jew: Paul and the Dialectics of Race.* LNTS 410. London: T&T Clark, 2009.

Seeley, David. *The Noble Death: Graeco-Roman Martyrology and Paul's Concept of Salvation.* JSNTSup 28. Sheffield: JSOT Press, 1990.

Segal, Alan. *Paul the Convert: The Apostolate and Apostasy of Saul the Pharisee.* New Haven: Yale University Press, 1990.

———. "Conversion and Messianism: Outline for a New Approach." In *The Messiah: Developments in Earliest Judaism and Christianity*, edited by J. H. Charlesworth, pp. 74-88. Minneapolis: Fortress, 1992.

Seifrid, Mark. *Christ, Our Righteousness: Paul's Theology of Justification.* NSBT 9. Downers Grove, IL: IVP Academic, 2000.

———. "For the Jew First: Paul's Nota Bene for His Gentile Readers." In *To the Jew First: The Case for Jewish Evangelism in Scripture and History*, pp. 24-39. Grand Rapids, MI: Kregel, 2008.

Shaw, David A. "Apocalyptic and Covenant: Perspectives on Paul or Antinomies at War?" *JSNT* 36 (2012): 155-71.

Sigal, Philip. *The Halakhah of Jesus of Nazareth according to the Gospel of Matthew.* Atlanta: SBL, 2007.

Silva, Moisés. "Historical Reconstruction in New Testament Criticism." In *Hermeneutics, Authority, and Canon*, edited by D. A. Carson, pp. 117-21. Grand Rapids, MI: Baker, 1986.

Sim, David C., and James S. McLaren, eds. *Attitudes to Gentiles in Ancient Judaism and Early Christianity.* LNTS 499. London: Bloomsbury, 2014.

Slee, Michelle. *The Church in Antioch in the First Century: Communion and Conflict.* LNTS 244. London: T&T Clark, 2003.

Smiles, Vincent M. *The Gospel and the Law in Galatia: Paul's Response to Jewish-Christian Separatism and the Threat of Galatian Apostasy.* Collegeville, MN: Liturgical, 1998.

Soards, Marion L. "Paul: Apostle and Apocalyptic Visionary." *BTB* 16 (1986): 148-50.

Sprinkle, Preston M. "The Old Perspective on the New Perspective: A Review of Some 'Pre-Sanders' Thinkers." *Themelios* 30 (2005): 21-31.

———. "Πίστις Χριστοῦ as an Eschatological Event." In *The Faith of Jesus Christ*, edited by M. F. Bird and P. M. Sprinkle, pp. 165-84. Milton Keynes, UK: Paternoster, 2009.

———. *Paul and Judaism Revisited: A Study of Divine and Human Agency in Salvation.* Downers Grove, IL: IVP Academic, 2013.

Standhartinger, Angela. "Die paulinische Theologie im Spannungsfeld römisch-imperialer Machtpolitik: Eine neue Perspecktive auf Paulus, kritisch geprüft anhand des Philippersbriefs." In *Religion, Politik und Gewalt*, edited by F. Schweitzer, pp. 364-82. Gütersloh: Gütersloher Verlag, 2006.

Stanley, Christopher D. *The Colonized Apostle: Paul through Postcolonial Eyes.* Minneapolis: Fortress, 2011.

Stanton, Graham. "The Law of Moses and the Law of Christ." In *Paul and the Mosaic Law*, edited by J. D. G. Dunn et al., pp. 99-116 Grand Rapids, MI: Eerdmans, 2001.

Stark, Rodney. *Cites of God.* San Francisco: HarperSanFrancisco, 2006.

Starling, David. *Not My People: Gentiles as Exiles in Pauline Hermeneutics.* BZNW 184. Berlin: Walter de Gruyter, 2011.

Stauffer, Ethelbert. *New Testament Theology.* Translated by J. Marsh. London: SCM, 1955.

Stegemann, Ekkehard. "Coexistence and Transformation: Reading the Politics of Identity in Romans in an Imperial Context." In *Reading Paul in Context: Explorations in Identity Formation*, edited by K. Ehrensperger and B. J. Tucker, pp. 2-23. LNTS 428. London: T&T Clark, 2010.

Stendahl, Krister. "The Apostle Paul and the Introspective Conscience of the West." *HTR* 56 (1963): 199-215.

Stephens, Mark B. *Annihilation or Renewal? The Meaning and Function of New Creation in the Book of Revelation.* WUNT 2.307. Tübingen: Mohr Siebeck, 2011.

Stockhausen, Carol. "2 Corinthians and the Principles of Pauline Exegesis." In *Paul and the Scriptures of Israel*, edited by C. A. Evans and J. A. Sanders, pp. 143-64. JSNTSup 83. Sheffield: Sheffield Academic, 1993.

Stowers, Stanley K. "Social Status, Public Speaking and Private Teaching: The Circumstances of Paul's Preaching Activity." *NovT* 26 (1984): 59-82.

———. *A Rereading of Romans: Justice, Jews, Gentiles.* New Haven: Yale University Press, 1994.

Strecker, Christian. "Taktiken der Aneignung: Politsche Implikationen der paulinischen Botschaft im Kontext der römischer imperialen Wirklichkeit." In *Das Neue Testament und politische Theorie: Interdisziplinäre Beiträge zur Zukunft des Politischen*, edited by E. Reinmuth, pp. 114-48. Stuttgart: Kohlhammer, 2001.

Strecker, Georg. *Theology of the New Testament.* Translated by M. E. Boring. Louisville: Westminster John Knox, 2000.

Strelan, Rick. *Paul, Artemis, and the Jews in Ephesus.* Berlin: Walter de Gruyter, 1996.

Stuckenbruck, Loren. "A Place for Socio-political Oppressors at the End of History? Eschatological Perspectives from *1 Enoch*." In *Reactions to Empire: Sacred Texts in Their Socio-political Contexts*, edited by J. A. Dunne and D. Batovici, pp. 1-22. WUNT 2.372. Tübingen: Mohr Siebeck, 2014.

Stuhlmacher, Peter. "Erwägungen zum ontologischen Charakter der καινὴ κτίσις bei Paulus." *EvTh* 27 (1967): 1-35.

Sturm, R. E. "Defining the Word 'Apocalyptic': A Problem in Biblical Criticism." In *Apocalyptic and the New Testament: Essays in Honor of J. Louis Martyn*, edited by J. Marcus and M. L. Soards, pp. 17-48. JSNTSup 24. Sheffield: Sheffield Academic, 2003.

Talbert, Charles H. "Paul, Judaism, and the Revisionists." *CBQ* 63 (2001): 1-22.

Tannehill, Robert. *The Narrative Unity of Luke-Acts: A Literary Interpretation.* 2 vols. Minneapolis: Fortress, 1990.

———. *The Shape of Luke's Story: Essays on Luke-Acts.* Eugene, OR: Cascade, 2005.

Taubes, Jacob. *The Political Theology of Paul.* Translated by D. Hollander. Stanford: Stanford University Press, 2004.

Taylor, Justin. "Why Were the Disciples First Called 'Christians' at Antioch? (Acts 11:26)." *RB* (1994): 75-94.

———. "The Jerusalem Decrees (Acts 15.20, 29 and 21.25) and the Incident at Antioch (Gal 2.11-14)." *NTS* 47 (2001): 372-80.

Taylor, Nicholas H. *Paul, Antioch and Jerusalem: A Study in Relationships and Authority in Earliest Christianity.* JSNTSup 66. Sheffield: JSOT Press, 1992.

———. "Apostolic Identity and the Conflicts in Corinth and Galatia." In *Paul and His Opponents*, edited by S. E. Porter, pp. 99-123. PS 2. Leiden: Brill, 2005.

Tellbe, Mikael. *Paul between Synagogue and State: Christians, Jews, and Civic Authorities in 1 Thessalonians, Romans, and Philippians.* ConBNT 34. Stockholm: Almqvist & Wiksell, 2001.

Thielman, Frank. *From Plight to Solution: A Jewish Framework for Understanding Paul's View of the Law in Galatians and Romans.* Leiden: Brill, 1989.

———. "The Story of Israel and the Theology of Romans 5–8." In *Pauline Theology*. Vol. 3, *Romans*, edited by D. M. Hay and E. E. Johnson, pp. 169-95. Minneapolis: Fortress, 1995.

———. "God's Righteousness as God's Fairness in Romans 1:17: An Ancient Perspective on a Significant Phrase." *JETS* 54 (2011): 35-48.

Thiessen, Jacob. *Gottes Gerechtigkeit und Evangelium im Römerbrief: Die Rechtfertigungslehre des Paulus im Vergleich zu antiken jüdischen Auffsangen und zur Neuen Paulusperspektive.* Frankfurt am Main: Peter Lang, 2014.

Tilling, Chris, ed. *Beyond Old and New Perspectives: Reflections on the Work of Douglas Campbell.* Eugene, OR: Cascade, 2014.

Tomson, Peter. *Paul and the Jewish Law: Halakha in the Letters of the Apostle to the Gentiles.* Minneapolis: Fortress, 1990.

Troiani, Lucio. *Il perdono cristiano e altri studi sul cristianesimo delle origini.* Brescia: Paideia, 1999.

Tucker, Brian J. *Remain in Your Calling: Paul and the Continuation of Social Identities in 1 Corinthians.* Eugene, OR: Pickwick, 2011.

Unnik, W. C. van. *Das Selbstverständnis der jüdischen Diaspora in der hellenistischen-römanischen Zeit.* Leiden: Brill, 1993.

VanderKam, James C. "Judaism in the Land of Israel." In *Early Judaism: A Comprehensive Overview*, edited by J. J. Collins and D. C. Harlow, pp. 70-94. Grand Rapids, MI: Eerdmans, 2012.

Vanhoozer, Kevin J. *The Drama of Doctrine: A Canonical-Linguistic Approach to Christian Theology.* Louisville: Westminster John Knox, 2005.

VanLandingham, Chris. *Judgment and Justification in Early Judaism and the Apostle Paul.* Peabody, MA: Hendrickson, 2005.

Vermes, Geza. *Jesus and the World of Judaism.* London: SCM, 1983.

Vielhauer, Paul. "Apocalyptic in Early Christianity." In *New Testament Apocrypha*, edited by W. Schneemelcher, pp. 542-69. Translated by R. McL. Wilson. Louisville: Westminster John Knox, 1992.

Wagner, J. Ross. *Heralds of the Good News: Isaiah and Paul in Concert in the Letter to the Romans.* Leiden: Brill, 2003.

Wallace, David R. *The Gospel of God: Romans as Paul's Aeneid.* Eugene, OR: Pickwick, 2008.

Wan, Sze-kar. "Does Diaspora Identity Imply Some Sort of Universality? An Asian American Reading of Galatians." In *Interpreting beyond Borders,* edited by F. F. Segovia, pp. 107-31. Sheffield: Sheffield Academic, 2000.

Watson, Francis. *Paul and the Hermeneutics of Faith.* London: T&T Clark, 2004.

————. "Constructing an Antithesis: Pauline and Other Jewish Perspectives on Divine and Human Agency." In *Divine and Human Agency in Paul and His Cultural Development,* edited by J. M. G. Barclay and S. J. Gathercole, pp. 99-116. London: T&T Clark, 2007.

————. *Paul, Judaism, and the Gentiles: Beyond the New Perspective.* Rev. ed. Grand Rapids, MI: Eerdmans, 2007.

————. "By Faith (of Christ): An Exegetical Dilemma and Its Scriptural Solution." In *The Faith of Jesus Christ,* edited by M. F. Bird and P. M. Sprinkle, pp. 147-63. Milton Keynes, UK: Paternoster, 2009.

Weatherly, J. A. "The Authenticity of 1 Thessalonians 2.13-16: Additional Evidence." *JSNT* 42 (1991): 79-98.

Webb, Robert L. "'Apocalyptic': Observations on a Slippery Term." *JNES* 49 (1990): 115-26.

Wechsler, Andreas. *Geschichtsbild und Apostelstreit: Eine forschungsgeschichtliche und exegetische Studie über antiochenischen Zwischenfall (Gal 2, 11-14).* BZNW 62. Berlin: Walter de Gruyter, 1991.

Wedderburn, Alexander J. M. *A History of the First Christians.* London: T&T Clark, 2005.

Weinfeld, Moshe. *Normative and Sectarian Judaism in the Second Temple Period.* LSTS 54. London: T&T Clark, 2005.

Wengst, Klaus. *Pax Romana and the Peace of Jesus Christ.* Translated by J. Bowden. Philadelphia: Fortress, 1987.

Westerholm, Stephen. *Perspectives Old and New on Paul: The "Lutheran" Paul and His Critics.* Grand Rapids, MI: Eerdmans, 2003.

————. "Paul's Anthropological 'Pessimism' in Its Jewish Context." In *Divine and Human Agency in Paul and His Cultural Environment,* edited by J. M. G. Barclay and S. J. Gathercole, pp. 71-98. LNTS 335. London: T&T Clark, 2007.

White, Joel. "Anti-imperial Subtexts in Paul: An Attempt at Building a Firmer Foundation." *Bib* 90 (2009): 305-33.

White, John L. *The Apostle of God: Paul and the Promise of Abraham.* Peabody, MA: Hendrickson, 1999.

White, L. Michael. "Capitalizing on the Imperial Cult: Some Jewish Perspectives." In *Rome and Religion: A Cross-Disciplinary Dialogue on the Imperial Cult,* edited by J. Brodd and J. L. Reed, pp. 173-214. Atlanta: SBL, 2011.

Wilckens, Ulrich. *Rechtfertigung als Freiheit*. Neukirchen-Vluyn: Neukirchener, 1974.

Wilken, Robert L. *John Chrysostom and the Jews: Rhetoric and Reality in the Late Fourth Century*. Eugene, OR: Wipf & Stock, 2004.

Williams, Sam K. "Against *Pistis Christou*." *CBQ* 49 (1987): 431-47.

———. *Galatians*. ANTC. Nashville: Abingdon, 1997.

Wilson, Stephen G. *Leaving the Fold: Apostates and Defectors in Antiquity*. Minneapolis: Fortress, 2004.

Wilson, Todd A. "The Law of Christ and the Law of Moses: Reflections on a Recent Trend in Interpretation." *CBR* 5 (2006): 129-50.

Windsor, Lionel J. *Paul and the Vocation of Israel: How Paul's Jewish Identity Informs His Apostolic Ministry, with Special Reference to Romans*. BZNW 205. Berlin: Walter de Gruyter, 2014.

Winninge, Mikael. *Sinners and the Righteous: A Comparative Study of the Psalms of Solomon and Paul's Letters*. Stockholm: Almqvist & Wiksell, 1995.

Winter, Bruce W. "Roman Law and Society in Romans 12–15." In *Rome in the Bible and the Early Church*, edited by P. Oakes, pp. 67-102. Carlisle, UK: Paternoster, 2002.

Witherington, Ben, III. *Paul's Narrative Thought World: The Tapestry of Tragedy and Triumph*. Louisville: Westminster John Knox, 1994.

———. *Grace in Galatia: A Commentary on Paul's Letter to the Galatians*. Grand Rapids, MI: Eerdmans, 1998.

Wright, N. T. "The Paul of History and the Apostle of Faith." *TynB* 29 (1978): 61-99.

———. *The Climax of the Covenant: Christ and the Law in Pauline Theology*. Edinburgh: T&T Clark, 1991.

———. *New Testament and the People of God*. COQG 1. London: SPCK, 1992.

———. "Gospel and Theology in Galatians." In *Gospel in Paul: Studies on Corinthians, Galatians and Romans for Richard N. Longenecker*, edited by L. A. Jervis and P. Richardson, pp. 222-39. JSNTSup 108. Sheffield: Sheffield Academic, 1994.

———. *Jesus and the Victory of God*. COQG 2. London: SPCK, 1996.

———. *What Saint Paul Really Said*. Oxford: Lion, 1997.

———. "Paul's Gospel and Caesar's Empire." In *Paul and Politics: Ekklesia, Israel, Imperium, Interpretation: Essays in Honor of Krister Stendahl*, edited by R. A. Horsley, pp. 160-83. Harrisburg, PA: Trinity Press International, 2000.

———. "A Fresh Perspective on Paul?" *BJRL* 83 (2001): 21-39.

———. "Paul and Caesar: A New Reading of Romans." In *A Royal Priesthood: The Use of the Bible Ethically and Politically*, edited by C. Bartholomew, J. Chaplin, R. Song, and A. Walters, pp. 173-93. Carlisle, UK: Paternoster, 2002.

———. "Romans." In *NIB*, edited by L. E. Keck, 10:393-770. 12 vols. Nashville: Abingdon, 2002.

———. *Paul: In Fresh Perspective*. Minneapolis: Fortress, 2005.

———. *Surprised by Hope*. San Francisco: HarperOne, 2008.

———. *The New Testament for Everyone*. London: SPCK, 2011.

―――. "Romans 2:17–3:9: A Hidden Clue to the Meaning of Romans?" *JSPL* 2 (2012): 1-28.

―――. *Paul and the Faithfulness of God.* COQG 4. London: SPCK, 2013.

―――. "Two Radical Jews: A Review Article of Daniel Boyarin, *A Radical Jew: Paul and the Politics of Identity.*" In *Pauline Perspectives: Essays on Paul, 1978-2013*, pp. 126-33. London: SPCK, 2013.

―――. "A New Perspective on Käsemann? Apocalyptic, Covenant, and the Righteousness of God." In *Studies in the Pauline Epistle*, edited by M. S. Harmon and J. E. Smith, pp. 243-58. Grand Rapids, MI: Zondervan, 2014.

―――. *The Paul Debate: Critical Questions for Understanding the Apostle.* Waco, TX: Baylor University Press, 2015.

―――. *Paul and His Recent Interpreters.* London: SPCK, 2015.

Yarbrough, Robert W. "Paul and Salvation History." In *Justification and Variegated Nomism.* Vol. 2, *The Paradoxes of Paul*, edited by D. A. Carson, P. T. O'Brien, and M. A. Seifrid, pp. 297-342. Grand Rapids, MI: Baker Academic, 2004.

―――. "Salvation History (*Heilsgeschichte*) and Paul." In *Studies in the Pauline Epistles*, edited by M. S. Harmon and J. E. Smith, pp. 181-98. Grand Rapids, MI: Zondervan, 2014.

Yinger, Kent L. "Reformation *Redivivus*: Synergism and the New Perspective." *JTI* 3 (2009): 89-106.

―――. *The New Perspective on Paul: An Introduction.* Eugene, OR: Cascade, 2011.

Zahn, Theodor. *Der Brief des Paulus an die Galater.* KNT. Leipzig: Deichert, 1907.

Zanker, Paul. *The Power of Images in the Age of Augustus.* Translated by A. Shapiro. Ann Arbor: University of Michigan Press, 1988.

Zetterholm, Magnus. *The Formation of Christianity in Antioch: A Social-Scientific Approach to the Separation between Judaism and Christianity.* London: Routledge, 2003.

―――. *Approaches to Paul: A Student's Guide to Recent Scholarship.* Minneapolis: Fortress, 2009.

―――. "Paul within Judaism: The State of the Questions." In *Paul within Judaism*, edited by M. D. Nanos and M. Zetterholm, pp. 51-52. Minneapolis: Fortress, 2015.

Index of Authors

Index of Subjects

Aegean mission, 96, 103-4
Aeneid, pattern of Paul, 221
anomos, 81-84, 103
apocalyptic, 9, 11-12, 27-28, 108-10, 114, 116, 119, 121, 123, 137, 157, 164, 166-67
apostleship, of Paul, 5, 14, 65, 82, 89, 96, 104
anti-imperial readings of Paul, 221-23
Antioch, incident, 29-30, 49, 94-95, 134, 170-71, 176, 179-82, 193, 196-97, 201, 203
Arabia, 87-89, 103
art, of Paul, 69
atheism, charge against Christians, 211-13
Augustus, 212, 218, 221, 229, 231, 233-34, 237-38, 244

background to Romans, 227-228
Barnabas, 91-95, 135, 164, 171, 173, 176-77, 181, 186, 190, 193, 201

calendrical inscriptions, and Romans, 220, 229
Christ, as climax of Israel's covenantal history, 150-51
Christ, as *princeps,* 217
Christ, title, in Roman context, 230-31
Christology, 7, 56-57, 111-12, 132-33, 140, 166; and covenant, 58
Christophany, 85-87, 90, 200
circumcision, 6-7, 22-23, 50-51, 64, 77-81,

92, 94-95, 112, 136, 161-62, 174, 179, 195-97
cosmic war, 129, 155
counterimperial motifs in Romans, 223-25
covenant, 59-60, 63, 101, 112, 130, 140, 146, 150, 174
covenantal history, 221
covenantal nomism, 37-41, 47, 67

Diaspora, 35-36, 63, 73, 101
dietary laws, 186-90, 192-93
dysangelion, 219

Edict of Claudius, 219
election: of Israel, 2, 13-14, 101, 118, 133, 167; of Gentiles, 24, 133
epistemology, 121
eschatology, 7, 11, 17, 22-24, 28, 39, 44, 56, 101; apocalyptic, 122, 166; two-stage, 129
ethnē, 71-74, 82-84, 99, 103-4
exodus, 125, 157

Gospel, Roman context, 229-30

Hellēn, 74-77, 84, 103
Herod, alliance with Rome, 215
"hidden transcripts" in Paul, 225-27

identity, of Paul: Jewish, 1-3, 16-17, 49-50; new, 3-4, 6, 12, 48, 97 imperial cult(s), 108, 212, 222, 229, 235, 238, 244, 247

Israel: of God, 46, 51, 163-66; *Sonderplatz*, 44; *Sonderweg*, 42-44

James, brother of Jesus, 179-80, 185, 189, 200

Jerusalem council, 30, 70, 87, 94, 134, 177-78, 180, 184, 191, 194, 197

Jesus: as new Adam, 240; as redeemer of Israel, 157; as son of David, 231, 233, 251-52; death, 14, 24, 108, 111, 115, 126-28, 137, 140; faithfulness of, 108, 137; resurrection, 14, 17, 24, 108, 111, 115, 125-26, 129, 140, 232, 240

judaize, definition, 197-98

justification, 135-40

Kyrios, against Caesar, 209, 242-43

law: as cause of slavery, 156-60; as custodian, 153-56, 168; as temporary, 151-53, 155; of Christ, 160-61, 168

legalism, Jewish, 8, 32-35, 39

Nero, 210, 213, 217, 229-31, 233, 241-42

new creation, 160-63, 168

New Perspective: an anomalous Jew, 25-27; defined, 8-10; a faithful Jew, 20-24; a former Jew, 10-12; a radical Jew, 24-25; a transformed Jew, 12-20

Paulus Fabius Maximus, inscriptions, 220

pax Christi, against pax Romana, 237-40

persecution, Jewish, 4-5, 98; of Christians, 210-12

Peter, 136, 164, 171, 174, 176, 178-81, 183-86, 189-93, 198, 200-201

pisteōs christou, 141-44

proselytes, integration, 136

rectification, divine, 138-39

rescue, 127

restoration of Israel, 158

resurrection, in Roman world, 232

righteousness of God, 233-36

Romans, as political theology, 228-29

Romans, political reading, 220

seed, of Abraham, 164-65

son: of Abraham, 132; of God, 158, 209, 219, 232

soteriology, 12, 14, 20, 29, 38, 60, 66, 114

Tertullian, on Caesar, 216

through the law, 145-47

Torah, 7, 14, 19, 22, 24, 35-37, 41, 58, 63, 65, 79, 115, 148-50, 184, 190, 193, 204

unity: in Christ, 44, 112, 146, 167-68; of Jew and Gentile, 11, 65-66, 80, 97, 102, 136, 163, 191-92, 199

will of God, 131-32, 134

works of law, 236-37

Index of Ancient Sources